Charaxes verae Nabokov
Montreux, Vaud  15.IV.68  ♂

Вотъ достойная годовщины
нежнѣйшая бабочка

♀

1925 - 68

Verina raduga Nab.

VN

Jan. 5, 1971

Montreux

For Véra

FROM VN

Montreux
Xmas 1969

VLADIMIR
NABOKOV

# VLADIMIR
# NABOKOV

SELECTED LETTERS

1940-1977

*Edited by Dmitri Nabokov*
*and Matthew J. Bruccoli*

HARCOURT
BRACE
JOVANOVICH

BRUCCOLI   CLARK   LAYMAN

*San Diego   New York   London*

FRONTISPIECE: Véra and Vladimir Nabokov, Montreux 1968
(*photo by Philippe Halsman, 1968;* © *Yvonne Halsman 1989*)

Copyright © 1989 by the Article 3 b Trust
Under the Will of Vladimir Nabokov.
Introduction © 1989 by Dmitri Nabokov.

Requests for permission to make copies of
any part of the work should be mailed to:
Copyrights and Permissions Department,
Harcourt Brace Jovanovich, Publishers,
Orlando, Florida 32887.

Library of Congress Cataloging-in-Publication Data
Nabokov, Vladimir Vladimirovich, 1899-1977.
    Vladimir Nabokov : selected letters, 1940-1977.
    Includes index.
    1. Nabokov, Vladimir Vladimirovich, 1899-1977—Correspondence.
2. Authors, Russian—20th century—Correspondence.
3. Authors, American—20th century—Correspondence.
I. Nabokov, Dmitri.
II. Bruccoli, Matthew Joseph, 1931-
III. Title.
PG3476.N3Z48   1989       813'.54 [B]        88-26793
ISBN 0-15-164190-0

Designed by Michael Farmer

Printed in the United States of America

First edition

A B C D E

# ACKNOWLEDGMENTS

Acknowledgment is made for the generous assistance of the following institutions and individuals: Bryn Mawr College Library; Cornell University Libraries; Harvard University Libraries; Hoover Institution on War, Revolution and Peace; The Library of Congress; Thomas Cooper Library, University of South Carolina, Interlibrary Loan: Daniel Boice, Yvonne Andrews, Cathie Gottlieb; Roger Angell; Alfred Appel, Jr.; Alison M. K. Bishop; Paul Carlton; Graham Greene; Alison Bishop Jolly; Pat Hitchcock O'Connell; Gina Peterman; Lord Weidenfeld. Prof. Brian Boyd generously volunteered to read this volume in typescript.

# CONTENTS

# INTRODUCTION

Dmitri Nabokov

> I have always had a number of parts lined up in case the
> muse failed. A lepidopterist exploring fabulous jungles
> came first. Then there was the chess grand master, then the
> tennis ace with an unreturnable service, then the goalie
> saving a historical shot, and finally, finally, the author of a
> pile of unknown writings—*Pale Fire, Lolita, Ada*—that my
> heirs discover and publish.
>> VLADIMIR NABOKOV, 1977 BBC interview

> ... turning to the title-page butterfly, its head is that of a
> small tortoise, and its pattern that of a common Cabbage
> White butterfly (whereas the insect in my poem is clearly
> described as belonging to a group of small blue butterflies
> with dotted undersides), which is as meaningless ... as
> would be a picture of a tuna fish on the jacket of *Moby
> Dick*. I want to be quite clear and frank: I have nothing
> against stylization, but I do object to stylized ignorance.
>> VLADIMIR NABOKOV, 1959 letter to publisher

> I do have a story for you—but it is still in my head;
> quite complete, however; ready to emerge; the pattern
> showing through the wingcases of the pupa.
>> VLADIMIR NABOKOV, 1946 letter to Katharine A. White

To give credits where credits are due, I express my gratitude to
friends and scholars for providing missing letters; to William
Jovanovich and Julian Muller of Harcourt Brace Jovanovich for their
patience during what was a long and sometimes fitful gestation; and,

above all, to Matthew Bruccoli, not only for his valuable collaboration, but also for his gentle encouragement and outward calm as deadlines passed like telegraph poles glimpsed from a speeding train.

Procrastination, however, can bear unexpected fruit. Thus, the appearance of this volume coincides felicitously with a kind of worldwide Nabokov renaissance. Editions ranging from the substantial to the complete are appearing in unprecedented abundance. Of special note abroad are the uniform Rowohlt series in Germany, the Anagrama books in Spain, Guanda's semi-annual cadence for some sixteen volumes together with Bompiani's projected plump two-volume Classici in Italy, and the Rivages editions and the forthcoming Pléiade in France. Russian versions of Nabokov's works—including various translations from his English—are proliferating. Here we have two basic categories: the meticulously prepared *Collected Works* in progress at Ardis of Ann Arbor (a product, as literature is called these days, of guaranteed fidelity) on one hand, and, on the other, the results of a Soviet rush to get Nabokov into print while *glasnost'* and paper supplies last. This second product varies wildly. There is a handful of refined, courageous scholars (one in particular) struggling for accuracy; there are well-meaning but shoddy reprints from whatever sources were available; there are some pretty awful translations from the English; and, alas for *glasnost'*, we see from the 1988 publication of *Dar* [*The Gift*], that the claws of political censorship are but half-clipped.

In Nabokov's adopted country there is good news indeed. Nearly all his fictional works are being assembled under the roomy roof of a new publisher, and an extensive, well produced, and properly distributed American Nabokov should soon be available.

The letters included in this volume represent only a small part of Nabokov's correspondence. They have been selected with certain general criteria in mind, and most of them reflect one or more of the following facets of Nabokov:

1. his evolution as a writer and insights into his creative process
2. his academic activity

3. his passions: lepidoptera and chess
4. certain important details of his life
5. his family relationships
6. his artistic and personal morality
7. the humor and originality with which he composed everything from a grocery list or the dressing-down of a derailed biographer to letters of importance regarding family or artistic matters.

The above are not dry scholastic categories, but themes that will fascinate the reader as they develop with the intricacy, symmetry, and suspense of a multifaceted novel by Nabokov. And *Lolita's* incredible adventures alone could be a novel.

When he was preparing his books for publication, Nabokov's occasional absent-mindedness during the physical process of writing was counterbalanced by microscopic attention to detail at the text's crucial stages: the exactitude of thought and often the research that creation entailed during the work's conception, and a final check of every word in proof. In the interim, the "passion of the scientist" could propel him past a lapse, but the "precision of the artist" compelled him to return eventually and fix that lapse. The occasional typo or other error will, of course, haunt the most carefully checked text, but Nabokov did all he could to forestall such mishaps, and a sampling of his corrections, particularly those to the proofs of the first edition of *Lolita*, is included to illustrate the meticulous care he gave a nascent work.

The preparation of these lists for the present volume meant, in effect, retracing every detail of Nabokov's 1955 revisions, to be certain that the ghosts of typos and rejects, as well as the author's emendations, had been properly resurrected.

Such attentive checking of Nabokov texts yields welcome by-products. One is reminded, for instance, that, no matter how many times one rereads his works, there is always some previously undiscovered surprise. Take the encounter with Rita described at the beginning of Chapter 26, Part Two, of *Lolita*. The episode is not a crucial element of the book, and the casual reader might tend to gloss over it. That would be a pity:

> She was twice Lolita's age and three quarters of mine: a very slight, dark-haired, pale-skinned adult, weighing a hundred and five pounds, with charmingly asymmetrical eyes, an angular, rapidly sketched profile, and a most appealing *ensellure* to her supple back—I think she had some Spanish or Babylonian blood. I picked her up one depraved May evening somewhere between Montreal and New York, or more narrowly, between Toylestown and Blake, at a darkishly burning bar under the sign of the Tigermoth, where she was amiably drunk: she insisted we had gone to school together, and she placed her trembling little hand on my ape paw.

The "Babylonian blood," the "asymmetrical eyes," the "rapidly sketched profile" are really not sketchy at all; they create a more specific sensation of everything about the girl than a page of toiled-over particulars. And Toylestown and Blake, and the "darkishly burning bar" (its name perhaps adjusted by Humbert for the image's sake) with its namesakes whirling and thumping about the neon sign, and the "depraved May evening" itself—*that* is original writing, where the concentrated image rules, where style and substance merge, as they should, to give the reader an agreeable spinal chill. Little pitfalls lurk, it is true, for the avid analyst with his deconstructionist lingo. Sometimes things are *exactly* what they seem; I think it is safe to say, for instance, that Humbert's "ape paw" has nothing to do with the animal laboring over a charcoal drawing in the author's afterword to *Lolita*, although someone's printout may dispute me. Then someone else, after more research, may conclude that the newspaper account cited by Nabokov as his inspiration for the book's theme never existed at all, and that the artistic animal was placed in the cage whose bars it is reproducing simply to enchant the unwary symbol-hunter.

The point, however, is the image, the "feel" one gets from the combination "ape paw," and how that combination came to be. The process went more or less like this: Nabokov had lived with the image, the "undeveloped film" as he once described it to me, for a long time. An embyronic Humbert was already waiting in the wings of *The Gift* (published in serial form as *Dar* in 1937–38) to be written into a book that one of the novel's characters was contemplating. This hairy, ape-like quality embodied to Nabokov both the grotesqueness and the pathos of the monstrous character that already lived within his artistic womb. A kind of Humbert, complete with those traits, came to life when the "film" was partially developed to yield *The Enchanter* (*Volshebnik*, written in 1939, not published until the posthumous French and English-language editions of 1986). When drafting *Lolita* Nabokov may have considered "apelike," even "simian." He may have considered a repetition of "hand," or even "arm." Yet he chose more simple, direct, and vivid words. In reply to a question much favored by interviewers, Nabokov would say that he thought in images rather than in any specific language. Nevertheless—and it is especially easy to find examples in the letters, particularly in the 1940s and early 1950s—he was still, at *some* level of consciousness, translating *some* images and locutions from their Russian (and occasionally their French) formulation. Not the meticulously studied strata of Americana amid which *Lolita* was finally set, but elements of the book, for instance, that had existed in his mind when he still had no idea he would one day become an American writer. Thus he instinctively ended up with the words "ape" and "paw"—but he wrote "ape's paw" and not "ape paw," for that felt somehow closer to the cozy Russian combination *obezyanya lapa* which he had long associated with the character. And only when he was correcting proofs (corrections list, 9 July 1955, 372:11)—the last chance, as it were, before the still adjustable creation in one's mind congeals into its first concrete form—did he reduce it to "ape," thereby avoiding the awkward and ambiguous double possessive "my ape's paw."

This peek through the magnifying glass is but one illustration of the infinitely diligent attention to detail that must accompany creative genius in order to produce a paragraph so concentrated and evocative, yet superficially so straightforward as the one cited above. And then, as one makes last-minute emendations to the proof of *this* very page, one's imagination is suddenly drawn through the magnifying glass into the looking glass. One pictures a future editor or scholar hunched, with his own lens, over a page of proofs that reproduce the corrections made by Vladimir Nabokov to the proofs of the Olympia *Lolita*, as corrected by Dmitri Nabokov for *Vladimir Nabokov: Letters, 1940–1977*, and destined for inclusion, say, in *Letters About Vladimir Nabokov, 1977–2001*. And, like the future selves of the astronaut in *2001* and the future kings in *Macbeth*, other editors and scholars loom, dimly reflected in the background of one's fantasy, as the looking glass multiplies into an infinite hall of mirrors, and time and place are neatly blurred into the timeless, placeless dream dimension that transpires, here and there, through the texture of the original Nabokov's texts.

At first, the present collection was to be limited, linguistically, to letters written in English and, chronologically, to those written after Nabokov came to America in 1940. It was subsequently decided to expand those parameters somewhat, both in order to set the stage for the American period, and to bring Nabokov's personal facets into sharper focus. Correspondence with members of the family and with other Russians was, except where noted, conducted in Russian. The English translations of these letters and of the occasional letter in French are by Dmitri Nabokov in collaboration with Véra Nabokov. Where there might have been doubt in the reader's mind as to the language used for an entire letter or for an individual expression, explanatory notes appear.

The Nabokov Archive has yielded such a wealth of material that at least one further volume is planned. It will include correspondence between Nabokov and émigré literary figures, his parents, and his wife, categories which are represented by only a few examples in the present collection.

Nabokov sometimes transliterated Russian letters into English characters simply to humor the faithful Royal typewriter that accompanied the family on travels across America and Europe. In other cases he did it for fun, as in a letter to his sister of 26 November 1967 that contains jocular Russian transliterations of Elena Sikorski's presumed jocular French pronunciation. Rendering such multilingual nuance in a manner comprehensible to the reader who might know neither Russian nor French was tricky. So was translating the little poem Nabokov wrote on a postcard to his sister in September, 1970, and the illustrations of Russian prosody, camouflaged in matter-of-fact sentences, that he sent to his brother Kirill in 1930. In such cases I have tried to provide English equivalents that preserve both sense and form, and prefer not to think of what will happen when translations into other tongues start rolling in. And it would not surprise me if some Soviet translator, without consulting us, were to attempt reconverting into Russian the letters that have been painstakingly Englished, for this has already happened with at least one Nabokov poem.

Transliteration is a thorny matter. I have followed the method set forth by Nabokov in his translation of *Eugene Onegin* (1964), but have done so somewhat nonexclusively. Generally accepted spellings of well-known names, titles, etc., have been left undisturbed. Nabokov's own usages varied widely over the years, and have not been altered. But enough gray areas remain—*Nikolai Gogol*, which in his "author's copy," VN retitled *Nikolay Gogol*; "Chernyshevski" in the English version of *The Gift* who, according to the rules, ought to be spelled "Chernïshevski"; other cases where several factors must be considered—to make consistency elusive. The Russian й and ы are particularly slippery characters, and no amount of revision seems to make y, ï, i, etc. represent them with total discipline.

With a couple of exceptions the letters from Nabokov to his sister Elena and to his brother Kirill are among those published in Russian under the title *Perepiska s sestroy* (Ann Arbor: Ardis, 1985). The correspondence with Edmund Wilson has been separately published as *The Nabokov-Wilson Letters*, ed. Simon Karlinsky (New York: Harper & Row, 1979).

There was often a reciprocal epistolary collaboration between Vladimir and Véra Nabokov. On occasion he would indicate the gist of a letter to be written, his wife would compose part or all of the text, and he would sign it. On other occasions he preferred, for one reason or another, that she sign a letter in which every word was his. Véra Nabokov was, among other things, her husband's typist for many years. By the late 1960s the escalation of correspondence and other matters made a secretary indispensable. Jacqueline Callier was engaged and has been of great assistance to the Nabokovs ever since. Russian-language typing has, over the years, been done almost exclusively by Véra Nabokov and Elena Sikorski.

Nabokov generally sacrificed most other pursuits to the pursuit of his art. When he did take the time to write letters, the stimuli were family ties, close friendship, and aesthetic, professional, or scientific matters that required the authority of his signature. He replied to critics only when his artistic or personal integrity was questioned. He wrote to newspapers and magazines on those rare occasions when an important matter of fact or of morality needed to be set right. He was moved by the letters of certain fans, but felt he could not sacrifice writing time to embark upon exchanges with them, and only seldom did he find some exceptional quality in a fan letter that caused him to break this rule. Among the most touching letters were those in which the return address had been deliberately omitted to make it clear that neither the author's time nor his signature was being solicited; I recall one in particular, signed "a little Nabokov." Then again, the whims of fate and filing caused the loss of a few special letters that had been set aside for reply, and no other trace of name or address remained. An exceptional letter from Israel, received and hopelessly misplaced many years ago, was one of those that caused Nabokov special chagrin.

In Montreux, in his later years, Nabokov often lacked the time to answer even the the most deserving letters. At the suggestion of Edmund Wilson—who even sent a sample—cards were printed containing a brief note of thanks and explanation for would-be correspondents.

Autograph hunters were a subspecies apart. Our files abound with cards to which are affixed reproductions of Nabokov photographs, of varying origin and quality, with space provided for the author's signature. Sometimes books would arrive with a request that they be inscribed and returned to some distant address. Or a waiter in some resort hotel would approach the Nabokovs' table, volume in hand, begging that it be signed for his boss or for some client. Nabokov despised the autograph industry, with its bookstore signature orgies and a commerce as brisk as that in baseball cards. He inscribed books only for relatives and close friends, and on certain other exceptional occasions. One of the few autographs he ever sent to an unknown postulant was the result of humanitarian compassion: the chap had written that it was the last wish of his father, condemned to imminent death by cancer. But a year or so later there was a new request, in the same forgetful hand: the last wish murmured by his doomed son was for a Nabokov autograph (or perhaps the order was inverse).

Of particular beauty and interest were the drawings with which Nabokov sometimes decorated letters or books destined for a small number of special people. The drawings that appeared on letters, or on separate sheets and cards, were sometimes figurative, sometimes fantastic, sometimes both at once, with a dash of the unique Nabokovian humor that colors his writing. In the book inscriptions, on the other hand, they almost always represented butterflies, generally nonexistent but often zoologically plausible, and sometimes with invented taxonomic appellations to match. A collection of Nabokov's drawings will appear in a volume of personal recollections, now in preparation.

Rather than overload this introduction with detail, Matthew Bruccoli and I have preferred to place explanatory notes wherever they might be most useful and most readily available to the reader, who will also encounter some amusing surprises. For instance, it has long been a mystery to me, who knew Nabokov well, how the notion could have been born among those unacquainted with him that he was austere, cold, somehow inhuman. Perhaps it was because of his intransigence in artistic matters, his intolerance of philistinism, and his disengagement from chic sociopolitical issues. Nabokov once said:

My characters cringe as I come near them with my whip. I have seen a whole avenue of imagined trees losing their leaves at the threat of my passage.

(1977 BBC interview)

Yet, in his real life and daily discourse, Nabokov was the warmest and most humorous of men, and even his writing took a back seat when he could directly intervene on behalf of an unfortunate man or beast. It is, perhaps, this very dichotomy that is beyond some readers, the kind who move their lips as they read, who are certain the author is giving them slices of his life, and seek out reflected slices of their own to "identify with":

> as if we were no longer able
> to write long poems
> on any other subject than ourselves!
> A. Pushkin, *Eugene Onegin*, tr. V. Nabokov
> (New York: Bollingen, 1964)

What upset Pushkin is true of prose as well, and true more than ever today. Letters, on the other hand, allow personality to transpire unrefracted, and these letters will afford the reader unprecedented glimpses of the private Nabokov.

We now have an autobiographical triptych of Vladimir Nabokov: *Speak, Memory*; *Strong Opinions*; and *Letters*. The first of the three books is a meticulously constructed real-life narrative of great beauty. The second is a fascinating collection of facts and sometimes iconoclastic views. The posthumously published third now gives us a direct and spontaneous portrait of the artist—Nabokov from the horse's mouth, as it were.

As for literary biography by other parties, there are, of course, various horses and various parts of horses. However, the reader is advised not to despair: a two-volume Nabokov book by Brian Boyd is due in 1990, and it promises to be a thoroughbred.

# EDITORIAL NOTE

The editorial headings provide bibliographical and archival information for each letter. Thus:

| Recipient (or writer) | Description & location of the document |
|---|---|
| Date (if not on the letter.) | Place of writing (if not on the letter) |

All unlocated letters are in the Vladimir Nabokov Archive, Montreux, Switzerland. ALS denotes an autograph (handwritten) letter signed; TLS denotes a typed letter signed; TL denotes an unsigned typed letter; CC denotes a carbon copy of a TL.

The placement and form of the return address and date on each letter have been retained except when the information is irregularly positioned; in these cases the information has been styled as place followed by date.

Typing or scribal errors have been silently corrected by Véra Nabokov or Dmitri Nabokov. Deletions made by Mrs. Nabokov or Dmitri Nabokov have been identified. Underlined words have been printed in italic type.

The letters often incorporate words from other languages. Russian and French words in English-language letters are translated, except for familiar French terms.

The footnotes have been provided by Véra Nabokov, Dmitri Nabo-kov, and Matthew J. Bruccoli. Footnotes of a personal nature written by Mrs. Nabokov or Dmitri Nabokov have been so identified. Judith S. Baughman assisted mightily in the preparation of this volume for publication.

M.J.B.

# CHRONOLOGY

| | |
|---|---|
| 23 April 1899 (New Style) | Birth in St. Petersburg, Russia, of Vladimir Vladimirovich, first child of V. D. Nabokov and Elena Rukavishnikov Nabokov. |
| 1914 | Private publication of one poem, untitled. |
| 1916 | Private publication of *Stikhi* [*Poems*]. |
| 1918 | Private publication in *Al'manakh: Dva Puti* [*Almanac: Two Paths*] of poems by VN and Andrei Balashov. |
| 15 April 1919 (New Style) | Departure from Russia. |
| 1919–1922 | Cambridge University. |
| 1922 | Settled in Berlin. *Grozd'* [*The Cluster*]. Berlin: Gamayun. |
| 28 March 1922 | Assassination of V. D. Nabokov. |
| 1923 | *Gornïy Put'* [*The Empyrean Path*]. Berlin: Grani. |

| | |
|---|---|
| 15 April 1925 | Marriage to Véra Slonim. |
| 1926 | *Mashen'ka* [*Mary*]. Berlin: Slovo. New York: McGraw-Hill, 1970. |
| 1928 | *Korol' Dama Valet* [*King, Queen, Knave*]. Berlin: Slovo. New York: McGraw-Hill, 1968. |
| 1929 | *Vozvrashchenie Chorba* [*The Return of Chorb*]. Berlin: Slovo. |
| 1930 | *Zashchita Luzhina* [*The Defense*]. Berlin: Slovo. New York: Putnam, 1964. |
| 1932 | *Podvig* [*Glory*]. Paris: Sovremennye Zapiski. New York: McGraw-Hill, 1971. |
| 1932 | *Kamera Obskura* [*Camera Obscura*]. Berlin: Sovremennye Zapiski. London: John Long, 1936. *Laughter in the Dark*. Indianapolis & New York: Bobbs-Merrill, 1938. |
| 10 May 1934 | Birth of Dmitri Nabokov. |
| 1936 | *Otchayanie* [*Despair*]. Berlin: Petropolis. London: John Long, 1937. New York: Putnam, 1966. |
| 1937 | Arrives in Paris. |
| 1938 | *Sogliadatay* [*The Eye*]. Berlin: Russkie Zapiski. New York: Phaedra, 1965. |
| 1938 | *Priglashenie Na Kazn'* [*Invitation to a Beheading*]. Paris: Dom Knigi. New York: Putnam, 1959. |

| | |
|---|---|
| 1940 | Arrives in America. |
| 1941 | *The Real Life of Sebastian Knight*. Norfolk, Conn.: New Directions. |
| Summer 1941 | Stanford University. Lecturer in Creative Writing. |
| Fall 1941 | Harvard University. Part-time position at Museum of Comparative Zoology. |
| Fall 1941-Spring 1942 | Wellesley College. Visiting Lecturer in Comparative Literature. |
| 1943-1948 | Wellesley College. Temporary Lecturer in Russian Language and Literature. |
| 1944 | *Nikolai Gogol*. Norfolk, Conn.: New Directions. |
| 1945 | *Three Russian Poets*, trans. VN. Norfolk, Conn.: New Directions. |
| 1947 | *Bend Sinister*. New York: Holt. |
| 1947 | *Nine Stories*. Norfolk, Conn.: New Directions. |
| 1948-1959 | Cornell University. Professor of Russian and European Literature. |
| 1951 | *Conclusive Evidence*. New York: Harpers. *Speak, Memory*. London: Gollancz. |
| 1952 | *Dar* [*The Gift*]. New York: Chekhov. New York: Putnam, 1963. |

| 1952 | *Stikhotvoreniya 929–95 [Poems 929–95]*. Paris: Rifma. |
| 1955 | *Lolita*. Paris: Olympia. New York: Putnam, 1958. London: Weidenfeld & Nicolson, 1959. |
| 1956 | *Vesna v Fial'te [Spring in Fialta]*. New York: Chekhov. |
| 1957 | *Pnin*. Garden City, N. Y.: Doubleday. |
| 1958 | Mihail Lermontov, *A Hero of Our Time*, trans. Dmitri Nabokov with VN. Garden City, N.Y.: Doubleday. |
| 1958 | *Nabokov's Dozen*. Garden City, N. Y.: Doubleday. |
| 1959 | Resigns from Cornell; travels in Europe. |
| 1959 | *Poems*. Garden City, N. Y.: Doubleday. |
| 1960 | *The Song of Igor's Campaign*, trans. VN. New York: Random House. |
| 1961 | Commences residence at Palace Hotel, Montreux, Switzerland. |
| 1962 | *Pale Fire*. New York: Putnam. *Lolita* film premiere. |
| 1964 | Aleksandr Pushkin, *Eugene Onegin*, trans. VN. New York: Bollingen/Pantheon. |
| 1966 | *The Waltz Invention*. New York: Phaedra. |

| | |
|---|---|
| 1966 | *Nabokov's Quartet.* New York: Phaedra. |
| 1969 | *Ada or Ardor: A Family Chronicle.* New York: McGraw-Hill. |
| 1971 | *Poems and Problems.* New York: McGraw-Hill. |
| 1972 | *Transparent Things.* New York: McGraw-Hill. |
| 1973 | *A Russian Beauty and Other Stories.* New York: McGraw-Hill. |
| 1973 | *Strong Opinions.* New York: McGraw-Hill. |
| 1974 | *Lolita: A Screenplay.* New York: McGraw-Hill. |
| 1974 | *Look at the Harlequins!* New York: McGraw-Hill. |
| 1975 | *Tyrants Destroyed and Other Stories.* New York: McGraw-Hill. |
| 1976 | *Details of a Sunset and Other Stories.* New York: McGraw-Hill. |
| 2 July 1977 | Death of VN in Lausanne, Switzerland. |
| 1979 | *The Nabokov-Wilson Letters,* ed. Simon Karlinsky. New York: Harper & Row. |
| 1979 | *Stikhi [Poems].* Ann Arbor: Ardis. |
| 1980 | *Lectures on Literature.* New York: Harcourt Brace Jovanovich/Bruccoli Clark. |

1981          *Lectures on Ulysses*. Columbia, S.C.: Bruccoli
              Clark.

1981          *Lectures on Russian Literature*. New York:
              Harcourt Brace Jovanovich/Bruccoli Clark.

1983          *Lectures on Don Quixote*. San Diego: Harcourt
              Brace Jovanovich/Bruccoli Clark.

1984          *The Man from the USSR and Other Plays*, trans.
              Dmitri Nabokov. San Diego: Harcourt Brace
              Jovanovich/Bruccoli Clark.

1985          *Perepiska s Sestroy* [*Correspondence with his Sis-
              ter*]. Ann Arbor: Ardis.

1986          *The Enchanter*, trans. Dmitri Nabokov. New
              York: Putnam.

# LETTERS WRITTEN IN GERMANY AND FRANCE

## 1923-1939

*These fifteen letters provide background on Vladimir Nabokov's family and the preparation for his emigration to the United States.*

19.vi.23
Soliès-Pont, Alpes Maritimes

My dearest,[2]

Today I received your dear card in which you say you only got two poems ("*Cherries*" and another one),[3] while, *before* them, I had sent you a long letter with the two poems "*Vecher*"[4] and "*Krestî*."[5] No problem if the poems get lost (I know them by heart anyway) but I'm sorry about the letter. . . . Now I send you two short poems (to be followed tomorrow by much better ones) and a longer one (about an actual occurrence; the song *en quéstion* was the romance "Within your eyes, within your wild caress-es . . . ").

It is evening now, with touching cloudlets in the sky. I took a walk around the plantation, behind the grove of cork oaks, ate peaches and apricots, admired the sunset, listened to a nightingale's twees and whistles, and both its song and the sunset tasted of apricot and peach.

In a large cage near the house, live, all together (and rather messily), chickens, roosters, ducks, peahens, and white rabbits. One of the rabbits was lying with its front paws extended, like a lop-eared sphynx. Then a chick climbed on its back, and both of them had a scare. . . .

All during these days I have felt drawn to the inkwell, but there's no time for writing. For that reason—and because, without you, the sun is not the same, am coming back no later than July 20. I have gained weight and gotten all dark, since I now wear nothing but

3

shorts when I work. I must say I am infinitely glad I came here, and infinitely grateful to Sol. Sam.ʼ... [6]

V.[7]

\*Solomon Samoylovich Krïm[8]

1. VN's mother.
2. VN subsequently penciled brackets around the salutation to indicate that it was to be deleted before the letter was shown to Andrew Field (see facsimile). The deletion was made out of gentlemanly reserve, respect for his late mother, and perhaps a soupçon of distrust. In response to VN's insistence that numerous gross blunders be expunged from the manuscript of Field's *Vladimir Nabokov: His Life in Part* (1977), Field implied that there were certain skeletons in the Nabokov closet and that he might be compelled by VN's recalcitrance to write another, more critical book. He even mentioned, perhaps in jest, the hypothetical title "He Called His Mum Lolita." When VN was safely dead, Field proceeded to use his unfounded conjectures about VN's relationship with his mother as one of the main themes of his *VN: The Life and Art of Vladimir Nabokov* (1986). On the strength of an inaccurate letter count, the transformation of a Slavic diminutive VN would never have used into a Spanish one no Russian would have used, plus what he thought was the trace of a "T," Field concluded that the excised "Radostʼ" ("dearest" or "beloved") was none other than "'Lolita,' surely." Then, assuming that the conjecture had been established as fact in the naive reader's mind, he proceeded to construct thereon a precarious house of marked cards for his psychocritical folly. DN.
3. For many years VN would give or send his poems to his mother, who meticulously transcribed them into albums that are now part of the Nabokov Archive in Montreux.
4. "Evening."
5. "The Crosses."
6. Final words omitted, for the same reason as "Radostʼ" had been. They are not "Farewell, Lolita." DN.
7. Translated from Russian by DN.
8. VN's footnote. Former chairman of the Crimean provisional government, absentee steward of Le Domaine de Beaulieu, estate in the south of France where VN worked as a farmhand in the summer of 1923.

*Evening*

*I heaved from my shoulder my pick and my shovel*
  *into a corner of the barn,*
*I dried off the sweat, ambled out to greet sunset*
  *a bonfire cool and rosy-hued.*

*It peacefully blazed beyond towering beeches,*
  *in between funereal boughs,*
*where fleetingly shimmered ineffable echoes*
  *of a vibrant nightingale.*

*And a guttural din, choirs of toads, gutta-perchalike,*
  *sang resilient on the pond.*
*It broke off. My forehead was trustingly, downily*
  *brushed by the flight of a passing moth.*

*The hills grew more somber: there, flashed reassuringly*
  *a twinkle of nocturnal lights.*
*In the distance, a train chugged and vanished. A lingering*
  *whistle lingeringly died....*

*The fragrance was grassy. Entranced I stood, thoughtless.*
  *And, when the nebulous hoot was stilled,*
*I saw night had fallen, stars hung close above me,*
  *and tears were streaming down my face.*[1]

1. Written during the same period as the opening letter; translated from Russian by DN.

Вторникъ.

19.VI. 23

[цд̃ Solies-Pont, A.M.] (19)

[Радость моя,]

      Получилъ сегодня твою дорогую карточку, гдѣ ты говоришь, что получила только два стиха ("черешни" и другой). Между тѣмъ до нихъ я писалъ тебѣ длинное письмо и два стиха: "Вечеръ" и "Кресты". Не бѣда если стихи пропадутъ (я ихъ впрочемъ помню) но жаль мнѣ письма... Теперь шлю тебѣ два снимка (послѣдуютъ завтра другіе гораздо лучше) и стихотворенье (истинное происшествіе. Писки ея diestis "была романсомъ въ твоихъ глазахъ, и твоихъ безумныхъ лас-кахъ")

      "Сейчасъ — вечеръ, трогательныя тучки. Я ходилъ по плантаціи, за пробковой рощей, или персики и абрикосы, смотрилъ на закатъ, слушалъ какъ цокалъ и свистѣлъ соловей — и у пѣсни его и у заката былъ вкусъ абрикосовъ и персиковъ.

      А въ большой клѣткѣ, у дома живутъ всѣ вмѣстѣ (и довольно грязно) куры, пѣтухи, утки, цезарки и бѣлые кролики. Одинъ такой кроликъ лежалъ вытянувъ переднія лапы: — лопоухій сфинксъ. Потомъ шлепнокъ въ лицъ ему на спину. — и оба испугались...

      Меня ты дни — все тянетъ къ чернильницѣ

а писать некогда. Поэтому — и ему
потому, что буд тебѣ солнце не в солнце
я возвращусь не позже 20го іюля.
Разсиралъ я и весь почернѣлъ, такъ
какъ работаю теперь въ однихъ кальсонахъ.
Вообще: я буквально радъ, что пріѣхалъ
и буквально благодаренъ Сол. Сам.⊕ (который
все не идетъ). [

В.                    ⊕ Соломонъ Самойловичъ
                              Крымъ

(19)

лысыи Холмы

дорога въ Керчь

рѣчка

плодовыи дерѣв.          плодовыи дерѣв. и т.д.

дорога къ Solis Port

домъ

рѣка

Крестимъ — мая окно

планъ „Beaulieu"

TO: **KIRILL NABOKOV**[1]                            ALS, 2 pp.
c. 1930                                           Berlin

Dear Kirill,

The poems you sent me are significantly better. The poem "To you, a stranger" ends well; the last two lines are good. The dragonfly etc. image is not bad in the poem about the window, and, thanks to the repetition of the letter P, there is a pleasant sound to the first line "one's soul, suffused with poems and passion." But there are also things that are not good: a flame cannot "flare up gradually" (flaring is an instantaneous phenomenon). Leave to Blok the act of "committing [those] shoulders to memory"; *okonnaya dvertsa* ["the window's doorlet"] is incomprehensible, and is there to rhyme with *serdtse* ["heart"], just as, incidentally, further on, *okontse* ["windowlet"] exists solely for the benefit of *solntse* ["sun"].

And, above all, beware of platitudes, i.e., word combinations that have already appeared a thousand times like "love's flame," "the Muses' creation" "to sing the beloved," "riotous agitation" and "tempestuous storm" (a pleonasm to boot), "jubilant sea," etc. There is a hackneyed sound as well in the rhythm itself of the poem "When in one's soul": first a stanza on "when," followed by one on "then"— this is mere rhetoric. As a general rule, try to find new combinations of words (not for the sake of their novelty, but because every person sees things in an individual way and must find *his own* words for them). Do not use epithets that no longer have any meaning ("noisy street"); do not fill in gaps, for a poem must be born whole and tightly packed, and if you must invent some adjective to plug a hole, that means the whole line is bad.

If you designate stressed syllables "/" and unstressed ones "-", here are all the schemes of Russian poetry (when written with regular meter):

The iamb: "- / - / - / - /" ("within my soul, those eyes of yours"). Every "- /" pair is called a foot, so here you have four-foot iambic meter, iambic tetrameter.

The trochee is the inverse of the iamb. Its foot is "/ -" ("trochees merit your attention").

8

There are, in addition, three types of meter whose feet consist not of two but of *three* syllables:

The amphibrach: - / - ("this too is a meter in which you should write").

The anapaest: - - / ("and this too is a meter in which you should write").

The dactyl: / - - ("also a meter toward which don't be squeamish").

Six-foot dactylic meter = hexameter.[2]

As you see, this is all simple and can be assimilated in five minutes, with no need for any textbooks.

Answer two questions for me:

1) Why, in the examples given, does the last foot not correspond to the scheme ("should write" and "squeamish")?

2) Why is an iambic line (or trochaic one, if you drop the first syllable) like "when imperturbably at work," in spite of its odd scheme of stressed and unstressed syllables ("- - - / - - - /"), nevertheless *iambic* (or, minus the first word, trochaic)? Try and answer.

Your V.[3]

1. VN's brother, who was attending the German university in Prague. Some of his poems were published in Russian émigré periodicals.
2. In Russian prosody, the term *geksametr* denotes a fundamentally dactylic hexameter. DN.
3. Translated from Russian by DN.

TO: **KIRILL NABOKOV**                                    ALS, 2 pp.
c. 1930                                                              Berlin

Dear Kirill,

Here is what it boils down to: are you writing poetry as a sideline, because everyone does it, or are you really drawn to it irresistibly, does it surge from your soul, do images and sensations naturally don the dress of poetry, crowding to emerge? If the former is the case, and a poem is only a carefree game to you, a pleasant fashionable entertainment, the desire to hand it with a grim expression to some girl, then forget it, for you are wasting your time.

If, on the other hand, it is the latter (and I would very much like it to be so), then one must first of all realize what a difficult, responsible job it is, a job one must train for with a passion, with a certain reverence and chastity, disdaining the seeming facility with which quatrains fall together (just tack on a rhyme and it's done).

Beware of stereotypes. Thus, for instance, the first verse of your poem (although it does contain errors, but more about that later) is far from being a stereotype, even though it contains discourse about a rose (but an original kind of discourse). What is a stereotype, and a bad one, is your way of rhyming. On more than one occasion I have written in *Rul'*[1] about ugly rhymes that irk the ear and create a comical impression through aural association. Thus, for example, you rhyme *mozg* ["brain"] and *roz* [a plural case of "rose"]; where the ear expects a rhyme, the aural sense involuntarily transforms *roz* into *rozg* [a plural case of "birch rod"], and these birch rods are comical. *Zhadny* ["greedy"] and *sada* [a case of "garden"] or *pozharishch* [a plural case of "site of a conflagration"] and *lapishch* [a plural case of "huge paw"] cannot rhyme at all, while *raztsvet* ["flowering" (n.)] and *tsvet* ["color"] or *kogti* ["claws"] and *nogti* ["nails"] rhyme too obviously, since they are almost identical words, which is bad. A rhyme must evoke astonishment and satisfaction in the reader— astonishment at how unexpected it is, and satisfaction with its precision or musicality.

Even more important, though, are images. You compare jealousy with an octopus, but the image you give of an octopus is incorrect: you endow it with "coils" and "huge paws" and "claws" and "nails," while actually an octopus is a gray bag with two goggled eyes and elongated feelers. In other words, this octopus of yours turned up quite by chance, and on top of it there is an admixture, from God knows where, of some "quagmire" and some "chastening hand," even though we had just been talking of "huge paws." Let us go through the poem again from beginning to end and see what other flaws it contains. Here—you have "the first color will . . . ripen." A fruit ripens, not a color. "A bird flies in on the wing." On what else would you expect it to fly? ... "In the abandonment of the garden" is a horrid Balmontism. It should be "in the abandoned garden" (an expression, incidentally, that is often found in romances). "The fire of *pozharishchi*": You are mistaken if you think *pozharishche* means "huge conflagration." It means "a place where a conflagration has occurred." "Ring ... paws" are too far apart. "With [one's?] mouth ... to sate one's thirst": with what else are you going to drink? In the fifth stanza for some reason you have a transposition of feminine and masculine rhymes. *Prevozmoch* ["to overcome"]—*noch* ["night"] is a very shabby rhyme.

Take all this into consideration and, if you have the urge to write, do so as conscientiously as you can and try to avoid the absurdities I have noted above.

Keep well.

V.[2]

1. *The Rudder*, émigré daily edited by Yosif V. Hessen and VN's father Vladimir Dmitrievich Nabokov.
2. Translated from Russian by DN.

TO: **ALTAGRACIA DE JANNELLI**[1]                                          CC, I p.

V. Nabokoff
Nestorstrasse 22
Berlin-Halensee
Germany
March 23d, 1935

Dear Mr. de Jannelli,

I am afraid I cannot very well send you a synopsis of the EXPLOIT[2] as its composition entails too much labour: the quality of this novel is in the way the plot is treated and not in the plot itself. Besides

I am very much against my books being judged by mere descriptions of their contents. As the EXPLOIT has not yet been translated into any language I offer you instead an option on another novel of mine KING QUEEN KNAVE, a German copy of which I am sending you by the same mail. As the option I gave you expires on the 1.V., I replace it herewith by a fresh one for KING QUEEN KNAVE to last until the 3.VII,1935.

I trust that this is the best we can do under the present circumstances and await your consent to my present offer.

Yours very truly

P.S. Schuster & Simon tell me that the book (Luzhin's Defence) has indeed been offered to them, but that they have not yet quite made up their minds about it. I shall keep you informed of further developments.

---

1. New York literary agent who was attempting to place translation rights to VN's work. She was the most energetic of the platoon of agents who homed in on Nabokov after wind of *Kamera obskura* (*Laughter in the Dark*) reached them from Europe. During the first two years of correspondence an amusing—and uncorrected—misunderstanding caused Nabokov to address de Jannelli as "Mr." Then the salutation changes to "Mrs." for Nabokov learned that his agent was female. Only in 1940, upon his arrival in New York, did he see her. She had an inkling of Nabokov's literary worth, but insisted that he attend to business details, and not squander his time writing more material when there were "deals" to be worked on. She shared the opinion of several publishers that what he did write should be relevant, as some would say today, to contemporary social and political issues, with characters and sufferings the reader could "identify with." Most of her efforts resulted in rejection slips, although, in 1938, she did succeed in getting *Laughter* published by Bobbs-Merrill. (In 1940 Houghton Mifflin rejected *Sie Kommt—Kommt Sie?* [*Mary*], explaining that "It isn't consistently good enough to warrant translation.") De Jannelli gave little Dmitri Nabokov his first camera, a Kodak Baby Brownie. DN.
2. Published as *Glory* (New York: McGraw-Hill, 1971).

> Vladimir Nabokoff-Sirin
> Nestorstrasse 22
> Berlin-Halensee
> 22nd May, 1935.

Dear Sirs,

Thanks for your letter of the 15th. I have noted that you are having the translation set up by your Printers and that I shall receive a set of proofs.[2] I certainly don't intend to make any superfluous corrections and generally I should not like to cause any delay. My demands are very modest. From the very beginning I have been trying to obtain an exact, complete and correct translation. I wonder whether Mr. Klement[3] informed you of the defects I found in the translation he sent me. It was loose, shapeless, sloppy, full of blunders and gaps, lacking vigour and spring, and plumped down in such dull, flat English that I could not read it to the end; all of which is rather hard on an author who aims in his work at absolute precision, takes the utmost trouble to attain it, and then finds the translator calmly undoing every blessed phrase. Please believe me that had the translation been in the least acceptable I would have passed it. And I am sure you will agree, in your quality of publishers, that a good translation is most important for the success of a book. So I hope that it has now been thoroughly improved and that it will not give rise to any objections of the above kind.

There is another bit of information for which I should be most grateful to you. Did you acquire from Mr. Klement together with "Camera Obscura" another novel of mine? And if so, was it "Despair" or "Luzhin's Defence" (entitled "La Course du Fou" in the French edition)? Please excuse me for bothering you with questions, but you will surely understand in what a ridiculous position I am. Mr. Klement has for months left all my letters without any reply. Possibly the man is dead. Now my point is that, as I hear, the American publishing firm Doubleday, Doran & Co. are desirous of publishing the latter book in collaboration with the British publishers, so that I should like to know who holds the English rights of this book.[4]

Yours very truly

P.S. Please do not omit "Berlin" when writing to me.

1. London publisher.
2. *Camera Obscura*, trans. W. Roy (London: John Long, 1936). Long was one of the Hutchinson imprints. Later translated by VN as *Laughter in the Dark* (Indianapolis & New York: Bobbs-Merrill, 1938).
3. Otto Klement, literary agent.
4. *The Defense* was published in New York by Putnam in 1964.

TO: **ALTAGRACIA DE JANNELLI**                          cc, 1 p.

V.Nabokoff
Nestorstrasse 22
Berlin-Halcnscc
August 11th, 1935

Dear Mr. de Jannelli,

I see from what you tell me that the American publishers all prefer to deal in a book where they can find an English partner. I therefore suggest your temporarily abandoning your attempts at finding a publisher for Podvig and La Course du Fou and trying your hand at Camera Obscura and Despair, those two books having already an English publisher in the firm of Hutchinson & Co. Ltd.

Camera Obscura, for one, is to appear this autumn under the firm of Long & Co. Its translation has already been completed, but there only exists till now one revised copy thereof.

Perhaps you could try to work on a Russian copy which I am addressing you together with this. I am also giving you an MS copy of Despair. The latter will probably appear in England next spring.[1]

Yours very truly

1. London: John Long, 1937; trans. VN.

TO: **HUTCHINSON & CO.**                                         cc, 2 pp.

Vladimir Nabokoff-Sirin<br>Nestorstrasse 22<br>Berlin-Halensee<br>August 28th, 1936

Dear Sirs,

After the publication of my book "Camera Obscura", the translation of which did not satisfy me—it was inexact and full of hackneyed expressions meant to tone down all the tricky passages—Messrs. John Long suggested that I should translate myself that other novel of mine they were supposed to publish,— "Despair". Though I am pretty well acquainted with the English language I did not care to take the entire responsibility and offered to make a translation which the publishers would have revised by some expert of their own. While they accepted this condition, Messrs. J. Long declared that they did not think they could "pay more than a fee of say 10/6d per 1000 words, as we should have to pay an additional fee to the person selected to edit it." Subsequently the fee was extended to 15/- per 1000 words, and I agreed.

They acknowledged the translation I sent them in the beginning of April 1936, but then left me for almost 2 months without any news. At length they informed me that they had not made any plans for the publication of the book as "some of our Readers' reports have

not been at all enthusiastic, especially in regard to your translation".
I did not point out to Messrs. J. Long the strangeness of their conduct,
but simply replied by a letter part of which please allow me to quote:

" . . . after careful consideration I think that perhaps your readers'
perplexity was not so much caused by an imperfect translation, as
by the peculiar character of the work itself and by a certain angularity
of style which was part of the author's deliberate intention. As a matter of fact among the Russian reviewers of the less sophisticated type
there occurred one or two who failed to penetrate beyond the "story"
and were frankly puzzled,—in spite of which the book very soon won
a reputation which my modesty forbids me to qualify. I quite understand that the book's "originality"—as the critics chose to put it—
may cause some perplexity after a superficial perusal,—the more so
as I have taken special pains to render exactly into English all that
I had taken similar trouble to convey to the Russian reader, a couple
of years before."

I also suggested that your firm might get in touch with McBride[1]
of New York whose manager Mr. Mangione wrote to my agent that
he was "enthusiastic about Despair preferring it, of course, to Camera
Obscura" and asked to consider its publication in case it should be
published in England.

To this letter of June 29th I have not yet had any answer.

While I do not think the whole attitude of Messrs. J. Long in this
matter to be beyond reproach, since they had engaged themselves to
have the translation edited and declared this to be the reason why
they offered me but a very moderate fee for my work, I, nevertheless, have now asked an English friend of mine (who is a professional translator) to revise my translation, so as to set things into
motion again; I hope to have the revised Ms. ready within a couple
of weeks.

I should like to add that some time ago I got acquainted with the
average production of Messrs. J. Long—and I feel somehow that
"Despair" would be far more in its place if you could publish it under
the imprint of Hutchinson instead of John Long. I am afraid that
the public for which Messrs. J. Long are working might fail to appre-

ciate "Despair" on account of its rather peculiar character as described in my letter quoted above.

Yours faithfully

1. Robert M. McBride & Co., New York publisher.

TO: **HUTCHINSON & CO.**                                          cc, 1 p.

Vladimir Nabokoff
Nestorstrasse 22
Berlin-Halensee
November 28th, 1936

Dear Sirs,

While leaving the final decision entirely with you, I think it my duty to repeat my attempt of persuading you that it is your interest as well as mine to publish "Despair" under your own imprint instead of John Long's.

I am getting gradually acquainted with John Long's latest publications, and I am afraid that my book would look among them like a rhinoceros in a world of humming birds. These publications are doubtlessly excellent in their own way, as they fully satisfy the wants of such readers who are looking for an amusing or thrilling tale, but who could hardly be expected to appreciate a purely psychological novel the merits of which lie not in its plot, but on a wholly different plane. My book is essentially concerned with subtle dissections of a mind anything but "average" or "ordinary": nature had endowed my hero with literary genius, but at the same time there was a criminal taint in his blood; the criminal in him, prevailing over the artist, took over those very methods which nature had meant the artist to use. It is *not* a "detective novel".

I cannot help feeling that "Despair", were it presented to the right sort of public, might prove quite a success for you and for me. Please believe me that I am not in the habit of praising my own work, and that if I draw your attention to some of its features (as noted by Russian critics), I do so out of business considerations only.

I cannot imagine why, inspite of my previous letters, you avoid discussing this matter with me, and I do hope to hear from you now.

Yours faithfully

TO: **VÉRA NABOKOV**[1]
20 February 1937

ALS, 2 pp.
Paris

My darling, my joy,

Yesterday I answered you by air mail, and now send an addendum. The more I think about it and listen to other people's advice the more absurd your plan seems (at the same time it is unbearable for me to think that Mother's peace of mind is *en jeu*, and that, in a general sense, some higher or inner law requires that, in spite of everything, we visit her and show her our little one—and all of it is such torture, I can't bear it, it is a constant strain on my spirit, and there is no place it can lie down for a rest). So think about everything I have written you, and about all my considerations. Is it possible that, after having expended such enormous efforts to establish a vital link with London and Paris, we must suddenly abandon everything to go to the wilds of Czechoslovakia,[2] where (psychologically, geographically, in every sense) I shall again be cut off from every possible source and opportunity of making a living? Just think—from there we shall never extricate ourselves to go to the south of France, and the London trip I have planned for the end of April will become impossibly complicated. I assure you that at Bormes[3] you will get peace and rest, and that the doctors there are just as good. Listen to reason, my darling, and make up your mind. *Because if you go on like that I shall simply take the next train to Berlin,*[4] i.e., I shall come to fetch you, which will certainly be neither wise nor cheap. I find it difficult to explain to you how important it is that we not lose contact with the shore to which I have managed to swim—to put it figuratively but accurately—for, after your letter, I really feel like a swimmer who has just reached a rock and is being torn from it by some whim of Neptune, a wave of unknown origin, a sudden wind or some such thing. Please take all this into account, my love. One of these days I should be getting a letter from Madame Chyorny. And on April 1 we shall meet in Toulon. *Incidentally, I am not particularly interested in the butterflies of that department—Var*[5]—for I have already collected there and am familiar with everything, so that I shall take care of my little one all day long and write in the evenings. And in May we'll find a cheaper arrangement. I think this time common sense is on my side. (To one thing I shall *definitely* not agree: *I can no longer stay without you and the little one.*)[6]

Long[7] writes me that Kernahan (a famous critic), to whom he showed *Despair,*[8] wrote him: *"Reviewers who like it will hail it as genius. . . . Those who don't like [it] will say that it is extremely unpleasant. . . . It is meant, I assume, to be the work of a criminal maniac, and as such is very admirably done"* etc.[9] Silly but flattering on the whole. Besides this he forwards an inquiry from an American publisher, which I am mailing to the Old Grace.[10]

*My dear love,* all the Irinas[11] in the world are powerless (I have just seen a third one, at the Tatarinovs'[12]—the former Mademoiselle. . .). The eastern side of every minute of mine is already colored by the light of our impending meeting. All the rest is dark, boring, you-less. *I want to hold you and kiss you.*[13] I adore you.

Don't forget the *tub* (or should I buy one here?). I delivered the books to Lyusia[14] yesterday. Had lunch at Petit's with Aldanov, Maklakov, Kerensky, Bernatsky,[15] and my two chaps.[16] *Write me in detail what the doctor said.*

I love you beyond words.

V.[17]

---

1. When my husband was absent from home he wrote me every day. I have selected four letters from those I received from him in 1937 during our longest "separation." Véra Nabokov.

19

2. VN's mother was living in Prague.
3. A town in the south of France where the widow of the poet Sasha Chyorny, a friend of the family, lived.
4. English in original.
5. English in original.
6. Last six words in English.
7. John Long.
8. Title in English in original.
9. English in original.
10. Pun on name of agent Altagracia de Jannelli.
11. Various ladies by that name who flirted with or had designs on VN.
12. *Rul'* staff writer Vladimir E. Tatarinov and his wife.
13. English in original.
14. Véra Nabokov's cousin Ilya Feigin.
15. Russian novelist Mark Aldanov; Vasily Alekseyevich Maklakov, last representative of the Russian Provisional Government in Paris; Aleksandr Kerensky, prime minister of the Russian Provisional Government; Bernatsky, unidentified.
16. Ilya Fondaminsky and V. M. Zenzinov. Fondaminsky was a political writer and activist, the main force behind the émigré literary journal *Sovremennye Zapiski*, and a close friend, with whom VN was staying. Zenzinov, in Russia a prominent Socialist Revolutionary and in the emigration an editor and critic, was also a close friend of VN.
17. Translated from Russian by DN.

TO: **VÉRA NABOKOV**
30 March 1937

ALS, 2 pp.
C/o Ilya Fondaminsky
130 av. de Versailles
Paris

My love, what's going on? This is my fourth day without a letter. Is the little one all right? Yesterday I picked up in my arms the three-year-old, red-curled, pensive-and-naughty nephew of Baroness Budberg[1] (also named Dmitri, and also addressed by a nickname), and was moved to tears by the recollection. . . . What a marvelous toy store there is on the Champs-Elysées—no comparison with our Czech stores—what trains! ("*le plus rapide train du monde des jouets*," with a "streamlined" engine and wonderfully made blue cars). I know you have a thousand worries, but still do write me more often!

Denis Roche is doing a fine translation of "Spring,"[2] which will soon be finished; yesterday I discussed various tricky passages with him. Budberg, on the other hand, could not cope with "Spring,"[3] so the collection will include either "The Return of Chorb," or I shall translate "Spring" myself (or Struve[4] will do "Pilgram"): the story must be delivered no later than August. Putnam[5] liked the autobiography[6] *very* much, and everybody advises me to agree to their running it in a review in serial form. I probably shall. Otherwise the rhythm will be broken; moreover, the size of the thing makes it very difficult to publish as a book. The same person (Budberg) has offered to have me meet Aleksey Tolstoy[7] today. I don't think I'll go. Maria Pavlovna,[8] a diminutive lady with a cigarette and laryngitis, rang and rang for tea, but to no avail, since it was Easter. I discussed with her a lecture tour in America, and she promised to help. She once collected butterflies in some wild spot with Avinoff.[9] Of . . . and . . . she said they were nice but *snobs*,[10] and this expression coming from *her* acquired for me a Proustian charm and, applied to them, a fresh and frightening forcefulness. Had dinner with Vilenkin,[11] who is hard at work arranging my London reading and promoting my book. (By the way, I learned quite by accident that *Luzhin*[12] is enjoying a very great—the word used was "phenomenal"—success in Sweden.) Tomorrow I shall see Mmes. Polyakov[13] and Sablin.[14] Tonight I am dining, together with six authors, at the house of some Maecenas. "The Present,"[15] which was published day before yesterday, turned out to be more than three hundred lines: four hundred twenty. That's fine. The next excerpt I shall entitle "The Reward," and again I'll squeeze in more lines than assigned. Oh, my darling, how I long to see you. . . . I'm filled with rapture when I think about May. Zyoka[16] tells me the little one is now even better looking. This past month Viktor[17] has gone through more than 200 francs. One of these days I shall visit Fayard, Lefèvre (*Nouvelles Littéraires*) and Thiebaut (*Revue de Paris*).[18]

*I adore you*,[19] it is very difficult for me to live without you, please write me very soon. It is three o'clock—I am off to see the doctoress, then I'll try to write for an hour or two. I love you, my life. . . .

V.[20]

1. Active literary lady and translator; companion first of Maxim Gorky, then H. G. Wells.
2. Into French. Published in English as "Spring in Fialta."
3. Into English.
4. Gleb Struve, authority on Russian émigré and Soviet literature and a close friend.
5. Of London.
6. Autobiographical sketches, never published in that form.
7. The historical novelist and poet.
8. Daughter of Grand Duke Paul.
9. At one time director of the Carnegie Museum in Pittsburgh.
10. English in original.
11. A college friend.
12. *The Luzhin Defense*, later published in English as *The Defense*.
13. A literary patroness.
14. Wife of the last head of the Russian diplomatic mission in London before England recognized the Soviet regime.
15. An excerpt from *Dar* [*The Gift*], Paris, *Poslednie Novosti* (28 March 1937).
16. George Hessen, a close friend.
17. A jocular appellation for himself.
18. Three publishers.
19. In English.
20. Translated from Russian by DN.

TO: **VÉRA NABOKOV**
15 April 1937

ALS, 3 pp.
130 av. de Versailles
Paris

My life, my love, *it is twelve years today*.[1] And on this very day *Despair* has been published, and *The Gift* appears in *Annales Contemporaines* [*Sovremennye Zapiski*].

Total success with *"The Outrage."*[2] It will appear in the May issue of *Mesures*, and our Viktor has already received a nice little thousand for it. The lunch at the villa of Henry Church (the publisher of *Mesures*, an American millionaire with a splendid boil on his nape, elderly, taciturn, with a literature-addicted wife of German extraction) turned out remarkably well. The rendezvous was at Adrienne

Monnier's bookstore on the Odéon, whence we proceeded by car to the Churches', out beyond St. Cloud (everything green and moist, almond trees in bloom, gnats swarming). I was much "feted" and was in great form. The writers were represented by Michaux.[3] I got on swimmingly with Joyce's publisher Sylvia Beach, who might help considerably with the publication of *Despair* in case Gallimard and Albin Michel *ne marcheront pas*. After lunch there was something on the order of a meeting of the *Mesures* editorial board, and a lady photographer took fifteen shots of us. Among the topics discussed was the possibility of using some kind of waves to identify the sounds emitted by plants. I maintained that the poplar's voice was a soprano, and the oak's a bass, but Paulhan[4] much more wittily declared that the oak apparently has exactly the same voice as a daisy—"*peut-être parce qu'il est toujours un peu embarrassé.*" Tomorrow I am having lunch with him, Cingria, Supervielle[5] and Michaux in Montmartre. My darling, I love you. The story about my little one ("for the shores")[6] is enchanting. Zenzinov can't stop laughing and is telling it to everybody. *Your letter to* Ilyusha[7] *is quite nice, my darling one.*[8] Your passport will be renewed in France as soon as you arrive. I am terribly distressed that the Prague project fell through again, but I never quite believed it would succeed. To England I shall go for a week at the end of the month. Tomorrow at five I shall call on Madame Sablin in order to arrange a Russian reading there. In any case I shall not leave before the 25th—the book must be given a little time to ferment, as both Budberg and Struve write. Have sent Long some more addresses that were given me by Sylvia Beach. My "Pushkin"[9] is having a very gratifying success. I've put on weight, gotten a tan, changed my skin, but am in a constant state of irritation because I have no place and no time to work. Tonight I am dining at the Kyandzhuntsevs'.[10] Am now going to phone the old man.[11]

*My love, my love,*[12] how long it's been since you've stood before me, and God, how many new things there will be about my little one, and how many births I have missed (of words, of games, of all sorts of things).

Wrote yesterday to Mrs. Chyorny. My love, be sure to prepare for your trip carefully so as to avoid any last-minute delays. How amusing about Frau V. Bardeleben.[13] Poor Ilf[14] has died. And, somehow, one visualizes the Siamese twins being separated. I love you, I love you. My stock has gone up a lot in France. *Paulhan est tout ce qu'il y a de plus charmant*, and something about him—his vivaciousness, his quick dark eye, his personality and his unshavenness—are reminiscent of Ilyusha. Give my greetings to Anyuta.[15] I am expecting a letter from her.

I embrace you, my joy, my tired little thing....

V.[16]

1. Since their marriage. English in original.
2. Title in English in original, but most likely refers to a French translation of the short story "Obida," later published in English as "A Bad Day."
3. Henri Michaux, French writer and critic of Belgian origin.
4. Jean Paulhan, influential French publisher and editor.
5. Charles-Albert Cingria and Jules Supervielle, French authors.
6. Probably something to do with a recitation by three-year-old DN of part of Pushkin's poem "For the Shores of Your Far Country."
7. Fondaminsky.
8. Sentence in English in original.
9. "*Pouchkine, ou le vrai et le vraisemblable*," essay written by VN in French and originally published in *Nouvelle Revue Française*, Paris, March 1937. Reprinted in *Magazine Littéraire*, Paris, September 1986, in issue dedicated to VN. Also reprinted as "Pushkin, or the Real and the Plausible," trans. DN in *New York Review of Books* (31 March 1988).
10. Saveliy Kyandzhuntsev, St. Petersburg schoolmate and close friend of VN's.
11. The reference is to Yosif V. Hessen, friend and political associate of VN's father, and father of VN's close friend George Hessen.
12. English in original.
13. Wife of German ex-military man who had rented rooms in his apartment at Luitpoldstrasse 27, Berlin, to the Nabokovs.
14. One half of the writing team of Ilya Ilf and Yevgeny Petrov, authors of the famous comic work *Zolotoy telyonok* [*The Golden Calf*] and other books.
15. Véra Nabokov's cousin Anna Feigin.
16. Translated from Russian by DN.

TO: VÉRA NABOKOV                                    ALS, 3 pp.
15 May 1937                            130 av. de Versailles
                                                Paris

My priceless joy—whom, it seems now, I shall soon manage to reach—the cable arrived yesterday *avec une allure* of a swallow. Today at ten I was already at the Czech Consulate (they close early on Saturdays). It turned out that the visa, though already sent, had not yet arrived. By the way, was the insufficient time reserve of my passport mentioned when the visa was sent? For it was sent not in response to my special request but to Mother's previous efforts. Or was it indicated anyway? I had asked that it be specifically mentioned and had sent the number of my file. From the consulate I rushed to the Czech Legation with a letter from Makl[akov], which it took him four days to write(!), to see the Envoy, but he was not there either, so I shall go to the consulate only on Tuesday morning and, if I get it, shall leave for Prague that same Tuesday. I dreamed tonight that our little one was walking towards me on the sidewalk, his cheeks dirty for some reason, wearing a dark-colored little coat. I asked him, referring to myself, "Who is this?", and he answered, with a sly smile, "Volodya Nabokov." My tooth was finished today—a temporary filling good for two or three months— but there's not enough time to extract the roots. Rinsing it with camomile has made the swelling subside somewhat. My beloved darling, I have, basically, only a very vague idea of your life in Prague; and feel that you are terribly uncomfortable and uneasy—the news about the bedbug [in the hotel room] told me a great deal, my poor love! ... Yesterday I squandered some four hours at the *Sûreté*, and they promised to make it possible for me to obtain a French passport[1] by Thursday, but, of course, if I get my visa on Tuesday, *I shall not stay here another second*, and anyway I no longer have any faith in these promises. I am totally exhausted by all this senseless torture, and even more by your worrying and waiting. Now about the money: Lusya[2] is holding 3100 francs and 105 pounds for me. Out of that I took 1100 francs for the two sums I sent to you (rounding out the amount with what I had in hand). Besides that I have one pound in coins, and two hundred francs. I'll probably be able to scrape together enough for the ticket without touching the reserve.

Today there was an intelligent review of *Dar* [*The Gift*] by Khodasevich.[3] He came to see me recently. Tonight I am going to the Russian Theatre to see the first performance of *Azef*.[4] All these past days I have been busy with "*Printemps a F[ialta]*"[5] so as to get it in perfect shape, and I believe I have, but there are a million corrections, each to be made three times. I continue with the radiation treatments[6] every day and am pretty much cured. You know—now I can tell you frankly—the indescribable torments I endured in February, before these treatments, drove me to the border of suicide—a border I was not authorized to cross because I had you in my luggage. My love, is it really true that I shall soon see you—in four days, if fate does not let me down? My dear love, I vow that you will have a good rest, and that life will be easier and simpler in general. My friendship with Ilya and V. M.[7] has grown even closer—they are wonderful. Without even mentioning how much I am obliged to Dr. Kogan-Bernstein,[8] whom I would owe over 5000 francs(!) if she were charging me anything (the usual charge for one treatment is 100 frs.!) *Try not to worry too much, my love. We shall soon be together anyway.*[9] Tell Mother I embrace her and am not writing her only because I am spending all my epistolary energy on you.

V.[10]

1. Not a regular French passport, but a "Nansen" passport issued, under an international convention, to stateless émigrés.
2. Ilya Feigin, brother of Anna Feigin.
3. Vladislav Felitseanovich Khodasevich, one of the greatest Russian poets of the century.
4. A play by Count Aleksey Tolstoy about a famous double agent in the service of the pre-revolutionary Russian government.
5. The French translation of "Spring in Fialta."
6. For psoriasis.
7. Ilya Fondaminsky and V. M. Zenzinov.
8. Doctor and personal friend, whom VN met through Fondaminsky.
9. Two sentences in English.
10. Translated from Russian by DN.

TO: **ALTAGRACIA DE JANNELLI**          VÉRA NABOKOV HOLOGRAPH COPY.

Hotel de la Poste, Moulinet
14 July 1938

Dear Mr. de Jannelli

I am writing from a small mountain resort.

On the whole I rather liked N.'s[1] description of *The Gift*, although it is very superficial—there is a lot more in my book both for the connoisseur and the lay reader. Here are some objections:

*The Gift* is thoroughly realistic, as it tells the story of a definite person, showing his physical existence and the development of his inner self. As he is an author, I naturally show his literary progress. Moreover, the whole story is threaded on my hero's love-romance, with the underground work of fate revealed—an essential point which N. has entirely missed. My style and methods have *nothing* in common with Joyce (though I greatly appreciate *Ulysses*). The novel is not "a crazy quilt of bits"; it is a logical sequence of psychological events: the movements of stars may seem crazy to the simpleton, but wise men know that the comets come back.

I don't understand why the reader should be "astonished" at the "insertion" of my hero's work (Chernyshevski's biography).[2] The preceding chapters lead up to it and, as samples are given of all my hero's literary production, it would have been an impossible omission to leave his chief book out. Moreover, at this point, my hero's interpretation of Chernyshevski's life (which, incidentally, took *me* four years to write) lifts my novel to a wider plane, lending it an epic note and, so to say, spreading my hero's individual butter over the bread of a whole epoch. In this work (Chernyshevski's life), the defeat of Marxism and materialism is not only made evident, but it is rounded out by my hero's artistic triumph.[3]

As to the interest which *The Gift* might represent to the foreign (American) reader, I want to repeat that I know how to translate the book in such a way as even to avoid the necessity of footnotes. "Human interest" means Uncle Tom's cabin to me (or Galsworthy's drivel) and makes me sick, seasick.

Your faith in my work is of the greatest value to me and I thank you warmly for your kind words.

Yours very truly,

1. Unidentified.
2. Nikolay Gavrilovich Chernyshevski (1828-1889), highly influential leftist political writer, subsequently very popular with the Soviets.
3. When *Dar* (*The Gift*) was published in installments in 1937–38 in *Sovremennye Zapiski* (Paris), Chapter Four, which consists entirely of Fyodor Godunov-Cherdyntsev's biography of Chernyshevski, was omitted because of pressures from part of the editorial staff. It was one of the few instances when Nabokov agreed (albeit with great reluctance) to a deletion, for he realized that this price had to be paid to have the novel published at all. It is also interesting that, in its March 1988 issue, the Soviet magazine *Ural* began serialized publication of what was announced as an unabridged version of *Dar*, with only a moderate obbligato of adverse comment to mitigate the viewpoints of Chapter Four, but nonetheless with other omissions and alterations. DN.

TO: **ALTAGRACIA DE JANNELLI**                    CC, 1 p.

Vladimir Nabokoff
Nestorstr. 22
Berlin-Halensee
November 16th, 1938?

Dear Mr. de Jannelli,

Many thanks for your nice long letter of October 12th. I quite understand what you have to say about "old-fashioned themes",—but let me be outspoken too. I am afraid that the "ultra-modernistic" fad is in its turn a little passé in Europe! That sort of thing was much discussed in Russia just before the revolution and in Paris just after the war, and we had a good many writers (most of them clean forgotten at present) doing a roaring trade by depicting the kind of "amoral" life on which you comment in such a delightful way. It may be curious, but what charms me personally about American civilisation is exactly that old-world touch, that old-fashioned something which clings to it despite the hard glitter, and hectic night-life, and up-to-date bathrooms, and lurid advertisements, and all the rest of it. Bright children, you know, are always conservative. When I come across "daring" articles in your reviews—there was one about condoms in the last Mercury—I seem to hear your brilliant moderns applauding themselves for being such brave naughty boys. Buster Brown has grown up. America is beautifully young and naif, and has a magnificent intellectual future, far beyond its wildest dreams, perhaps. But I am afraid that at present the kind of modernism you mention is only another form of conventionality—old as the hills.

I am not writing this in defence of my novels. They belong to Russia and her literature, and not only style but subject undergoes a horrible bleeding and distortion when translated into another tongue. The German version of "King, Queen, Jack" is a cheap travesty; "Camera Obscura" which, in Russian, was meant as an elaborate parody, lies limp and lifeless in John Long's and Grasset's torture-houses; and "Despair" which is something more than an essay on the psychology of crime turns out to be a half-baked thriller—even when I translate it myself. Strange indeed are the "fata" of my books! I feel sure, however, that with your help, sympathy, and wonderful understanding, I shall find in America at last the readers who, I know, are awaiting me there.

Yours faithfully

P.S. I have just received your latest report. Thank you. I have sent you a second copy of "La Course du Fou"[1] some time ago.

1. Paris: Fayard, 1934; later published in English as *The Defense*.

FROM: **IVAN BUNIN**                                                    TLS, I p.

April 1st 1939

To whom it may concern:

Mr. Vladimir Nabokoff (nom de plume V. Sirin) is a very well known Russian author whose novels (some of which have been translated into German, English and French) enjoy a high reputation among Russian intellectuals abroad. He is the son of the late V.D. Nabokoff, the eminent Russian Liberal Member of the first Russian Parliament and Professor of Criminology. After leaving his country (in 1919) Mr. Nabokoff went to Cambridge where he obtained his B.A. degree in foreign languages (French and Russian) with distinction. He is not only a novelist of quite exceptional talent, but also a profound student of Russian language and literature. As an instance of this I may signify that in one of his works he contributed to the elucidation of certain literary questions referring to the Russian sixties of which he made a long study. All this, together with his mastery of English and great experience in lecturing would make him a teacher of Russian literature and thought of quite exceptional quality at any English or American University. I recommend him very warmly for such a post as I really think that it would be hard to choose better.

Signed
Ivan Bunin[1]
Prix Nobel 1933

1. Bunin and Nabokov were friends.

# LETTERS
# 1940 - 1977

TO: ELIZABETH MARINEL ALLAN          ALS, 4 pp. M. Juliar.
     AND MARUSSYA MARINEL[1]          West Wardsboro, Vt.


25 August 1940

Dear friends,

We received both your letters, and avidly but sadly absorbed every word. I value highly your lines about *Invitation*[2]; your fate worries us deeply; the incident of the harp is symbolic and appalling.

I wrote a letter to Pyatigorsky[3] about you, detailed and insistent. We fervently hope that you may move to this country. We too have a feeling of some kind of interplanetary remoteness, some ungodly distance separating us from the dearest and most precious of friends. Our normal everyday existence, in contrast, seems the height of luxury, like some millionaire's coarse dream. That dreamlike, complex day of our departure, the panic-stricken, gaping suitcases and the whirlwind of old newspapers, Mitya's[4] forty-degree fever, and you amid our bedlam—how shamefully distant it all is. And one begins to feel as if he had silently slipped away without sharing his foresight with others. So that, on the whole, it is embarrassing to repose—as I do now—on a blanket in a meadow amid tall grass and flowers, hearing from afar the peaceful sounds of a solitary country house, children's exclamations, the thud of a ball. We are staying amid marvelous green wilds with the wonderfully kind Karpoviches,[5] where one can go around half-naked, write an English novel, and catch American butterflies (soon I'll have to start using your sweater: fall is on the way). My position is maddeningly undecided, so far nothing has worked out, and the thought of winter is rather frightening, but, by comparison, it is a genuine paradise here. It was a torment to imagine your feelings, your poor mother's situation; one would like to know many more details. I feel so sad, so distressed for you. We recall all your gentle kindness, the delightful hours we spent together, and we talk so very often about you.

My literary (or, rather, anti-literary) agent[6]—a short, fearsome, bandy-legged woman, her hair dyed an indecent red—demands from me a genteel book, with agreeable protagonists and moral landscapes. What I am composing now will hardly satisfy her. She also forbade me to write in Russian: that part of my life, she says, is definitely over; I don't believe I shall obey her for long.

Write to us again, please. In a few days we shall return to New York. Our address remains unchanged—the Tolstoy Foundation. I kiss your hands. Keep well.

Yours,
V. Nabokov[7]

1. Elizabeth (Lisa) Gutman—who later married Aron Allan—was an old and dear friend of the Nabokov family. She and her two sisters, Marussya and Ina, performed as a harp trio, under the stagename Marinel. This letter was written when Elizabeth and Marussya were trying to get out of Europe.
2. *Invitation to a Beheading.*
3. Gregor Pyatigorsky, cellist.
4. Dmitri Nabokov.
5. Mikhail Mikhailovich Karpovich, representative to the U.S. from the Provisional Government after the first 1917 revolution; later professor of Russian literature at Harvard and long-time editor of *Novïy Zhurnal.* He helped the Nabokovs to emigrate by furnishing a necessary affidavit.
6. Altagracia de Jannelli
7. Translated from Russian by DN. The original includes a fourth page by Véra Nabokov.

to: **JAMES LAUGHLIN**[1]                    TLS, 2 pp.

V. Nabokov
35 W 87th St
New York
January 24th, 1941

Dear Mr. Laughlin,

I thank you for your letter and shall be delighted to show you some of my work; but first of all I want to be quite frank about my very singular predicament. In modern Russian literature I occupy the particular position of a novator, of a writer whose work seems to stand totally apart from that of his contemporaries. At the same time, owing to my books being banned in the Soviet Union, they can circulate only among the limited group of emigre intellectuals (chiefly in Paris). Out of a dozen novels I have written (under the penname of Vladimir Sirin) during the last fifteen years my best are "The Lujin Defense" (of which there exists a miserable French translation and an—unintelligible to me—Swedish one), "Invitation to Beheading" and the 120,000 word "Gift" (neither of the two translated). One of my worst novels "Camera Obscura", translated into half-a-dozen languages, has been published here by Bobbs-Merrill under the title of "Laughter in the Dark" in my own translation. I also translated into English a better novel of mine, "Despair" which was published in England. Moreover, I have in manuscript form a novel, "The Real Life of Sebastian Knight".[2] I wrote it in English and rather like it.

Would you like me to send you the typescript of "Sebastian Knight", the English "Despair" or the French "Lujin Defense"?

Yours sincerely
V. Nabokov

1. Head of New Directions.
2. Norfolk, Conn.: New Directions, 1941.

TO: **ELIZABETH MARINEL ALLAN**       ALS, 2pp. M. Juliar.
    **AND MARUSSYA MARINEL**

26 January, 1941
35 West 87th Street
NYC

My dear and unforgettable friends,

Now we have also received your preceding letter and the newspapers; I answered immediately. Perhaps by now my letter, too, has limped to its destination; medieval landscapes remain undisturbed by the passing of airplanes. In mind and spirit we are constantly with you, and it is most distressing to realize that we cannot manage to give your fate the proper nudge. I wrote twice to Pyatigorsky. Besides that I asked an influential person to write him, and that was done too. I shall still try to act through my cousin, whom I shall visit in a few days. The silence of this man who could, of course, have helped you, is completely repellent. Another great friend of mine is faced with a similar situation. It is terrible to think that, not getting any help from here, people who are dear to me might think my concern for them is scattered by the wind of my own worries. For some time now it has been amazingly difficult to obtain results in matters of this kind here. But please believe me—I am trying and shall continue trying. Everything you write about your existence, about its Neanderthal hardships, about your poor mother, is so frightening that I am ashamed to write you about our life here. I shall only say that never before have I had to work so much as this winter over here— translations, preparation of lectures, magazine articles—and all of it in English, nothing but English, so that the demon of my own language sits, enveloped in his wings, and only yawns from time to time, with its dear black gullet gaping. Véra and Dmitri have both been ill these past months. As I wrote you, he has acquired some English and is happy at the excellent school he is attending.

I don't lose hope that we shall soon see you here.

Love,
V. Nabokov[1]

1. Translated from Russian by DN. The rest of the letter is by Véra Nabokov and has been omitted.

TO: JAMES LAUGHLIN                                    ALS, 2 pp.

10-II-41
35 W 87

Dear Mr. Laughlin,

I am sending you in a few days "Despair" and "Sebastian Knight." I think the second is more amusing.

I liked your list. Kafka and Rimbaud—that's the stuff. Yes, *Pasternak* is a real permanent poet; his verse is hard to translate so as to
retain both music and suggestion (and association of images), but it
can be done. There are not many other poets or poems in Russia now
worth the trouble: I recall only one poem by *Maiakovsky* which is
really good (i.e. transcending propaganda), only one by *Bagritsky*,
several by *Zabolotsky* and *Mandelshtam*. There's also *Essenin* and
*Selvinsky*. By far the best poets of recent times are Pasternak and
*Khodassevich*: a collection of Russian modern poems ought to be
based, I think, on the work of these two and though "politically" the
latter was an emigre (he died two years ago) the best in poetry produced in Soviet Russia is closely linked with (and influenced by) his
work. The same connection exists between, say, Selvinsky and a brilliant young poet (who died recently, in Paris) *Poplavsky*.

The most representative kind of collection would be 10 Khodassevich, 10 Pasternak and 20 The Rest.

I am dreadfully busy these days with lectures etc so please excuse
me for the hastiness of these suggestions. My own impression is that,
inspite of political distress, the best poetry produced in Europe
(—and the worst fiction) during these last twenty years has been in
the Russian language, so that a volume of Russian poetry would be
a very good thing.

Yours sincerely
V. Nabokov (Sirin)

TO: JAMES LAUGHLIN                                                    TLS, 1 p.

19 Appleby Road
Wellesley
Mass.
Sept. 29th 41

Dear Laughlin,
Thanks for your two letters. I am translating Hodassevich and will

send you a sample very soon. I was also very much interested by your other suggestion and think it so kind of Wilson[1] to have praised my painful efforts. I have, as a matter of fact, numerous translations of Pushkin, Lermontov, Tyutchev and Fet. I am looking forward to see The Poet of the Month[2] as I don't know what form my work must take.

I am a little worried about not getting the proofs of Sebastian Knight as it is almost October already. I lunched with Weeks[3] the other day and he assured me they would mention Sebastian in their book notice column. My Aurelian[4] will appear in their Christmas number. But generally speaking you are quite right, I have never been able to push my books—even gently.

Is there any chance of our seeing each other soon? I have such a pleasant memory of our meeting.

Yours truly
V. Nabokov

1. Edmund Wilson.
2. Series published by New Directions. VN's *Three Russian Poets* was published by New Directions in 1944.
3. Edward Weeks, editor of *The Atlantic Monthly*.
4. "The Aurelian," VN story translated by VN and Peter Pertzov from Russian.

TO: JAMES LAUGHLIN                                         TLS, 1 p.

19 Appleby Road
Wellesley, Mass
November 27th, 1941

Dear Laughlin,

I have received a letter from Doubleday Doran & Co., presumably a publishing firm, who write that after seeing my story in the Atlantic they "certainly don't want to intrude if I am all tied up for my book ideas but that if I should have some free they would be most interested in hearing about them".

Before answering them I would like to know whether you are interested in the following three books (which are best suited for translation purposes):

1) La Course du Fou, Fayard Publ., Paris., the story of a chess player who was crushed by his genius.

2) Despair, John Long Publ., London, the story of a queer fellow who thought he had found his double, who was not, and

3) my longest novel the untranslated "Dar" (Gift) which is the story of a great writer in the making. (Nothing to do with Sebastian).

The translation of Invitation to a Beheading is progressing at a very slow pace. Should you care to start with La Course du Fou I would need a good translator from the Russian (under my supervision, of course). I would like you to read the book in French (bearing in mind that the translation is hideous) and if you like it inspite of those garbled passages, maybe you could find a good translator.

I hope you had a pleasant trip back West.

Yours very truly
V. Nabokov


TO: JAMES LAUGHLIN                                TL, 2 pp.

19 Appleby Road
Wellesley, Mass.
April 9th 1942

Dear Laughlin,

I have been wanting to write to you for quite a long time, but I have been working hard these last weeks (both as an author and as an entomologist, and my correspondence has been rather neglected. I think I did not even thank you for the plump and juicy anthology. Some of the translations (Maiakovsky especially) are very good, so is the story about the Soviet Bureaucrat, and I particularly liked your own verse which you so modestly printed in diamond. The author of the letter you sent to me is quite right about Hodassevich who was strongly anti-Soviet and lived abroad. But his influence on the best Soviet poets was tremendous. Yes, I am looking forward to that chess match provided Mr. Z. comes to Wellesley. (Incidentally: Bunny Wilson[1] has a very cute but absolutely erroneous theory that "Sebastian" is composed on the lines of a chess-game).

I am rather in low spirits lately because I have not the vaguest idea what is going to happen to my family and me next. My Wellesley year ends practically in June and I have not been able to find any academic post for the next season. I do not know what plans to make for Summer or indeed what kind of Summer we can afford. I feel a little tired because I seem to be doing too many things at once—my new English novel, two short stories, translations for my lectures, some Russian stuff and a huge scientific paper about certain butterflies I have discovered. I think I told you that the Atlantic has finally acquired "Mlle O".[2] I have also sold two poems to the New Yorker.

When would you like to get my book of translations?

There are rumors that you are going to get married. If so I congratulate you most cordially—it is a very pleasant state as far as my own experience goes.

When shall I see you?

Sincerely

1. Edmund Wilson.
2. "Mademoiselle O," VN story translated by VN and Hilda Ward from Russian.

TO: **JAMES LAUGHLIN**                                    TLS, 1 p.

V. Nabokov c/o Prof. M. Karpovich
West Wardsboro, Vermont.
July 16th 1942

Dear Laughlin,

Vermont is very pleasant and beautiful—although beautiful in a kind of gobelin way, and of course lacking the floral versatility of the West. The other day I got a butterfly here which has never been recorded yet from this state: *Colias interior* Scudder which was first found by Agassiz on the North shore of Lake Superior.

I have turned part of the attic into a most comfortable studio; but although I devote to Gogol from eight to ten hours a day of solid work, I now see that I shall never have the book ready before the Fall.[1] I shall probably need two months more and then at least a fortnight to dictate it. What causes this irritating delay is the fact that I have to translate every scrap of quotation myself: most of the Gogol material (letters, articles etc.) is not translated at all, and the rest is so abominably botched that I cannot use it. I have lost a week already translating passages I need in the "Inspector General" as I can do nothing with Constance Garnett's dry shit. I have a bad habit (not really bad, just being coy) of choosing the most difficult path in my literary adventures. This book on Gogol will be something new from beginning to end: I disagree with the bulk of Russian critics of Gogol and use no sources except Gogol himself. My book will make the Oliver Allstons[2] very mad, I hope. It is a pity that I cannot publish it in Russian as well. The emigre book market is not worth the trouble and, as you know, my works are banned in Russia.

A propos: I have made up my mind to get my best Russian novel (The Gift) translated and published. It is about 500 pages long. What I would like you to supply me with first of all is a good translator as I have no time to do the job myself. I need a man who knows English better than Russian—and a man, not a woman. I am frankly homosexual on the subject of translators. I would revise every sentence myself and keep in touch with him all the time, but I *must* have somebody to do the basic work and then to polish my corrections. The Gift was published serially in the "Annales Contemporaines" (the great Russian review that appeared in Paris during 20 years, since 1920), but the war, or rather the complete destruction of Russian intellectual life in Paris by the German invasion, has made its appearance in book form impossible—naturally.

To be quite frank with you, both as a publisher and as a friend, I cannot help feeling that the intense and rather devastating work which Gogol is giving me is worth more than the remuneration you suggested. I have had to postpone writing an essay which Weeks asked me to do, and other things too. The enervating part is that the translations of Gogol I have to make require another section of the brain than the text of my book and switching from one to another by means of spasmodic jumps causes a kind of mental asthma.

Yours cordially
V. Nabokov

1. *Nikolai Gogol* (Norfolk, Conn.: New Directions, 1944).
2. Reference to *The Opinions of Oliver Allston* by Van Wyck Brooks (1941).

TO: JAMES LAUGHLIN                          ALS, 1 p.

8-VIII-42
West Wardsboro
C/o Prof. Karpovich
Vermont

Dear Laughlin,

I have seen Yarmolinsky's[1] and his wife's translations of Pushkin: their work is conscientious, reasonably exact and careful but they lack my main desiderata: style and a rich vocabulary. Without a good deal of linguistic and poetical imagination it is useless tackling my stuff. I shall control the translation as to the precise meaning and nuance, but my English is not up to my Russian, so that even had I the necessary time I would not be able to do the thing alone. I know it is difficult to find a man who has enough Russian to understand my writings and at the same time can turn his English inside out and slice, chop, twist, volley, smash, kill, drive, half-volley, lob and place perfectly every word; Yarmolinsky will gently pat the ball into the net—or send it sailing into the neighbour's garden. But difficult though it is, I think that such a person can be found. What about inserting an advertisement in some literary or professional review?

I am eager—viciously eager—to see "Home Life."[2] It is like calling a version of "Fleurs du Mal"—"The Daisychain."

> Yours very cordially
> V. Nabokov

---

1. Avrahm Yarmolinsky, former director of the Slavonic Section of the New York Public Library. Translator, with his wife, Babette Deutsch, of Russian classical verse. He would supply a literal text on which she based the English version.
2. Gogol's *Dead Souls*, translated by Bernard Guilbert Guerney as *Chichikov's Journeys; or Home Life in Old Russia*; introduction by Clifton Fadiman.

TO: JAMES LAUGHLIN                                                    ALS, 2 pp.

> Nov. 13th, 42
> car 522

My dear Laughlin,

I am writing this in a train somewhere in Illinois. I want to tell you how dreadfully sorry I am for the Gogol delay. This lecturing tour (which financial discomfort forced me to undertake) has greatly interfered with the completion of my book. I have been travelling since the first days of October and shall go on doing so well into December. At this moment I am going for a couple of days to Cambridge before resuming my peregrinations.

I still hope to be able to send you the MS by Christmas. The book is almost finished. Had I a quiet fortnight for a final spurt and another ten days to dictate the thing to my wife (I cannot type) then I would be quite sure of having it ready by that time. I have read one of its passages to Wilson and his reaction was highly satisfactory.

A hasty perusal of the new edition of "Dead Souls" ("Home Life"!) disclosed that—apart from Fadiman's idiotic introduction and the rather self-conscious slang occurring here and there in the translation—the latter is far better than anything that has been published before. True, it lacks the poetic and musical (and nightmarish!) qualities of the original, but it is fairly exact and is the work of an honest mind. In fact it might be a good idea to try and get him to translate my "Gift"—with my assistance.

I have had another poem in the "New Yorker" and Weeks is publishing "Mlle O" soon. I apologize for this wobbly handwriting.

Yours very cordially  
V. Nabokov

TO: *LIFE*[1]                                        CC, I p.

8 Craigie Circle  
Cambridge, Mass.  
31st March 1943

Sir,

I have just seen your Russian issue.[2] It would be unfair both to Russia and to your readers if the following corrections were not made.

Pushkin, the greatest Russian poet (and not merely a "poet-aristocrat") never "joined officers' conspiracy against Tsar", was not "exiled to Caucasus" and did not write the abominable libretto of the opera "Eugene Onegin". Tsar Alexander III's death was not due to "terror". Ambassador Davies' ridiculous collection is not Russian art but solely an exhibition of Ambassador Davies' bourgeois taste ("Snow and Revolution"). People might be puzzled too by the queer confusion of limbs suggested by the activity you attribute to the fellow in the part of Tsar Peter who "s i n g l e h a n d e d, b o o t e d Russia towards progress".

Incidentally I do wish you had not published the picture on P. 106;[3] it is the kind of thing which is apt to make Americans shake with

profane laughter instead of leading to the "sympathy and understanding" which optimism and ignorance so honestly advocate.

Yours faithfully

1. This letter was not published.
2. 29 March 1943.
3. Tableau of Russian women athletes in front of Stalin's portrait.

TO: JAMES LAUGHLIN                          TLS, 1 p.
Cambridge, Mass.

26th May 1943.

Dear Laughlin,

I have just mailed you my "Gogol through the Looking-Glass".

This little book has cost me more trouble than any other I have
composed. The reason is clear: I had first to create Gogol (translate
him) and then discuss him (translate my Russian ideas about him).
The recurrent jerk of switching from one rhythm of work to the
other has quite exhausted me. The book has taken me exactly one
year to write. I never would have accepted your suggestion to do it
had I known how many gallons of brain-blood it would absorb; nor
would you have made the suggestion had you known how long you
would have to wait (I think that your patience has been that of a
true artist).

There are probably some slight slips of the pen here and there.
I would like to see the Englishman who could write a book on Shakespeare in Russian. I am very weak, smiling a weak smile, as I lie in
my private maternity ward, and expect roses.

Thanks for your delightful note about the cook. We are planning
to start on the 16th.

I got a letter from Guerney in reply to mine. He could begin in September.[1] What is the next move?

Yours cordially
V. Nabokov

1. A projected translation of *The Defense*; the project was dropped.

TO: **BERNARD GUILBERT GUERNEY**[1]                                    CC, 1 p.

8 Craigie Circle
Cambridge 38, Mass.
8th February 1944

Dear Mr. Guerney,

Thanks for your long and delightful letter. If your translation of IGOR[2] had been supplied with scholia then your choice in this or that case would have been at least explained to the inquisitive reader. In spite of the references you give *in lit*. I think "linnet" is wrong and that either a cuckoo or a swallow is meant. It is also extremely improbable that the bard would have used the rather local and inconspicuous flying squirrel in a sequence containing the traditional grey wolf and eagle. "Dove-blue" is not so bad as it looks and is employed by ornithologists to define the color of a certain species of hawk. "Tawny" suggests to me the color of a lion or a dingo-dog and not of the Russian wolf. I still emphatically object to a flying squirrel being able to "soar": what it executes is at best a long gliding hop.

This is what I am going to answer if you challenge me to a *rencontre* in the New Republic and shall also add that all this is of little importance, the important thing being that you have put so much creative thought and poetical care into your admirable translations.

I am sorry that you came across my dwarf story in the Esquire.[3] I wrote it exactly 25 years ago and it is an absolute failure of the lurid juvenile type. In the thirties a friend of mine, then in America, translated it into English, sold it and mailed me a cheque to Menton—that's all; I am not responsible for anything in the transla-

46

tion. Incidentally and quite objectively I have a faint feeling that your knowledge of my Russian works is not as complete as it ought to be in view of your general deep knowledge of Russian letters.

Thanks again for your interesting letter. I loved that bit about your having certain little sigils to check pilfering—like Sherlock Holmes upsetting the ashtray.

Yours cordially

1. Translator of Russian literature.
2. Twelfth-century Russian epic. Later translated by VN as *The Song of Igor's Campaign* (New York: Vintage, 1960).
3. "The Potato-Elf," trans. Serge Bertensson and Irene Kosinka, *Esquire*, 12 (December 1939), 70–71, 228, 230–235. VN's first American publication. This story was subsequently retranslated by VN and DN and republished in the October 1973 *Esquire*; collected in *A Russian Beauty and Other Stories* (New York: McGraw-Hill, 1973).

TO: MRS. THEODORE SHERWOOD HOPE[1]                    CC, 1 p.

8 Craigie Circle
Cambridge 38, Mass.
8th February 1944.

Dear Mrs. Hope,

Thanks for your letter and kind invitation to address your Society.

I have read with interest the account of your German studies—I liked the bit about Goethe—but the end has puzzled me greatly. I have lived in Germany for 17 years and am quite sure Gretchen has been thoroughly consoled by the secondhand, somewhat bloodstained, but still quite wearable frocks that her soldier friend sent her from the Polish ghettos. No, I am afraid we shall never see the Barnard statue in a German impersonation. It is useless looking at a hyena and hoping that one day domestication or a benevolent gene will turn the creature into a great soft purring tortoiseshell cat. Gelding and Mendelism, alas, have their limits. Let us chloroform it—and forget. I am sorry of course for music and gemütlichkeit—but not very much, not more in fact than I am for the lacquered what-nots and cherry-trees in bloom (trashy perhaps but sweet) which gemütlich little Japan has contributed.

When I lecture on Russian literature I do so from a writer's point of view, but upon reaching modern times cannot avoid stressing the fact that Communism and its totalitarian rule have prevented the development of authentic literature in Russia during these last twenty five years.

My fee is considerably higher than the one you suggest.

Sincerely yours

1. Chairman of the New York Browning Society.

TO: **DONALD B. ELDER**[1]                                    cc, 2 pp.

8 Craigie Circle
Cambridge 38, Mass.
March 22nd 1944

Dear Mr. Elder,

I am sending you at last a short account of the remaining chapters of my novel.

The subject of *The Person from Porlock*[2] is not easy to define concisely. If I say that its writing requires a considerable amount of critical and original research in such different fields as Shakespearean lore (mainly *Hamlet*) and certain aspects of Natural Science, this will only vaguely define the limits of the matter. I propose to portray in this book certain subtle achievements of the mind in modern times against a dull-red background of nightmare oppression and persecution. The scholar, the poet, the scientist and the child—these are the victims and witnesses of a world that goes wrong in spite of its being graced with scholars, poets, scientists and children. I am putting this rather bluntly, I am afraid, as it is difficult to give a synopsis of something, the rhythm and atmosphere of which are more essential than a physical outline. And the difficulty is increased by the fact of the idea of the book being far more than the discomfort experienced by free minds on the worst curves of a bumpy century; its idea being, in fact, something fundamentally new and thus demanding a treatment incompatible with the bare description of a general theme. Although I do not believe in message of hope books whose intention is to solve the more or less transient problems of mankind, I do think that a certain very special quality of this book is in itself a kind of justification and redemption, at least in the case of my likes.

As has been adumbrated in the first chapters, the main character of the book, Prof. Krug, is a man of genius and the totalitarian government of his country is extremely anxious to have him on its side. I am especially satisfied with the scene depicting his conversation with Paduk, the Ruler of the State,—Paduk who has been his schoolmate (an account of their school days is given in the chapter following the part already submitted). Krug refuses to collaborate in any way and the next step of the government is trying to find out by what means he may be forced to do so. Finally his weak point is discovered, and this weak point is his love for his child. The boy is taken from him—and he who had been aloof and sarcastic in his dealings with the government, now accepts to bend his philosophy and his University work to the government's needs. Unfortunately (for the government) the child is taken by mistake to a camp for defective children (whom the state is anxious to get rid of) and, being sick at the time, dies. Krug has now nothing to lose and refuses to collaborate.

I find difficult to go on with this bald account at this point. Anyway, the problem with which the reader now thinks Prof. Krug is faced, is the problem of responsibility, since the government now tries to break Krug by offering, in case he submits, to set free all his numerous colleagues and friends who have been imprisoned (and to let them remain free as long as he continues to submit). In the meantime, however, Krug, who in the months following his wife's death, had begun to work at a book about death and resurrection, has a most prodigious illumination (coinciding with his imprisonment after the boy's death), the dawning of a certain great understanding—and this is the most difficult bit to explain—but to put it bluntly, he realizes suddenly the presence of the Author of things, the Author of him and of his life and of all the lives around him,—the Author who is *myself*, the man who writes the book of his life. This singular apotheosis (a device never yet attempted in literature) is, if you like, a kind of symbol of the Divine power. I, the Author, take Krug to my bosom and the horrors of the life he has been experiencing turn out to be the artistic invention of the Author.

There is of course much more in the book, and these bald notes are quite inadequate and unworthy of it. When, in a most dramatic chapter, Paduk the Ruler brings together Krug and his friends in the old schoolroom of yore, and his friends plead with him to yield and thus save them from the firing squad, Krug tries to explain to them what he has discovered—*my* presence and the disappearance of all problems. And when finally Krug is taken up a hill, through the vineyards, to be shot—and is shot according to the local conceptions, I, the Author, intervene,—but the special way in which I manage this intervention, cannot be explained without actually producing the completed manuscript of the book which will be ready in a few months.

Very sincerely yours

1. Editor at Doubleday, Doran.
2. Published as *Bend Sinister* (New York: Holt, 1947). The working title refers to the billcollector who interrupted Coleridge's work on "Kubla Khan."

TO: **JAMES LAUGHLIN**                     ALS (XEROX), 3 pp.

*NB*                     10-VII-44

*Ship it to:* V. Nabokov
Museum of Comparative Zoology
Harvard   Room 402
Cambridge

Dear Laughlin,

I want you to do something for me. I noticed with dismay that

I have somehow mislaid samples of plants which I brought from Utah—and namely the pabulum of two allied forms of butterflies—a thing I call *vetch* on which *melissa* breeds and the species of lupine— the food plant of *annetta*. I need these plants badly to identify them quite exactly. There are several species of lupine around Alta. I need the one growing in the haunts of *annetta* (Locality N° 2 on the chart I append). As *annetta* lives in symbiosis with ants I would also like to have a few, half-a-dozen, say, specimens of ants from the anthill (or anthills) shown on the map. Both lupine and ant must come from that precise spot. Kill the ants with alcohol or carbona or any other stuff handy (just drown them, do not squash) and put them into a small box with cotton wool. The plants can be mailed in a carton or in any other way, but try to keep them flat (they might also be placed in some book etc). The other plant, the "vetch" (I am not quite sure whether it is vetch, but it has pods), although growing in the vicinity of Walker's Lane, along the roads, *must come from the limited locality N°* . Mrs. Laughlin once saw me collecting there, and another time I pointed out these flowers to you on our way down. *Melissa* is well out and on the wane, little blue butterflies fluttering about that vetch, but nowhere else higher up. *Annetta* may be just emerging. It will be in full force towards the end of the month. You will do me a great favour if you can send me these plants (and a few ants)!

Sincerely yours V. Nabokov

! Please, give me the approx. altitude of the *Vetch locality* (6000?) and its distance from Salt Lake City and Alta. Also, please, the altitude of *Walker's Lane* [where another form of *melissa* occurs in June and in August (also as "noted")].[1]

---

1. Last paragraph written along left margin of letter.

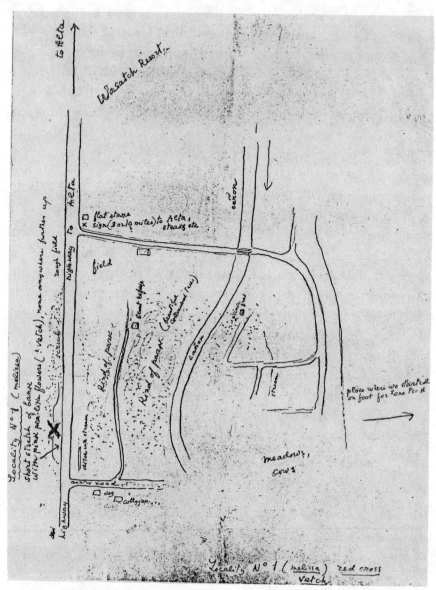

Nabakov's maps accompanying his 10 July 1944 letter to James Laughlin.

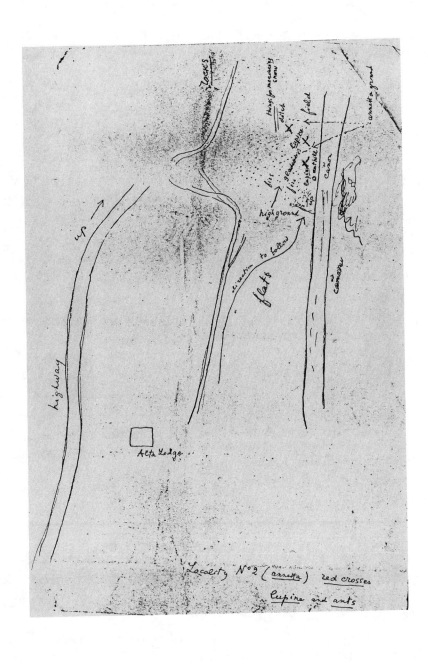

Locality No 2 (_arretta_) _red crosses_
_lupine_ and _ants_

TO: **KATHARINE A. WHITE**[1]     TLS, 1 p. Bryn Mawr College.

8 Craigie Circle
Cambridge 38, Mass.
28 September 1944

Dear Mrs. White,

I am a little shocked by your readers' having so completely missed the point of my story.[2] Apart from that, I quite fail to see how it may be confused with the "projections into the future made by would-be American satirists" since there is no projection and not the faintest trace of satire in my story—either "half-exposed" or otherwise. For all I know or care the 21st century may be less "enlightened" than our time, which may or may not be "crude" etc.—but again all this has nothing whatever to do with the point of the story.

I shall certainly continue to show you the things I happen to write.

Sincerely yours
V. Nabokov[3]

1. *New Yorker* editor.
2. "Time and Ebb," *The Atlantic Monthly* (January 1945). Collected in *Nine Stories* (New York: New Directions, 1947) and *Nabokov's Dozen* (New York: Doubleday, 1958).
3. Butterfly drawing below signature.

TO: **KATHARINE A. WHITE**[1]     TLS, 1 p. Bryn Mawr College.
c. 2–3 June 1945     8 Craigie Circle
Cambridge

Dear Mrs. White,

I am mailing you the proofs in haste.[1] *Please* give them your personal attention if you have time. I do not think news of H's death[2] would interfere with passages in the story since it all happened a month ago. The French consul has been simplified. Other things I have altered or added (gently put back in some cases) are utterly essential. The two sentences I have deleted in the last section are quite unnecessary—I mean any good reader can insert mentally the two little explanations your reviser inserted in print.

Thanks for the news about Bunny—I felt somehow unhappy about him.

This is the *first* letter I have typed out myself in my life. Took me 28 minutes but came out beautifully.[3]

> Yours very sincerely
> V. Nabokov

---

1. "Double Talk," *The New Yorker* (23 June 1945). Retitled "Conversation Piece" when collected in *Nine Stories*.
2. Adolf Hitler.
3. This sentence added in holograph.

TO: **PROF. WILLIAM T. M. FORBES**[1]     TLS, 1 p. Cornell University.

> Letterhead: Harvard
> Museum of Comparative Zoology.
> September 24, 1945

Dear Professor Forbes:

Many thanks for gifting these excellent little Lycaenids (*faga, ramon*, some *hanno* specimens) and for the loan of the rest. Also, for the return and dissection of the *mollicularia* specimen.

Your material comes out as:

*Itylos (sensu stricto)* Koa Druce, 2♂, 2 ♀

*Pseudolucia endymion* Blanchard (forma *chilensis* Blanchard), 4♂, 1♀

*Pseudolucia collina* Philippi, 1♂

*Pseudothecla faga* Dognin, 4♂ (one labeled "*excisicosta*")

*Echinargus martha* Dognin, 1♂, "Huacapistana", 1♀ *sic*! "Matucana".

*Hemiargus ramon* Dognin, 2♂, 1♀

*Hemiargus hanno* Stoll (various forms, the *Paramaribo* one being the typical one), 10♂, 5♀

I was especially pleased with the loan of *martha* (I think it *is* the *Lycaena martha* of Dognin, judging by his woodcut etc.). Genitalically (and in a way macroscopically) it is beautifully intermediate between *Echinargus isola* from Central America and *Echinargus n.sp.* from Trinidad. One hind wing (in the ♂) was loose. I shall return the loaned specimens (and genitalia preparation) together with the *Lycaeides* forms previously borrowed, if this is convenient to you.

Yours sincerely,
Vladimir Nabokov

1. Department of Entomology, Cornell University Agricultural Experiment Station.

TO: **PROF. GEORGE R. NOYES**[1]                         TLS, 2 pp.

8 Craigie Circle
Cambridge 38, Mass.
24th October 1945

Dear Professor Noyes,

Many thanks for your kind letter and interesting article in the Slavonic Review. It gives a very clear picture of what has been done and is being done in Russian at Berkeley.

I am glad you liked my translations.[2] Yes, I do read *Iphigenia* in five syllables, but as this made it impossible to fit her into my line, I consulted some American poets who were of the opinion that under the circumstances it would be permissable to imply a contracted reading to the exclusion of the second "i" in I'ph(i)geni'a.

As to Gogol I do not think that your point of view is so widely divergent from my own. I never meant to deny the moral impact of art which is certainly inherent in every genuine work of art. What I do deny and am prepared to fight to the last drop of my ink is the deliberate moralizing which to me kills every vestige of art in a work however skillfully written. There is a deep morality in the

Overcoat which I have tried to convey in my book, but this morality has certainly nothing whatever to do with the cheap political propaganda which some overzealous admirers in nineteenth century Russia have tried to squeeze out of, or rather into it, and which, in my opinion does violence to the story and to the very notion of art.

By the same token, though you may be right that Gogol did not object to serfdom, the interior moral standards of the book bristle against it. And the reader is more impressed by the bodily serfdom of the peasants and the inevitably following spiritual serfdom of the owners than by the petty roguery of Chichikov.

In my opinion, the fact that *The Kreutzer Sonata* and *The Power of Darkness*[3] were written with a deliberate moral purpose largely defeats their purpose, killing the inherent morality of uninhibited art.

I thank you for the steps you have kindly taken on my behalf. I am glad you understand that I should not be offered a low-salaried job. And I fully understand that the considerations you describe may influence in many ways the final choice among the applicants. But please bear in mind that I am very much interested.

I shall certainly treat as confidential all the information which you have indicated as such in your letter.

Sincerely yours,
V. Nabokov

1. Slavic Department, University of California, Berkeley.
2. Probably English translations from Pushkin's *Eugene Onegin, The Russian Review* (Spring 1945).
3. Both by Tolstoy.

TO: **ELENA SIKORSKI**[1]        ALS, 2 pp. Elena Sikorski.
26 November 1945        Cambridge, Mass

My Dear Elenochka,

We received three letters of yours—one bearing a postmark (15 October), a second one thanks to opportunity, and now another, dated 8 November. Thanks, my dearest. Write me more fully and more often. Your delightful letters are a great joy to me. I cannot even begin to tell you how precious the snapshots are for me.

You asked me to describe my day for you. I wake up at eight or on the near side of eight, and always as a result of one and the same noise: Mityushenka going to the bathroom.

[floorplan of apartment]

He has a propensity for pensiveness and dawdling, so there is always a chance he will be late for school. At 8:40 the school car picks him up at the corner. Véra and I watch through the window (marked by an X) and see him striding toward the corner, looking very trim, wearing a gray suit and a reddish jockey cap, with a green bag (for his books) slung over his shoulder. At about half-past-nine I too set out, carrying my lunch (a flask of milk, two sandwiches). It is about a quarter hour's walk to the museum, along tranquil streets (we live in a suburb, in the Harvard area), then past the university tennis courts—a multitude of courts, totally overgrown with gigantic weeds during the war years, when there has been no one to care for them. My museum—famous throughout America (and throughout what used to be Europe)—is the Museum of Comparative Zoology, a part of Harvard University, which is my employer. My laboratory occupies half of the fourth floor. Most of it is taken up by rows of cabinets, containing sliding cases of butterflies. I am custodian of these absolutely fabulous collections. We have butterflies from all over the world; many are type specimens (i.e., the very same specimens used for the original descriptions, from the 1840s until today). Along the windows extend tables holding my microscopes, test tubes, acids, papers, pins, etc. I have an assistant, whose main task is spreading specimens sent by collectors. I work on my personal research, and for more than two years now have been publishing piecemeal a study of the classification of American "blues"[2] based on the structure of their genitalia (minuscule sculpturesque hooks, teeth, spurs, etc., visible only under a microscope), which I sketch in with the aid of various marvelous devices, variants of the magic lantern. When the weather is good I take a short break around midday. Other curators, from various floors, of reptiles, mammals, fossils, etc.—all wonderful people—also gather on the steps. My work enraptures but utterly exhausts me; I have ruined my eyesight, and wear horn-rimmed glasses. To know that no one before you has seen an organ you are examining, to trace relationships that have occurred to *no one* before, to immerse yourself in the wondrous crystalline world of the microscope, where silence reigns, circumscribed by its own horizon, a blindingly white arena—all this is so enticing that I cannot describe it (in a certain sense, in *The Gift*, I "foretold" my destiny—this retreat into entomology). Around five I come home, already in the blue darkness of winter, the hour of evening newspapers, the hour when . . . are rolling home, and radio phonographs burst into song in the illumined apartments of large ivy-colored buildings.

The school delivers Mityushenka at about the same time. He lays out on the table what he calls his "sour little papers"—sheets of paper with drawings that are the result of chance and grades that are not. He does extremely well at school, but that is thanks to Véra who goes over every bit of homework with him in detail—his assignments in Latin, mathematics, etc. His exceptionally gifted nature includes a dose of indolence, and he can forget everything in the world to immerge in an aviation magazine—airplanes, to him, are what butterflies are to me; he can unerringly identify types of aircraft by a distant silhouette in the sky or even by a buzz, and loves to assemble and glue together various models. During our travels in the Rocky Mountains and in Utah he accompanied me on my hunts, but he does not have a real passion for butterflies. He sees letters in color as Véra and I do and as Mother used to, but each of us has his own colors: for instance my M is a flannel pink, while his is light-blue. He is exceptionally musical, takes music lessons, and sings charmingly. He is vain, quick-tempered, pugnacious, and flaunts American expressions (which are sometimes pretty crude) current among schoolboys here—but, next to them, he is a white-and-silver little crow, infinitely gentle and generally very lovable. Something I find particularly touching is that he tells us absolutely *everything* with a naive kind of truthfulness. After an early dinner I lie down for a rest with a book or a final bit of unfinished (museum) work; around nine there is a loud noise—a harplike glissando on the other side of my wall; it is Mityushenka rattling on the uprights at the head of his bed, summoning me to come say goodnight. This is when he is especially nice and warm.

Twice a week I travel far out of town for the whole day to Wellesley, a women's college where I give two courses (for four hours straight). That wears me out even more than the museum. Thus I have only Saturday and Sunday left for my literature. I shall definitely send you what I have written during this period but there are certain "buts": let me figure a few things out—I have to be very careful with my writing hand, and your health concerns me too.[3] What you say about your little one is perfectly adorable—I especially like the little animal game. What a joy that you are well, alive, in good spirits. Poor, poor Seryozha . . . ![4]

If it were possible to transplant you over here, I think that after struggling along for a year or so you could find something. Your type of profession, diploma, etc., carry a lot of weight here. How do you envisage such a move? You with your child and husband, or Rostik[5] and E.K.[6] as well, i.e., do you associate the latter with the former—or would the three of you arrive first and would we then join forces to bring over R. and E.K.? I am agonizingly anxious to have them here. . . . I shall never forget how we struggled to get out of black 1940 Paris, what nightmarish difficulties they caused us (straight out of *Invitation*), the agonizing procedure of collecting money for the tickets, the 40 degree fever Mityenka had the day of our departure— we bundled him up and set out, and Yosif Vladimirovich[7] (who later died over here) and Aunt Nina[8] (who died last year in Paris; Nik. Nik.,[9] on his way home from the funeral, was hit by a car and killed) saw us off. In New York, Natasha[10] . . . met us and put us up at her place; then we went to the Karpoviches' farm in Vermont; then I worked all winter (gratis) at the American Museum of Natural History in New York and wrote reviews for a magazine. Then I was invited to lecture by a certain university enticed by my having once translated *Alice in Wonderland* into Russian. Then I was invited to Stanford University in California, and here things got a bit easier. Brains and talent are highly valued over here (and you have them).

Today I was a professor (it is Tuesday), am very tired, and am not writing clearly, but I'll write again soon. It is evening, Mityenka is in bed, Véra is reading to him (Gogol's "Terrible Vengeance"). Did I write you that I have gained a huge amount of weight, and have begun to look like Apukhtin?[11]

Dearest, I embrace you, and I am confident that we shall see each other. Regards to your husband.

Your V.[12]

1. VN's sister.
2. In this connection it is interesting to note the bizarre comments of Professor Emeritus Frank Carpenter (who was not a lepidopterist), a colleague of whom VN had thought as a friend, and of certain other "wonderful people" whose cordiality toward Nabokov seems to have altered in inverse proportion to the latter's fame. In the July-August 1986 issue of *Harvard Magazine*, dedicated in part to reminiscences of Nabokov's entomological work at Harvard, Carpenter is quoted as saying, with a soupçon of patronizing envy: "He was seriously interested in butterflies, but the level of his interest was that which we find in the majority of amateurs. Of course, within two or three species of the so-called Blues, he obviously knew what he was doing . . . It's an Old World tradition, particularly in the wealthy families. . . . " Assistant Professor Deane Bowers, current curator of lepidoptera at the Harvard Museum of Comparative Zoology, clarifies matters by explaining in the same article, that, while he published in professional journals, Nabokov was not a professional scientist only in a strictly academic sense: he was not armed with a Ph.D. in biology and "didn't work full-time in entomology." He did invent a radically new paradigm for the classification of an entire group of Blues, and his scientific approach in general, ahead of its time in certain ways, has gained increasing respect against a background of changing scientific perspectives. A splendid exhibit entitled "Nabokov's Butterflies" has subsequently been mounted at Harvard, and a collection of VN's entomological studies will be published in France. DN.
3. References, veiled of necessity, to the obstacles of Iron-Curtain censorship and retribution.
4. VN's brother Sergey, who died in a German concentration camp.
5. Rostislav, son of VN's sister Olga.
6. Evgeniya Konstantinovna Hofeld (1884–1957), governess of VN's sisters Olga and Elena from 1914 on, who had accompanied the family to Prague. She, VN's mother, and his sister Olga were to remain there until their deaths.
7. Yosif V. Hessen.
8. Nina Dmitrievna Kolomeytsev, VN's aunt.
9. Nikolay Nikolaevich Kolomeytsev, admiral, husband of Nina Dmitrievna.
10. Natalia Alekseevna Nabokov, wife of Nikolay Dmitrievich Nabokov, VN's first cousin.
11. Aleksey Apukhtin, a plump society poet.
12. Translated from Russian by DN, with a few deletions for personal reasons.

Дорогая моя Еленочку.

1947? 48?

Мы получили три твоих письма, одно со жемчежена (от 15го октября), а последнее оказіей. И теперь от 3го ноября. Спасибо, дорогая. Пиши мне побольше и почаще, твои прелестные письма для меня громадная радость. Не стану говорить как мне дороги снимочки.

Ты просишь меня описать тебе мой день. Я просыпаюсь в 8, или около восьми сидри, от всегда одного и того же звука: Митюшенька идеть в ванную.

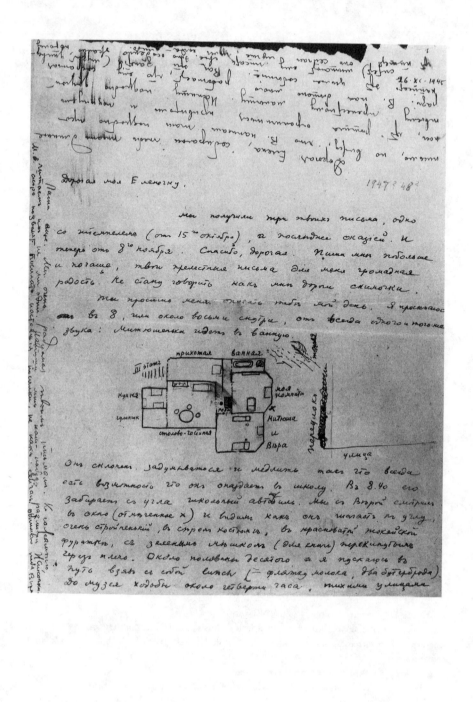

Он склонен задумываться и медлить так что всегда есть вероятность что он опаздает в школу. В 8.40 его забирает с угла школьный автомобиль. Мы из второй смотрим в окно (отмеченное x) и видим как он шагает к углу, очень стройненький, в спром костюмчик, в красиватой нокейской фуражк, с зеленым мышком (для книг) перекинутым через плечо. Около половины десятого я пускаюсь в путь взяв с собой линеь (= фляжу молока, два бутерброда) до музея ходьбы около четверти часа, тихими улицами to: **The Reverend Gardiner M. Day**[1]  cc, 1 p.

8 Craigie Circle
Cambridge 38, Mass.
21st December 1945

Dear Sir,

I regret to inform you that Dmitry cannot comply with your request to take part in a collection of clothing for the German children.

I sincerely endorse the idea of help and forgive—in regard to our enemies. In my opinion, however, this rule can only stand if what we give comes from depriving ourselves, not from depriving our friends.

Since this country has not enough to feed and clothe the children of both our allies and our enemies, I consider that every item of food and clothing given the Germans must necessarily be taken from our allies, who not only have begun suffering at a time when the Germans were having a very good time, but who, moreover, suffered for a just cause.

When I have to choose between giving for a Greek, Czech, French, Belgian, Chinese, Dutch, Norwegian, Russian, Jewish or German child, I shall not choose the latter one.

Very sincerely yours,

1. Rector of Christ Church, Cambridge, Mass.

to: **Kirill Nabokov**  ALS, 2 pp.
1945  8 Craigie Circle
Cambridge, Mass.

Dear Cyril,

I was very happy to get news from you and learn that you are safe. Almost simultaneously a letter came from Evg. Konst.[1] (do get in touch with her) telling me that Sergey perished in the Neuengamme concentration camp. This is very dreadful. I am writing to Nika[2] who is on a mission in Germany (X-0005 HQW S.S.B.S. Morale Division, APO 413) to try and find out something more about him—but I am afraid it is useless to pursue any glimmer of hope under the circumstances. Please let me know all you can discover in regard to this monstrous matter.

I find it difficult to write much about my own mode of life. Taken all in all it is much the same as it had been in Europe, but I am much happier in this country than I was in France.

Véra and Mityusha are in fine shape. He is eleven now. I work as Research Fellow at Harvard Univ. (Museum of Comparative Zoology) and also teach at Wellesley College. During these last years I have had published three books in English (A novel called *The Real Life of Sebastian Knight*, a biography of Gogol, and a small volume of translations from Pushkin, Lermontov, Tyutchev) and have contributed poetry and prose to the *New Yorker* (several poems) and the *Atlantic Monthly* (several stories). Most of my time, however, is taken up by scientific papers on butterflies, some of which I have discovered myself during collecting trips in Arizona and Utah.

I am out of town at present but shall have some of my stuff forwarded to you as soon as I get back to Cambridge (a small university town near Boston) where we live.

Keep well, write, I am tremendously happy that you have made it safe and sound through these awful years.[3]

Your V.

1. Evgeniya Konstantinovna Hofeld.
2. VN's cousin, composer Nicholas Nabokov.
3. Final paragraph in Russian.

TO: **KATHARINE A. WHITE**        ALS, 1 p. Bryn Mawr College.
Cambridge, Mass.

1–I–1946

Dear Mrs. White:

Thanks for your charming letter. I do have a story for you—but it is still in my head; quite complete, however; ready to emerge; the pattern showing through the wingcases of the pupa. I shall write it as soon as I get rid of my novel, i.e. in a couple of months.

Rebecca West's account of the trial of J. was admirable.[1] So was Irwin Shaw in the last issue.[2] So was a very funny *critique* by Gibbs (mimicking a very good story by Thurber).[3]

I think I shall come to N.Y. at the end of next week.

Very sincerely yours
V. Nabokov

I (and my son) enjoyed hugely your husband's last book.[4] I have admired his art ever since his red barn cast that blue shadow (in Harper's?)

1. "A Reporter at Large: The Crown versus William Joyce" (29 September 1945).
2. "A Reporter at Large: Stuff of Dreams" (5 January 1946).
3. Wolcott Gibbs, "Outline of Victoria" (15 December 1945).
4. *Stuart Little* (New York & London: Harper, 1945).

TO: **ELENA SIKORSKI**        ALS, 2 pp. Elena Sikorski.
Cambridge, Mass.

24 February 1946

My dear Elenochka,

It was very sad to learn of your operation. Write me quickly how it all went.

*Love at the closing of our days*
*is apprehensive and very tender.*
*Glow brighter, farewell rays*
*of our last love in its evening splendor.*

*Blue shade takes half the world away:*
*through western clouds alone light is slanted.*
*O tarry, O tarry, declining day,*
*enchantment, let me stay enchanted!*

*The blood runs thinner, yet the heart*
*remains as ever deep and tender.*
*O last belated love, thou art*
*a blend of joy and hopeless surrender.*

Do you recognize this?[1]

I traveled to New York (to speak on the radio about Gogol) and came back with influenza, but now I'm all right. I weigh 195 pounds—I don't know how much that is in poods.

It is snowing, and the weather here is rotten. The bathroom window is covered against drafts with a piece of Father's white robe with the light-blue stripes, which he used to wear in 1921 and 22. Mityushenka is blissfully immersed in the colored *funnies*[2] in today's (very fat, Sunday) Boston paper. Everything you write about the *most lovable little man*[3] is charming. It's so good to be in contact now.

Nika[4] writes that in Paris he was invited to Marshal Zhukov's box.[5] I am snowed under with various work, am doing too many things simultaneously, and would like to retreat into a little lair and work on my novel. I embrace you, my dearest, and hope your husband is feeling better.

Your V.

Give me some advice: I am quite unable to judge from here how much help E.K. needs for her and Rostislav to manage. The packages arrive so undependably—perhaps money transfers might be better?

I could send something (15–20 dollars a month). That is about what I spend on the packages. Surely it is impossible to buy what I send for that money, and many things are not available at all. When the packages do arrive, they of course make life a lot easier for her. Advise me what to do. Maybe it should be one-half money and one-half merchandise? We have also bought Rostik a suit and a sweater—probably that would be prohibitive in Prague, wouldn't it?[6]

1. Tyutchev's poem "Last Love." English translation by VN. Copyright © 1944 Vladimir Nabokov.
2. Original in English.
3. Original in English.
4. Nicholas Nabokov.
5. Soviet general during World War II.
6. Translated from Russian by DN.

TO: ELENA SIKORSKI             ALS, 2 pp. Elena Sikorski.

Cambridge, Mass.
14 May 1946

My dear Elenochka,

It was sad to read about your operation. I thought the book I sent would get there in time for your convalescence, but apparently it has fallen behind schedule.

Thanks for the information about E.K.'s needs. That's how we'll do it, then.

The last page you copied was no. 48 ("cloud" and "whisper to me," etc.). I treasure your charming letters in a special folder. How I'd like to have a look at the "warm" little lion cub!

I have been included for the second time in *Best American Stories*. The other day the Harvard library made some phonograph recordings of my voice—several poems.[1] I've been spending a lot of time lately on a long and terrifying novel,[2] and hope to finish it in a month. It is a little along the lines of *Invit.[ation] to a B.[eheading]* but for bass voice, as it were.

Mityushenka is doing well at school. But we don't like Saturdays and Sundays, for he takes off somewhere on his bicycle, and plays and fights with the neighborhood kids. He just came back, threw his baseball mitt and bat into a corner, and rode off again.

Véra has gone out to post three letters and now there will be another. I generally stay in bed on Sunday.

When I'm done with the novel I'll get going on a detailed autobiography, something I have long wanted to write.

Oh, how I would like to send you certain of my recent Russian poems, but it's not possible—my hand is a little sore, and I cannot copy them.[3]

Keep well, my dearest, and a handshake to your husband.

V.

Tomorrow is our wedding anniversary—21 years, if you can believe it.[4]

1. The first of several live and studio recordings that VN made at Harvard over the years, material from which was issued on cassette in 1988 by the Harvard Poetry Room. DN.
2. *Bend Sinister*.
3. An allusion to Iron-Curtain censorship and the perilous consequences for a Prague recipient of such material. DN.
4. Translated from Russian by DN.

TO: ELIZABETH MARINEL ALLAN
AND MARUSSYA MARINEL                    ALS, 1 p. M. Juliar.

8 Craigie Circle
Cambridge 38, Mass.
22 May, 1946

Dear Marussya and Lisa,

This paper is quite undescribably lovely. Thank you!

I want you to know that I have just now finished an enormous, difficult novel[1] that I have been writing for three or four years. Its general atmosphere resembles *Invitation to a Beheading* but is even more catastrophic and jolly. I don't know yet who will publish it, but it is a great relief. I repose like a brand-new mother bathed in lace, with slightly damp skin, so tender and pale that all the freckles show, with a baby in a cradle beside me, his face the color of an inner tube.

The academic year ends in a few days and I shall be able to have a rest. Yesterday I went to see the doctor, who found me overworked. I really want to see you.

Yours,<br>
V. Nabokov[2]

1. *Bend Sinister.*
2. Translated from Russian by DN.

TO: **KENNETH D. MCCORMICK**[1]    CC, 1 p.
Cambridge, Mass.

22nd September 1946

Dear Mr. McCormick,

I am writing you to explain a few things about my next book.[2]

This will be a new kind of autobiography, or rather a new hybrid between that and a novel. To the latter it will be affiliated by having a definite plot. Various strata of personal past will form as it were the banks between which will flow a torrent of physical and mental adventure. This will involve the picturing of many different lands and people and modes of living. I find it difficult to express its subject matter more precisely. As my approach will be quite new, I cannot affix to it one of those labels of which we spoke. By being too explicit at this point I should inevitably fall back on such expressions as "psychological novel" or "mystery story where the mystery is a man's past", and this would not render the sense of novelty and discovery which distinguishes the book as I have it in my mind. It will be a sequence of short essay-like bits, which suddenly gathering momentum will form into something very weird and dynamic: innocent looking ingredients of a quite unexpected brew.

I am certain that I could complete this book in about 1½–2 years.

Our frank and friendly talk has made a very pleasurable impression upon me. I greatly appreciate your interest in my work. You have discerned, I believe, its permanent value. From this point of view SOLUS REX[3] (I shall probably change the title) is a perfectly safe bet. On the other hand, my previous Russian experiences (I am the author of some ten books in Russian) have proved to me that only after one work is published am I freed from its obsession and can attack my next one with real vigor and appetite.

Sincerely yours,

1. Editor at Doubleday.
2. *Conclusive Evidence—A Memoir* (New York: Harper, 1951); retitled *Speak, Memory*.
3. The work originally destined to bear the title *Solus Rex* was never completed. Portions of it were published as two short stories, "Solus Rex" and "Ultima Thule," in Russian émigré journals in 1940 and 1942, and in English, translated by VN and DN, in *A Russian Beauty* (1973). "Solus Rex", as used here, was also a working title for *Bend Sinister*, which Holt published in 1947.

TO: **ALLEN TATE**[1]     cc, 1 p.

Cambridge, Mass.

13 October 1946

Dear Allen,

An unexpected thing has happened: they do want the book. They want to buy SOLUS REX and also an option on the novel I am writing now.[2] But the advance they offer to pay for SOLUS REX ($1.500) does not seem to indicate that they are sufficiently interested to make a good job of it.

Before answering them, I wish to discuss the matter with you. If Holt can make me a better offer concerning SOLUS REX, I shall be glad to consider it. There is, of course, the question of those passages that seemed to you obscure. Could you give me in your letter one sample of the kind of thing you have in mind? This does not mean that I shall not come over to New York for a personal discussion. I could come next Saturday, the 19th, if this is convenient to you.

And here is another suggestion. I have been thinking lately that if I could give up teaching (as I do now in Wellesley) and could devote all my time to writing, I would complete my new novel within 1½ years or so and would also finish a volume of short stories. Do you think that Holt could be interested in signing an agreement with me along these lines (concerning the three books: Solus Rex, the new novel and the short stories) allowing a sufficient yearly advance to take care of me and my family of two, while I attend to the business of writing?

Very sincerely yours,

1. Poet, at that time employed as an editor at Henry Holt.
2. See 22 September letter to Kenneth D. McCormick. VN's novel in progress was *Lolita* in its earliest stages.

TO: **FREDERICK STARR**[1]                                                            CC, 1 p.

8 Craigie Circle
Cambridge 38, Mass.
22nd October 1946

Dear Mr. Starr,

I have just returned to Cambridge from a trip to New York and found here your very kind letter of October 18th waiting for me.

The more I think about this matter, the more convinced I become that I am not the right man to address your audience. I fully share your opinion that a war with Russia would have been a terrible and unnecessary disaster, but I do not think that unless we face boldly all the facts, this country can evolve a sincere and constructive international policy.

On the other hand, while I feel certain that there is nothing in

my lecture that could have come in conflict with your purposes, I
do not like the idea of having to speak under any restrictions whatever, for this would give me the sensation of having deliberately un-
dertaken to dissimulate part of the truth and thus of somehow deceiv-
ing my audience as to my true attitude. I therefore suggest in the
friendliest manner that my engagement to address your Society be
cancelled.

I am sorry you did not write me about it all at an earlier date,
before my name was announced on your program, and while you still
had a long time to find another lecturer. But considering the great
number of Russian scientists and writers now living in New York,
I feel sure that you will have no difficulty in finding the right sort
of man.

Very sincerely yours,

1. Of the American Society for the Study of Russian Culture.

TO: **MUCIO DELGADO**[1]                                                    cc, 1 p.

8 Craigie Circle
Cambridge 38, Mass.
17 November 1946

Dear Mr. Delgado,

Thank you for your letter.

The Editorship-in-Chief is even more attractive to me than administrative work. It would, however, interest me to know how
independent I should be in my selections and decisions. If possible,
I would like to know who is going to be Head of the Department
and what would be the exact separating line between his authority
and mine.

As to the salary, I am afraid that $7,500 would be the minimum
I could accept. Since I sent in my application there has been a very

large increase in prices. I have also found out that moving to New York must cost much more than I had thought.

Sincerely yours,

1. Chief, Radio Program Branch, International Broadcasting Division, Department of State.

TO: **ALLEN TATE**                                                    cc, 1 p.

8 Craigie Circle
Cambridge 38, Mass.
28 January 1947

Dear Allen,

I am very much bored with Laughlin of the New Directions. Do you think Holt might be interested in buying from him all my contracts in toto? All the advances have already been covered, and the editions pretty near sold out. If you think that this might work, I shall suggest to Laughlin my buying back all my rights from him. This will probably result in lower price than if another publisher made the inquiry. But I should only do this at the present time, if Holt would back me. Laughlin has now three books of mine: SEBASTIAN, the GOGOL book and LAUGHTER IN THE DARK which he bought from Bobbs-Merrill, the original publisher. THE THREE POETS contract has expired.

Has anything been done about the dust jacket for B.S.?[1] I should like it to be as sober as possible.

And finally: you would very much oblige me if you now could have the second half of the advance sent to me.

Sincerely yours,

1. *Bend Sinister.*

TO: ELIZABETH MARINEL ALLAN
AND MARUSSYA MARINEL                    ALS, 1 p. M. Juliar.

8 Craigie Circle
Cambridge 38, Mass.
27 April, 1947

Dear Marussya and Lisa,

The downy "bird"[1] and the enchanting present gave me tremendous pleasure. Thank you, dear friends! In response to Roshchin's breezy piece about Odessa you will soon read in *Noviy zhurnal* a poem I have recently composed.[2] As for Russian prose, I seem to have completely lost the knack, but I can still manage verse. It is a poem about a three-day clandestine sojourn—or anyway a brief sojourn—of mine in Leningrad. In short, you'll see. I am very pleased with this little thing.

I have to devote this windy spring Sunday to diligent study of some sixty compositions by my students.

Keep well. How sad that we get together so seldom.

Yours,
V. Nabokov[3]

1. The "bird" is drawn from a popular jingle that was improvised upon for various festive occasions and probably refers to a gift sent for VN's birthday. DN.
2. "To Prince S.M. Kachurin," published in VN's English translation in *Poems and Problems* (New York: McGraw-Hill, 1970).
3. Translated from Russian by DN.

TO: MRS. DOUGLAS HORTON[1]                    CC, 1 p.
Cambridge, Mass.

28th October 1947

Dear Mrs. Horton,

I have just come back from a trip to Ithaca where I talked with the President and with the Head of the Modern Languages Department. Cornell is interested in my joining the Faculty as Associate Professor of Literature. The offer tempts me particularly because the arrangement would be permanent.

Before getting too deeply involved with Cornell, I want to be clear about my position at Wellesley. Is it hurrying things too much if I ask for a prediction from you: do you see the possibility of a permanent appointment for me at Wellesley College beginning with September 1948?

Very sincerely yours,

1. President of Wellesley College.

TO: **MORRIS BISHOP**[1]                                                           CC, 1 p.

8 Craigie Circle
Cambridge 38, Mass.
1st November 1947

Dear Bishop,

Many thanks for your good letter and the charming enclosures.

Here are the answers to your questions:

Yes, my only academic degree is B.A. Cambridge University (Trinity College), England, 1922.

Though my time between then and 1940 was mainly devoted to literature, I also

1. gave instruction in Russian, French and English literature, in the beginning to individual pupils, later to small groups interested in these subjects;

2. accepted invitations from clubs and organizations to give one or more lectures on literary subjects. Such invitations arrived in increasing numbers from France, Belgium, Czechoslovakia, Austria and England, and also from various German towns where there existed (before the war) more or less numerous colonies of Russian émigrés;

3. wrote reviews of prose and poetry, first for the Russian émigré

newspaper RUL (Berlin), regularly for a number of years,—then, in a more scattered way, for various Russian (émigré) and foreign publications (such as the NOUVELLE REVUE FRANÇAISE, leading French magazine of literary criticism, for which I was asked to write an essay on Pushkin illustrated by my own verse translations into French, or LE MOIS, which asked me for a general short survey of new trends in literature, etc.). This kind of activity I continued after coming to the United States, where I contributed during the winter of 1940–41 pretty regularly literary reviews to the NEW REPUBLIC (under its old management), and less regularly to some other publications such as the N.Y. SUN and TIMES.

My major opus in the field of criticism is a critical biography of NIKOLAI GOGOL (New Directions Publ., 1944).

In 1941 I read at the Annual Meeting of the New England Modern Language Association an essay which was later published in the Bulletin of the organization under the title THE CREATIVE WRITER. An article THE LERMONTOV MIRAGE, with my own translations from the poet, was published in the RUSSIAN REVIEW, issue of November 1941.

I enclose a detailed list of publications.

Sincerely yours,

1. Chairman, Department of Romance Literature, Cornell University.

TO: **KATHARINE A. WHITE**                    TLS, 1 p. Bryn Mawr College.

8 Craigie Circle
Cambridge 38, Mass.
10th November 1947

Dear Mrs. White,

As I wrote to you at the time, I deeply appreciated your sympathetic handling of "My Uncle".[1] It is the principle itself of editing that distresses me.

I shall be very grateful to you if you help me to weed out bad grammar but I do not think I would like my longish sentences clipped too close, or those drawbridges lowered which I have taken such pains to lift. In other words, I would like to discriminate between awkward construction (which is bad) and a certain special— how shall I put it—sinuosity, which is my own and which only at first glance may seem awkward or obscure. Why not have the reader re-read a sentence now and then? It won't hurt him.

I repeat, however, that I appreciate your attitude and would gladly go over the story with you. If it is not too much trouble for you to come to Boston, it would be a great help, since I have had to go away on a trip a week ago and a repeated absence would be difficult to organize. It is extremely kind of you to suggest your coming here.

Very sincerely yours,
V. Nabokov[2]

1. "Portrait of My Uncle," *The New Yorker* (3 January 1948); collected in *Conclusive Evidence*.
2. Signed with butterfly drawing.

TO: MRS. DOUGLAS HORTON                                    cc, 1 p.
Cambridge, Mass.

November 30, 1947

Dear Mrs. Horton,

Believe me I deeply appreciate your hope that it would be possible for me to continue my present work at Wellesley College and at the Harvard museum. In regard to the latter, I wish to say that the interruption will be only spatial since I shall be able to go on with my scientific research in Cornell's excellent entomological laboratory. I shall find there my good and celebrated friends, Professors Forbes and Bradley, and one of the finest entomological libraries in the country.

As to Wellesley the matter is different. You know how very much attached I am to the College. It is quite a wrench to leave it. However, certain very attractive aspects of the work I am offered at Cornell, together with the security of the position, lead me to accept their offer.

It is with the utmost reluctance that I now submit my formal resignation beginning with the 1st of September 1948.

Very sincerely yours,

TO: **PROFESSOR T. G. BERGIN**[1]                                                          cc, 1 p.

8 Craigie Circle
Cambridge 38, Mass.
30th November 1947

Dear Professor Bergin,

Many thanks for your very kind letter. It was a pleasure to meet you and Mrs. Bergin at that delightful party you gave.

What you say about the Literature course seems to me very attractive. I have been turning it over in my mind and I think I could prepare a course consisting of two parts echoing each other: Writers (Teachers, Storytellers, Enchanters) and Readers (Seekers of Knowledge, Entertainment, Magic). Of course, this is only a rough outline of the plan. I would include writers of various countries and categories. In planning the course, it is essential for me to know how many hours are to be devoted to it. I would also like to know the exact number of times my other classes are to meet during the term.

Very sincerely yours,

P.S. I wonder if it would be possible, when making out my schedule, to have me lecture in the afternoons or, should this not be possible, at least not earlier than 10–11 a.m.

1. Division of Literature, Cornell University

TO: **MORRIS BISHOP**                                         CC, 1 p.

8 Craigie Circle
Cambridge 38, Mass.
28th December 1947

Dear Bishop,

Yes, everything is perfectly clear now. I am sorry to have been so obtuse.

I suggest the following wording for the announcement:

101, 102. Survey of Russian Literature with emphasis on the XIX century. Throughout the year. Credit three hours a week. Prerequisite, proficiency in Russian. M.W.F. 11. Mr. Nabokov.

Lectures in Russian and classroom excercises on the development of Russian literature.

201, 202. Renaissance of Russian Poetry (1890–1925) Neo-romanticism and neo-classicism. From Blok to Pasternak and Khodassevich. Throughout the year. Credit three hours a week. Prerequisite, proficiency in Russian. Mr. Nabokov. Hours to be arranged.

Extensive study of the poets of the period, matter and manner.

I am pleased to note that my lectures in 101, 102 will be at 11 (or was it just a sample of time?). Bergin writes me that my Div. of Lit. course is tentatively put down for M,W and F at 2. If my other Russian course could be at 12, immediately following the first, that would be a splendid arrangement. But please, if possible, do not put me down for an hour earlier than 11.

We both wish you both a very happy New Year. I was delighted to hear of your receiving the "rosette".[1]

Sincerely yours,

1. Lapel emblem of the Légion d'Honneur.

TO: **COL. JOSEPH I. GREENE**[1]

CC, 1 p.
Cambridge, Mass.

January 14, 1948

Dear Colonel Greene,

My husband has asked me to thank you for your letter of January 2, notifying him that the United States Government has elected the option on the German-Austrian translation and publication rights of his novel BEND SINISTER. He hopes that his book may help the re-educational program of the Government, though, knowing the Germans as we do, we cannot help entertaining some doubts as to their susceptibility to re-education.

At this point my husband thinks it essential to submit to you the following considerations:

One of the main subjects of BEND SINISTER is a rather vehement incrimination of a dictatorship—any dictatorship, and though the dictatorship actually represented in the book is imaginary, it deliberately displays features peculiar a) to nazism, b) to communism, c) to any dictatorial trends in an otherwise non-dictatorial order. It would be very easy for a biased translator to upset this balance. This, my husband believes, should be borne in mind when selecting the German translator. It would be even better, if the author could be given a chance to peruse the translation prior to publication.

Sincerely yours,

1. *Infantry Journal,* Washington, D.C.

TO: **PROF. WILLIAM T. M. FORBES**    ALS, 1 p. Cornell University.
Cambridge, Mass.

12 II 1948

Dear Professor Forbes

I have great pleasure in informing you that I am joining your Faculty (as Associate Professor) and shall come to Cornell some time in summer.

I want to ask you whether it would be possible for me to go on with my lepidopt. research work at the Agric. Exper. Station? Could I have the use of microscopes (binoc. and mono.)? Do tell me if this is all feasible.

I am looking forward to seeing a lot of you next year.

> Very sincerely yours,
> V. Nabokov

TO: THE AMERICAN CONSUL
PRAGUE, CZECHOSLOVAKIA                                cc, 1 p.

> 8 Craigie Circle
> Cambridge, Mass.
> U.S.A.
> 26 February 1948

Dear Sir,

I am trying to arrange the immigration to the United States of my nephew, Rostislav Petkevich (Petkevic),[1] aged 17, at the present time domiciliated at 12 Koulova, Prague, Dejvice. Owing to financial difficulties, his parents have never been able to take care of him so that he has always lived with my mother until she died in 1939. Since that time it has always been my wish to have him join me, but the fulfillment of this plan had to be postponed on account of the war. In 1940, I immigrated to the United States bringing with me my wife and son. In 1945 we became American citizens. Since my arrival in the United States I have, by degrees, achieved a position which, though still modest, appears sufficiently secure to warrant bringing my nephew over.

From the reports I have been getting, I believe that he is not only a gifted, but also an honest and decent lad, and one who deserves the chance that I wish to give him. I am convinced that, given the opportunity, he will develop into a good, and possibly a valuable, citizen who will serve his adopted fatherland to the best of his strength and ability.

Upon arrival to this country he will reside at the Reed Farm of the Tolstoy Foundation.

I hope that you will find it possible to approve my nephew's application for an American visa.

Yours faithfully,

I am enclosing Affidavits of Support and all supporting documents with required number of copies.

1. The son of VN's sister Olga did not emigrate.

TO: **DEAN C. W. DE KIEWIT**[1]                                              cc, 1 p.

8 Craigie Circle
Cambridge 38, Mass.
21 March 1948

Dear Dean de Kiewit,

Many thanks for your kind letter. It is very interesting to hear that you have definite plans for the development of Russian studies at the University.

I entirely agree with you that courses in Russian Literature should not be limited to those given in Russian. Indeed, I know from experience that a course in this subject given in English has a strong appeal for students who have a general interest in literature,—the enrollment in such a course which I am giving currently at Wellesley College (they call it "Russian Literature in Translation") is one of the largest in the College. I would therefore welcome the arrangement originally suggested by Professor Bishop, namely that I give two courses in Russian (a general survey course and one more specialized, such as for instance on Russian poets of the revival period) and one in English (a general survey with emphasis on the XIX century). At one time it has been suggested that the idea of this latter course be abandoned and that instead I should give a course, or rather one section of a course in General Introduction to Literature. To this I agreed most reluctantly. Russian literature (both theory and practice of it) is my special field and I feel sure that this is the field in which students would profit most from my lectures. I was therefore highly gratified when the idea of a Russian Literature course given in English was recently revived. This arrangement—two courses in Russian and one in English—will, I believe, provide the best opportunity for me to offer and for the interested students to absorb the wealth of material represented by Russian literature and its history. I am very much looking forward to this work.

On the other hand, though sorry to disappoint you, I must tell you quite frankly that I am entirely lacking in administrative talents. I am a hopelessly poor organizer, and my participation in any committee would be, I am afraid, pretty worthless. I would, however, be delighted to assist in the selection of literary material, in Russian and in translation, worth being reproduced in microprint for the University library.

Very sincerely yours,

1. College of Arts and Sciences, Cornell University.

to: **David Higham**[1]                                                    cc, 1 p.

8 Craigie Circle
Cambridge 38, Mass.
24 March 1948

Dear Mr. Higham,

I wonder if you have seen the THREE POETS volume produced by Lindsay Drummond? While using my translations, bought from me as a collection, the publishers deemed it proper to present the book as "PUSHKIN, LERMONTOV, TYUTCHEV, POEMS, RUSSIAN LITERATURE LIBRARY 8" (on the dust jacket); the same thing minus the "Russian Literature Library 8" figures on the binding and again the same thing plus "Lindsay Drummond Limited, London, 1947" on the inside cover. Somewhere in between my name modestly appears following that of the lady who supplied a number of entirely awful and out-of-place illustrations. Finally, a list of their publications, appended at the end under the heading "RUSSIAN LITERATURE LIBRARY EDITED BY STEFAN SCHIMANSKI", makes mention under "8" of "PUSHKIN, LERMONTOV, TYUTCHEV, POEMS. ILLUSTRATED BY DONIA NACHSHEN"—period. I nearly forgot to mention that the same list figures on one of the fly leafs, in smaller characters and this time omitting the illustrator.

There is no mention of me in the blurb. A Mr. Stefan Schimanski is named as "editor"—who the deuce is Mr. Schimanski and what has he been "editing" in my book? Apart from a couple of hideous misprints, due to the fact that I never saw the proofs, the translations appear exactly as I made them. Incidentally, since I get nowhere any credit for the three introductions, that credit automatically goes to the mythical editor.

Can you suggest what is to be done about it? Never in my life have I been subjected to the cavalier treatment these publishers seem to reserve for their authors. Frankly, I would very much prefer not being published at all in England to being published like this! Tell me what is to be done in order to stop them. Can you obtain that they display prominently, on all copies still in their possession, my name as the author of the translations *and introductions*? Can you stop them from ever repeating this offensive blunder, should another batch of the book be printed? And—should they be willing to present the book with due mention of what had been done by me in all the places where it is natural to do so—could you prevail upon them to divorce the text from the incredible illustrations? If all or any part of these conditions cannot be accepted by the publishers, what can you do towards cancelling the agreement? I signed it very much against my better judgment and sorely regret having done so. I urge you in the first place to examine the book and form your own opinion which, I feel certain, will not differ from mine. I hope to hear from you very soon.

Sincerely yours,

1. Literary agent in London.

TO: COL. JOSEPH I. GREENE                                    cc, 2 pp.

957 East State Street
Ithaca, New York
24 August 1948

Dear Colonel Greene,

I have been on the move and your letter took some time to catch up with me—hence the delay. I have now looked through the typescript you have kindly sent me and am absolutely appalled by it. The translation is so bad that were I to check and correct all the blunders and boners in it, it would take me as much time and labor as it would to translate the whole thing anew. My idea was that I would look through the translator's work and assist him in rendering those (not very numerous) passages which might stump a person not familiar with certain modern literary trends or liable to misunderstand allusions to local features of American life. As things stand, however, I would have to revamp almost every sentence.

1) The translator's knowledge of English is vague and he seems to rely throughout on a pocket dictionary. When the pocket dictionary fails him, he is helpless.

2) His German vocabulary is miserably poor.

3) He does not bother about accuracy and is satisfied with any approximative meaning at hand.

4) He has no sense of style. My imagery is absolutely lost upon him. He does not see what I want the reader to see and simply does not understand the literary and scholarly side of the book.

Note please that these observations of mine are based on a perusal of what I would term the easiest portion of the book, I shudder to think what would happen if he were allowed to tackle the Hamlet part.

Although this may clash with the traditional modesty of authors, I want to draw your attention to the fact that my book is a lasting contribution to American literature and the German publisher should be warned not to give it to a hack to tamper with in this way. Insofar as you are including my work in your program, I think it is in your interest as well as in mine to preserve in it those qualities and values which alone bring out the main points of the novel. Why not look for a translator in New York, some German émigré writer (perhaps Mann might suggest somebody), whose English would be adequate to the task? I am not hoping for a translator of genius, but I think I am justified in wanting somebody who would be both a scholar and a talented stylist.

I am returning the typescript with a list of a few typical errors in the first and last pages. I did not think it necessary to go on and devote any more time to the annotation of the blunders (just as numerous) in the rest of the pages.

I have also to say a few words anent the publisher's letter:

1) The titles they suggest are ridiculous (quite in line with the inept translation).

2) The rest of the queries and suggestions are not worth while dealing with at the present moment since there are countless other stumbling blocks which have tripped up the translator (with the publisher not noticing it) but anyway the translator has no idea whatever of what the sentences on pp. 56, 49 and 73 mean. I repeat that when I am given a competent translator to deal with, I shall be delighted to give him every assistance in translating these and other passages which may seem to him obscure.

I am sorry if this will delay the publication of the book but I am sure you will forgive me for being so bitterly frank on a subject which is of the utmost importance to me as the author of the book.[1]

Very sincerely yours,

I have transferred my school from Harvard to Cornell where I have accepted a professorship in literature.[2]

1. The project was dropped. *Bend Sinister* appeared in German as *Das Bastardzeichen*, trans. Dieter E. Zimmer (Reinbek: Rowohlt, 1962).
2. This sentence in holograph.

TO: **EDWARD WEEKS**
October 1948

cc, 1 p.
802 E. Seneca St.
Ithaca, N.Y.
Tel. 6834

Dear Weeks,

I have received your letter of September 30 and can only excuse its contents by assuming that you were in your cups when you wrote it. I have never published any story called "The Proud Castle" or "The Professor's Return", as you seem to imagine. I *never* send editors anything that I consider to be of inferior quality. In fact, the piece[1] I sent you is better than those I have published in the New Yorker so far. Your letter is so silly *and* rude that I do not think I want to have anything to do with you or the Atlantic any more. I am sending you a cheque for $800 and shall send the rest as soon as I am able to.

Yours faithfully,

1. On 30 September Weeks declined a section of *Conclusive Evidence* for the *Atlantic Monthly* and reproached VN for reserving his best work for the *New Yorker*.

TO: JOHN FISCHER[1]                                     cc, I p.

802 E. Seneca Street
Ithaca, N.Y.
14 December 1948

Dear Mr. Fischer,

Many thanks for your letter and the kind things you say about my work.

I would be delighted to have my book published by Harper and Brothers, when it is completed. In the meantime, I would like to apply for a Saxton fellowship and am returning with this letter the filled out questionnaire.[2] I am answering question 17 below, which also covers the question in your letter.

Sincerely yours,

*To question 7.*

The book I have already begun to write will be, I think, about 200–250 pages long. It is an inquiry into the elements that have gone to form my personality as a writer. Starting with several phases of childhood in northern Russia, it will wind its way through the years of Russian revolution and civil war, thence to England (Cambridge University), to Germany and France, and finally to America (1940). All I have written up to now has been published in *The New Yorker* and should give the reader a fair idea of the method used. However, the necessity to select for writing such passages as could be published separately, has led to a somewhat jerky development of the theme. In the course of integrating these fragments in the book various alterations will take place, but the manner will remain the same. In other words, the flow of the book I contemplate is more ample and sustained than the sharp pieces carved out of it for magazine publication might suggest. It is a most difficult book to write, not only because it necessitates endless forays into the past, but also because the blending of perfect personal truth with strict artistic selection[3]

1. Editor at Harper & Brothers.
2. VN did not receive the fellowship.
3. End of letter missing in carbon copy.


TO: **PROF. DAVID DAICHES**[1]
                          CC, I p.
                               Ithaca, N.Y.

8 January 1948 [1949]

Dear Mr. Daiches,

I had thought of having a little talk with you but perhaps this is a more practical way of dealing with the following matter.

Since I came to Ithaca, I have gradually discovered that I simply cannot make ends meet on my present salary. Here are some of the reasons. The housing situation here compelled me to pay a much higher rent than I had expected. I also never thought that there would be high deductions for old age insurance etc., as proved to be customary at Cornell. In result of various deductions my actual salary amounts to about $4170 for the year.

I have not done any writing at all since the beginning of the academic year as I had to reorganize completely my courses.

In result of all this, I am in a bad financial fix. Do you think something could be done about it soon?

Sincerely yours,


1. Chairman of the Cornell Division of Literature.


TO: **KATHARINE A. WHITE**
                                   CC, I p.
                                   Ithaca, N.Y.

4th March 1949

Dear Mrs. White,

Many thanks for your charming letter. As you see, I have been very meek (though I also said "Jesus!" a few times as Ross[1] did) and have omitted or changed some of the "long" words.[2] I do hope that you will be able to retain a few things in the beginning, especially the last letters of the alphabet and the reference to the Maertz dictionary. The point is that this *New Yorker* issue will certainly be quoted by psychologists interested in colored hearing—do think of them a little.

I always appreciate your delicate, sympathetic and careful way of dealing with my prose.

I also wish to thank you for several other things,—for speaking to Mrs. Leiper of Simon and Schuster, from whom I received an inquiry about the book, for having the bookkeeping check the amount, and also for discussing the comparative advantages of Harper v. Rinehart.

I was very sorry to hear that you have been ill. Are you quite well now?

Sincerely yours,

I am enclosing my notes, your notes and both copies of text. Please, return one of them with the proofs.[3]

Kindly accelerate printing (during March)[4]

1. Harold Ross, editor of *The New Yorker*.
2. "Portrait of my Mother," *The New Yorker* (9 April 1949). Collected in *Conclusive Evidence*.
3. Final twelve words are in holograph.
4. Holograph note in Russian at bottom of copy.

TO: **HERBERT LYONS**[1]                    CC, 1 p.

802 E. Seneca Street
Ithaca, N.Y.
31 March 1949

Dear Mr. Lyons,

I shall be glad to do an occasional review for you. I have been wanting for a long time to take a crack at such big fakes as Mr. T.S. Eliot and Mr. Thomas Mann; apart from this, any new work by a well-known writer, American, English, French or Russian, would be welcome.

May I add that if you could pay me more for this kind of work, I would be able to devote more time to it.

Sincerely yours,

1. On the staff of the *New York Times Book Review*.

TO: **ROBERT M. GLAUBER**[1]                    CC, I p.
Ithaca, N.Y.

9 April 1949

Dear Mr. Glauber,

Yes—I am a great admirer of Mirsky's work. In fact, I consider it to be by far the best history of Russian literature in any language including Russian.[2] Unfortunately I must deprive myself of the pleasure of writing a blurb for it, since the poor fellow is now in Russia and compliments from such an anti-Soviet writer as I am known to be might cause him considerable unpleasantness.

Sincerely yours,

1. Editor at Alfred A. Knopf.
2. D. S. Mirsky, *A History of Russian Literature*, 1927; republished by Knopf in 1949.

TO: **HERBERT LYONS**                                         CC, I p.

802 E. Seneca Street
Ithaca, N.Y.
24 April 1949

Dear Mr. Lyons,

This is the first time in my life that something written by me has
been pruned by others without my consent.[1] When you asked me to
write the article, the very first thing I did was to draw your attention
to the fact that I would have to be consulted before any cuts were
made. This was a condition—otherwise I would not have written the
article at all. If the editor or editors thought that this or that passage
might better be omitted, there was plenty of time (about a month)
for acquainting me with your qualms. Whoever edited the article,
has doctored it in such a way that the reader may get the impression
of my disliking only this "first try" of Sartre and loving the rest. In
other words, it is all hopelessly botched and butchered and in gaping
disaccord with my signature. I repeat that never before has any publication acted with such utter *sans-gêne* towards me. I cannot believe
that you are responsible for this mess. Still I would like to have some
explanation from the Times in regard to this cavalier treatment.

Incidentally they still owe me a quarter of the fee.

Sincerely yours,

1. Review of Sartre's *La Nausée, New York Times Book Review* (24 April 1949).

TO: **PHILIP RAHV**[1]                                          CC, I p.

> 802 E. Seneca Street
> Ithaca, N.Y.
> 21 May 1949

Dear Rahv,

I have written a piece—half-essay half-review—on the famous Russian epic "La Geste d'Igor" and on the latest translations of it into several languages. It is about 3,500 words long. Would the Partisan care to publish it?[2]

There is something I would like to ask you. If you have not yet made any arrangements for bringing out "The First Poem" thing in the June or July issue, I would prefer to have it appear in August or September.[3] You would greatly oblige me if you could comply with this *pros'ba* [request].

I am sorry you did not ask me what I think of the disgusting and entirely second-rate Mr. Pound,—and Mr. Eliot who is also disgusting and second-rate.

> Sincerely yours,

1. Editor of *Partisan Review*.
2. Not separately published; incorporated in VN's edition of *The Song of Igor's Campaign* (1960).
3. *Partisan Review* (September 1949). Collected in *Conclusive Evidence*.

TO: *LIFE*                                                     CC, I p.[1]

> Res.: 802 E. Seneca St.
> 12 November 1949

Sirs,

It may interest a few of your readers to learn that the butterfly wings in the third panel of the Bosch tryptich, so beautifully reproduced in your issue of November 14, can be at once determined as belonging to a female specimen of the common European species now known as *Maniola jurtina*, which Linnaeus described some 250 years after good Bosch knocked it down with his cap in a Flemish meadow to place it in his Hell.[2]

Yours truly,
Vladimir Nabokov.

1. Published in edited form by *Life*, 27 (5 December 1949).
2. A reference to Hieronymus Bosch's triptych "The Garden of Delights." DN.

TO: **KATHARINE A. WHITE**                                    CC, 2 pp.

802 E. Seneca St.
Ithaca, N.Y.
27 November 1949

Dear Mrs. White,

Many thanks for your very sweet wire, for your kind words about my piece and for the check. The arrangement you suggest is O.K. I am sending you another piece that may amuse you, "Lantern Slides".[1] Here is a complete list of the pieces forming the book:

| Chapter 1 | Perfect Past | New Yorker |
|---|---|---|
| Chapter 2 | Mother | New Yorker |
| Chapter 3 | Uncle | New Yorker |
| Chapter 4 | English Education | New Yorker |
| Chapter 5 | Mademoiselle | Atlantic |
| Chapter 6 | Butterflies | New Yorker |
| Chapter 7 | Colette | New Yorker |
| Chapter 8 | Lantern Slides | |
| Chapter 9 | Russian Education | New Yorker |
| Chapter 10 | Curtain Raiser | New Yorker |
| Chapter 11 | First Poem | Partisan |
| Chapter 12 | Tamara | New Yorker |
| Chapter 13 | Student Days | |
| Chapter 14 | Exile | |

| Chapter 15 | Second Person | in progress |
|---|---|---|
| Chapter 16 | Third Person | |

Some, such as Chapter 5 (which you saw and rejected before you developed a real taste for me) and Chapter 3 (which, I confess, was badly written) have been altered and expanded.

I wonder if you find "Lantern Slides" acceptable. After that—three more pieces, and the book is finished. I shall soon submit all three to you: Chapters 14 (Exile), 15 (Second Person) and 16 (Third Person). Of these the first is concerned with émigré life in Western Europe and has a great deal about literary mores. The second is couched, so to speak, in the second person (being addressed to my wife) and is an account of my boy's infancy in the light of my own childhood. The last is, from my own point of view, the most important one of the series (indeed, the whole book was written with this conclusion and summit in view) since therein are carefully gathered and analyzed (by a fictitious reviewer) the various themes running through the book—all the intricate threads that I have been at pains to follow through each piece. Incidentally, this chapter will include some very nice things about my delightful association with the New Yorker. I do not think, though, that this last piece will be suitable for separate publication. All this is confidential for the time being.

It is just possible that I shall do after all a special chapter on my father—if I manage to get to Washington where the material I require exists. Pullman plus a couple of nights at a good hotel adds up to a sum I do not possess at present.

I hope you have completely recovered from your grippe. The little thing about Eagles and Bears was quite admirable[2] (my son arrived for Thanksgiving with a copy, all a-chuckle), except the three unnecessary and lame lines from "Bears didn't" to "in the mind" at the top of the first column of page 24—if I may express a frank opinion. Otherwise it is one of the very best things I have read on the subject.

Best regards from both of us to you both.

Sincerely,

1. *The New Yorker* (11 February 1950). Collected in *Conclusive Evidence.*
2. "Notes and Comments," *The New Yorker* (26 November 1949). An unsigned fable by E. B. White about international relations.


TO: **KATHARINE A. WHITE**                                    CC, 1 p.
Ithaca, N.Y.

28 January 1950

Dear Mrs. White,

Many thanks for that nice cheque.

I was planning to go to Washington next week but as I have to go to Toronto to deliver a lecture, the Washington trip has to be postponed. Anyway I am having some trouble with the last chapters of my book[1] and have had to do a good deal of reshaping and adding to the first chapters. I may drop altogether the idea of writing a special piece about my father since various material concerning his activities finds adequate niches here and there in my book.

May I ask you for a piece of very confidential advice. I am determined to make some money with the book and think of enlisting the services of a good press agent—I wonder if you could assist me in finding out where and how one finds such people? Or perhaps you would advise me against any such move? All my previous books have been such dismal financial flops in this country that I don't trust the pure fate of unaided books any more.

Sincerely yours,

1. *Conclusive Evidence.*

TO: **PASCAL COVICI**[1]                                          CC, I p.

802 E. Seneca Street
Ithaca, N.Y.
February 3, 1950

Dear Mr. Covici,

I find your conditions acceptable. As soon as I have completed an autobiographical work which has to go to Harper Brothers this spring, I shall prepare for you 50 pages from the Karamazovs, four excerpts from four different chapters.[2]

If you decide to have me do the whole book, perhaps you would agree to the following three points:

1. If you contemplate an introduction I would like to be the one to write it;

2. A number of notes—explanations, comments and so on—would be appended by me for the scholarly reader;

3. For income tax reasons I might have to ask you to divide the total payment equally between 1950 and 1951.

I would also ask you then to send me a copy of the best available edition of the BROTHERS in Russian.

Sincerely yours,
Vladimir Nabokov

1. Editor at Viking Press.
2. VN's projected translation of Dostoevsky's *The Brothers Karamazov;* VN relinquished the project in April after he was hospitalized.

TO: **KATHARINE A. WHITE**                                    CC, I p.

Ithaca, N.Y.

20 March 1950

Dear Mrs. White,

I am returning the tawny paper with "The Room".[1] Have corrected two misprints. I want to tell you again how grateful I am to the New Yorker for their generosity. I hope you can use the poem soon since Mr. Churchill is getting on in years and any accident or sickness that might happen to him would perhaps interfere with the publication of my good-natured dig.

Incidentally, I tried strophe 9 on two friends of mine and really there does not seem any possibility of ambiguity whatsoever, as to the meaning of the last two words.[2]

We had a marvellous time at the New Yorker party, but it was a terrible disappointment that you were not there. Véra and I hope that you are making a speedy recovery.

You will soon get two stories, "Exile" and "Gardens and Parks".[3] I wonder if you have had an opportunity to glance at Amy Kelly's charming and scholarly book, "Eleanor and the Four Kings"?[4] I understand it was sent to your office.

Best regards to your husband.

Cordially yours,

1. *The New Yorker* (27 January 1951). Collected in *Poems* (1959) and *Poems and Problems* (1971).
2. "From Glen Lake to Restricted Rest." The last two words refer to the practice of refusing accommodations to Jews.
3. See 24 March 1950 letter to White.
4. *Eleanor of Aquitaine and the Four Kings* (Cambridge: Harvard University Press, 1950).

TO: **KATHARINE A. WHITE**
cc, 1 p.
Ithaca, N.Y.

24 March 1950

Dear Katharine,

I hope you will be quite well by the time this reaches you. But just in case you are still resting I am sending a duplicate of this letter to your home address while enclosing the stories with the original addressed to you at the New Yorker office.

I have followed your example and am in bed with a temperature above 102°. No bronchitis but grippe with me is invariably accompanied by the hideous pain of intercostal neuralgia. However, I have managed to put the finishing touches to two pieces, "Exile"[1] and "Gardens and Parks",[2] which constitute Chapters XV and XVI of my book. Its title will be "Conclusive Evidence". Chapter XIV will be a new venture, a kind of essay on women and love. And Chapter XVII will be a critical survey of the whole book.

To be quite frank in regard to the following matter: Sirin, the writer I detachedly describe in one passage, is I; it is the *nom-de-guerre* under which I used to write in Russian and it seemed to me that this was the most unobtrusive way to render an important period in my life, especially since the name "Sirin" conveys absolutely nothing to American readers.

When coming to the last pages of the piece "Exile", please remember that the frontispiece to the first edition of "Alice in the Looking Glass" carries a very subtle and difficult chess problem, and I would not like to think that New Yorker readers could be more bewildered by my chess problem (which occupies only a few lines) than Dodgson's little readers.

Véra and I send our very best greetings to you and Andy.

Sincerely yours,

1. *Partisan Review* (January–February 1951).
2. *The New Yorker* (17 June 1950).

TO: **JAMES LAUGHLIN**                                          cc, 1 p.

802 E. Seneca Street
Ithaca, N.Y.
27 April 1950

Dear Laughlin,

I have been sick for more than a month and only now am beginning to get back to normal conditions. One of my first concerns is that unfinished business of the LAUGHTER IN THE DARK reprint. Quite independently of whether or not the deal is a profitable one for you and me, it is essential for me to keep my records straight, and this I cannot do unless I know the exact text of your contract with the New American Library. It is very important for me, so please give it your attention. Please have a copy of the agreement sent to me without further delay. I am at a loss to understand why you have not done it before. After all, literature is not only fun, it is also business.

I thought THE SHELTERING SKY an utterly ridiculous performance, devoid of talent.[1] You ought to have had the manuscript checked by a cultured Arab. Thanks all the same for sending me those books. I hope you don't mind this frank expression of my opinion.

Sincerely yours,

1. By Paul Bowles (New York: New Directions, 1948).

TO: JOHN FISCHER                                                   CC, I p.

802 E. Seneca Street
Ithaca, N.Y.
9 May 1950

Dear Mr. Fischer,

I shall not pretend that I am not disappointed by your decision.[1] Some of the reasons that made me wish for an early publication I have explained in my last letter. There were others that it would take too long to explain in writing. I leave them unsaid for I realize that it is now too late for you to change your decision.

I hope this does not signify that you are losing interest in my book. I am enclosing herewith a piece of it which perhaps Harper's Magazine would care to purchase. Please let me have your reaction as soon as you conveniently can as I am anxious to place this piece before I go away for the summer.

There is also another question which I would like to discuss with you. As you surely know, before coming to this country and becoming an American writer, I have published a number of novels in Russian. Two of these have been translated into English and published by John Long (London), and one of these two was published by Bobbs-Merrill more than ten years ago and recently reissued by the New American Library ("Laughter in the Dark"). Besides the English translation there have been translations of this and others of my novels into French, German, Swedish and Czech, and recently also in Italian, Spanish and Dutch.

The second[2] of the two that were published in England by Long before the last war, as well as a couple of others, should, I think, be sometime published in this country, preferably within a few years. I never raised this question before with any publisher, with the exception of New Directions some ten years ago. . . . Please let me know whether your firm could be interested in such a project. I have a letter from a firstrate agent who seems to be interested in this matter but before dealing with him I would like to hear from you.

Sincerely yours,<br>
Vladimir Nabokov

---

1. On 21 April VN asked Fischer to publish *Conclusive Evidence* in the fall of 1950—not early in 1951.
2. *Despair.*

TO: **DR. JOSEPH BEQUAERT**[1]                                    CC, 2 pp.

802 E. Seneca Street
Ithaca, N.Y.
6th July 1950

Dear Bequaert,

I am sending you a little memorandum that may be useful to Dr. McDunnough when he arrives. As you know, a serious illness in the spring of 1948 prevented me from winding up my lepidopterological affairs to my satisfaction before I left for Ithaca. I have now looked through my correspondence and notebooks and have jotted down the following items for your and McDunnough's information.

1. I am responsible for the arrangement of the Nearctic butterflies. Very possibly Dr. McDunnough will disagree with some of my taxonomic ideas but at least the series are in good order now. It was not an easy job since the specimens were scattered all over the place. I also classified most the Palearctic butterflies of the Weeks collection which were originally in glassless trays when I first examined the collection in 1941–42. As you also know, I was never officially curator of the Lepidoptera, and what I did in that line was solely in appreciation of Barbour's sympathy and generosity in giving me the possibility to indulge in research work dealing with certain Lycaenids, which resulted in various papers published in "Psyche", "The Entomologist" and the "MCZ Bulletin".

2. A chest near the bookcase contains numerous vials with male genitalia (mainly Lycaenids) coated with glycerine in a mixture of alcohol and water. I had hoped to arrange them more permanently (using the jar system, as I do not believe in slides for these things) but I did not have the time to do so before my departure. The numbers affixed to these vials correspond to numbers on *yellow* labels affixed to Lycaenids in the collection. Most of them refer to the *Lycaeides* (the "scudderi-melissa" group) that is temporarily set apart with "do-not-disturb" notes (opposite the Nearctic collection) since there are still specimens that I have to return to my correspondents. The numbers in pencil on white labels affixed to the butterflies refer to my files where each specimen has a card of its own, and should

not be confused with the aforesaid numbers on yellow labels referring to the vials with genitalia. I shall be in Boston sometime in September and shall finish sorting out the specimens to be returned. The Frank Chermock batch is ready but he does not answer my letters and I do not know where to send it to him (it contains a holotype-allotype pair among other valuable things).

3. Some Lycaenids occurring in North America, but really belonging to the Neotropical group, will be found together with specimens of the latter in one of the cabinets (nearest to the windows) containing West-Indian butterflies. I placed them there temporarily while working on the Neotropical *Plebejinae*.

4. Also temporarily, for safety's sake, while boxes were continuously opened and handled, I removed Scudder's Lycaenidae specimens, among which there are a few types, to the "green" cabinet and attached large labels "Scudder's collection" to the cases.

5. The following material had been loaned through me and I do not know if it has been returned since I left (there are notes pinned in the corresponding empty spots in the cases):

> To Avinov, Carnegie Museum, 15-VI-1943, 6 females of *Phoebis argante* race from Cuba.
> To Franklin Chermock, 18-IV-1945, a specimen of *Colias occidentalis* Scud.
> To W.P. Comstock, A.M.N.H., 7-IX-1946, nine specimens of *Anaea* and, in 1945, some sixty or more *Heliconius charithonius* (you should have the list, if I remember correctly).
> To R.M. Fox, Carnegie Museum, 25-IX-1946, about 1900 specimens of *Ithomine* (his count, 1878, is short of ours by 32).
> To A.B. Klots, College of the City of New York, Dep. of Biology, 22-IV-1948, 1 *Boloria freija*.

6. I have given to the MCZ all the abundant lepidopterological material spread and incorporated in the Nearctic section, that I collected in 1943 and 1947 in Utah and Colorado besides a smaller collection I made in various Eastern localities.

7. I have been also responsible for obtaining specimens for the Mu-

seum from various correspondents of mine (you have the list of these accessions) such as Stallings, Grey, Eff and many others.

There are some other, minor, matters but they can wait until I see you in the fall.

Sincerely yours,
Vladimir Nabokov

1. Of the Museum of Comparative Zoology, Harvard University.

TO: JOHN FISCHER                                        CC, 1 p.

802 East Seneca Street
Ithaca, N.Y.
20 July 1950

Dear Mr. Fischer,

Thanks for your two kind letters. Am enclosing the copy. Good, accurate work on the part of the copy editor.

*Re* the subtitle. The addition "of a vanished era" will not do at all. The book is not about an era, but about a person, and in that sense the past cannot be said to have "vanished". If you have any other suggestions for a subtitle, let me know. I am completely out of mental funds.

The jacket copy is, as you say, not a success. I object strongly to the following points: 1. Sitwell, a ridiculous mediocrity, does not belong here.[1] 2. The paragraph stressing the "immeasurable wealth"[2] etc. is impossible—sets my teeth on edge. 3. Nabokov does *not* tell about the assassination of his father with "good humored detachment". 4. The sentence about the ironically appropriate butterflies is too silly for words.[3] 5. The quotation from Proust is bad English and anyway irrelevant.[4]

*Re* the "style sheet". The name Colette has one "l".

Here are some notes relating to the copy-edited typescript: p. 14, premonitary (not . . . . . tory); p. 33, overboard; pp. 43, 46 and 55, schoolroom; pp. 81 and 89, yes, quite right, "moth" should not be capitalized; p. 110, yes, "confront"; p. 125, bonnet; pp. 159 and 172, Alexandr (but Alexandre on p. 113 and 162); p. 170, reinstate *gaffe*; p. 176, yes—idiotic; p. 186, nonexistant; p. 187, buttoned sweater etc.; p. 191, had possessed; p. 191, "Claws" is intentional and so is "Butcher" in the same sentence; p. 200, sung is o.k.; p. 299, yes, 1916–1900 B.C.—excellent idea; p. 211, reinstate catacumbal.

I am enclosing with this letter a last chapter (XVI) which I find difficult to decide whether to add or not to my book.[5] I am sending it to you mainly because it contains, among other matter, all that is necessary to say in the blurb. The "reviewer" and "Miss Braun" are of course fictitious people, and there is no such book as "When Lilacs Last". If this chapter be added, then the parenthetic "Bishop to c2" on p. 219 should of course be deleted. I like this chapter XVI well enough but for some reasons I still hesitate to include it. However, as I say, your blurbist is free to fish out whatever he finds suitable. I would suggest making the blurb as prim and prosaic as possible: after all the reader will find out all about the author in the book itself.

Sincerely yours,

1. The proposed jacket copy compared VN to Sitwell—presumably Edith.
2. A reference to the pre-Revolution affluence of the Nabokov family.
3. "It was, perhaps, ironically appropriate that a passion for butterflies should determine the pattern of his new life in exile."
4. " . . . as Proust has observed, they 'bear unfaltering, in the tiny and almost impalpable drop of their essence, the vast structure of recollection.' "
5. A final chapter in guise of a review of the book was not included in *Conclusive Evidence*.

TO: **KATHARINE A. WHITE**    cc, 1 p.
Ithaca, N.Y.

23 July 1950

Dear Katharine,

Just a word of summer greetings. We hope you are well, all three of you, and enjoying vacation. Have heard from the Bishops that you were in Nova Scotia.

I am engrossed in the preparation of a new course. Have finished annotating "Bleak House" and "Mansfield Park" and now shall have to translate—at least in parts—"Madame Bovary": what there is in this line is a mess. In connection with "Mansfield Park" I have been reading Walter Scott, Cowper, Shak.'s "Henry VIII" and Inchbald-Kotzebue's "Lovers' Vows". Am anticipating my students' surprise when I tell them that they will have to read all that too in order to appreciate Jane. My plan is to teach my 150 students to *read* books, not just to get away with a "general" idea and a vague hash of "influences", "background", "human interest" and so forth. But this means work.[1]

We shall probably spend all summer here. Our boy is in Evanston, attending a five-week course in Debating given by Northwestern to a selected group of highschoolers. He enjoys it.

Did I tell you that my university piece[2] will be in Harper's Magazine? The MS of the book went to Harpers, and I am now feeling as flat and empty as a young mother.

My wife joins me in sending you and yours our best regards.

1. See VN's *Lectures on Literature* (New York: Harcourt Brace Jovanovich/Bruccoli Clark, 1980).
2. "Lodgings in Trinity Lane," *Harper's Magazine* (January 1951).

TO: **KATHARINE A. WHITE**                                CC, I p.
                                                          Ithaca, N.Y.

November 13 [1950]

Dear Katharine,

I want to add to Véra's letter that I have found some extraordinary things, plays and articles, in the Soviet periodical "Zvezda" for 1949 that cast a brilliant and terrible light on Soviet-American relations. Would you like me to write a piece of 4000–5000 words on the subject? It would contain samples of the Soviet notion of the American way of life culled from some plays and a remarkable warning, in August 1949!—of their Korean policy. I could have the article ready within a month's time. It might fit either into the body of the New Yorker or into its book-reviewing head.

TO: JOHN FISCHER                                                    cc, 1 p.

802 East Seneca Street
Ithaca, N.Y.
November 14, 1950

Dear Mr. Fischer,

Here are a few questions I would like to discuss:

1. Time is passing, and I still have not seen either blurb, jacket or binding. Who is designing the jacket? I trust there is no "Russian" stuff—churches, pagodas, samovars—being considered. I am raising this question only because I have had something of the sort inflicted upon me by an English publisher.

2. What are you doing in the way of publicity? Santa Claus is putting on his jackboots. When are you sending out that announcement? Incidentally, I hope there has not been a misunderstanding—if I mentioned the Russian-language publications in New York, it was only because I took for granted that you would take care of the American ones anyway. The bulk of my readers is American, not Russian.

3. Perhaps I have mentioned the following matter before. Have you tried to get any of the so-called "book clubs" interested in CONCLUSIVE EVIDENCE? I am told one can make a bit of money that way.

4. I hope that Harper's Magazine will publish my story in its December issue, thus making some publicity for the book *before* Christmas.

Thank you for sending a set of proofs to Bonnier's.

About two months ago I wrote to the French film company by registered mail. The letter was not returned but no answer came. You might be luckier. The name of the firm is "SEDIF", in case you care to write them. The "adresse provisoire" (the only one I have) is 65–67,

Champs-Elysées, Paris. Their letterhead, however, also lists addresses in Marseilles, Bordeaux, Lille, Lyon and Brussels.

Sincerely yours,
Vladimir Nabokov.


TO: **KATHARINE A. WHITE**                    cc, 1 p.
Ithaca, N.Y.


November 19, 1950

Dear Katharine,

I would be very glad to do an article, or a series of articles, on the lines Ross suggests.[1] His idea not only does not clash with mine but rather amplifies it and I think I am the right man for it since I know exactly all the moves in the Soviet anti-American game.

Next week I shall send you a list of the material I have at my disposal here. After to-morrow I am going to Cambridge for three or four days and shall see what the Widener has.

Sincerely yours,


1. Harold Ross's 15 November memo to White: "Could he expand his source field? Shawn and I have had other writers in mind for our idea, and Nabokov might be the man. But, on the other hand, he wouldn't be doing the idea he had in mind, and it might be better not to tamper with that idea. You might ask him about this. In any event, we should certainly like to see whatever he writes on this subject, regardless, and would be willing to hold up doing anything here pending receipt of that."


TO: **KATHARINE A. WHITE**                    cc, 1 p.
Ithaca, N.Y.


December 7th, 1950

Dear Katharine,

Many thanks for the cheque. A 25% deduction is a very good way of repayment.

I have noted that you want me to wait with that article on Russia until you have dealt with the "Soviet Image of the United States" book. I am not going to write it at all unless you are interested.

The article about Pavlov[1] is vividly written but the author does not seem to be aware that Pavlov was after all a crank, that most of the results of his experiments might have been clear a priori, and that the whole matter has been severely and deservedly criticized by leading scientists abroad.

On the other hand, Rebecca West's piece[2] is admirable and I am eagerly waiting for its continuation.

Sincerely yours,

P.S. My New Yorker is arriving later and later (Monday or even Wednesday). This has been happening since September but somehow I kept forgetting to mention it.

1. "Ivan Petrovich Pavlov," *The New Yorker* (2 December 1950).
2. "The Annals of Crime: London Masque," *The New Yorker* (2, 9, 16 December 1950).

TO: **KATHARINE A. WHITE**                                CC, I p.
                                                    Ithaca, N.Y.

December 30, 1950

Dear Katharine,

First of all I want to thank you for the generous cheque,—or have I done so already when I returned the signed double of the agreement?

Barghoorn's book ("The Soviet Image of the United States") does not barge into anything I might say on the subject. His information stops at 1947 while I was thinking in terms of 1949 and 1950. It is a very poor book written by a man who, judging by a terrible mistranslation on p. 46 for instance, hardly knows any Russian. The whole thing sounds as if it had been written by a graduate student with an average of 77 in his undergraduate days. Finally, he is mainly interested (and lugubriously unspecific at that) in political Soviet articles whereas I had in mind a racy and artistic piece on the way America and Americans look in Soviet stories, novels, plays and "literature-culture" articles in Soviet magazines.

A collection of excerpts in the Times Book Review by Schwarz[1] is somewhat nearer in general trend to the color of the water in which I see my subject floating while it still has gills.

If Mr. Ross and Mr. Shawn would like me to tackle the matter, would they be willing to give me some guarantee that my time would not be a complete loss in case some unexpected circumstance were to prevent the publication of the piece?

And what about the length? Say, three instalments?

Wishing you a happy New Year, I remain, dear Katharine,

Yours very cordially,

1. Harry Schwartz was a frequent reviewer of books on Russia.

TO: **HAROLD ROSS**                                                     cc, 1 p.

802 East Seneca Street
Ithaca, New York
December 6, 1950
[for 6 January 1951]

Dear Mr. Ross,

Thanks for your nice letter—it covers all the points. Yes, a single piece of 5000–6000 words would be just the thing. The extraneous circumstance I had in mind was the possible though improbable appearance of an article on the same subject and lines in some other periodical before I had quite finished mine.[1]

I did have the pleasure of meeting you. In fact I came all the way, across some hilly country, to the anniversary reception at the Carlton last March and said to you (in allusion to our indirect meetings through Katharine White in all kinds of verbal jungles): "Dr. Ross, I presume?" You said you were not a doctor.

I hope to have an opportunity to see you again.

Sincerely yours,
Vladimir Nabokov

1. Ross to VN, 3 January 1951: "I can conceive of no circumstance extraneous to the piece itself (or the pieces) precluding their publication, except the dropping of an atom bomb that would put us out of business, and in that event it is possible that the management would recognize pending undertakings." VN informed White on 10 March that he was postponing the article indefinitely.

TO: JOHN SELBY[1]                                        CC, I p.

802 East Seneca Street
Ithaca, N.Y
January 17, 1951

Dear Mr. Selby,

Two years ago you wrote to me about my book but to my regret at that time we did not arrive at an understanding. To-day I am writing you on an entirely different matter which, I hope, will interest you.

I am teaching a course in European Fiction at Cornell University and have selected as a permanent item Flaubert's "Madame Bovary". In September I ordered, for a class of 133 students, copies of your edition of that novel, through the university book shops. I devoted seven class meetings to the discussion of the novel, and at least 10 minutes of every such period had to be spent in correcting the incredible mistranslations (more exactly, only the worst of them). In point of fact every page of the book contains at least three or four blunders—either obvious mistakes, or slovenly translations giving a wrong slant to Flaubert's intention. His lovely descriptions of visual things, clothes, landscapes, Emma's hairdo etc. are completely botched by the translator. I had to revise all this, going through each word of the book with a copy of the French first edition before me and have found, in addition to the various blunders due to the translator's insufficient French, a number of misprints due, in most cases, to faulty proofreading ("beads" for "meads", "came" for "cane"— that sort of thing) and, in other cases, to the translator's faithfully copying the misprints in the French first edition (which were corrected in the later French editions).

My intention was to use the book next year and in later years. As my classroom analysis of Flaubert's style is a close one, and as my students are not expected to have enough French to turn to the French original, the situation is an alarming one. I thought you might be interested to know all this. My suggestion is that before you make a new printing of your edition (the one "based on the Eleanor Marx Aveling translation with corrections and modernization by the editor", 1946), you accept from me a list of more than 1000 corrections. If this suggestion interests you, please let me know what terms you could offer me.[2]

I have also come to the conclusion that a number of notes elucidating local, literary and historical allusions, which are absolutely incomprehensible to the American student, ought to be added to the English translation of the book (provided that all mistranslations are corrected); and this I would also be willing to do.

With one thing and another I have almost completed a small book on the structure of "Madame Bovary" for students. Would you be interested in publishing it?

Sincerely yours,
V. Nabokov

1. Rinehart editor.
2. The project was dropped.

TO: **PATRICIA HUNT**[1]                                            cc, 2 pp.

> 802 East Seneca Street
> Ithaca, New York.
> February 6th, 1951

Dear Miss Hunt,

Your suggestion interests me hugely. All my collecting life (45 years—I started at 6) I had been dreaming of somebody's taking photographs of the marvels I saw, and the skill of a Nature Reporter and a photographer from LIFE combined with my knowledge of butterflies and their ways would make a simply ideal team. It is really a wonderful idea and I am absolutely at your service in this matter, if we agree on terms.

There are the following considerations to be taken into account. The environs of Ithaca are hopeless; and so is New England. Indeed, the whole east (except Florida which, however, represents a totally different, tropical, fauna related to the Antilles) is extremely poor in butterflies. There are a few interesting things far up in the north of Maine but none of them are showy. The few showy ones that occur throughout the eastern states (the Monarch, two or three Swallowtails, Admirals) have been pictured ad nauseam. The few rare species, dingy or dazzling, are extremely local and cannot be counted upon to show up at a fixed time and place. There is one little thing, a perfect jewel (and one of the rarest butterflies in the world) of which only some thirty or forty specimens have been taken since it was turned up by Edwards' Negro gardener almost a hundred years ago; at the present time two or three collectors know of a locality for it in Vermont, in early May—but the exact place is a secret. A very local blue butterfly which I have named myself can be found in a pine barren between Albany and Schenectady but nothing else of popular or scientific interest is to be found in that neighborhood. The only eastern butterfly that combines marvelous beauty with comparative rarity (a good female costs two or three dollars) is a large Fritillary which is found here and there in June in the hills of the south-eastern states. To try and get pictures of these things would mean traveling from one place to another and being subject to the whims of weather and collector's luck.

Not so in the west (where I have extensively collected during several summers). I am thinking especially of S. Colorado and Arizona—but some gorgeous things can be easily found in fair numbers anywhere in the Rockies. I would dearly want to have photographs taken of a charming middle-size butterfly that I discovered and named ten years ago in the Grand Canyon, a few minutes walk down the Bright Angel Trail. The Tetons where I collected for two months in 1949 are also splendid. Then, of course, there is Alaska, where I have not been, but which I know to be full of nice things easy to photograph.

I have had in mind for years a list of positions and perching places in regard to various not too shy and very photogenic butterflies. Flowerheads, leaves, twigs, rocks, treetrunks. In certain spots, a number of interesting and gaudy things have, on hot days, a habit of congregating on damp sand and are not easily disturbed in their tippling. Many other species settle with outspread wings on short alpine flowers or bask in the sun on stones. (I take it for granted that your photographer is prepared to do some crawling and wriggling and to ignore completely the possible presence of snakes). Others with closed wings revealing in profile beautiful undersides can be photographed very nicely since dozens of them can be seen at a time on the blossoms of thistles along quite accessible roads in canyons. All these western butterflies can make wonderful pictures and such pictures have never been taken before.

Some fascinating photos might be also taken of me, a burly but agile man, stalking a rarity or sweeping it into my net from a flowerhead, or capturing it in midair. There is a special professional twist of the wrist immediately after the butterfly has been netted which is quite fetching. Then you could show my finger and thumb delicately pinching the thorax of a netted butterfly through the gauze of the netbag. And of course the successive stages of preparing the insect on a setting board have never yet been shown the way I would like them to be shown. All this might create a sensation in scientific and nature-lover circles besides being pleasing to the eye of a layman. I must stress the fact that the whole project as you see it has never been attempted before.

When collecting, my general system is to go by car to this or that locality which may be a bog or a mountain pass or the shore of a lake or the beginning of a trail leading to alpine meadows. I do not care to camp out but usually stay at one of the good motels which abound in the west. The best time to collect is from the end of June to the beginning of August though of course this varies with altitude, latitude etc. I have not quite made up my mind where I shall collect this summer. It will depend to some extent on the money my book— (CONCLUSIVE EVIDENCE to be brought out by Harper on the 14th of this month—you may have seen parts of it in The New Yorker, Harper's Magazine or the Partisan) will bring me. It may also depend on what LIFE would decide to spend on this project.

> Sincerely yours,
> Vladimir Nabokov

1. Patricia Hunt, a member of *Life's* Nature Department, wrote VN on 31 January asking for his assistance with a projected article about his butterfly collecting. Nothing came of it.

TO: **KATHARINE A. WHITE**                      CC, 4 pp.
                                                Ithaca, N.Y.

March 17, 1951

Dear Katharine,

I am sorry the New Yorker rejected my story.¹ It has already been sent elsewhere, so that I feel free to discuss certain points without being suspected of trying to persuade the New Yorker to reconsider their decision.

First of all, I do not understand what you mean by "overwhelming style", "light story" and "elaboration". All my stories are webs of style and none seems at first blush to contain much kinetic matter.

Several pieces of "Conclusive Evidence", for instance, which you were kind to admire were merely a series of impressions held together by means of "style". For me "style" *is* matter.

I feel that the New Yorker has not understood "The Vane Sisters" at all. Let me explain a few things: the whole point of the story is that my French professor, a somewhat obtuse scholar and a rather callous observer of the superficial planes of life, unwittingly passes (in the first pages) through the enchanting and touching "aura" of dead Cynthia, whom he continues to see (when talking about her) in terms of skin, hair, manners etc. The only nice thing he deigns to see about her is his condescending reference to a favorite picture of his that she painted—frost, sun, glass—and from this stems the icicle-bright aura through which he rather ridiculously passes in the beginning of the story when a sunny ghost leads him, as it were, to the place where he meets D. and learns of Cynthia's death. At the end of the story he seeks her spirit in vulgar table-rapping phenomena, in acrostics and then he sees a vague dream (permeated by the broken sun of their last meeting), and now comes the last paragraph which, if read straight, should convey that vague and sunny rebuke, but which for a more attentive reader contains the additional delight of a solved acrostic; I C-ould I-solate, C-onsciously, L-ittle. E-verything S-eemed B-lurred, Y-ellow-C-louded, Y-ielding N-othing T-angible. H-er I-nept A-crostics, M-audlin E-vasions, T-heopathies—E-very R-ecollection F-ormed R-ipples O-f M-ysterious M-eaning. E-verything S-eemed Y-ellowly B-lurred, I-llusive, L-ost. The "icicles by Cynthia" refers of course to the setting at the beginning of the story and is a message, as it were, from her forgiving, gentle, doe-soul that had made him this gift of an iridescent day (giving him something akin to the picture he had liked, to the only small thing he had liked about her); and to this, in eager, pathetic haste, Sybil—a little ghost close to the larger one—adds "meter from me, Sybil", alluding of course to the red shadow of the parking meter near which the French professor meets D.

You may argue that reading downwards, or upwards, or diagonally is not what an editor can be expected to do; but by means of various allusions to trick-reading I have arranged matters so that the reader almost automatically slips into this discovery, especially because of the abrupt change in *style*.

Most of the stories I am contemplating (and some I have written in the past—you actually published one with such an "inside"—the one about the old Jewish couple and their sick boy)[2] will be composed on these lines, according to this system wherein a second (main) story is woven into, or placed behind, the superficial semitransparent one. I am really very disappointed that you, such a subtle and loving reader, should not have seen the inner scheme of my story. I do not mean the acrostic—but the coincidence of Cynthia's spirit with the atmosphere of the beginning of the story. When some day you re-read it, I want you to notice—I hope with regret—how everything in the tale leads to one recurving end, or rather forms a delicate circle, a system of mute responses, not realized by the Frenchman but directed by some unknown spirit at readers through the prism of his priggish praises.[3]

I have yet something else to say. I do not think that the remarks jotted down in pencil came from you. They are not in your style. On page 15, I start preparing the reader for the last paragraph by describing the kind of thing millions of cranks have done with Shakespeare's sonnets—reading the initial letters of the lines to see if they made some esoteric sense. What on earth has this to do with the remark in the margin that Shakespeare's sonnets have the rhyme scheme ABBA or ABAB?

On page 4 the annotater finds it unusual that a college girl wears a hat at an exam. They all do it when they want to catch a bus or a train immediately afterwards. I skip some other queries, such as the one on page 6 "how he knows"—anent the lovers of the lady. But I cannot understand how any reader can be stumped by "ultimate island" on page 7, clearly a reference to Ultima Thule. There are other things, but let them ride.

I am really quite depressed by the whole business. The financial side is an entirely separate trouble. But what matters most is the fact that people whom I so much like and admire have completely failed me as *readers* in the present case.

I expect to be in New York end of May, and I hope that Véra and

I will have an opportunity to see both of you then. Before then I hope to send you another story which will come back to me in a "Rush" envelope, on yellow paper.

Sincerely yours,

1. "The Vane Sisters," *Hudson Review* (Winter 1959). Collected in *Nabokov's Quartet* (New York: Phaedra, 1966).
2. "Signs and Symbols" (15 May 1948).
3. White to VN, 21 March: "We did not work out your acrostic, to be sure, that being rather out of the New Yorker's line, but otherwise, even after reading your letter, we believe that we did understand at least the general purpose of your story. The big difference to us between this one and the story of the old Jewish couple is that the latter aroused our emotions about your characters whereas the story about the Vane sisters did not. I think it's fine to have your style a web, when your web is an ornament, or a beautiful housing, for the content of your text, as it was in 'Conclusive Evidence,' but a web can also be a trap when it gets snarled or becomes too involved, and readers can die like flies in a writer's style if it is unsuitable for its matter. I shall have to stick to my guns on that and on the fact that we did not think these Vane girls worthy of their web."

TO: **SHEILA HODGES**[1]                                                CC, I p.

802 East Seneca Street
Ithaca, New York
March 22, 1951

Dear Miss Hodges,

I am delighted to learn that your firm wants my book. I shall hear of it, no doubt, from Harpers within a day or two.

I had several titles in mind for the book and selected the most abstract one as I hate to have a drop of a book's life blood exuded upon its cover. But of course I understand your point of view, especially as none of my friends liked "Conclusive Evidence". So here are a few other titles from which you can choose: "Clues", "The Rainbow Edge", "Speak, Mnemosyne!" (this one is my favorite), "The Prismatic Edge", "The Moulted Feather" (from Browning's poem), "Nabokov's Opening" (a chess term), "Emblemata".[2]

Very truly yours,
Vladimir Nabokov

1. Representative of English publisher Victor Gollancz.
2. The title of the Gollancz edition was *Speak, Memory* (1951).

TO: **FRANCIS BROWN**[1]                                              CC, 1 p.

Res.: 802 East Seneca Street
Ithaca, N.Y.
April 19, 1951

Dear Mr. Brown,

I remembered the Chehov and Tolstoy portraits included in the Bunin memoir[2] you kindly sent me and hoped that the other portraits would be on the same high level. Unfortunately they are not.

If I undertook to write an article on this book, I would certainly do so in a destructive vein. However, the author, whom I used to know well, is now a very old man, and I do not feel that I should demolish his book. As I cannot praise it, I would rather not review it at all.

I am sorry to have caused you this slight delay and am returning the book to-day, under separate cover.

Yesterday I wrote you asking you to let me review Klots' book on butterflies, which I know is an important and interesting work. I hope that this idea will appeal to you.[3]

Sincerely yours,
Vladimir Nabokov

1. Editor of the *New York Times Book Review*.

2. Ivan Bunin, *Memories and Portraits* (Garden City, N.Y.: Doubleday, 1951).

3. Alexander Barrett Klots, *A Field Guide to the Butterflies of North America, East of the Great Plains* (Boston: Houghton Mifflin, 1951). VN did not receive the assignment.

TO: **PROF. JOHN H. FINLEY, JR.**[1]                                    CC, 1 p.

Ilease reoly 802-East Seneca Street
It aca, N.Y.
June 12, 1951

Dear Irofessor Finley,

Many t anks for your delig tful letter. Yes, I think I would be able to arrange a course of t e general tyoe you suggest, orovided you allow me some individual latitude. In my lectures I emo asize t e artistic side of literature. I visualize a course t at would not clas wit your conceot of t e connections between narrative genres. It would deal wit questions of structure, develooment of tec nique, t emes (in t e sense of "t ematic lines"), and imagery and magic and style. I certainly could link uo my study of nineteent century fiction wit t ematic lines running t rough such initial masteroieces as t e Iliad— or t e Slovo; but my main ouroose would be to analyze suc artistic structures as Mansfield Iark (and its fairy-tale oattern), Bleak ouse (and its c ild-and-bird t eme), Anna Karenin (and its dream-and-deat symbols), t en t e "transformation" t eme, as old as t e oldest myt s, in one lumo consisting of t ree stories (Gogol's Overcoat, Stevenson's Jekyll and yde and Kafka's Metamoro osis), and finally the jardins suoerooses of Iroust's style in is first volume Swann's Way. If t is is too muc , eit er Bleak or Mansfield may be sacrificed. It seems to me t at t is orogram does not really deviate from yours since in t e long run it deals with t e istorical evolution of symbols, of images, of ways of seeing t ings and conveying one's vision. After all, Homer, and Flaubert, and Gogol, and Dickens, and Iroust are all members of my family. I only hooe t at t e "added stiooend" will be adequate—if, of course, my course outline meets with your aooroval.

In any case I am looking forward to seeing a lot of you and Harry Levin next soring.

Sincerely yours,

I.S. T is tyoewriter is falling aoart but a new one is on its way.

1. Finley, of Harvard, had invited VN to teach Humanities 2 as a visiting professor in 1952.

TO: **ELENA SIKORSKI**        ALS, 2 pp. Elena Sikorski.

623 Highland Rd.
Ithaca, N.Y.
6.IX.1951

My dear Elenochka,

There has been a slight lightening of my "workload," and I hasten to put this respite to good use. Your description of your co-workers was highly entertaining. I enclose a money order for 30 d. (20 for IX and 10 on account for X). I'll try to do likewise in XI. Véra wrote you at my behest, but your letters must have crossed. It was a bit awkward that you asked P. for help before I sent you the money, but probably my inefficiency is mainly to blame. Please confirm whether you have received everything, including this little check of mine.

Last spring we got rid of the house on Seneca St., which was ruining us, sold the furniture that was ours including the upright piano, and, lightly laden, set out for the whole summer in our aging car, across swollen rivers and through unbelievable thunderstorms, for the West. Now, having returned, we occupy a far more agreeable house, and, come next semester (February—June), shall have to go temporarily to Harvard University, in Cambridge, where I am going to give two courses in Russian literature and one in general literature.

Mityusha is already attending Harvard; he is seventeen and enormous, he sings bass in an Episcopalian church choir, and he is interested, in the following order, in: mountain climbing, girls, music, track, tennis, and his studies. At the same time he is gifted, intelligent, knows his way around every intellectual area, and has written his first poem and his first short story. Yet in many ways he is still the little boy he was when, all golden, he played on the beach in Menton or Santa Monica. See—you must grab and hold in the fist of your soul everything about Zhikochka[1] today: that way it will all shine through him, too, for a long time.

We traveled to Colorado, then to Montana. Mityusha would take the numerous terrifying curves, overlooking precipices, with a graceful but somewhat exhausting flourish, after which it was bliss to return to Véra's wonderful, steady tempo.

He left us to take part in the national forensic championship in Los Angeles, then joined us in Telluride, a little old mining town in the San Juan Mountains of Southwestern Colorado. I went all that way over unpaved, broken-up mountain roads in specific search of a butterfly that I myself had described in 1948 on the basis of nine museum specimens; I had an overwhelming desire to see it live and discover its unknown female. The altitude of Telluride is 9000 feet (3000 meters), and from there I had to climb on foot every morning to 12,000 feet (4000 meters), and I am fat and heavy, although I still have my soccer calves. It will not be hard for you to understand what a joy it was for me to find at last my exceedingly rare goddaughter, on a sheer mountainside covered with violet lupine, in the sky-high, snow-scented silence. *Je fais mon petit Sirine*[2], as you can see.

Incidentally, *Sebastian Knight* is being published in French by Albin Michel and *Conclusive Evidence* (*Speak, Memory*), which has brought me a lot of fame but little money, is coming out in England, and there will also be a slim volume of verse in Paris.[3]

Thereupon Mityusha was driven to Grand Teton Park, in western Wyoming, where he lived in a portable tent and performed fearsome ascents with famous climbers on mountains that correspond to the most difficult ones in Europe and Asia—with ropes, pitons, rappels, etc.—while Véra and I lived alone on an isolated ranch in the Yellowstone Park area. Now, too, we are living in a very silent place among sumptuous, half-orange foliage, and not a sound except for the crickets. It is with unbearable sadness that I think of E.K.[4] and R.[5], to whom I dare not write.[6]

I embrace you.

V.[7]

1. Elena Sikorski's son, Vladimir. Elena Sikorski was now in Geneva, while Evgeniya Konstantinovna Hofeld and Rostislav had remained in Stalinized Prague. DN.
2. "I'm doing my little Sirin number": a reference to the care VN had dedicated to the style and rhythm of the preceding passage, as he had always done with his Russian poetry and prose, generally signed "Vladimir Sirin," or, in the French spelling, "Sirine." DN.
3. *Stikhotvoreniya 929-95* (Paris: Rifma, 1952).
4. Evgeniya Konstantinovna Hofeld.
5. Rostislav.
6. Because of the potentially dangerous consequences of such correspondence in the police-state atmosphere in which they lived. DN
7. Translated from Russian by DN.

TO: **PROF. M. M. KARPOVICH**[1]

cc, 6 pp.
Ithaca, N.Y.

October 12, 1951

Dorogoi Mikhail Mikhailovich,

Many thanks for your charming and comprehensive letter. I shall take up your points in the same order as you have listed them.

I think you are quite right in dealing with Turgenev in the first part of the course.[2]

I intend to refer to Ostrovski, Saltykov and Leskov *in passing*; but am not planning to make the reading of their works obligatory.

I shall use my own prose translations in the case of Nekrasov. I am grateful to you for letting me have Tyutchev whom I like to tie up with Fet and Blok, all in my own translations.

Dostoevski: "The Double", "Zapiski iz Podpol'ya" [*Notes from the Underground*], "Crime and Punishment".

Tolstoi: "Death of Ivan Il'ich" and "Anna Karenin".

Chehov: "Lady with the Dog", "The Ravine", "Dom s Mezaninom" ["House with Mezzanine"] and one other story; "Chaika" [*The Seagull*].

A detailed analysis of all these works will be interlarded with background lectures and general discussions. Of Gorki I shall only mention the Volga-ferry story when comparing his clumsy technique to that of Chehov.

I do not plan to devote special lectures to Bunin, etc., but shall take care of them in a general lecture. Of recent authors, I shall deal with Blok, Hodasevich, Belyi. I will omit Sologub, Remizov, Balmont, Bryusov although I may refer to them in a general way with grains of salt from my own salt lick. I also plan a couple of lectures on Soviet literature as a whole.

In many cases I shall use my own mimeographed translations. Obligatory textbook: Guerney's Treasury.[3] And as a general reference book: Mirsky.

This is how I visualize the main matter of the course, with connecting lectures of the kind you suggest. If you find any serious flaws in my plan, please let me know, and with a grunt of reluctance I shall add some of the dreadful translations of Ostrovsky and Leskov. I have corrected most of Anna Karenin's important chapters and the Dostoevski material.

I seem to have come to terms with Finley. Proust has been dropped, and I start with Don Quixote.

Thanks for the schedule. Yes, I should like a midterm exam in addition to the final one. I have nothing against the early hours. Tatiana Nikolaevna, to whom we both send our most cordial greetings, is wrong here. I am getting old and go to bed around 10 o'clock. I either do not sleep until the following night or get up (after taking a pill on the eve) around 8 a.m. as fresh as an English daisy or a Russian rose. I find it very convenient to have the Humanities 2 lecture immediately after the Slavic 150 b. I have the same arrangement here.

As to the Pushkin course I do not mind having one hour on Monday or Wednesday in the early afternoon and the other hour (two hours per week in all) at 10 on Saturday, since assistants take over in my Humanities course on the third day. However, I have another suggestion. Would it not be possible to have a two-hour session any time on Monday or Wednesday? This is the method I follow here, but of course I have but a small bunch of students. I presume that the Pushkin students can all read Russian, although I also have all my material in translation.

I seem to have covered the course reading assignment that you list on the yellow sheets. If you do want me to take Ostrovsky and Leskov, I would choose The Storm and perhaps The Enchanted Wanderer. Blok's The Twelve I shall translate in class. Chehov's stories would come in Yarmolinsky's translation, with my corrections.

In speaking of a complete edition of Pushkin's works (the pièce de résistance will be "Evgenyi Onegin", then the Diminutive Dramas, "The Queen of Spades", some fifty lyrics). I was thinking of a six-volume set in buff bindings, more or less recently brought out by the Soviets ("Academia", 1936). I have also heard of a new edition of "Evgenyi Onegin" with more notes than the usual ones have.

I think this is all anent academic matters. I read with interest your remarks concerning the Ford Foundation. I do hope they take "Dar."[4]

Your plans for the summer are splendid; and we certainly hope to visit you at Cambridge before you leave. Now about the house. Your offer is very tempting and I wonder when is the deadline for giving you our decision? The only possible drawback would be the question of temperature. Would the expense of 25–30 keep the house comfortably warm? Since there is only two of us, we could do well with a smaller—and less expensive—place. On the other hand I find that I can work only when surrounded with an almost Proustian silence. What chance in your opinion do we have of finding a smaller, and preferably cheaper, place that would also be very, very quiet? However, I repeat, your proposal is most attractive and I would like a little time to decide.

This year Mitusha is taking Biology, Latin Lit., Music and History of Civilization, besides English A. He is not taking any Russian Lit.—my friends thought he had enough Nabokov at home. I hope that next year he will be able to take the Russian Survey course with you. I am writing him to drop in at your office, you will be amazed at his altitude.

Véra and I send our best love to both of you.

P.S. I am applying to the Guggenheim Foundation for a grant which would allow me to prepare a scholarly prose translation of Evgeni Onegin for publication. I have been bold enough to mention you as one of my references.

One more consideration regarding the house. Would you want to rent it for the period February to June? We would probably want to leave on June 15 or 30th, at the latest.

I do not quite understand the "reading period" business, for which I have suggested a few titles on a separate sheet. How are the students tested on this reading? Do I understand rightly that the final exam should cover the whole term course including the reading period material?

COURSE READING ASSIGNMENT

Tyutchev, poems

Nekrasov, poems

Fet, poems

Dostoevski, The Double, or Zapiski iz Podpol'ya; Crime and Punishment.

Tolstoi, Death of Ivan Il'ich, Anna Karenin

Chehov, Lady with the Dog, The Ravine, Dom s Mezaninom, One other story; Chaika.

Blok, Hodasevich, Mayakovski, poems.

**READING PERIOD ASSIGNMENT.**

One of the following:

Chehov, The Duel

    "   The Three Sisters

Tolstoi, Haji Murad

Olesha, Zavist'

Andreev, (perhaps) The Seven Who Were Hanged

Bunin, The Gentleman from San Francisco

Zoshchenko, ?

Blok, Balaganchik

Belyi, Fragments.

1. Department of Slavic Languages and Literatures, Harvard.
2. Slavic 150b: Modern Russian Literature to 1917, which VN taught at Harvard in Spring 1952.
3. Bernard G. Guerney, *A Treasury of Russian Literature* (New York: Vanguard, 1943).
4. First published as a book in Russian (New York: Chekhov Publishing House, 1952) and translated into English in 1963.

TO: **PASCAL COVICI**                       cc, 2 pp.

623 Highland Road
Ithaca, N.Y.
November 12, 1951

Dear Mr. Covici,

Many thanks for your charming letter. I shall be in New York on December 8, arriving late on Friday, the 7th, and leaving Sunday afternoon. I am delivering a lecture Saturday evening, but otherwise will be free and delighted to meet you.

I shall teach in the spring term at Harvard. One of my courses

(Humanities II which is attended by more than 500 students) will include Don Quixote, and I shall certainly recommend your magnificent Putnam[1] to those who can afford it.

I hope to discuss with you in New York my literary plans, but here is a little preview: I have two books for publication, one that could be brought out rightaway (a collection of short stories) and the other (a book of criticism entitled The Poetry of Prose) which could be ready for print within a few weeks.

The collection would comprise the following eleven stories: The Assistant Producer; The Aurelian; Double Talk; Cloud, Castle, Lake; Spring in Fialta; In Aleppo Once; A Forgotten Poet; Time and Ebb; Signs and Symbols; The Vane Sisters; Lance. Eight of these were included in the Nine Stories booklet published by New Directions in a small edition long since out of print.

The book of criticism, The Poetry of Prose, will consist of 10 chapters: I. Cervantes: Don Quixote; II. Jane Austen: Mansfield Park; III. Pushkin: The Queen of Spades; IV. Dickens: Bleak House; V. Gogol and Proust; VI. Flaubert: Madame Bovary; VII. Tolstoi: Anna Karenin, The Death of Ivan Il'ich, Haji Murad; VIII. Chehov: The Ravine, The Lady with the Spitz and other stories; IX. Kafka: Metamorphosis; X. The Art of Translation.[2]

Moreover, I am engaged in the composition of a novel, which deals with the problems of a very moral middle-aged gentleman who falls very immorally in love with his stepdaughter, a girl of thirteen.[3] However, I cannot predict its date of completion since I have to combine this work with short-term productions in order to vegetate.

Very sincerely yours,
Vladimir Nabokov

---

1. Samuel Putnam's translation of Don Quixote (New York: Viking, 1949).
2. See Lectures on Literature (1980), Lectures on Russian Literature (1981), Lectures on Don Quixote (1983)—all published by Harcourt Brace Jovanovich/Bruccoli Clark.
3. The first explicit mention of Lolita in this correspondence.

TO: **ARCHIBALD MACLEISH**[1]                              CC, 1 pp.

> 623 Highland Road
> Ithaca, New York
> December 2, 1951

Dear Mr. MacLeish,

Thanks for your charming letter. I shall be delighted to take part in your readings program.

I knew from Harry Levin that you would be away during the spring term and this is a very keen disappointment. I take this opportunity to tell you what you surely must know (for we all know mutually who likes our stuff and who does not) that I am a great admirer of your poetry. There is that movement of light in one of your most famous poems that invariably sends a shiver of delight up and down my spine whenever I think of it.

> Sincerely yours,
> Vladimir Nabokov

1. Boylston Professor of Rhetoric and Oratory at Harvard.

TO: **HENRY ALLEN MOE**[1]                              CC, 4 pp.

> temporary address: 9 Maynard Place
> Cambridge 38, Mass.
> permanent address: Cornell University
> Dept. of Russian Lit.
> Ithaca, New York
> April 5, 1952

Dear Mr. Moe,

I thank you for your letter of April 1st which has just been forwarded here from Ithaca. I find it a little easier to explain to you my financial situation in a letter rather than by filling the form enclosed with your letter.

My salary at Cornell, after taxes and withholdings, amounts to $4.450.00 (before taxes etc. it is $5.500.00). If I were granted a fellowship, I would ask the College for a leave of absence (without pay) for one half of the academic year, and my salary would be reduced accordingly by about a half, $2.250

| | |
|---|---:|
| I have a son in college (Harvard) who costs me about (in a year) | $2.000 |
| The cost of living for me and my wife for last year was about | 3.600 |
| I help support a nephew in Europe at a cost of $20 a month | 240 |
| This puts my basic expenses at about | 5.840 |

Then there are also such incidental expenses as doctors' bills, state income tax, payments on the car etc.

Ordinarily I just manage to balance my budget by literary earnings.

The whole point of my application for a fellowship is that, in order to complete the English "Evgenii Onegin" as I have it in mind, with exhaustive commentaries etc., within a year, I should have to set aside all other literary work.

By dint of stringent economy, I hope to keep down my expenses for the year to around 5.500–6.000.

I wonder if a grant of $3.500 would be too much to apply for under the circumstances described above? If granted, I would like to receive it in twelve monthly payments, from August 1952 to August 1953.

I would like to plan the order of my work in the following way: part of the time to research at Cornell University Library, the Harvard Libraries, the Library of Congress and possibly other libraries and at least half-a-dozen months in actual composition, settling down for this purpose at some quiet, secluded, hay-fever-less spot.

Sincerely yours,
Vladimir Nabokov

P.S. I have not applied for a Fulbright or any other award.


PLAN FOR STUDY.

I am contemplating a complete, richly annotated prose translation of Pushkin's novel in verse "Eugene Onegin" (1823–1831). It is the first and fundamental Russian novel: Its general atmosphere, the logical and harmonious development of its plot from the esssential features of the characters, the retrospective and introspective rambles of the writer's thought, are rightly considered by critics to have "given the cue and pattern to the great Russian novelists of the XIX century" (Mirsky, History of Russian Literature).

The following points require elucidation:

1. There does not exist any edition in any language (not excepting the original one) with the exhaustive commentaries that the text should have for adequate understanding and enjoyment.

2. The several translations into English that have appeared since the latter half of the last century have been attempts to render "Eugene Onegin" in verse, with the result that the elaborate rhyme scheme of the original, the fluency of the Russian iambic tetrameter and the conciseness of the sonnet-like stanzas of which the cantos consist, forced the translators to plunge into a jungle of jingles (I have been there too in my time) that transformed one of the most brilliant works ever composed into a vague, lame, third-rate concoction with rhymes of the "pleasure-leisure", "heart-part" sort. Since there is no way of transforming the complex Russian structure of the piece into adequate English verse, I propose to offer not only a literal prose translation but to accompany it by profuse notes explaining as thoroughly as possible the musical impact of the Russian line and various points of Pushkin's technique.

3. There will also be notes on Russian customs, literary events, and other matters referring to Pushkin's time.

4. The introduction will contain a brief Life of Pushkin and an evaluation of the novel's place in West European literature.

5. In recent years a great number of fragments and new readings

of various passages have been discovered, and all this will be incorporated in my translation.

6. "Eugene Onegin" is as great a world classic as "Hamlet" or "Moby Dick", and the presentation of it will be as true to the original as scholarship and art can make it.

I have had the project in mind for a considerable time. Every year, in class, I am reminded of the sore need that exists for it, since this novel, the backbone of any study of Russian literature, cannot be adequately taught, or appreciated by the students, in the absence of an acceptable translation. However the pressure of current work has prevented me from doing much more than jotting down rough drafts of a few passages. Although I have no publisher in view, I have no doubt that, once completed, such a work would win the indorsement of some University Press. I would work on my project in the United States and, if given the means to concentrate on it, could probably complete it within a year or so.[2]

1. Secretary, John Simon Guggenheim Memorial Foundation.
2. VN received the grant for 1952–1953. The translation of *Eugene Onegin* was published by the Bollingen Foundation in 1964.

TO: **PASCAL COVICI**                                        CC, 2 pp.
                                                    Cambridge, Mass.

                                                    May 16, 1952
Dear Covici,

I am sorry to be so late with my answer to your kind letter of April 16 * * blame for it the stress of that end-of-term business which, for me, is always like something of a sprint at the end of a long run.

I have been working, however, at some of my projects, and here is a general "*aperçu*" of what I hope to accomplish in the near future:

1). The "Slovo" (Russian epic of the late 12th century, of which I spoke to you) should be ready by fall. The book I would offer you then would contain 1. The basic Slavic text (about 25–30 pages), 2. My translation (about 40–50 p.), 3. My notes (about 40 p.), 4. Historic and linguistic commentaries by Prof. Jakobson of Harvard Univ. and Prof. Szeftel of Cornell Univ. (about 100 pages).

The whole book will be under 200 pages.

2). "Eugene Onegin", the Russian novel, early 19th century. This is, as I think I have been telling you during our most pleasant interview in Cambridge, the greatest work of fiction in Russian literature, and it has never been properly translated into any language, while even in Russian no edition exists as yet with complete notes and commentaries. This is exactly the kind of edition I have in mind. I could never hope to complete it if I had not been granted a Guggenheim fellowship for the coming year. The work itself will take about 100 pages (it will be in prose with the possible exception of a few samples rendered in verse). I expect that the commentaries and notes will take about three times as much space. And, of course, there would have to be a complete Russian text (this too has never been properly assembled and published in toto in Russian) *au verso* or in the end. The translation, I think, will be ready in about a year. The comments will take a few months more than that.

3). My book of literary criticism I hope to polish off for print within the same time. You have its plan.[1]

4). The reminiscences shall take a couple of years to write.

5). And I am also working on my new novel, on and off, but I would rather not discuss any definite time limits (or even indefinite ones) for the present. I shall keep you informed as I progress along.

In about a month we shall leave Cambridge for the summer, though I do not know yet our exact itinerary. My permanent address will remain "Prof. V. Nabokov, Goldwin Smith Hall, Cornell University, Ithaca, N.Y.".

One more thing I would like to mention. The Chekhov Publishing House of the Ford Foundation has just published my novel "*DAR*" ("The Gift"). This book deals with the development of a writer of genius. It contains his early poetry, the material he assembles for his second book (which he does not write), his first great book which is the biography of a famous Russian critic of the sixties (this biography, for some reason, created something of a furore in the Russian émigré circles, though it was never published until the recent edition by the Ford Foundation), and a happy love story involving my young man and his half-Jewish fiancée. Would you be interested in publishing a translation?

Sincerely yours,
Vladimir Nabokov

1. This sentence is in holograph.

TO: **ROSALIND WILSON**[1]                                                     CC, 1 p.

Dubois, Wyo.
July 24, 1952

Dear Rosalind,

Vladimir has asked me to answer your letter of July 1st for him, and, even before I do so, to apologize for the lateness of his reply.

The question of mimicry is one that has passionately interested him all his life and one of his pet projects has always been the compilation of a work that would comprise all known examples of mimicry in the animal kingdom. This would make a voluminous work and the research alone would take two or three years. If this sort of thing corresponds to what Houghton Mifflin have in mind, Vladimir is your man. Should they, however, think of a much slighter work meant for the amusement of the lay reader in his more ambitious "scientific" moments, this, Vladimir says, would not be in his line.

We shall be on the move before the end of this week, destination yet undecided. The best address to use would be Goldwin Smith Hall, Cornell University, Ithaca, N.Y., but a letter to General Delivery, Dubois, Wyo., will also follow.

It was a great disappointment to us that we could not fit a visit to Wellfleet into our schedule this spring. We hope to catch up on this in the fall. If you go there in the course of the summer, please give our love to the whole family.

Best regards from both of us.

Sincerely,

P.S. I don't think I made it sufficiently clear that the book on mimicry Vladimir would like to write would present, in the first place, his own views in this very complicated matter, based on the classified presentation of all the known examples.

1. Daughter of Edmund Wilson; she was with Houghton Mifflin.

TO: **HENRY ALLEN MOE**                                                   cc, 1 p.
March 1953                                                              Ithaca, N.Y.

Dear Mr. Moe,

I have devoted two months to research at the Widener Library for my "Eugene Onegin", and have found more fascinating material than I expected or hoped. As I see it now, the work will consist of an introduction of about sixty pages, the translation proper (some two hundred printed pages) and over three hundred pages of various notes and commentaries. It will be the most comprehensive work on "Eugene Onegin" in any language.

I have completed so far about two thirds of my library research, a preliminary draft of some seventy per cent of the stanzas, and have organized my notes relating to the first two chapters. There are in all eight basic chapters and fragments of two more.

Now I am going to the South-West and shall stay there till September working on the translation proper, which calls for intense concentration. I hope to have finished the translation by the beginning of the fall semester at Cornell, after which I shall still have a considerable amount of work to do, organizing and shaping commentaries for Chapters III–VIII and the fragmentary IX and X. Normally

I manage to combine some creative work (fiction or poetry) with my academic duties, but this Pushkin thing has become an obsession with me, and I feel I must get it out of my system before starting anything else. I feel sure I could bring my project to an end sometime early in 1954, if I could devote to it all my time which is not occupied by academic duties. I would therefore like to apply for a prolongation of my Fellowship for six months.[1] I would be very glad to show you a portion of my work in its more or less final form, such as the sets of commentaries belonging to the first two chapters.

Sincerely yours,
Vladimir Nabokov

1. VN's request was too late for that year's competition.

TO: **PROF. HARRY LEVIN**[1]                              CC, 2 pp.

Portal, Arizona
May 2, 1953

Dear Harry,

We are in the south-east corner of Arizona, on the border of New and Old Mexico. The nearer mountains are maroon, spotted with the dark green of junipers and the lighter green of mesquites, and the far mountains are purple as in the Wellesley song. From eight a.m. to noon, or later, I collect butterflies (only Wells, Conan Doyle and Conrad have portrayed lepidopterists—all of them spics, or murderers, or neurotics) and from two p.m. to dinner time I write (a novel). We spent two months in Cambridge—or rather Widener. I found even the book of dreams Tatiana used in "E.O.". My commentaries to the novel have grown to some 300 pages. I have read all the books Pushkin refers to in "E.O.". Even Burke. Even Gibbon. Of course, Richardson and Mme Cottin. And moreover, I have read all the stuff

(Richardson, Shakespeare, Byron) in French, since this is what Push-kin had done.

Did I thank you for your book? We shall talk of it at length when we meet again. It is brilliant and erudite.[2]

I am re-reading "Tom Jones" and finding him horribly dull.

We saw a good deal of the lovable James'es and Sweeneys in Cam-bridge. Bollingen has bought for a handsome sum my "Igor" and Ro-man's comments. Roman arranged the whole matter with wonderful charm. We also saw, of course, a lot of the Karpovichs. And the Kerby-Millers, and many other friends. We missed the Levins.

I wonder if your account of your trip will make me Europe-sick, or at least France-sick. I know that every time I come to this dear West, I feel a pang of recognition, and no Switzerlands could lure me away from Painted Canyon or Silver Creek.

Véra joins me in sending you both our warmest greetings and says she is about to write Lena.

Yours,

1. Department of Comparative Literature, Harvard University.
2. Probably *The Overreacher* (Cambridge: Harvard University Press, 1952).

TO: **BURMA-VITA CO.**[1]                                                      TLS, 1 p.

Goldwin Smith Hall
Cornell University
Ithaca, New York
August 22, 1953

Gentlemen:

I am writing to offer you the following jingle for your entertaining collection:

He passed two cars; then five; then seven;
and then he beat them all to Heaven.

If you think you can use it, please send cheque to address given above.[2]

Yours truly,
Verá Nabokov
(Mrs. Vladimir Nabokov)

1. Burma-Shave advertised with jingles on roadside signs.
2. The company replied that it had more jingles than it could use.

TO: **ELENA SIKORSKI**                                        ALS, 2 pp.

29 September 1953
957 East State St.
Ithaca, N.Y.

My dear Elenochka,

yes, I repent, I ought to have written you a long time ago. I have been working for about a year now on four books simultaneously, and in the intervals try to forget that there exists such a thing as a pen.

Poor Rostik. It is touching, but also very silly.[1] I'm afraid that E.K.[2] will end up being nanny to a third generation. . . .

You always write so vividly and so well about Zhikochka. Ours has run his third car into the ground and is getting ready to buy a used plane. During the summer he took part in a Harvard expedition to almost totally unexplored mountains in British Columbia, before which he worked building highways in Oregon and handling a gigantic truck. He is absolutely and somehow brilliantly fearless, popular with his comrades, endowed with a magnificent brain, but disinclined to study. We found him in his bivouac tent on the shore of a lake in the Tetons (western Wyoming), and from there he drove off to Colorado. He does up to 1000 miles (1600 km.) a day in his car—it's unbelievable!—sometimes driving twenty or thirty hours at a stretch. Véra and I spent the spring in Arizona, and the summer in Oregon, worrying constantly about him—I doubt if we'll ever get used to it. We saw him the other day at Harvard; he has grown a splendid blondish, shovel-shaped beard and looks like Alexander III.

Véra and I have settled in Ithaca in the same house we had in 1948, and it's all very comfortable. I have about 300 students in all, and teach about eight hours a week—three lectures on European literature, three on Russian liter., and an hour and half devoted to Pushkin, for special students. I think I shall finish my enormous Eug. Oneg. sometime this winter. Now my novel is being typed. I am working on a series of stories for the *New Yorker*. I have more or less completed and sold an Engl. translation of *Slovo o polku igor*.[3] Soon I must deliver to the Chekhov Publishing House in New York the Russian translation I did with Véra of my *Conclusive Evidence*.[4] I have stopped reading newspapers and magazines—there is simply no time for everything.

I think, if everything goes well, we'll fly over to Europe some time—but first I must finish my *travaux*. I am fairly fat, just as before (190 pounds), I have false teeth and a bald pate, but I am capable of walking up to 18 miles a day in mountainous terrain and usually do ten, and I play tennis better than I did in my youth. The passion for butterflies has turned into a real mania this year, and there have been many interesting discoveries. In general everything is going wonderfully well, and I would so much like everything to be fine with you. Keep well. Véra is enclosing a poem.

I embrace you, my dearest.

Your V.[5]

---

1. Rostislav, who had no steady job and very little money, was about to become a father.
2. Evgeniya Konstantinovna Hofeld.
3. *The Song of Igor's Campaign.*
4. *Drugie Berega* [*Other Shores*].
5. Translated from Russian by DN.

TO: **KATHARINE A. WHITE** CC, I p.

Ithaca, September 29, 1953

Dear Katharine,

I would have returned the proofs sooner if—because of my long absence—I had not been more than ordinarily occupied with college work.

Many thanks for your charming letter, the cheque, and the Pnin proofs. Apparently I did not make the conductor's gesture (note 7) clear enough, and obviously your suggestion about the forest ride (note 9) is a misprint. Otherwise, everything is O.K.

The Pnin story is the first chapter of a little book (ten such chapters in all) that I hope to complete within a year or so. It is not the enormous, mysterious, heartbreaking novel that, after five years of monstrous misgivings and diabolical labors, I have more or less completed.[1] CONCLUSIVE EVIDENCE and PNIN have been brief sunny escapes from its intolerable spell. This great and coily thing has had no precedent in literature. In none of its parts will it be suitable for the New Yorker. According to our agreement, however, I shall show it to you (sometime in New York) under the rose of silence and the myrtle of secrecy.

The rest of this winter will be devoted to bringing into shape my Guggenheim book on Pushkin and to translating into Russian (!) my CONCLUSIVE EVIDENCE for the Ford Foundation.[2] I am looking for a patron who would arrange things so that I could give up teaching—or for a university that would pay me, say, 12 thousand dollars for a few annual lectures based on my books.

As you see, I do not quite know when you will get the next Pnin story, but you will. If by any chance you decided to publish the first instalment without waiting for the rest, I would welcome it.

Véra and I would like to see you both very much.

Best love.

1. *Lolita*.
2. *Drugie Berega* (New York: Chekhov Publishing House, 1954).

TO: **MORRIS BISHOP**                    MS, 1 p. Mrs. Morris Bishop.

> *To Morris Bishop*
> *The old man who devised the Roomette*
> *Now in Hades is bedded, I'll bet:*
> *To make water, his bed*
> *He must prop on his head—*
> *—A ridiculous doom, or doomette.*
> *Vladimir Nabokov*
> *Night train NYC—Ithaca*
> *2.XI.53*

> *There was a young lady who met*
> *A gentleman in a roomette.*
> *She said of the case:*
> *"We had both the same space,*
> *Et il fallait que je me soumette!"*
> *M. G. B.*[1]

1. Morris Bishop's reply. Both limericks are in holograph.

TO: **MORRIS BISHOP**                    TS, 1 p. Cornell University.
1953

For Morris Bishop

> *There wás a housebúilder named Jímmy Ricks,*
> *Who built hóuses for mákers of límericks,*
> *But becaúse of a stútter*

*B's he tried not to útter,*
*And when aśking for bricks would say "Gímme 'ricks."*

—Vladimir Nabokov

TO: **KATHARINE A. WHITE**                    CC, 1 p.
Ithaca, N.Y.

December 23, 1953

Dear Katharine,

It was nice to hear about your grandbaby. I hope everything continues to go well with mother and child.

I shall try to explain about the book. Its subject is such that V., as a college teacher, cannot very well publish it under his real name. Especially, since the book is written in the first person, and the "general" reader has the unfortunate inclination to identify the invented "I" of the story with its author. (This is, perhaps, particularly true of the American "general" reader).

Accordingly, V. has decided to publish the book under an assumed name (provided he can find a publisher) and wait for the reviews before divulging his identity. It is of the utmost importance to him that his incognito be respected. He would trust you, of course, and Andy, if you promise to keep the secret. Now, suppose you decide that there is nothing in LOLITA to interest the New Yorker, would the MS still have to be read by the other members of the editorial staff, or would it be possible for you to make a final decision without it? If the MS has to be read by anyone besides you, would it be possible for you to keep V.'s name secret? Could you be quite sure that there would be no leaks?

V. is very anxious to hear from you about it and have your assurance of complete secrecy before he sends you the MS. Moreover, the nature of the plot being what it is, he hesitates about mailing it. Should he make up his mind to visit New York in January, he would prefer to bring the MS personally to your house. Would it be possible to keep it away from the office? V. has been asked by a Russian club to give a reading in January. If he accepts, it will pay for his trip, and then he will bring the MS to New York. If not, we shall find some other way to get it to you within a few weeks. He doubts, however, that any part of the book can be suitable for the New Yorker. But he would like you to read it.

Best wishes from both of us to both of you.

Sincerely,

TO: **PASCAL COVICI**                                      CC, 1 p.

101 Irving Place
Ithaca, N.Y.
February 3, 1954

Dear Pat,

Please return the little girl[1] to the *above address*, using the Railway Express (not the regular mail).

I am sending you the first two chapters, 52 typewritten pages, of my Pnin novel. The first chapter appeared in the New Yorker (November 28, 1953). It will be a book of about 225–250 pages and—as I see it now—will consist of ten chapters of unequal length in all. In the next eight chapters, the insecurity of Pnin's job becomes evident while simultaneously it transpires that owing to some juggling, which Dr. Eric Wind blames upon his first wife, Eric's marriage to Liza is invalid, and in the midst of her intrigue with "George" she returns for a while to Pnin. Owing to a further impact of circumstances, Pnin finds himself solely responsible for the welfare of Liza's boy. There are some surprises and alarums. Then, at the end of the novel, I, V.N., arrive in person to Waindell College to lecture on Russian literature, while poor Pnin dies, with everything unsettled and uncompleted, including the book Pnin had been writing all his life. This is a very spare outline, and of course as little an expression of the book's beauty as Aphrodite's skeleton would be of hers; but I give it you just as a general notion of my general plans.

There is a good chance that the novel will be finished in June and I intend to send parts of it to the New Yorker as I go.

I would wish to reserve all foreign rights, as well as cinemato-graphic, television etc. (all subsidiary) rights. The New Yorker writes me that Pnin is a great hit with their readers. I would nevertheless wish a substantial publicity budget included in the agreement. The main reason for my falling out with Harpers was the way they han-dled CONCLUSIVE EVIDENCE. I would further wish the book to appear between fall and Christmas 1954.

I have no doubt that you have in mind a "good" contract and that this is going to be a long and fruitful connection.[2]

With best wishes,

Sincerely,
Vladimir Nabokov

1. *Lolita.*
2. *Pnin* was declined by Viking and published by Doubleday in 1957.

то: **JAMES LAUGHLIN**                                          cc, 1 p.

101 Irving Place
Ithaca, N.Y.
February 3, 1954

Dear Laughlin,

Would you be interested in publishing a timebomb that I have just finished putting together? It is a novel of 459 typewritten pages.

If you would like to see it, the following precautions would have to be observed:

First of all, I would have to have your word that you alone would read it. Everything else could be settled later. You would further have to give me an address where the MS could reach you personally and directly. This is a very serious matter for me, as you will understand after reading the work.[1]

> Sincerely,
> Vladimir Nabokov

---

1. Laughlin was out of the country and unable to read the typescript of *Lolita*.

TO: **WALLACE BROCKWAY**[1]                                        cc, 1 p.

> 101 Irving Place
> Ithaca, N. Y.
> March 18, 1954

Dear Mr. Brockway,

My wife and I very much enjoyed your visit to Ithaca. I shall be in New York and could have lunch with you on Saturday, April 3rd, if this is convenient to you.

Yesterday I sent you by Express the MS I told you about. I need hardly remind you that I am submitting it to S. & S. on a highly confidential basis.

> Sincerely yours
> Vladimir Nabokov

---

1. Simon & Schuster editor; also associated with the Bollingen Foundation.

TO: **JAMES LAUGHLIN**                                         CC, I p.

General Delivery
Taos, N.M.
July 4, 1954

Dear Mr. Laughlin,

Vladimir asks me to find out if you have returned from your Asian trip, and if you would care to read his manuscript now, in spite of the very rigid conditions he is forced to stipulate about this Ms.

If you think you can find time to read it *yourself*, he will have it sent to you. Should you feel that you want it for publication after having read it, you might naturally want to have the opinion of one of your readers. But Vladimir would like to be sure that you will not show it to anyone unless you are reasonably certain that you desire to publish the book. The sender named on the package will be a friend of ours living in New York.

I hope you have had an interesting and successful journey.

Sincerely

TO: **WALLACE BROCKWAY**                                      CC, I p.

General Delivery
Taos, New Mexico
July 15, 1954

Dear Mr. Brockway,

I have finished working on Part One of ANNA KARENIN[1] and am having the thing typed. It will be in your hands before the end of the month.

There will be ninety six notes of varying length; and I have corrected the numerous blunders in Garnett's text. I have also finished the foreword for Part One and a brief expose of the main introduction.[2]

Thank you very much for your efforts on behalf of LOLITA.[3] Would you mind taking care of the MS until you hear from me again, which will be soon? I want to have the thing published and am looking for an agent. Incidentally, would you happen to know of one who would undertake to place the book? I would be willing to let him have up to twenty five percent.

Sincerely,
Vladimir Nabokov

1. VN's edition was not published. (He insisted that the correct translated form of the title was *Anna Karenin*.)
2. These notes plus ten more were later included in *Lectures on Russian Literature*.
3. Brockway had suggested that *Lolita* be submitted to Grove Press.

TO: **WALLACE BROCKWAY**                                          cc, 1 p.

General Delivery
Taos, New Mexico
July 25, 1954

Dear Mr. Brockway,

I received your wire on Monday but the "reader's report" you mentioned has not arrived. So I have decided to mail you the stuff, partly because I have to turn my attention at once to some other work that has been waiting, and partly because I may move to another place soon and would appreciate receiving the 450 dollars before I leave.

I am sending you: 1. A list of points to be made in the Main Introduction; 2. A Foreword to Part One (22 pages) (from this Foreword some items may be transferred eventually to the Main Introduction), consisting of six sections (Characterization; Imagery; Calendar; Time Elements; Names; List of Characters in Part One)—the last of these sections (the list of characters) may be amalgamated later with a List covering all eight parts; 3. A collection of 104 notes, on 44 pages, (two of these notes may need some revision: the purchasing power of the dollar in 1872 should be checked, and I would dearly like to obtain a plan of the 1872 St. Petersburg-Moscow "sleeper"); 4. A list of absolutely necessary corrections of the Garnett translation. (The page and line are given for each correction, and in every given line the new version begins one word before and ends one word after the corrected text; there are dots before and after the corrected text unless the correction begins or ends the line).

You will find that the number of notes is twice as great as that of your queries, so I assume that you will find answers to some of the questions in the reader's report that I have not yet received.

Many thanks for forwarding the MS.

Sincerely yours,

TO: **GERTRUDE ROSENSTEIN**[1]                          CC, 1 p.

General Delivery
Taos, New Mexico
July 25, 1954

Dear Miss Rosenstein,

Thanks for your kind letter. I wish you had asked me to translate for you the libretto of "Boris Godunov" or even any of the Rimski-Korsakov operas based on Pushkin's text. But, unless you know Russian, you can have no idea of what Chaykovski (and his brother) did to the Pushkin verse novel when preparing their vile libretto for "Eugene Onegin". Lines from the greatest poetical work ever written in Russian were picked out at random, mutilated at will and combined with the tritest concoctions of Peter and Modest Chaykovski. The resulting libretto is an absurdity and an abomination. It consists of vulgar and, in my view, criminal inanities. To my sincere regret, I cannot associate my name with it in any way whatsoever. The only thing I could have done would have been to compose an entirely new libretto to fit the music, basing it on the true "Eugene Onegin" as written by Pushkin. However, this would have been a very different kind of job from the one you have in mind.

Sorry.

Sincerely yours,
Vladimir Nabokov

1. With TV Opera, National Broadcasting Company.

TO: **KATHARINE A. WHITE**                                      cc, 2 pp.

Taos, August 11, 1954

Dear Katharine,

Five months have elapsed since you wrote me about the second Pnin chapter—do forgive me for this long silence!

I was immersed at the time in a most harrowing work—a Russian version and recomposition of *Conclusive Evidence*. I think I have told you more than once what agony it was, in the early 'forties, to switch from Russian to English. After going through that atrocious metamorphosis, I swore I would never go back from my wizened Hyde form to my ample Jekyll one—but there I was, after fifteen years of absence, wallowing again in the bitter luxury of my Russian verbal might. Hardly had I finished that book, when I had to put into shape for eventual publication a series of lectures on Kafka, Proust and Joyce. And finally, a New York publisher suggested I revise and annotate an English translation of *Anna Karenin*. The footnotes for the First Part alone took me two months to collect and compose, and there had to be a foreword and other commentaries. I have just finished this First Part, and it is with some relief that I turn to your old and new letters: thanks for being so kind to a taciturn contributor.

As you know I sold the *Pnin* rights (with, of course, the obvious New Yorker stipulation) to Viking—on the strength of the first two chapters. They paid me well; but I do not know when I shall be able to deliver to them the completed MS.

When I started this letter, I intended to answer—and refute—your criticism of Chapter 2 point by point; but I feel now that the five-month delay has dulled that urge. Let me say merely that the "unpleasant" quality of Chapter 2 is a special trait of my work in general; you just did not notice in Chapter 1 the same nastiness, the same "realism" and the same pathos. The disgusting Wind pair are there to stay, I am afraid—and I can assure you that my psychotherapists differ from those of other writers on the subject.

I shall send you sometime in September a chapter on Pnin's vacation with Russian friends in New Hampshire, his return to the university and his discovery that he is about to lose his job, and another chapter, dealing with the nasty experiences of the Wind child at St. Matthew's, a private New England episcopalian school.

Chance and certain lepic considerations have led us to an adobe house ten miles north of Taos, an ugly and dreary town with *soi-disant* "picturesque" Indian paupers placed at strategic points by the Chamber of Commerce to lure tourists from Oklahoma and Texas who deem the place "arty". There are, however, some admirable canyons where most interesting butterflies occur.

Some extremely unpleasant circumstances, which I shall explain to you later, make it imperative for us to leave Taos for New York (a grave sickness in the family). I shall telephone you at the New Yorker next week on the chance you may be there. There is a number of things that I would like to discuss with you.

Best love to you and Andy.


TO: **PROF. REUBEN BROWER**[1]                       cc, 1 p.
                                                Ithaca, N. Y.


                                            September 10, 1954
Dear Mr. Brower,

My husband has asked me to give you a short description of his paper. He has had many unexpected matters to attend to and is afraid that you might not get a copy of the thing in time.

The main theme of his paper is that "the clumsiest literal translation is a thousand times more useful than the prettiest paraphrase". This is illustrated by observations gathered during his work on a translation of EUGENE ONEGIN. The paper is divided into seven parts:

1. Description of the novel and explanation of its dependence on certain western literary traditions.

2. Explanation of the peculiarities of Russian prosody.

3. A demonstration of how Pushkin's imagery and language are derived from XVIII-century French poetry, all of which must be taken into consideration when transferring them to English or back to French.

4. How a translator chooses his medium.

5. Defects of some existing translations.

6. The translator's workshop is shown, and some difficult passages are translated to the best of the translator's ability, after the necessity for rejecting some plausible solutions has been demonstrated.

7. Conclusions:

That it is impossible to translate ONEGIN in rhyme;

That it is impossible to describe in a series of notes the modulations and rhymes of the text as well as its associations and special features;

That it is possible to translate ONEGIN with reasonable accuracy by substituting for the original 14-line stanza, fourteen unrhymed lines of varying length, from iambic dimeter to iambic pentameter.

From this fact as applied to ONEGIN, some general conclusions are drawn.

I hope this will help you to some degree. My husband wants me to tell you that he is very much looking forward to meeting you.

Sincerely yours,

1. Editor of *On Translation* (Cambridge: Harvard University Press, 1959) to which VN contributed "The Servile Path."

TO: **ROGER W. STRAUS, JR.**[1]

cc, 1 p.
Ithaca, N.Y.

October 15, 1954

Dear Mr. Straus,

Some time ago you wrote me kindly expressing interest in my new novel. I could not do anything about it at the time for I had promised James Laughlin of New Directions to let him see it first, even though I did not expect him to want to publish it.

I have just heard from him as expected, and am asking him now to forward the MS to you.

For reasons you will easily understand after reading the book, I would wish to publish it under a penname. And for the same reasons, I would like to ask you to do me the favor of reading it yourself and not having it read by anyone else unless, after you have read it, you come to the conclusion that you wish to consider its publication.

I hope I may hear soon from you.

Yours truly,
Vladimir Nabokov

1. President of Farrar, Straus & Young.

TO: **JAMES LAUGHLIN**

TLS, 1 p.

Goldwin Smith Hall
Cornell University
Ithaca, N.Y.
October 15, 1954

Dear Laughlin,

Thanks for your letter. I understand your point and shall in all probability take your advice regarding publication abroad.[1] Any concrete suggestions you would care to make regarding such publication would be appreciated.

Before I ship her to France, I would like to show L. to Farrar,

Straus & Young, 101 Fifth Avenue. A short while ago Mr. Straus wrote me and asked to read my latest. Would you please do me the favor of forwarding the MS to him (Mr. Roger W. Straus, Jr.) by Railway Express (or messenger, if you prefer), making sure that the package goes to him *personally*. I would be much obliged to you if you could do it without delay, since I have written him about it.

Sincerely,
Vladimir Nabokov

1. Laughlin reported to VN on 11 October that he and Robert MacGregor "feel that it is literature of the highest order and that it ought to be published but we are both worried about possible repercussions both for the publisher and the author. Your style is so individual that it seems to me absolutely certain that the real authorship would quickly be recognized even if a pseudonym were used."

TO: **JASON EPSTEIN**[1]                                        CC, 1 p.

Goldwin Smith Hall
Cornell University
Ithaca, N.Y.
November 3, 1954

Dear Mr. Epstein,

Thank you for your letter. I am shipping you the MS by Railway Express. Please bear in mind that, if published, I would want this novel to appear under a penname. I would therefore appreciate (for the sake of preserving my incognito) if you reduced to a minimum the number of people who will read the MS for you, and, if you would withold, even from them, the true identity of the author. May I assume I have your word that you will respect this wish of mine?

EUGENE ONEGIN is still far from being completed. The translation itself will take up only about one third of the finished MS. The rest will consist of detailed notes and commentaries. The whole will come up to about six hundred pages. I would want to incorporate *en regard* a photostatic reproduction of the original edition (the Houghton Library at Harvard possesses a copy of it); one or two portraits of the author; Pushkin's discarded stanzas in footnotes at the bottom of the page. There will be an Introduction discussing various features of ONEGIN and, as already mentioned, about 250–300 pages of commentaries to be placed at the end of the volume. If you believe that such a publication might be of interest to you, please let me know, and I shall show you the work when it is ready.

Sincerely yours,
Vladimir Nabokov

1. Doubleday editor.

TO: **PHILIP RAHV**                                                     CC, 1 p.

700 Stewart Avenue
Ithaca, N.Y.
November 20, 1954

Dear Rahv,

I shall be happy to let you publish parts of the novel in the Partisan Review. But before sending you the eighty pages you suggest, I would like to make sure that, in case you decide to go ahead with it, you will agree to my using a penname.

For reasons of my own, I do not wish to publish it under my name, for the time being, at least. Will you agree to respect my incognito?[1]

Sincerely,
Vladimir Nabokov

1. Rahv replied on 28 November that it would be impossible for the *Partisan Review* to publish an excerpt from *Lolita* pseudonymously.

TO: **PASCAL COVICI**                                    CC, 1 p.

Ithaca, N.Y.

January 23, 1955

Dear Pat,

I have a very wonderful young translator from Russian into English for you. Moreover, I would undertake to check his work free of charge. Would you be interested, I wonder, in publishing Lermontov's celebrated novel The Hero of Our Time? The three old English versions of it that I know are execrable. Or anything else?

I am working intensively on PNIN.

I hope you and your family enjoy perfect health.

Sincerely,

Vladimir Nabokov

1. VN's translation in collaboration with Dmitri Nabokov was published by Doubleday in 1958.

TO: **PASCAL COVICI**                                    CC, 1 p.

Goldwin Smith Hall
Cornell University
Ithaca, N.Y.
February 22, 1955

Dear Pat,

Many thanks for the Trilling book[1] (incidentally, it went to an address where I do not live any more and travelled around for a while; your letters arrive at the right address, but your books do not).

The Hero of Our Time is an exciting novel, always fresh and readable. It is part of every course in Russian literature, and this alone should help to sell it. But it also should appeal to the general public if properly presented in English. It has elements of American frontier tales, mirages of yellow rocks and some thunderous romantic situations and adventures. And its hero is a picturesque character that catches one's fancy. Oleg Maslenikov is a complete mediocrity. I have not seen his "Hero" but I doubt that he can have produced anything but a very pedestrian version. For good measure the "Hero" might be published together with a new translation of "The Queen of Spades" by Pushkin, of which the usually so careful and brilliant Guerney has made a sad mess in his "Treasury". My young friend could not undertake a translation unless something definite can be worked out before. I would like you to mark that this is a very special offer on my part for ordinarily I do not revise other people's work gratis. If you do not approve of such a striking volume as the "Hero" and the "Queen" combined, perhaps you would prefer to suggest something else?

Here is more news about Pnin. The New Yorker has taken another chapter. I am now in the middle of the next one. I am not sending you anything yet because I want to show you a larger piece.

Sincerely,

Vladimir Nabokov

1. Lionel Trilling, *The Opposing Self* (New York: Viking, 1955).

TO: **KATHARINE A. WHITE** CC, 5 PP.

700 Stewart Ave.

March 5, 1955

Dear Katharine,

Thanks for the proof¹ and the chubby check. It is nice to know that Andy is out of the hospital.

I have cheerfully agreed to accept some thirty minor alterations, and have attended to some other details you wanted cleared up; but a few items I cannot accept, especially: 7 + 8 (explanation), 11 + 11a (transition), 19 (the head! Pnin's head!), 25 (the squirrelized tree), 32 (transition) and 34 (explanation). Such changes would affect the inner core of the piece which is built on a whole series of inner organic transitions; it would be agony even to contemplate replacing some of them at random by mechanical inorganic links when I have taken such pains with the inner linkage and balance. I hope you will agree with me in this as you have agreed in the past.

I am enclosing your Notes, my Notes and the Proofs.

With best wishes.

Sincerely,

PNIN'S DAY, Notes to notes.

1. O.K.

2. O.K.

3. She is very much alive. Pnin is not a widower. The reference further (3a) is to Pnin's father and mother.

4. "Here" refers to Waindell College, to his Assistant Professorship.

5. O.K.

5a. base plugs. This sounds O.K., but I do not know the word. It *does* mean the two holes into which you insert the two-pronged attachment at the end of a lamp's cord?

6. O.K.

6a. I think "them" seems clear enough since it is immediately followed by "like two old friends". But you may replace "them" by "the pair" or "this pair".

7. I really do not think that you should insert "the Clements' daughter, Isabel" here. No, I cannot accept this. My plan is to bring her presence in gradually, through various impressions and suggestions (and if the reader does not quite understand at first, he certainly will further on) and this explanation spoils the modulated approach completely.

8. O.K. (Bed head is good English. You will find it in the Oxford dictionary. But "bed headboard" is better, I admit.)

8a. Please put back "married daughter" (see 7)

9. O.K.

9a. "Prepared" seems O.K. to me, and means here exactly the same as "made preparations",

10. O.K.

10a. O.K.

10b. The date should be "1940", of course. A slip in my script.

11. I cannot insert anything here. The next paragraph takes him to the classroom automatically. We even learn that he meets on the way somebody who offers him a lift.

12. The English "non", of course (as in "nonstop"). If not clear, change "non" to "o" in "not". If still not clear, cut from "acquiring" to "non", and put instead "sounding positively Italian". Perhaps, this would be simpler and better.

12a. O.K. Or better italicize the "nun" of "after*nun*".

13. motuweth frisas. A reference to the sequence "Monday, Tuesday, Wednesday, Thursday" and the weekendish "Friday, Saturday, Sunday" as abbreviated in a memorandum book or calendar. It seems so clear. Let us keep it please, if possible ("on a Montuewed-thursday-Frisatsunday" basis would not have the neatness of my formula).

11a. I am quite sure I would not like any little bridge here. Readers should learn to leap.

14. Superfluous, since it has been translated three lines earlier.

15. I have thought about it, but came to the definite conclusion that nothing could be added. However, an exclamation mark after "Berlin" might settle the point.

16. Low boy file *is* the right term. See Beckley-Cardy's (Chicago) School Buyer's Guide of Furniture-Supplies-Equipment, Catalog No. 96, School year 1953–1954. Administrator's edition, p.17, No. D 250, "all-in-one lowboy file", illustr. "Filing case" is acceptable. It is further referred to (same paragraph) as "small steel file".

17. O.K.

18. O.K.: With the help of the janitor he screwed onto the side of the desk a pencil sharpener.

18a. No caps, please.

18b. O.K.: to match

18c. O.K.

19. Stet: head. He had no hair (see Galley Four). Head *must* remain. The story collapses otherwise.

20. "His compatriot" is redundant then. I would keep "compatriot", eliminate "Komarov" after it, and dispense with the explanation "the only Russian" etc. But do as you please.

21. "antique", or "antiquated", or quite literal "antiquarian"

22. to "slapper-slip" is dialect English for a double slip. But, if not clear, just put "slipped",

23. Yes.

24. "Circular flock" is good ornithological English. It is essential here.

25. It was not a typo. The squirrel goes so fast that it merges with the tree. I must have the tree scrabble. Please, stet.

25a. I have switched around two words, otherwise the "him" is dim.

26. A reference to the Pushkin quoted earlier. I have inserted now the translation.

26a. Please, stet. Pnin translates everything from the Russian. He wants to express the notion "something" but says "something or other"—as many Russians do.

27. O.K.

3a. Pnin would have been a very small Pnin forty years ago! This refers to his parents. I have made it clearer now.

28. You are quite right. I have simplified matters. After "Library": "Wearing rubber gloves . . . . . shelving, Pnin would go to those books and gloat over them: obscure magazines" etc.

29. O.K.

29a. "interested"

30. The reference is to the same Kroneberg translation. Vengerov was the editor of Shakespeare's collected plays in Russian.

31. O.K. Good suggestion.

32. O.K. (Although not really necessary) No, on second thoughts, it is dreadful. Please, eliminate.

32a. "Chapleted" is correct.

33. I have made this a little clearer.

33a. No parenthesis. This was all on the banners (I have seen that film).

33b. Eliminate this "shown", please.

34. This insertion is impossible. Nothing should be added here. I worked for a month on this passage.

35. No date, please!

36. I have rearranged this.

1. "Pnin's Day," *The New Yorker* (23 April 1955).

TO: **JASON EPSTEIN**                                      CC, 1 p.

Goldwin Smith Hall
Cornell University
Ithaca, N.Y.
March 12, 1955

Dear Mr. Epstein,

Here is a short list of works which ought to be retranslated and which might be presented in the following form:

1. A volume which might be titled "Three Duels", and which would contain

Pushkin's THE PISTOL SHOT
Lermontov's PRINCESS MARY
Chehov's THE SINGLE COMBAT.

2. "Three Fantasies"—a trio of fantastic tales—

Pushkin's THE QUEEN OF SPADES
Gogol's THE NOSE
Dostoevski's THE DOUBLE (by far the best thing Dostoevski ever wrote)

My favorite project, however, is Lermontov's THE HERO OF OUR TIME, a novel consisting of five stories (of which PRINCESS MARY is one).

If you are interested in any of these works, I shall explain in more detail what is wrong with the old translations (for instance, with

Yarmolinski's "The Pistol Shot" or Guerney's "The Queen of Spades").

My protege is none other than my son who will be graduated from Harvard this spring. He is a young Russian scholar and a budding American author in his own right. He has done some very creditable translations for me, and I would undertake to control and revise and work on the lines suggested here.

Sincerely yours,
Vladimir Nabokov

TO: **DOUSSIA ERGAZ**[1]            cc, 2 pp.
June 1955            Ithaca, N.Y.

|  | INSTEAD OF: | SHOULD BE: |
|---|---|---|
| *Forword* | | |
| p.2 | inGray | in Gray |
| *Part One* | | |
| p.2 | died died | died |
| p.3 | hotel Mirana | Hotel Mirana |
| p.4 | *que j'avais déniché* | that I had filched |
| p.5 | fat powdered | fat, powdered |
| p.8 | "Annabel" phase an | "Annabel" phase the |
| p.9 | *Alors* she | She |
| p.12 | cringe and hide.) | cringe and hide!) |
| p.19 | humiliating sordid taciturn | humiliating, sordid, taciturn |
| p.23 | wear before I touched her | wear, before I touched her, |
| p.29 | lawyers favors, | lawyer's favors, |
| p.38 | being presumably the maid) | being presumably the maid), |
| p.42 | Ramsdale journal | Ramsdale Journal |
| p.45 | and bathe, and bask but a | and bathe, and bask; but a |
| p.53 | Her little doves seemed | Her little doves seem |
| p.54 | real zest)? no. | real zest)? No. |
| " " | Lola, Lolita. | Lola, Lolita! |
| " " | Does fate *trame quelque chose?* | Is it Fate scheming? |
| p.56 | to report, save primo: | to report, save, primo: |
| p.60 | Dr. Blanche Schwarzman | Dr. Blanche Schwarzmann |
| " " | torrentially talking to | torrential talk with |
| p.65 | lawyer has acalled | lawyer has called |
| p.66 | herself free, recoiled and lay | herself free, recoiled, and lay |

| | | |
|---|---|---|
| p.81 | I convinced myself that Louise left, got into Lo's bed | Having convinced myself that Louise left, I got into Lo's bed |
| " " | | |
| p.89 | That is when I knew she was | It was then I knew she was |
| p.103 | Humbert. *Mais comment?* | Humbert. But how? |
| p.109 | *faisant la coquette.* | coquettishly. |
| p.110 | *je ne sais pas à quoi* | *je ne sais à quoi* |
| p.119 | other, and went back to the | other, and returned to the |
| p.121 | doublebreatsed | doublebreasted |
| p.122 | ticketing illegally parked Beale car as she slipped and fell . . . . while hurrying | ticketing the illegally parked Beale car as she was hurrying |
| " " | | |
| p.128 | Mrs. H.H. trajectory | Mrs. H.H.'s trajectory |
| p.129 | slipped and plunged | slipped on the freshly watered asphalt and plunged |
| p.137 | her wool joursey | her wool jersey |
| " " | figures of children with snubbed noses, dun-colored | figures of snub-nosed children with dun-colored, |
| p.183 | *C'était quelque chose de tout-à-fait spécial,* | It was something quite special, |
| p.200 | (tale left, white eyelashes | (tail left, white eyelashes |
| p.212 | —o Beaudelaire!— | —oh Baudelaire!— |
| " " | coach (a husky | coach, a husky |
| p.218 | Shewent on | She went on |
| p.220 | *kollega* | comrade |
| p.222 | Alps no more possess | Alps no longer possess |
| " " | and in so many *cabanos* | and in so many *cabanes* |
| p.223 | semi-extant dragons— | semi-extant dragons!— |
| " " | withdrew. *J'étais dévozé par un désir suprème, comme dit l'autre.* Beneath the laprobe | withdrew. Beneath the laprobe |
| p.257 | killedin | killed in |
| " " | her mother, eh?) | her mother, eh?). |
| p.276 | nonsensedespite | nonsense despite |
| p.278 | cockcureness | cocksureness |
| p.286 | other alternative that to | other alternative than to |
| p.290 | whow as | who was |
| p.324 | counrty | country |
| p.342 | Saguaro deserts | saguaro deserts |
| p.360 | Goddness, | Goodness, |
| p.390 | forty at one minute and a hundred the next. | forty, one minute, and a hundred, the next. |
| p.409 | and not not after to-morrow, | and not after to-morrow, |
| p.412 | emeralkd | emerald |
| p.418 | all at one, | all at once, |
| p.423 | Godd bless our | God bless our |
| p.439 | "Quilty", *dis-je,* | "Quilty", I said, |
| p.442 | disorganized by by a drug | disorganized by a drug |

| " " | the cowmen and the sheepmen | the cowman and the sheepman |
|---|---|---|
| p.447 | howl and clutched at his brow | howl and hand pressed to his brow |

Chere Madame, j'ai relu LOLITA et voici quelques petites fautes, coquilles etc. que j'ai corrigees. Vous voudrez bien noter que j'ai supprime plusieur phrases françaises. Veuillez remettre cette liste a M. Gerodias afin qu'il puisse l'incorporer dans le texte avant la composition.

Bien a vous,

1. Corrections lists for *Lolita*; Mme. Ergaz was VN's French agent. In this and the following lists, holograph marks indicating the status and fate of certain corrections have been omitted.

TO: **MAURICE GIRODIAS**[1]　　　　　　　　　　cc, 6 pp.

Ithaca, N.Y.

| page;line | INSTEAD OF: | SHOULD BE: |
|---|---|---|
| 2;1 | *Je suis né en* 1910 | I was born in 1910, |
| 6;14 | build | built |
| 14;7 | analysists | analysts |
| 15;23 | *charmant* | *charmante* |
| 20;17 | moustach /everywhere/ | mustache |
| 21;18 | *qui sait,* | who knows, |
| 21;26 | *le bonhomme* | the good man |
| 25;5 | patient | patiently |
| 27;1-2 | pack up up | pack |
| 30;25 | debur | debut |
| 33;13 | importance | important |
| 35;5 | cousins | cousins, |
| 35;6 | wife | wife, |
| 35;26 | was | seemed |
| 35;27 | insured | insured it |
| 36;5 | En route | *En route* |
| 36;14 | white-framed | white-frame |
| 36;21 | *Que pouvais-je faire?* | What could I do? |
| 37;1 | bottom | end |
| 39;18 | I'll | "I'll |
| 43;14 | sily | silky |
| 44;5 | no, | now, |

| 45;16 | *et moi* | and I |
|---|---|---|
| 50;14 | me | my |
| 53;19 | full skirted | full-skirted |
| 53;23 | *dans de vieux jardins* | in old gardens |
| 53;22 | pyjamas | pajamas |
| 54;14 | does not deny | denies |
| 54;24 | tried out | tried on |
| 58;5 | that | this |
| 65;25 | numbleness | numbleness |
| 73;25 | "She's | "She'd |
| 80;5 | You | Your |
| 81;9 | full page | full-page |
| 86;16 | Inacrnadine | Incarnadine |
| 90;1 | heck | the heck |
| 91;4 | semblance | resemblance |
| 91;22 | thirty-year old | thirty-year-old |
| 99;9 | picnic ground | parking area |
| 99;12 | when in quest | in quest |
| 100;12 | intend | intended |
| 102;3 | *decide* | *décide* |
| 102;23-24 | picnic ground | parking area |
| 103;3 | sun-dappled privvy | a sun-dappled privy |
| 103;10 | but chance can | chance, however, can |
| 110;15 | laquered | lacquered |
| 111;13 | In | "In |
| 111;16 | Hotel,) | Hotel!) |
| 111;22 | somewhat set her | set her somewhat |
| 116;7 | parctically | practically |
| 117;8 | awoken | awoke |
| 123;18 | a quiet | as quiet |
| 126;10 | *que c'etait tout comme).* | that it might be implied). |
| 130;16 | pseudo-celtic | pseudo-Celtic |
| 130;17 | all | every |
| 131;2 | novelist | novelist, |
| 131;3 | dog | dog, |
| 131;11 | carved Indian's | carved-Indian |
| 131;18 | nursing already | already nursing |
| 133;14 | Herald— | Herald, |
| 134;10 | find instead another | find, instead, another |
| 134;11 | than God | thank God |
| 135;23 | Bee | bea |
| 136;6 | Know Your Child | Know-Your-Child |
| 136;7 | dislike | dislike, |
| 138;8 | four-hours' | four-hour |
| 139;3 | headache daily | daily headache |
| 140;4 | to do | to go |
| 140;11 | 8.30 | 9.30 |

| | | |
|---|---|---|
| 140:16 | a horseshoe | horseshoes |
| 140:19 | worn out | worn-out |
| 140:25 | And afterwards to somebody | And perhaps afterwards she would say to somebody |
| 141:18 | and seemed taller | and taller |
| 141:22 | bwteen | between |
| 142:3 | maedlein | *mädlein* |
| 147:17 | srossing | crossing |
| 148:19 | Lolia | Lolita |
| 149:26 | way I had | way in which I had |
| 151:7 | Through | Under |
| 155:24 | | of girlish |
| 166:2 | Venetial | Venetian |
| 167:9 | pharmaceupist, | pharmaceutist, |
| 167:22 | tome | time |
| 183:15 | taken all | taken in all |
| 184:5 | has | had |
| 188:7 | fried chicken bones | fried-chicken bones |
| 191:10 | naivete | naiveté |
| 191:12 | exhasperating | exasperating |
| 191:13 | disogranized | disorganized |
| 194:15 | Holme | Holmes |
| 196:20 | should | had |
| 198:19 | Lorraine | Lorrain |
| 201:1 | *en grand,* | on a grand scale, |
| 201:14 | these Magnolia Gardens | that Magnolia Garden |
| 202:18 | zootsuiter | zootsuiters |
| 203:12 | Mississippian | Mississippi |
| 204:3 | run down in | run in |
| 204:12 | (*Je m'y connais, en montagnes*) | /omit/ |
| 208:3 | We learned | We came |
| 208:9 | moustach | mustache |
| 209:3 | they | it |
| 209:3 | children | children's |
| 210:10 | and | or |
| 210:21 | *Ou bien* | Or else |
| 211:18 | than | but |
| 211:22 | morning | mourning |
| 213:9 | dust | dust, |
| 215:1 | heft | left |
| 219:10 | *de plus atrocement cruel* | more atrociously cruel |
| 222:18 | cabanes | *cabanes* |
| 222:23 | forstfloor | forest floor |
| 223:5 | heavenly hued | heavenly-hued |
| 224:5-6 | and I suspect | and, I suspect, |
| 227:17 | dispair | despair |
| 232:1 | that first wild | that wild |

| | | |
|---|---|---|
| 232;2 | to the Lolita | to Lolita |
| 233;4 | since as I have once remarked, | since, as i have once remarked |
| 239;8 | fieldglasses, | binoculars, |
| 240;7 | both—I omitted to find out—would | both, would |
| 241;17 | *maedlein* | *mädlein* |
| 242;5 | get | got |
| 249;19 | burglar | burgle |
| 249;19 | srutinize | scrutinize |
| 249;21 | eight dollar | eight one-dollar |
| 250;6 | participation | permission to participate |
| 258;7 | had been rather looking forward to | had looked forward to meet, |
| 260;19 | burdened by | burdened with |
| 263;10 | again | again" |
| 263;14 | them | them, |
| 264;1 | uou | you |
| 264;12 | weather | face |
| 265;6 | mind | mind, |
| 265;7 | fold on fold | fold on fold, |
| 269;20 | martirize | martyrize |
| 269;24 | wronb | wrong |
| 272;11 | girl | girls |
| 274;21 | three girls and five | two girls and four |
| 281;19 | *sers* | *serre* |
| 286;7 | three quarter way | three-quarter-way |
| 286;16-17 | I saw by her own lights a | I saw a |
| 286;21 | that | than |
| 290;10 | *il parait,* | I hinted, |
| 288;15 | (a storm | (A storm |
| 288;16 | admrable | adorable |
| 288;23 | smashed | slammed |
| 288;24 | window-pane. | window. |

July 6, 1955

Dear Mr. Girodias,

I am sending you:

1. The missing page 195.

2. A copy of a short list of corrections I sent Madame Ergaz for you a week or so ago (in case it has already reached you, please return the second copy to me).

3. A new set of corrections where I have taken into account what you say about the over-abundance of French phrases in the MS. Of

your list of sixty I have cancelled or translated one third, but this is as far as I can go.

I am delighted that you are doing LOLITA. Please rush the proofs and I shall rush them back.

Humbert's French, the French he uses himself, should, of course be correct. This also applies to Gaston's French and that of the other French people in the book. I hope there are no slips there. Elsewhere there are bits of deliberately faulty French.

Sincerely yours,
Vladimir Nabokov

1. Proprietor of the Olympia Press, Paris, which published both avant garde literature and pornography in English. *Lolita* was published by the Olympia Press in September 1955.

TO: **MAURICE GIRODIAS**        cc, 6 pp.

Goldwin Smith Hall
Cornell University
Ithaca, N.Y.
July 9, 1955

Dear Mr. Girodias,

I have just discovered another page (p.429) which, I suppose, is missing from the copy you have. I am sending it enclosed, and am adding a few corrections pertaining, chiefly, to the last pages of the book.

Please let me know if you have received my previous letter with corrections and p.195.

Sincerely yours,
Vladimir Nabokov

PS. If you mail the proofs before July 20th, address them to 700 Stewart Avenue, Ithaca, NY.; this might save time since the university mail is not distributed on weekends. I shall, however, abandon the Stewart Avenue apartment around July 25th.

| page:line | INSTEAD OF: | SHOULD BE: |
|---|---|---|
| 144:20 | backfisch | *backfisch* |
| 147:7 | shadographs | shadowgraphs |
|  | *tour* | not underlined [note in Russian] |
| 192:10 | perhaps | —perhaps |
| 192:11 | mannerisms | mannerisms— |
| 298:22 | moustached | mustached |
| 301:18 | into this his pregnant | his pregnant |
| 301:19 | in with her | into it with her |
| 303:23 | Charlotte's and Mine | my and Charlotte's |
| 304:2 | though I | though, I |
| 304:7 | I of course | I, of course, |
| 305:12 | in winter | in the winter |
| 306:7 | or both | or both, |
| 306:18 | Somebody I imagined | Somebody, I imagined, |
| 307:10 | sunglasses | sunglasses, |
| 307:21 | trousers | trousers, |
| 308:7 | moustach | mustache |
| 308:24 | the worst | "the worst |
| 308:24 | is | would be |
| 309:24 | behind me | behind me, |
| 309:25 | moustach | mustache |
| 312:24 | me—I | me, I |
| 314:13 | rogue's | rogues' |
| 315:6 | And moreover | And, moreover, |
| 316:11 | beau!" what a tongue-twister. | beau", "Qu'il t'y"—what a tongue twister! |
| 317:10 | noncommittent | noncommittal |
| 317:14 | crossed | cross |
| 321:18 | The rest | The rest, |
| 322:2 | mobile-white bloused | mobile-white-bloused |
| 322:21 | been followed | been, followed |
| 323:17 | moustach | mustache |
| 323:23 | protruding, | protruding |
| 325:1 | after | after, |
| 325:21 | and impossible | and was impossible |
| 330:8 | celluloid | celluloid, |
| 330:25 | playing | acting |
| 331:12 | part left | part, left |
| 331:15 | have) | have), |
| 332:2 | Gaston | Gaston, |

| | | |
|---|---|---|
| 332:9 | memories— | memories, |
| 332:10 | mine— | mine, |
| 333:7 | Lo had | Lo, had |
| 333:13 | readymade tennis short, | tennis shorts, |
| 334:22 | discovery | discovery, |
| 335:12 | quartette | quartet |
| 335:13 | prepositions | propositions |
| 335:14 | Birdsley; | Beardsley; |
| 335:15 | it could not | they could not |
| 338:18 | towel around his neck | towel that was around his neck, |
| 338:22 | moustach | mustache |
| 339:6 | anjoyed | enjoyed |
| 339:8 | swung at | made for |
| 339:10 | air— | air; |
| 339:18 | counteract and get over his | counteract his |
| 342:4 | zigzaging | zigzagging |
| 343:15 | acceeding | exceeding |
| 344:14 | year old | year-old |
| 346:24 | come for | come, for |
| 346:25 | strain it was | strain it had been |
| 347:7 | thirteen-dollar | thirteen-dollar-a-day |
| 347:8 | part-time young | young part-time |
| 347:22 | who, in the act | who was in the act |
| 349:6 | works | "works |
| 349:8 | At the moment I knew | I knew |
| 350:1 | rolly-polly | roly-poly |
| 350:19 | there was | they had |
| 351:14 | and was | and on the following day I was |
| 351:15 | solid next day for | solid, for |
| 352:6 | festivity | celebration |
| 353:10 | toticed | noticed |
| 355:3 | stood out and | stood out, and |
| 356:2 | where to | where, to |
| 357:9 | stayed at | stayed, at |
| 357:11 | ley, only one | ley, one |
| 362:11 | as old friend | an old friend |
| 362:11 | Charlotte's | Charlotte's, |
| 363:7 | that after | that, after |
| 363:12 | fiend | fiend, |
| 363:12 | taken | taken, |
| 363:12 | complicated | complicated, |
| 363:13 | vague | vague, |
| 365:25 | and merely | and, merely |
| 366: | "Dolores Disparue" | "Dolorès Disparue" |
| 367:11 | Valery | Valéry |
| 368:13 | *t'offrait* | *t'offrais* |
| 369:8 | and after | and, after |
| 370:33 | psychally analyzing | psychoanalyzing |

| | | |
|---|---|---|
| 372:11 | ape's | ape |
| 372:14 | sport that | sport, that |
| 373:3-4 | suspenders and painted tie-home-town | suspenders-and-painted-tie-home town |
| 373-5 | | |
| 373:22 | her Valechka | her, Valechka |
| 381:10 | correspondents, I | correspondents—I |
| 381:10 | recollect | recollect, |
| 382:13 | be re-ribbed | revert to a rib |
| 384:12 | hot-dog-stand | hot-dog stand |
| 384:21 | Ramsdale, he would hand them | Ramsdale he would hand |
| | turn over instead of hand | |
| 386:4 | withhelding | withholding |
| 388:18 | car had | car, had |
| 390:19 | forty | 40 |
| 390:20 | at one minute and a hundred | one minute and 100 |
| 392:9 | hollow-cheeked | hollow-cheeked, |
| 392:10 | watered-milk white | watered-milk-white |
| 396:12 | sketch | sketchy |
| 399:3 | nausea. *C'était l'autre que j'égorgerai.* He was | nausea. He was |
| 399:11 | but their shape at the | but the |
| 399:17 | *Bon.* | Good. |
| 400:22 | did they you | did you |
| 402:5 | dod | did |
| 404:19 | baby, | baby |
| 404:21 | and know as | and know, as |
| 406:13 | matter (a reprieve, I | matter" ("A reprieve", I |
| 406:14 | Anyway | "Anyway |
| 407:3 | coming with me. | coming with me? |
| 407:24 | remark—: | remark: |
| 408:2 | rejoin: I | rejoin: "I |
| 408:7 | that so as to | that in order to |
| 409:3 | you will come to | you will not come to |
| 409:6 | hope (to that effect)". | hope" (to that effect). |
| 410:7 | judging by the | according to |
| 410:8 | scale of my map. | my map. |
| 410:10 | However the | However, the |
| 410:16 | country if any was | country, if any, was |
| 414:6 | been proven | be proven |
| 416:9 | sunset | sunset- |
| 416:18 | automaton's | automaton |
| 418:21 | heavy unattractive, affectionate child | heavy, unattractive, affectionate child, |
| 419:11 | played | played, |
| 419:18 | Suddenly | Suddenly, |
| 419:19 | casual arm | casual arm, |

| | | |
|---|---|---|
| 420:2 | ankle | ankle, |
| 420:2 | forward— | forward, |
| 420:3 | preparotary | preparatory |
| 420:6 | Avis | Avis, |
| 420:6 | pink dad | pink dad, |
| 420:10 | Lolita | Lolita, |
| 421:13 | her) | her), |
| 422:10 | *Bon zhur,* | *Bonzhur,* |
| 423:3 | years-old | year-old |
| 423:5 | years-old | year-old |
| 423:8 | policement | policemen |
| 425:9 | when with | when, with |
| 425:15 | nieces, onto | nieces onto |
| 425:16 | call out to me | call to me |
| 426:23 | years- | year- |
| 429:8 | that in hope | that, in hope |
| 429:18 | launched himself in the glory of | launched on a glorious |
| 429:19 | a long-range | long-range |
| 430:14 | blonds, | blondes, |
| 431:6 | Road twelve | Road, twelve |
| 431:7 | and as | and, as |
| 431:14 | warned, | foretold, |
| 431:14 | a moment and | a moment and, |
| 432:7 | vagues | vague |
| 432:11 | of mine, | of mine |
| 432:12 | bobbie pin | bobby pin |
| 433:10 | Manor, | Manor |
| 434:19 | old one had | old one, had |
| 434:18 | were and | were, and |
| 435:2 | dishevelled, | dishevelled |
| 436:5 | evidebt | evident |
| 436:22 | bipedal trickster | trickster |
| 437:5 | with those | about those |
| 437:13 | Patagonia. *Je paie a travers le nez.* | Patagonia. |
| 437:14 | or rather, I refuse | I refuse |
| 439:15 | and with a | and, with a |
| 439:17 | paralytical | paralyzing |
| 441:16 | the same to keep | the same time to keep |
| 441:17 | my eye on him. | an eye on him. |
| 442:3 | readers, among | readers |
| 442:4 | them a lovely lacy old lady with pale ovel eyes, will | will |
| 442:5 | this point, the | this point the |
| 442:6 | their, and her, childhood | their childhood |
| 442:7 | fistycuffs, | fisticuffs, |

| 443:5 | it's verse. | it's in verse. |
|---|---|---|
| 444:29 | protegée | protégée |
| 445:6 | offer you | offer you, |
| 446:12 | painted yellow— | painted yellow—" |
| 448:20 | elexir | elixir |
| 449:22 | The glass had gone | The crystal was gone |
| 453:8 | Clare Obscur | Clare Obscure |
| 453:10 | it gave me, was | it gave me was |
| 455:3 | (Hi, | ('Bye, |
| 455:19 | and than, thinking | and then, thinking |
| 456:8 | beyond the town | beyond the town, |
| 456:13 | to the eye | to the eye, |
| 456:22 | voices, majestic | voices—majestic |
| 456:22 | majically near, | magically near, |
| 458:10 | But even so, | But, even so, |
| 458:15 | when the reader | as the reader |

to: **PHILIP RAHV**                                      cc, 1 p.

700 Stewart Avenue
Ithaca, NY.
July 13, 1955

Dear Rahv,

LOLITA is to be published in English, under my name, by the Olympia Press in Paris,[1] presumably before the end of August. I am in the midst of correcting the proofs. All this happened very suddenly. They are rushing the publication because they want to take advantage of the tourist trade.

You have been very kind to my little girl. You suggested at the time that you would publish fragments if I signed them. I would now, since it is coming out under my own name anyway. If you are still interested, I could send you a piece at once, provided you can make room for it on your nearest issue. Later, it would become more complicated since the consent of the publishers would have to be secured.[2]

I would appreciate having your reaction as soon as possible. In case you are interested, perhaps you could remember what part of the book you wanted.

Sincerely,

Vladimir Nabokov

PS. Incidentally, what about that little piece on translation that I gave you?[3]

---

1. Maurice Girodias subsequently claimed that it was he who persuaded VN to put his name on *Lolita*. See DN, "A Few Things That Must Be Said on Behalf of Vladimir Nabokov," *Nabokov's Fifth Arc*, ed. J. E. Rivers and Charles Nicol (Austin: University of Texas Press, 1982).
2. *Partisan Review* did not publish *Lolita* excerpts.
3. "Problems of Translation: *Onegin* in English," *Partisan Review* (Fall 1955).

TO: **WALLACE BROCKWAY**                                    CC, 1 p.

Goldwin Smith Hall

Cornell University

Ithaca, N.Y.

July 15, 1955

Dear Mr. Brockway,

I have just written a letter to you and Mr. Simon jointly, regarding ANNA, for I was not sure that you were in town or on vacation. I would very much appreciate hearing from you (as member of the Simon & Schuster firm) at your earliest convenience on that subject.

Now let me talk to you in your capacity of editor with Bollingen. Mr. Epstein, of Doubleday, has just written me about his talk with you *re* my ONEGIN. I would be very happy if Bollingen could be interested in the publication of this thing. Mr. Epstein, I take it, has explained to you that this work will consist of 1. a rhythmic, but not rhymed, translation of the complete novel, including all existing fragments of the "Tenth" chapter, rejected by Pushkin, as well as Onegin's Journey and Onegin's Album, both of which exist in fragmentary form. 2. elaborate notes and comments resulting from an exhaustive research into the roots of Pushkin's prosody and imagery (French XVIII-century poets), fact and fiction in connection with his African descent etc. etc. I envisage this publication as a strictly scientific opus. I believe that a complete Russian text should be included, as well as a reproduction of at least the title page of the original edition (one of the very few copies known to exist is in the Houghton collection, Harvard) and of some of the poet's drawings. Please let me know what you think of it.

Sincerely yours,
Vladimir Nabokov

TO: MAURICE GIRODIAS              CC, 1 p.
Ithaca, N.Y.

July 18, 1955

Dear Mr. Girodias,

I am returning the corrected page proof 429. Many thanks for sending it to me.

By now you must have received the corrected twenty galleys covering the beginning of Part One, and all the galleys of Part Two. I quite understand that it would be too complicated for you to insert my corrections in Part Two *after* it had been set. You will see, however, that I have taken care of the matter in the proofs I have returned.

I am leaving to-day on a lecture engagement but shall be back on Friday, the 22nd, and shall immediately attend to whatever proofs arrive in my absence, so that you will certainly have them back early next week.

I am delighted that you have set such an early date for publication. I hope you have already started a publicity campaign. What are you doing about publicity in the U.S.? When sending out review copies, are you including the following publications: 1. The Partisan Review

(Philip Rahv, an admirer of LOLITA, 513 Sixth Avenue, New York 11, NY); 2. The New Yorker (be *sure* to address that copy to Edmund Wilson, c/o the New Yorker); 3. The New York Times Book Review (Harvey Breit, that is the only fellow I know in that shop); 4. Saturday Review of Literature (?); 5. The New York Herald Tribune. That's all I can think of. I am sure you have some other periodicals in mind.

You and I know that LOLITA is a serious book with a serious purpose. I hope the public will accept it as such. A *succès de scandale* would distress me.

Sincerely yours,
Vladimir Nabokov

TO: **JASON EPSTEIN**                                                   CC, 1 p.

Goldwin Smith Hall
Cornell University
Ithaca, NY.
August 27, 1955

Dear Mr. Epstein,

First of all let me thank you somewhat belatedly for the Lermontov agreement and advance. Next, I wish to apologize for my long silence: after losing eight days at the hospital, I had to devote all my time to PNIN. *That* book I finished yesterday.

*Eugene Onegin.* I have had no answer from Brockway. I wonder if I should write someone else at Bollingen's or just give them up altogether and go to some university press. I have just learned that, thanks to a new fund, Cornell might want to do the initial, large-size, edition. Is there anything you might want to suggest in this connection? Would Doubleday, for instance, want to share the expense and responsibility with the Cornell Press (or some other university press)? Would you like to be put in touch with the Cornell Press? Or are you interested in a later, smaller, edition only? In any case, I accept the idea of a smaller edition to appear after the larger one has been out for a reasonable length of time, provided the details can be settled in a satisfactory way between you, the original publisher and me. Do you think it might do any good to try and ring up Brockway once more? Would you be kind enough to do so?

*Anna Karenin*. I have had another look at the various translations of this novel. Some sentences and passages have been turned and twisted so many times by the different translators that they will inevitably remain as they are either in one or another version. On practically every page, however, there are blunders, omissions or clumsy turns which have to be rehandled. Under these circumstances, I am inclined to think that an advance for a new translation could be set at $2000. This would not cover notes and comments for which I would want a separate agreement between you and me (the translation would be done by my son). Neither Simon nor Brockway have answered my last letter. I am now going to write them that I consider myself released from my understanding with them. In any case, I am free to undertake a new translation (my son even more so), since they never considered a new translation anyway.

*Theatre*. In my painfree moments I have been re-reading a number of Russian plays. Unfortunately, all those that are worth translating are in verse (Griboedov, Pushkin, Lermontov, Blok), a fact I had entirely overlooked. This project will have to be shelved—for the time being at least.

*Language book*. I am afraid, this project does not interest me as I am interested in literary matters only. Thank you, anyway, for asking me. It sounds very good, but I just don't have the time for this sort of thing.

Sincerely,
Vladimir Nabokov

Goldwin Smith Hall
Cornell University
Ithaca, NY.
August 29, 1955

Dear Pat,

I am sending you the complete book under the provisional title of MY POOR PNIN.

I hope you will like it. I realize, however, that the MS is shorter than you expected. There is nothing I can do about this: books set their own limits, as you surely know, and any more chapters would be nothing but padding, adding nothing to characterization or plot. I may do another book on Pnin later on but it would have to be set in entirely new surroundings.

Should the length prove a major consideration, and should you want the agreement cancelled and your money returned, I would accept your decision, of course.

I would like to hear soon from you.

With best wishes,

Sincerely,

PS. The New Yorker has bought Chapter 4; Ch. 5 was too functional for them, and I don't know yet their reaction to Chapters 6 and 7.

TO: **PASCAL COVICI**                              cc, 2 pp.

Goldwin Smith Hall
Cornell University
Ithaca, NY.
September 29, 1955

Dear Pat,

I am glad you like the book, and nothing would please me better than to have it published by you.[1]

The question of money is a minor one. I do not agree with your definition: it certainly is *not* a collection of sketches. But it is much shorter than you had the right to expect, and I shall accept a reduction of the advance, but would like you to set aside a substantial sum for publicity.

The other question you raise is much more important. When I began writing PNIN, I had before me a definite artistic purpose: to create a character, comic, physically inattractive—grotesque, if you like—but then have him emerge, in juxtaposition to so-called "normal" individuals, as by far the more human, the more important, and, on a moral plane, the more attractive one. Whatever Pnin is, he certainly is least of all a clown. What I am offering you is a character entirely new to literature—a character important and intensely pathetic—and new characters in literature are not born every day.

Throughout the years I worked at this book, I discarded many vistas that opened before me, abandoned many alluring but unneccessary sub-plots and generally pared my material to the bone, eliminating everything that was not strictly justified in the light of art. I am saying this in order to stress with absolute finality that I cannot tamper with either the plot or the construction of the thing.

To be specific:

1. There is no confusion about Pnin's addresses, and I can send you a complete consecutive list of them.
2. The beginning of Ch.3, you say, anticipates Ch.2, but then goes beyond it. Why should it not?
3. We can't know more about Victor. By the end of the book he is fifteen, and is in Italy with his mother.
4. By the end of the "summer camp" chapter every bit of meaning has been squeezed out of it.
5. If you turn to p.161, you'll find the mangy little dog introduced for the very purpose of having him exit from Waindell in Pnin's car and exchange glances with the cocker whom the "I" of the story has taken along on his morning ramble—while Pnin does not notice his friend.
6. It is an absolute necessity for me to concentrate on Victor in Ch. 4, and to introduce "myself" in Ch.7.

On the other hand, I shall be glad to submit to you a complete calendar of Pnin's life (I have one), a list of his consecutive addresses and any other information you may want. I shall be glad to eliminate unnecessary repetitions, if any, and to correct all slips of grammar or punctuation.

Only one major change is possible: I have in my MS an alternate ending for Ch. 6—two paragraphs that take the place of the passage wherein Pnin writes his letter to Hagen. Both endings are equally satisfying to me. I sent you the one that seemed more amusing, but you can have your choice.

One more consideration. You seem to regret that the book is, as you put it, "not a novel". I do not know if it is or not. According to popular definitions, the main thing it seems to lack is length. What is a novel? Is Sterne's Sentimental Journey Through France a novel? Is Proust's Sentimental Journey Through Time a novel? I do not know. All I know is that PNIN is not a collection of sketches. I do not write sketches. But must we pigeonhole him into any kind of category?

I would like to have your reaction to this letter before I go into further details. If you would like me to come to New York to discuss the matter *viva voce*, I could do so in the first half of October. I shall be glad to consider any minor details that may bother you, but unless you can publish the book as it is please feel free to reject it—though, of course, I would very much regret this.

Cordially yours,
Vladimir Nabokov

I am still recovering from a severe attack of lumbago and am dictating this letter to my wife.

1. On 22 September Covici wrote to VN proposing a reduction in the advance for *Pnin* and explaining that Viking's decision to publish the volume would be contingent upon VN's agreement to perform further work on the material.

TO: **PASCAL COVICI**                    CC, I p.

> Goldwin Smith Hall
> Cornell University
> Ithaca, NY.
> October 29, 1955

Dear Pat,

Many thanks for your letter. I will be glad to come and have lunch with you, Malcolm Cowley and Marshall Best, if you think I can convince you and them that adding anything whatsoever to my book would mean padding (and therefore spoiling) it. Before we meet, I would like to know if you would still want the book under these circumstances. If you do, I will be glad to come and discuss any details that seem repetitive or not clear to you (though I may ask you to pay my traveling expenses).

On the other hand, if you are convinced that the book needs major alteration and that without it you would rather not publish it, please do me the favor to say so quite frankly and without further ado, and we shall cancel the agreement, and remain good friends. And I shall, of course, reimburse you.[1]

With kindest regards,

> Sincerely,
> Vladimir Nabokov

---

1. On 23 November Covici informed VN that Viking had decided it would be a disservice to VN to publish *Pnin*.

TO: **KATHARINE A. WHITE**                    CC, I p.
                                        Ithaca, N.Y.

                                        24 November 1955

Dear Katharine,

Your decision has distressed me[1] I look back at our cloudless association and it is most painful to think that it will be different from now on. Your kindness, your gentleness and understanding have always meant so much to me. On the other hand, I cannot help realizing that the pace and concentration of your work must have claimed sacrifices and involved a strain that could not be kept up for ever.

It was a great pleasure for both of us to see you in the halls of the New Yorker. We cherish your personal friendship and look forward to many happy meetings with you.

I thank you for promising me your continued sympathy and support in the New Yorker. To my regret, I don't think I can have anything to show you in the course of the next six weeks, since I am working fiercely on the last batch of commentaries for my "Eugene Onegin".

I shall make it a point to let you know well in advance of a possible visit to New York so that we might have the opportunity to discuss any matter in which I might be of use to you. I suspect that I may be coming to New York in the course of the winter either in connection with my books or to make a record of "Onegin" that I promised to the BBC.

Our love to both of you.

Yours ever,

1. Mrs. White had retired as fiction and verse editor, although she remained on the *New Yorker* staff.

TO: **CASS CANFIELD**[1]  cc, 1 p.

Ithaca, N.Y.

8 December 1955

Dear Mr. Canfield,

I am glad to show you my book on Pnin. Please note that it is not a novel in any routine sense. It is a short book—180 pages (typescript), divided into seven chapters, four of which (Chapters One, Three, Four and Six) have appeared in the New Yorker.

Each of the seven chapters is concerned with a separate incident in Pnin's life at Waindell College, until he is fired. All these chapters, although slanted and illumined differently, fuse to form a definite unity at the end.

In Pnin, I have created an entirely new character, the like of which has never appeared in any other book. A man of great moral courage, a pure man, a scholar and a staunch friend, serenely wise, faithful to a single love, he never descends from a high plane of life characterized by authenticity and integrity. But handicapped and hemmed in by his incapability to learn a language, he seems a figure of fun to many an average intellectual, and it takes a Clements or a Joan Clements to break through Pnin's fantastic husk and get at his tender and lovable core. It is this combination of the grotesque and the gentle that makes him so pleasingly bizarre. And this is also what apparently endeared him so much to the readers of the New Yorker. I have never had so much fan mail from readers with my other stories as I had with the four Pnin chapters.

There is an intricate interplay in recurrence of themes throughout the book that can be appreciated only if read carefully. I hope you will read MY POOR PNIN yourself; or, if it must be read by some of your readers, that you will pick some sensitive and intelligent people for this task.

From the response the published chapters have had so far, I am convinced that this book may have a bright commercial success, if launched properly.

Sincerely yours,
Vladimir Nabokov

1. President of Harper & Brothers.

TO: **KIRILL NABOKOV**                                ALS, I p.
                                                 Cambridge, Mass.

                                                29 February 1956

*Dorogoy* Kirill,

It was most kind of you to send me those viatic details and amiable suggestions. Various (tedious) considerations have made us postpone the trip [to Europe]—till next summer, at least. We shall probably go to California in April to hunt butterflies.

Your remarks concerning LOLITA are by far the most intelligent and artistic ones yet made about the poor child.

Dmitri finished Harvard last year, and stands over 6′5″ in his socks. He has an admirable bass voice and an MG racing car.

We are staying here for another month, so as to be near the Harvard Library. I am finishing a huge book on EUGENE ONEGIN. My Russian stories are to be published next month by the Chekhov Publ. House, and the French translation of my memoirs is coming out in Paris sometime in autumn.

Was it November?—yes, I think it was November last year: in the course of a polemic Russian exchange in *Novoe Russkoe Slovo*[1] involving Yanovski, Marc Slonim and Kuskova,[2] you were mentioned as one of the gifted poets of the Prague group in the old days. Have you written anything lately?

*Sincères amitiès* to both of you from us both.

                                                   *Tvoy* V.


PS. We shall remain here for another month but my permanent address remains (please note): Goldwin Smith Hall, Cornell University (not Campbell) Ithaca (not Itaca), NY.

1. *The New Russian Word*, Russian-language New York daily.
2. Yuriy Yanovsky, Ukrainian short-story writer and novelist; Marc Slonim, critic, editor, and educator; Ekaterina Kuskova, well-known political personality before the Revolution.

TO: MORRIS BISHOP    TLS, 1 p. Mrs. Morris Bishop.

16 Chauncy St.
Cambridge
6 March 1956

Dear Morris,

It was a pleasure to receive your letter and that drab little view of Nice 1906. Thanks also for depositing the check. We hope to see both of you here. In a few minutes we are setting out for New York, where I shall make to-morrow a recording of "ONEGIN", Canto One, for the BBC's Third Program. We plan to be back Thursday night.

I have just learned that Gallimard wants to publish LOLITA. This will give her a respectable address. The book is having some success in London and Paris. Please, cher ami, do read it to the end!

Frankly, I am not much concerned with the "irate Paterfamilias". That stuffy philistine would be just as upset if he learned that at Cornell I analyze "ULYSSES" before a class of 250 students of both sexes. I know that LOLITA is my best book so far. I calmly lean on my conviction that it is a serious work of art, and that no court could prove it to be "lewd and libertine". All categories grade, of course, into one another: a comedy of manners written by a fine poet may have its "lewd" side; but "LOLITA" is a tragedy. "Pornography" is not an image plucked out of context; pornography is an attitude and an intention. The tragic and the obscene exclude each other.

You know all this as well as I do—I am just jotting down these remarks at random because you happened to conjure up the possibility of an attack.

We are both very much interested in Alison's[1] exhibition. You will have to tell us all about it.

Best love to all three of you.

V

1. Bishop's wife.

TO: PASCAL COVICI                                     CC, 1 p.

I am on sabbatical leave and shall stay at Cambridge until mid-April, after which I shall go to California until fall.

16 Chauncy Street
Cambridge, Mass.
29 March 1956

Dear Pat,

Thanks for your kindly letter.[1] I do not think there is any cause for concern. LOLITA is doing very well. I have already signed a contract with Gallimard for the French rights, and a large piece of it will appear in the Nouvelle Revue Française. There is a good chance, moreover, of its being published in this country.

As a friend and one of the few people who have read the book, you will, I am sure, slap down such rumormongers as contend that the book is pornographic. I know that LOLITA is my best book so far. Calmly I lean on my conviction that it is a serious work of art, and that no court could prove it to be "lewd and libertine". All categories grade, of course, into one another: a comedy of manners written by a fine poet, or a satirical poem in the genre of Pushkin's "Gavriliad", may have its "lewd" side; but LOLITA is a tragedy. Pornography is not an image plucked out of context. Pornography is an attitude and an intention. The tragic and the obscene exclude one another.

I don't say anything about PNIN but may have something to tell about him another time.

As ever,
Vladimir Nabokov

1. On 23 March Covici wrote expressing concern about the effect *Lolita* might have on VN's Cornell position.

TO: **JASON EPSTEIN**

cc, 1 p.

Mt. Carmel, Utah
May 25, 1956

Dear Mr. Epstein,

Your letter of May 3 has caught up with me at the above address. I expect to remain here for about two months.

The translation of "A Hero of Our Times" is practically finished. I am going over it now and expect to have it retyped for you by July. It is going to be the first exact translation of this curious book. When the typescript is ready, I shall confer with you about a few brief notes to the translation.

I shall have completed my "Eugene Onegin" by September.

I shall be glad to enter into an agreement with you concerning a translation (with a few commentaries essential for students) of *Anna Karenin*. It would be based in the main on the Garnett version, with all the blunders corrected, and with all the images and special Tolstoyan locutions faithfully restored. Let me know your reaction to this plan.

Let me confess that your suggestion about a book on butterflies appeals to me tremendously. It would contain my adventures with leps in various countries, especially in the Rocky Mountains states, the discovery of new species, and the description of some fantastic cases of adaptation. I think I could achieve a perfect blend of science, art and entertainment.

My wife and I have rented a beautiful little cottage here, in a strategic position between the Grand Canyon, Sion and Bryce National Parks. We plan to move to Maine in about two months: Dmitri has a singing engagement with the Arundel Company in Kennebunk Port.

Best regards from both of us.

Sincerely,
Vladimir Nabokov

P.S. Viking, after long consideration, has turned down my "My Poor Pnin", claiming it is not a novel—which is right. I claim it is a complete work, whatever label be attached to it. Would you like to have a look at it? About half of it appeared in the "New Yorker".[1]

1. *Pnin* was published by Doubleday in 1957. The last sentence of the P.S. is in holograph.

TO: **JASON EPSTEIN**                                                    CC, 1 p.

Mt. Carmel, Utah
June 13, 1956

Dear Mr. Epstein,

Many thanks for your friendly letter and kind suggestions.

A couple of days ago I shipped to you MY POOR PNIN. In case you decide not to publish it, could you please keep the MS until I return East.

I want to ask you to allow me a little more time for pondering the butterfly book.[1] Your conditions suit me; but before definitely committing myself I would like to evolve a precise plan for the book and can only do so after Lermontov is out of the way. When I get back to Cornell, where my papers are, I shall show you some of my own drawings illustrating my theories regarding wing patterns in butterflies.

Any arrangement regarding the repayment of the $750 will be, of course, acceptable.

Regarding A HERO OF OUR TIMES: I shall need a few notes to explain certain geographical, ethnological, and historical allusions. I would like also to write a short introduction—four or five typescript pages—explaining some peculiarities of Lermontov's style and drawing the reader's attention to the structure of the work.

I am faced with one little difficulty. The translation is based on the Soviet edition "Gosizdat Hudozhestvennoy Literaturi", Moskva,

1951, 135 pp., and it is absolutely necessary to have this text checked against the edition of Lermontov (Complete Works) published by "Academia" in 1936–1937. The HERO is in vol. 5 of this edition. The Cornell Library does not have this edition, and I think it is difficult to obtain. I wonder if you could help me in this. If you cannot obtain it at the Four Continents or Mrs. Rosen's, perhaps you could borrow it for me at the NY. Public Library or Columbia? I would not need to keep it for more than ten days or so. If I could get it by July 1, I would be finished with it before leaving Mt. Carmel. Or I might check the text later, in the proofs. I am delighted you liked my poor Lolita.[2]

Yours,
Vladimir Nabokov

1. The project was dropped.
2. The last two sentences are in holograph.

TO: HENRY ALLEN MOE                                                    CC, 1 p.

Goldwin Smith Hall
Cornell University
Ithaca, NY.
September 24, 1956

Dear Mr. Moe,

Indeed, I have an excellent candidate for a Guggenheim Fellowship. Her name is Sylvia Berkman. She teaches literature at Wellesley College. She has published a biography of Katherine Mansfield and a number of very good stories in Harper's Bazaar and Botteghe Oscure. Her work is subtle and of real literary value. But she is a writer who makes great demands of herself and therefore her work is time-consuming. She finds it almost impossible to combine writing with teaching and has so far been able to persuade the college to allow her to teach on a half-yearly basis, devoting the other half of the year to writing. The very quality of her work makes it difficult for her to make a living by writing alone. I am convinced that one whole year of security, devoted exclusively to creative writing, may result in a valuable book.

My other suggestion is in the nature of a query. Would you consider awarding a *third* fellowship to a split personality, Twiddledee and Twiddledum in one, or better say a Dr. Jekyll and Mr. Hyde combined, one half writer, the other half entomologist? I have written the better part of a novel ("Bend Sinister") and a considerable part of a book on Pushkin's "Eugene Onegin", including a translation of the work, on two Guggenheim awards, in 1943 and in 1953, respectively. The Pushkin book has suffered some delays since then but will be ready for publication by Christmas.

On the other hand, I have devoted many years to entomological research and am the author of several monographs and papers on Lepidoptera, a list of which I attach to this letter. I have completely re-classified a group of Lycaenidae (as you can see from "A Field Guide to the Butterflies of North America" by Alexander B. Klots, of the City College of New York and the American Museum of Natural History). I have described and named a number of species and subspecies, and other scientists have named lepidoptera after me.

For several summers now I have been studying the lepidopterous fauna of the Rocky Mts. To complete these studies, I would need to examine certain collections, both in America and Europe, and then do some laboratory work. I might add that for six years I have been a Research Fellow in Entomology on the staff of the Muscum of Comparative Zoology, Harvard.[1]

Sincerely yours,
Vladimir Nabokov

1. VN did not receive the grant.

TO: JASON EPSTEIN                                          CC, 2 pp.

Ithaca, N.Y.

1 October 1956

Dear Mr. Epstein,

I have just received the sketches. They are executed with talent, the picture as art goes is first-rate, but in regard to my Pnin it is wrong: The sketch looks like the portrait of an underpaid instructor in the English department or like a Republican's notion of a defeated Adlai, when actually he should look like a Russian muzhik clean-shaven. I am sending you some photographs of Pnin-like Russians, with and without hair, for a visual appreciation of the items I am going to discuss.

1. The head should look quite bald, without any dark margin, and must be ampler, rounder, smoother, more dome-like. Note Zhavoronkov and Yegorov for the type of head, which however should be bigger in Pnin's case, not egg-shaped. Maslov would be perfect, minus hair.

2. The glasses should be definitely tortoise-shell ones, with heavier, somewhat squarish frames.

3. The nose is very important. It should be the Russian potato nose, fat and broad, with prominent nostril curves. See Zhukovski for nostrils, and Obrastsov for a replica of Pnin's fat glossy organ; but Pavlov and Maslov are also good.

4. The terribly important space between nose and upper lip. This must be simian, large, long, with a central hollow and lateral furrows. See Zhavoronkov, Baykov, Yegorov, Zhukovski. The latter's lips are very Pninian. Pnin's bad teeth should not show.

5. The cheeks and jowls. Jowls and jaw should be large, broad, massive. See Baykov, Zhavoronkov, Yegorov.

6. The shoulders should be very broad, square, padded. Pnin wears a ready-made American suit of four years age.

7. The tie should be a flamboyant one.

Now, instead of all this, the sketches show a puny professor Milksop, with an egg-shaped face, flat nose, short upper lip, non-descript chin, sloping shoulders, and the necktie of a comedy bookkeeper. I have noticed long ago that for some reason illustrators do not read the books they illustrate. In my book, all the details listed above are mentioned in the first chapter, and repeated further on.

The lettering, title and name, is very handsome in both sketches. The larger one is perhaps more pleasing.

Splendid idea to have Pnin hold a book. The title on the book he holds should read

## ПНИН
### В.НАБОКОВ[1]

I shall certainly not make any arrangements for LOLITA in this country before discussing them with you. Everything you have done for LOLITA until now delights me. I hope you will publish the thing in its entirety some day.[2]

I approve in advance whatever selection you make for the *Anchor Review*.[3] It might be difficult for me to help there since in my mind I see the book as a whole.

We shall arrive in New York on Monday, the 15th, in the evening, and would like to see you on the 16th (any time is convenient) or on the 17th (evening only). We shall leave early on the 18th. It would be helpful if you could let me know now what is your preference, for I would like to plan the rest of my stay.

Yes, I have met Fred Dupee, though not in the Partisan Review, but years ago on a little peak in Darien.

The signed agreements must have reached you by now.

Sincerely yours,
Vladimir Nabokov

1. PNIN/V. NABOKOV. The Russian words were added in VN's hand.
2. "There was considerable enthusiasm among the Doubleday editors for *Lolita*, though we were all apprehensive about possible legal consequences. As I recall, Ken McCormick, the editor-in-chief at the time, would have agreed to publish it if Douglas Black, the president of the company, authorized it. But Black was so strongly opposed that he refused even to read the manuscript." Jason Epstein to Sally Dennison, 23 February 1982; Dennison, *(Alternative) Literary Publishing* (Iowa City: University of Iowa Press, 1984), p. 175.
3. The June 1957 issue of *The Anchor Review* (Doubleday) included an excerpt from *Lolita* and articles about the novel by VN and F. W. Dupee.

TO: **HOWARD NEMEROV**[1]

CC, 1 p.
Ithaca, N.Y.

November 9, 1956

Dear Mr. Nemerov,

A correspondent has sent me a clipping—your delightful letter in a recent issue of the N.Y. Times. I think it is a very friendly and gallant gesture on your part. I wish I could send you a copy of "Lolita" but I too find it difficult to obtain copies. I have never been officially notified, however, that the book has been actually banned. You would do me a great favor if you could give me additional details.

Cordially yours,

1. Poet, then on the faculty of Bennington College. Nemerov's letter published in the 30 October *New York Times* protested against the ban on importation of *Lolita* into the United States. The Olympia Press *Lolita* was not banned from the United States. Two copies were confiscated by U.S. Customs in 1956 but subsequently released. Thereafter the novel was legally circulated here. See Maurice Girodias, "A Sad, Ungraceful History of *Lolita*," *The Olympia Reader*, ed. Girodias (New York: Grove, 1965).

TO: **JASON EPSTEIN**

CC, 1 p.

Goldwin Smith Hall
Cornell University
Ithaca, NY.
13 November 1956

Dear Jason,

Véra and I thank you for your letter. The jacket is absolutely splendid—I never imagined that an illustrator could render an author's vision so accurately.[1] I am afraid I was a little bitter about the preliminary sketch.

Thanks for the Nemerov letter. He is a gifted author and his sympathy was very welcome. I do not know him personally but I have a pleasant image of him.

Mrs. K.N. Rosen, bookseller, of 410 Riverside Drive, has just sent me a clipping, presumably from a trade publication, from which I quote:

"OLYMPIA PRESS BANNED TITLES

"Practically all English titles printed by Olympia Press in "Paris (sorry, we cannot give the address) have been banned "in England and America. Latest to be banned by U.S. Customs "is 'Lolita', a new novel by Vladimir Nabokov, which was "called 'one of the best novels in 1955' by Graham Greene "in *The Sunday Times*."

Do you think you could do without any quotations from Edmund?[2] He never wrote anything of value about me except in the case of "Sebastian Knight" his misinterpretation of which he greatly admired. We are very close friends, I admire and respect him greatly, but it is not a friendship based on a similarity of opinions and approaches.

Our best regards to Barbara and you.

Sincerely,

1. *Pnin*.
2. Edmund Wilson.

TO: **MAURICE GIRODIAS**                                        CC, 1 p.

Goldwin Smith Hall
Cornell University
Ithaca, NY.
November 15, 1956

Dear Mr. Girodias,

I thank you for your kind letter of November 12 with the promise not to dispose of the English-language rights of LOLITA without my written consent.

I was interested to learn that the US. Customs seems to have nothing against the book. If this situation endures, we shall probably have no trouble to find an American publisher for a new edition to be made here.

You go on to say that you intend to advertise and distribute the book in the US. I most earnestly entreat you to abstain from any such action. Please, read carefully the reason which compells me to do so.

The book is protected by an "Ad Interim" copyright only. This affords protection for five years, provided not more than 1500 copies of the book are entered into the US. Should you import more than this number of copies, the protection becomes void, both you and the author lose all rights in the book, and anyone can publish and sell it at will. As I have tried to explain before, this situation stems from the fact that I am an American citizen residing in the US. A book by such an author, if published abroad, can only be protected by a temporary (5-year) copyright, and not more than 1500 copies of such an edition can be imported at any time. A regular 28-year copyright can be substituted for the temporary one, if, within 5 years from date of original publication, a new edition is manufactured and published inside the US. This edition must be manufactured by American labor. This law is an outgrowth of the elaborate legislation protecting American labor against foreign competition. It is a rigid law and there is nothing that can be done about it. The five-year copyright is given only as a temporary protection between original publication and the bringing out of an American edition. The 1500 copies limit cannot be extended. If we exceed it, we lose all protection. Please check on this at the American Consulate in Paris if you wish any additional clarification. But by all means do so before you undertake anything to step up the importation of the book into the US.

Sincerely yours,

TO: JASON EPSTEIN                                              CC, 1 p.

Goldwin Smith Hall
Cornell University
Ithaca, NY.
20 November 1956

Dear Jason,

Thanks for sending the LOLITA excerpts and the Dupee article. At first glance, it all looks fine. I shall devote more time to this matter during the Thanksgiving vacation. You will have it all back early next week.

Would the $400 honorarium cover both excerpts and article? If so, I would accept $200 for the excerpts and $200 (or more) for the article.[1] I am writing to Paris to make sure that they won't mind my signing the agreement with the Anchor Review for the reprint of the LOLITA pieces. I think it will be all right and you can prepare the agreement. Send me an extra copy, if possible, so that I can send it to my agent for Olympia.

The two PNIN notes will also be returned to you within a few days now. It is a pity I cannot come to New York at this time. I shall regret having missed meeting my English publisher. Véra and I would be delighted if he decided to come to Ithaca.

It never occurred to me that you might want to use a particular comment by Edmund (I was thinking of an entirely different one).[2] This is a general appraisal, and a very warm and kind one, and I have no objection whatsoever if you think it appropriate for use in the present occasion. You might want to skip the reference to Conrad, since he did not start upon his literary career in his native (Polish) language (as I did, in Russian).

Yes, I too liked the photograph of Edmund in the Book Review. We spent a delightful afternoon with him and Elena in Talcotville.

Take all the time you want with the Lermontov notes. In the meantime I have thought of another short novel I would like to translate for you sometime, "The Blackamoor of Peter the Great" by his great-grandson, Aleksandr Pushkin, with a fifty-page biography of that Moor.

I am sending you under separate cover the French translation of my novel "Lujin's Defense" ("La Course du Fou") which I have just received from Paris. The French edition is out of print, so I would like this copy back after you have read it.

I read with great interest what you had to say about the Anchor Review issue. It sounds wonderful.

Sincerely
Vladimir Nabokov

1. "On a Book Entitled Lolita," *Anchor Review*, #2 (New York: Doubleday, 1957).
2. ... [Nabokov] turns out to be a master of English prose ... the most extraordinary phenomenon of the kind since Conrad. ... [He is] something like Proust, something like Franz Kafka, and, probably, something like Gogol ... [but he] is as completely himself as any of these other writers...." Edmund Wilson

TO: **MAURICE GIRODIAS**

CC, 1 p.
Ithaca, N.Y.

December 14, 1956

Dear Mr. Girodias,

I thank you for your letter of November 20th. I would have answered sooner but I wanted to obtain the opinion of some literary friends in New York with regard to your plans.

I can give you no guarantee, but the general opinion is that you will have no difficulty in disposing in this country of your quota of 1500 copies (or whatever remains of this quota) at, say, $10 a copy.

If you intend to make any publicity, would you let me see and approve your copy, as well as the list of publications in which you plan to advertise?

You and I understand perfectly well that LOLITA is not the kind of book that should appeal to the kind of people you euphemistically call "amateurs". In fact, my friends here are waging an intensive campaign to establish the book as a literary achievement of artistic value and lasting importance, and to counteract the unfortunate publicity it received at the outset. Only after this has been achieved can one hope to have LOLITA published in this country.

As you know, some good reviews have already appeared in The Partisan Review and The Hudson Review.[1] As you also know, lengthy excerpts will be published in The Anchor Review, which is to appear in early June. These excerpts will be accompanied by a wonderful article written by a well-known literary critic, F. Dupee, who thinks very highly of LOLITA. On my part, I am contributing to the same issue of The Anchor Review an essay explaining the author's point of view. Everybody recommends caution in selecting the right kind of publicity for your campaign.

Within a few days I shall be writing Mme Ergaz on some other aspects of the question and shall ask her to communicate with you.

There is something else I would like to mention: I have received no statement of accounts from you on either of the two dates on which they were due. I would appreciate receiving one now.

Sincerely yours,
Vladimir Nabokov

1. John Hollander, "The Perilous Magic of Nymphets," *Partisan Review* (Fall 1956); Louis Simpson, "Fiction Chronicle," *Hudson Review* (Summer 1956).

TO: **GRAHAM GREENE**                                   CC, I p.
Ithaca, N.Y.

31 December 1956

Dear Mr. Greene,

From various friends I keep receiving heart-warming reports on your kindness to my books. This is New Year's Eve, and I feel I would like to talk to you.

My poor Lolita is having a rough time. The pity is that if I had made her a boy, or a cow, or a bicycle, Philistines might never have flinched. On the other hand, Olympia Press informs me that amateurs (amateurs!) are disappointed with the tame turn my story takes in the second volume, and do not buy it. I have been sent copies of the article, in which, about a year ago, a Mr. Gordon[1] with your witty assistance made such a fool of himself. It would seem, however, that a clean vulgar mind makes Gordon's wonderfully strong, for my French agent tells me that the book (the English original) is now banned by governmental decree in France. She says: "La réponse de James Gordon à l'article de M. Graham Greene a indigné certains puritains et ... c'est le Gouvernement anglais qui a demandé au Ministre de l'Intérieur (of France) de prendre cette décision."

This is an extraordinary situation. I could patter on like this till next year. Wishing you a very happy New one, I remain,

Yours very sincerely,

1. In response to Greene's listing the Olympia *Lolita* as one of the best books of 1955, John Gordon, chief editor of the *London Sunday Express*, pronounced it "about the filthiest book I've ever read," setting off a Greene-Gordon feud and fueling the campaign to ban the book in England. It was not banned.

On 17 June 1957 Max Reinhardt, Managing Director of The Bodley Head, wrote VN at Greene's recommendation requesting an option to publish *Lolita* in England in two or three years. The delay was necessitated by a new obscenity bill pending in Parliament.

FROM: **GRAHAM GREENE**                                      ALS, 1 p.
January 1957

Thank you very much. I thought Lollita a superb book + I am now, as a director of a publishing firm in England, trying to arrange its publication. In England one may go to prison, but there couldn't be a better cause!

Graham Greene

то: **Katharine A. White**  CC, I p.

Goldwin Smith Hall
Cornell, Ithaca, NY.
February 5, 1957

Dear Katharine,

Here is a little note for The New Yorker. I shall send you my ballad in the course of this week. Many thanks for your charming letter.

Department of Mimicry

In The New Yorker of February 23, 1957, page 31, Mr. Hellman writes that if the two butterflies he mentions, a skipper and a Lycaenid (the correct genus of this "shasta comstocki" is by the way *Icaricia* Nabokov, 1944), are not named after John Henry Comstock, Professor of Entomology in Cornell University, he will eat his cyanide jar. Since these butterflies are named after Dr. John A. Comstock, renowned for his excellent work in the life history of Californian lepidoptera, I can only hope that Mr. Hellman's jar is not loaded. Incidentally, pinching the thorax is a much simpler way of dispatching a butterfly.[1]

I hope you are enjoying Florida.

Sincerely,
Vladimir Nabokov

1. Unpublished.

то: **Maurice Girodias**  CC, I p.

Goldwin Smith Hall
Cornell, Ithaca, NY., USA.
February 12th, 1957

Dear Mr. Girodias,

Many thanks for your interesting letter and enclosures. I am following the developments of the case with keen interest. Apart from my personal involvement I can also sympathize with your predicament and the injustice of which you are the victim.

I very much regret that I lack the funds to attack the ban independently, as you suggest. I simply do not make enough money with my books to permit such action, much as I would like to undertake it. Apart from this, I wish to give you every assistance in your campaign. You may use in your pamphlet, described in your letter of February 8, my essay written for Doubleday's Review.[1] I have also obtained from them the permission to use in your pamphlet Prof. Dupee's article on LOLITA.[2] I am sending you enclosed both pieces. Doubleday were at first opposed to allowing Dupee's article to be used and they consider it a favor that they have finally agreed to have you use it. Of course, we assume that both pieces will be used in a French translation only.

I have no objections to your using in your pamphlet parts of the French translation of LOLITA provided Gallimard agrees to this. I would very much prefer if you did not stress too much my being a professor at Cornell. I am a writer primarily, and this is the important point. I do not mind being referred to as "university professor teaching literature in a great American university". But I would prefer you not to call Cornell by name.

I am enclosing photographs. Return them after use, if this is possible. You will also find enclosed a short curriculum vitae and a list of my published works both of which you may use at your discretion.

I hope you will let me have two copies of your pamphlet,[3] one for me, the other for Doubleday.

Wishing you success in this struggle for a just cause,

Sincerely yours,

1. "On a Book Entitled *Lolita*," *The Anchor Review*, #2 (1957), 105–112.
2. F.W. Dupee, "A Preface to *Lolita*," *Anchor Review*, #2 (1957), 1–14.
3. *L'Affaire Lolita* (Paris: Olympia Press, 1957).

TO: **KATHARINE A. WHITE**                          CC, 1 p.

Goldwin Smith Hall
Cornell, Ithaca, NY.
February 16, 1957

Dear Katharine,

Thanks for your letter and enclosures. I was sorry to hear of Andy's illness. I hope Florida will do you both a lot of good.

I long to finish my huge Pushkin opus and go back to fiction. That monster has grown far beyond whatever I planned originally but I am glad now that I did not shrink from the task—eight years ago. It is not only going to make "Eugene Onegin" accessible to the foreign reader but will also give the American reader, and the English-reading Russian, a unique and exhaustive work on the subject.

PNIN is about to come out. In fact, I have already received an advance copy from Doubleday. The date is March 7.

I am sorry you never read the LOLITA I sent you. Fascinating things have been happening to it in France. The British Home Secretary begged the French Ministre de l'Intérieur to help him look after the morals of the British tourists by prohibiting 25 books published by The Olympia Press (LOLITA included). The French Minister obliged invoking, in the absence of a suitable law, the law against subversive political publications(!). Taking advantage of this, The Olympia Press instituted action against the Minister's decree. And the French press went wild over this attempt against the freedoms. They make a special case for LOLITA, "le célèbre roman de Vladimir Nabokov". They refer to the whole thing as "l'affaire LOLITA", and Gallimard will have it out within a couple of months. Of course, the ban is only for the English-language edition published in France. With the exception of The Daily News(!) American periodicals ignore the whole business.

I am sending you for a second look a little ballad you turned down in 1953.[1] I still think it is one of the best things I ever wrote. On second thought—tell me first if I may send it again.

If I find any potential New Yorker contributors in my classes, I shall tell them to go ahead and shall advise you of my discovery.

Véra joins me in sending you both our very kind regards.

Yours,
Vladimir Nabokov

1. "The Ballad of Longwood Glen." The following sentence is in holograph.

TO: **HOWARD NEMEROV**                                                        CC, 1 p.
Ithaca, N.Y.

February 18, 1957

Dear Mr. Nemerov,

I have just read with great interest and enjoyment your novel *The Homecoming Game*.

It is a full of true wit, and its structure—the intricate and satisfying interlacings of themes—is admirable. I missed a little description of the football game, which was a kind of *scène à faire*, but on second thought its omission is subtle.

May I draw your attention to the fact that your man is called "Asher" two or three times by his interlocutors?

It was so very kind of you to send me your book. I hope to have the opportunity of having a good chat with you some day.

Sincerely yours,
Vladimir Nabokov

TO: **JASON EPSTEIN**                                        CC, 1 p.

Goldwin Smith Hall
Cornell, Ithaca, NY.
February 20, 1957
I have received from Philadelphia
six more handsome PNINS

Dear Jason,

Would you be willing to advise me on a rather puzzling affair. Girodias (Olympia Press) wants me to sue the French government on account of LOLITA. He thinks it will help his own action if I join the fray. He rather bluntly states that matters would be helped by showing to the judges that "the author of Lolita is an absolutely honorable and authentic writer" and by having "respectability, responsibility and good manners" represented in the affair.

I do not expect to win the "heavy damages" he wants me to sue for. Neither can I lose (financially, that is) since Girodias offers to assume all expenses which will be reimbursable to him only in case I win.

I am rather loath of exposing myself in the company of The Olympia Press. But I am also rather at a loss to find a point of view from which to consider the whole thing.

I have to take into account the fact that so far Cornell has been very tolerant. The matter simply has not been discussed, and no questions have been asked. But might not matters be made worse if I start a litigation, and possibly lose it?

On the other hand, I wish, of course, to give every possible support to Olympia, though personally I do not care if the ban will be lifted or not, since Gallimard is going to publish the French translation anyway.

I would be very grateful if you gave me your opinion on the various aspects of the affair. I trust your judgment, and do not know anyone else whom I would like as much to consult. I hope this will not be too much trouble.[1]

Girodias is very happy about Dupee's article and my material. He is going to publish, he says, 2000–2500 copies (he mentioned 500 in his previous letter) and sell 1000 numbered copies to defray the costs. Gallimard has agreed to allow him to include excerpts from LOLITA.

Girodias is going to distribute the rest of his pamphlets gratis. Do you have any suggestions to whom he should send copies in this country? He asks me this.

Many thanks for the Lermontov.

Sincerely,
Vladimir Nabokov

1. On 25 February 1957 Epstein advised VN against initiating the suit and urged him to remain aloof from the legal question until it clarified itself.

to: **MAURICE GIRODIAS**                    cc, 1 p.

Goldwin Smith Hall
Cornell University
Ithaca, N.Y.
March 1, 1957

Dear Mr. Girodias,

Please excuse me for not having answered sooner your letter of February 16th. Before arriving at a decision with regard to a separate action by me in defense of LOLITA before the French courts, I wanted to hear the opinion of some wise and experienced friends of mine. This involved some correspondence with New York.

I have been advised against taking such action, mainly because of the distance, and because I could not possibly come to Paris in the near future. Perhaps even more important is the consideration that my university might not like the idea.

I thank you for your generous offer to finance the litigation and am sorry it is not possible for me to avail myself of it.

Many thanks for the interesting clippings. Please keep me informed of any further developments.

Here are a few people to whom it would be good to send copies of your brochure on LOLITA:

Jason Epstein, Doubleday & Company, 575 Madison Ave., NY 22, NY

Harvey Breit, NY. Times Book Review, NYC

Mrs. Katharine White, The New Yorker, 25 W. 43 St., NY.36, NY

Bennet Cerf, Saturday Review of Literature, 25 W. 45 St., NY

Edward Weeks, The Atlantic Monthly, 8 Arlington St., Boston, Mass.

Philip Rahv, The Partisan Review, 513 Sixth Ave., NY.11, NY.

Edmund Wilson, 16 Farrar Street, Cambridge, Mass.

Prof. Harry T. Levin, 14 Kirkland Place, Cambridge, Mass.

Bertrand Thompson, Calle Rio Negro 1216, Montevideo, Uruguay

F.W. Dupee, Eliot House F 24, Cambridge 38, Mass.

I shall probably think of other names too. Perhaps you could mail me a few copies so that I can dispose of them as I think best.

Sincerely yours,
Vladimir Nabokov

TO: **JASON EPSTEIN**                                                CC, 1 p.

Goldwin Smith Hall
Cornell, Ithaca, NY.
March 5, 1957

Dear Jason,

We received your letter[1] while I was explaining the arrangement of a sleeping car on the Moscow-Petersburg express train, (in 1872, in connection with Anna Karenin's journey in the first book of the novel which you should some day publish with my notes)—to a class of 146 bored and 4 enthusiastic students.

We came home, had a light lunch, and about half past two received the visit of Mr. Ivan Obolensky from New York.[2] We were in the midst of an animated soliloquy[3] when you telephoned.

His firm is tremendously eager to acquire the American rights of LOLITA at once and to publish it in the course of this spring. Your letter has, of course, cast a chill shadow on my reaction to this plan. On the other hand, I am sure you understand my situation. I only hope they will not make it irresistibly attractive—but they seem to be planning just that.

My experience with Harpers has been disappointing, I am not sure I would consider any offer coming from them. As to Random, I have never had any dealings with them. What I would like best of all, would be to get an offer from you. Two or three weeks will certainly elapse before anything is signed and settled, but Lolita is young, and I am old.

I apologize once again for not having opened your package at once and for causing you all this additional bother.

Now that the hills of Ithaca are blue and silver in the spring sun, when will you and Barbara come and see us here?

I have written to Paris saying I would not sue in "l'affaire Lolita".

Edmund[4] has just written me from Cambridge.

Sincerely,

1. On 1 March Epstein wrote urging VN to seek a long-established American publisher for *Lolita* and advising him to wait until current Supreme Court obscenity cases were settled.
2. Partner in the New York publishing house of McDowell, Obolensky.
3. It is possible that VN meant to write "colloquy." It is also possible he meant, tongue-in-cheek style, that a soliloquy was going on. DN.
4. Wilson.

to: MAURICE GIRODIAS                                    cc, 2 pp.

Goldwin Smith Hall
Cornell University
Ithaca, N.Y., U.S.A.
March 5, 1957

Dear Mr. Girodias,

The possibility has arisen that a new publisher in New York may want to bring out LOLITA.

As you remember, several months ago there had been a considerable interest on the part of several American publishers, none of whom came through with an offer. One of the largest houses in US came close to making an offer, but gave up, partly in fear of unavoidable court proceedings, partly because of your insistence on "a genuine partnership agreement". At the time they wrote refusing to consider such an agreement and saying that in their opinion no serious American publisher would do otherwise.

Moreover, their lawyers warned them that my agreement with Olympia does not establish your right to license an American edition, and that before buying the American rights they would have to insist that this agreement be amended. I did not follow up this matter at the time since that particular firm gave up negotiations anyway, having been put off by all these complicated circumstances and an American edition of LOLITA became, at best, an extremely remote possibility.

I now hear from another firm who wants to make a definite offer and bring out the book without delay.[1] This is a newly created firm, and they seem willing to undertake the risk of litigation, hoping that LOLITA could help them to make a name for themselves. I suggest therefore that you and I attend now to the rewording of our agreement, to avoid delays when their offer arrives.

Please understand me correctly. I quote from a legal opinion obtained on this subject: "It is clear in the contract that Olympia has the exclusive right to sell its version in the English language throughout the world. At the same time, the contract does not specify that

Olympia has the right to license an American edition. According to the agreement, it can sell only its own edition here."

I suggest that we amend our agreement in such a way as to make possible the sale of American rights to an American publisher. Would you send me a new contract or would you like me to send you a draft of such a contract? It would have to comprise a clause authorizing me to dispose of the American rights to our mutual advantage, and stipulating your terms in case I succeed in doing so. Or else you could say that you would be willing to give up your American rights in the book for a consideration, and I suggest that you quote a lump sum and also an alternate arrangement.

Please bear in mind that 1) this is not an old, opulent firm and 2) that we have to create conditions under which an American edition can be brought out, since otherwise you could only bring in 1500 copies of the original edition—after which, by September 1960, the copyright will expire, and the loss will be yours as well as mine.

I hope to hear from you at your earliest convenience.

Sincerely yours,
Vladimir Nabokov

1. McDowell, Obolensky.

TO: **KATHARINE A. WHITE**                              CC, 1 p.

Goldwin Smith Hall
Cornell, Ithaca, NY.
March 6, 1957

Dear Katharine,

I am sending you *The Ballad of Longwood Glen*, which I wrote in 1953.[1] Ever since then I have been reworking it, so that this final product differs considerably from the one which The New Yorker rejected some three years ago. I want to ask you to consider it very carefully. With my usual modesty I maintain it is the best poem I have composed—far superior, for instance, to the *Evening of Russian Poetry*.

At first blush this ballad may look to you like a weird hybrid between Shagall and Grandmother Moses. But please stick to it as long as you can bear, and by degrees all kinds of interesting shades and underwater patterns will be revealed to the persevering eye. If you still hate it, please feel no qualms—just send it back. I hope to have something else, in prose, for you soon.

> Very cordially yours,
> Vladimir Nabokov

Encl.

1. *New Yorker* (6 July 1957).

TO: **JASON EPSTEIN**                                               cc, 1 p.

> Goldwin Smith Hall
> Cornell, Ithaca, N.Y.
> March 10, 1957

Dear Jason,

Your letters are always a delight to me, both in matter and form. As you well know, nothing in the world would please me better than to have Doubleday bring out LOLITA.

I realize the difficulties and dangers you describe if LOLITA were to come out without due preparation. There is one important fact, however, that I am compelled to consider right now. I have been working on my Pushkin for the last two years with fantastic concentration which excluded all other literary pursuits (the only vacation I took was to attend to the Lermontov book). The New Yorker paid me exceedingly well—up to 2500 for every Pnin installment—but I have not had anything to sell since I finished that book. I cannot possibly live on my Cornell salary only. Now comes this unexpected offer from Obolensky. As I intimated to you over the telephone, my reaction to it is not a matter of principle but a matter of money. I am not particularly impressed by his firm but I cannot afford to miss the opportunity of not missing the opportunity to sell the book.

I am delighted about the new plan you adumbrate. I shall not enter into any agreement with Obolensky for a couple of weeks, in the course of which time I hope to have your decision.

Sincerely,
Vladimir Nabokov

TO: MAURICE GIRODIAS

cc, 1 p.
Ithaca, N.Y.

March 10, 1957

Dear Mr. Girodias,

I have carefully read your letter of March 5, wherein you urge me to reconsider my decision in regard to lolitigation.

You say that you fail to understand why Cornell might not like the idea of my intervention etc. To this I would like to say that the fact that my academic standing was introduced into the controversy was very embarrassing to me. I have an established literary reputation on both sides of the ocean, and I published this book as a writer, not as a university professor.

My moral defense of the book is the book itself. I do not feel under any obligation to do more. However, I went further and wrote the essay on LOLITA, a copy of which is now in your hands. On the ethical plane, it is of supreme indifference to me what opinion French, British or any other courts, magistrates, or philistine readers in general, may have of my book. However, I appreciate your difficulties.

Before I can reopen the question of litigation, I would have to have your answer to my letter of March 5. It might influence my decision considerably if you made it possible for me to sell the American rights and the British rights of LOLITA.

Of course, if I did reconsider the question, I would have to have from you a legal document exempting me from any financial responsibility whatever to lawyers and courts in France, even in case Olympia decided to go out of business or any other disaster occurred.

Sincerely yours,
Vladimir Nabokov

TO: **IVAN OBOLENSKY**                                          CC, I p.
                                                        Ithaca, N.Y.

March 23, 1957

Dear Prince Obolensky,

Many thanks for your kind letter. I had planned to go to New York during spring vacation but a bad cold forces me to postpone my trip again. I shall definitely be in New York for a day or two in the middle of April.

I have given much thought to the plans you suggested for LOLITA and have consulted several friends whose opinion I value. I have also been in touch with my publisher in Paris. The unanimous opinion is that this is not the right moment to publish LOLITA in the United States. I am terribly sorry to disappoint you. Here are a few reasons against publication:

1. Everybody seems convinced that LOLITA would be banned if it were to be published now, without further preparation. Even if you are willing to assume the costs of a legal fight which may run into 50.000 or 60.000 dollars, you may eventually lose the case, and then LOLITA would be lost irretrievably.

2. Should the book get into trouble, the NY. Times would at once refuse to advertise it, and every important publication in the country would follow suit. Nor would the Post Office let you announce the book directly through the mails if the legal action were begun under a federal statute.

3. When you suggested that you would get in touch with a reprint house it became clear to me that you did not realize all the implications of this case. Could you visualize LOLITA as a little paperback being offered for sale on the newstands?

Let me repeat that I am terribly sorry that this will be a disappointment to you. But I have become convinced that the publication has to be put off at least until I see how the Anchor Review fares, how the Paris litigation is settled, and what decision the Supreme Court takes in some similar cases now before it.

Sincerely yours,
Vladimir Nabokov

TO: JASON EPSTEIN                                             CC, 1 p.
                                                        Ithaca, N.Y.

I take this opportunity to send                    March 24, 1957
you the envelope of a letter which
has just been forwarded from
Cambridge.

You seem to have at your office
some patriotic Bostonian who refuses to let me leave Cambridge.

Dear Jason,

My main creature, an ex-king, is engaged throughout PALE FIRE in a certain quest. This quest, or research (which at one point, alas, involves some very sophisticated spiritualism), is completely divorced from any so-called faith or religion, gods, God, Heaven, Folklore, etc. At first I thought of entitling my novel THE HAPPY ATHE-IST, but the book is much too poetical and romantic for that (its thrill and poetry I cannot reveal to you in a short and matter-of-fact summary). My creature's quest is centered in the problem of heretofore and hereafter, and it is I may say beautifully solved.

The story starts in Ultima Thule, an insular kingdom, where a palace intrigue and some assistance from Nova Zembla clear the way for a dull and savage revolution. My main creature the King of Thule, is dethroned. After some wonderful adventures he escapes to America. Certain political complications lead President Kennedy to answer evasively when questioned about the displaced personage.

He lives more or less incognito, with the lady he loves, somewhere on the border of Upstate New York and Montario: the border is a little blurry and unstable, but there is a bus to Goldenrod, another to Calendar Barn, and on Sundays the Hudson flows to Colorado. Despite these—on the whole quite innocent—little defocalizations, the locus and life-color are what a real-estate mind would call "realistic", and from the picture window of my creature's house one can see the bright mud of a private road and a leafless tree all at once abloom with a dozen waxwings.

The book is regularly interrupted, without any logical or stylistic transition, right in the middle of a sentence (to be blandly continued a few lines further) by glimpses of an agent, a Mr. Copinsay, from Thule, whose job is to find and destroy the ex-king. Mr. Copinsay, who is of Orkney descent, has some dreadful troubles of his own, and his long journey (through all the drains[1] the book) is full of nightmare difficulties (he gets entangled in a West-Indian cruise at one point). However, he does reach Goldenrod in the final chapter—where a surprise awaits the reader and him.[2]

I am writing this in a hurry, have to correct exams. But I want to add that I am delighted with PNIN's progress.

Yours,

1. The CC reads "drains"; it is impossible to emend this typing error.
2. At this stage of the novel's development, Ultima Thule had been inherited from *Solus Rex*, a novel Nabokov was writing in France at the outbreak of World War II, and never completed. Two chapters from it, entitled "Ultima Thule" and "Solus Rex," were published in Russian journals in the early 1940s and later appeared in *A Russian Beauty* (1973). When *Pale Fire* was published by Putnam in 1962, its loci, characters, and themes had gone through many stages of evolution, and the structure of the novel had assumed a different and totally original form: All the real or imagined events of the Kingdom of Zembla and the story of its ex-monarch are contained in a presumably mad commentator's notes to a 999-line poem composed for the occasion by an invented poet. DN.

TO: **PROF. MARK SCHORER**[1]  CC, I p.

Goldwin Smith Hall
Cornell, Ithaca, NY.
March 24, 1957

Dear Schorer,

I shall be glad to make my contribution to the D.H. Lawrence Fellowship Fund, although, between you and me, I dislike Lawrence as a writer and detest Taos, where, in 1954, I had the misfortune of establishing my headquarters when collecting butterflies in the N. Mexico mountains.

I would like you to know how much I appreciated your eyespot on Pnin's underwing.

Véra and I remember with pleasure our meetings with you and your wife in Cambridge.

Sincerely yours,
Vladimir Nabokov

1. Department of English, University of California, Berkeley.

TO: **ROBERT HATCH**[1]  CC, I p.

Goldwin Smith Hall
Cornell University
Ithaca, New York
March 29, 1957

Dear Mr. Hatch,

I would have gladly demolished this fraud if I had time but unfortunately I haven't. This NOT BY BREAD ALONE[2] is something on the lines of a third-rate Upton Sinclair book and has no literary value whatsoever. I am not interested in the political or publicistic side of novels.

Sincerely yours,
Vladimir Nabokov

1. Editor at *The Nation*.
2. By Mark Dudintsev.

TO: **KATHARINE A. WHITE**          CC, 1 p.
Ithaca, N.Y.

April 4, 1957

Dear Katharine,

I am delighted you want my little ballad. Yes, of course, couldn't is better rhythmically than could not.

Let me thank you very warmly for your frank and charming letter about LOLITA. But after all how many are the memorable literary characters whom we would like our 'teen-age daughters to meet? Would you like our Patricia to go on a date with Othello? Would we like our Mary to read the New Testament temple against temple with Raskolnikov? Would we like our sons to marry Emma Rouault, Becky Sharp or *La belle dame sans merci*?

You would do me a great pleasure and favor if my poem could appear before June 1. I think I told you already that about one quarter of LOLITA, and two essays on it (one by me, the other by Fred Dupee), will appear in a few weeks' time in the ANCHOR REVIEW. I liked very much the elegant PNIN ad in your recent issue. The dear man seems to be doing very well.

I was sorry that The New Yorker decided not to use my entomological correction.[1] The blunder in that article must have grievously hurt the Comstock of California, eminent author of BUTTERFLIES OF CALIFORNIA,—a touchy old man whom I respect. The Cornell Comstock, with whom Helmann confused him, was a much inferior scientist, whose specialty, moreover, was not lepidoptera.

We enjoyed the glimpse you gave us of your Florida vacation. I hope you both came back in perfect condition.

Our picture window is a veil of vertical snow, and the junipers look like albino camels.

Yours,

1. See VN's 5 February 1957 letter.

TO: **PROF. ROMAN JAKOBSON**                                    CC, I p.

Goldwin Smith Hall
Cornell University
Ithaca, N.Y.
April 14, 1957

Dear Professor Jakobson,

After a careful examination of my conscience, I have come to the conclusion that I cannot collaborate with you in the proposed English-language edition of the SLOVO.[1] Frankly, I am unable to stomach your little trips to totalitarian countries, even if these trips are prompted merely by scientific considerations.

I am asking the publisher to return to me my material. I must also ask you not to use my manuscript translation of the SLOVO in your Harvard classes.

Do not worry about the financial aspect of the matter, I am taking it up directly with the publisher.

Very truly yours,
Vladimir Nabokov

1. Jakobson and VN had planned to collaborate on a translation of *Slovo o polku Igoreve*, which VN translated alone as *The Song of Igor's Campaign* (1960).

Goldwin Smith Hall
Cornell, Ithaca, NY.
April 22, 1957

Dear Jason,

Véra and I are both delighted with LOLITA at Anchor.[1] Despite your self-disparaging remarks, the cover is splendid and most enticing. Your arrangement and selection of the LOLITA excerpts is above all praise. I also find that the rest of the material in the review is excellent (except Auden's piece:[2] incidentally, somebody ought to have told him that *monde* in French is masculine so that no French poet could ever have said "Le monde est ronde". It is the same nonsense as his famous slip in an earlier essay "acte gratuite" instead of "acte gratuit". Moreover, the slogan "highbrows and lowbrows, unite!", which he had spouted already, is all wrong since true highbrows are highbrows because they do *not* unite).

The piece about Sartre[3] is simply marvelous. I chuckled all the way, especially as I was probably the first writer in America to debunk him (in an article on the English translation of the "Nausée" in the NY. Times Book Review, in 1950).

Many thanks to you and Doubleday!

Many thanks, too, for your helpful and constructive reply to my appeal. I am not sure I can afford to consult a lawyer (I am absolutely pennyless at this moment and owe my bank 800 dollars), but I am writing my Paris agent asking her to act along the lines you suggest.

By the way, she is offering me a contract with Mondadori[4] for LOLITA—150.000 Fr. frs. advance, 8% up to 3000 copies, 10% to 5000, 12% after 5000—and with Rowohlt for the German rights—150.000 Fr. frs. advance, 8% up to 5.000 copies, 10% up to 10.000, 12% over 10.000. Does this seem reasonable to you?

She also complains she never received the two PNIN copies you sent her from me. Could you check?

Sincerely,
Vladimir Nabokov

1. *The Anchor Review, #2.*
2. W. H. Auden, "The Dyer's Hand: Poetry and the Poetic Process."
3. Herbert Lüthy, "The Void of Jean-Paul Sartre."
4. Italian publisher Arnoldo Mondadori.

TO: **MAURICE GIRODIAS**

CC, 1 p.
Ithaca, N.Y.

May 14, 1957

Dear Mr. Girodias,

You know as well as I do that publishing LOLITA in the US under your own imprint would mean asking for trouble. Nor can you fail to realize that a second-rate publisher would be no use since he would not be able to defend the book. Some ten years ago Doubleday spent more than $60000 on the defense of HECATE COUNTY by Edmund Wilson. Costs have gone up since then and are beyond the means of a second-rate publisher.

Since you know all this, and also know that we have here all sorts of Watch and Ward Societies, Catholic Legions of Decency, etc., and that, moreover, every post master in the country can start censorship trouble, I feel sure that you do not seriously contemplate the course of action you suggest in your letter. I wish to add that it also is in complete contradiction to what Madame Ergaz tells me that you promised her.

I agree that our interests are identical insofar as we both want the book to be published here, and to sell. While it remains true that no first-rate publisher will agree, as a matter of policy, to publish jointly with you, or with anyone else, yet there are other ways in which your claims could be satisfied, provided those claims are just and reasonable. The bigger the American publisher, the better your chances of reaching an agreement satisfactory to you.

I can only repeat that the course to follow is first of all to wait for Doubleday to make up their mind. If they decide that they want to publish LOLITA as a book, I shall put you in touch with them in due course. If they decide against publication, I shall put you in touch with the other important publisher who is willing to do the job the way it should be done. Whoever publishes LOLITA here will have to agree to defend it, at his own expense, and to carry this defense through the courts as far as the Supreme Court, if necessary.

I am sure you are getting a lot of offers right now from all kinds of mediocre firms. So am I. This is not what we need.

If you cooperate with me, and if publication in the US is eventually arranged on terms satisfactory to me, I shall likewise cooperate and shall agree to amend our contract so that you can without question license the American publisher.

*Re* translation.[1] *Capeline*, which is not at all the kind of hat I meant, is the least error among the numerous blunders.

On p. 23: The *acte de naissance* is meaningless; on the same page the translator has not understood that the allusion is to Poe's "Annabel Lee". There is no *couronne d'épines*.

On p. 24: The description of the *carte postale* is wrong. It should be *à vues d'un bleu verni*. The *vaux et monts* is meaningless, it should be *dans les chemins creux*. *Cornés* should be *bordés*.

On p. 25: *Aux barres* is nonsense. It should be *au petit jeu de paume*. And so on, at a rate of at least three on every page.

I was especially annoyed that on p. 30 the skit on Eliot did not come out at all.

Sincerely yours,

1. *Lolita*, trans. E. H. Kahane (Paris: Gallimard, 1959).

TO: **JASON EPSTEIN**                                    CC, I p.
                                                      Ithaca, N.Y.

                                                      June 10, 1957
Dear Jason,

The more I think about it the more convinced I feel that I should not be the one to transmit your offer to Olympia. His last letter on the subject was curt—to put it mildly. He will certainly say no, if

I submit your offer to him, and he may even choose not to answer at all.

While giving the matter more thought I have also come to doubt there is any reason for Mr. G. to accept. What you offer, in effect, is an unlimited option as against an advance of $1500 to be divided between Olympia and me. I am very much interested in having Doubleday publish LOLITA. Moreover, I would be glad to know that Olympia is tied by your contract and cannot publish the book here in a way that would be undesirable to me. But even I would like to put on record that an advance of $1500 does not seem adequate. There would be no point in discussing the advance before having Mr. G.'s reaction to the whole plan, however.

I do not think that your writing to him could prejudice my rights, especially if you make your offer "subject to the author's approval". I also feel much less worried about Mr. G.'s possible blunders since you say yourself that he could hardly arrange for publication without asking me for a reduction of royalty.

I would very much prefer, of course, if you could buy the American rights from G.—whether outright or on the basis of some kind of royalty, even if this meant some reduction in my 10% rate in an agreement I could then sign with you. But if this cannot be done, by all means write to him, and then we shall see what he really expects from a deal.

I do hope you will agree to tackle Girodias yourself.

Sincerely,
Vladimir Nabokov

TO: **VAUN GILLMOR**[1]                                           TLS, 1 p.
Letterhead: Cornell University.

June 26, 1957

Dear Miss Gillmor,
    I am sending you in two folders* part of my work on EUGENE

ONEGIN, namely: some introductory material, the translation of EO, Chapter One, an appendix on prosody, and the commentary to Ch. One. You have in your hands a second appendix related to Chapter One, L, on the subject of Pushkin's Abyssinian ancestor. All this represents one third of the whole work: the commentaries to the other chapters (Two to Eight) and additional fragments are much less bulky than the commentary to Ch. One which contains much general information.

I must apologize for sending you to read the Commentary in a carbon copy: the main one is still being used to make an Index.

If after perusing this MS you find you are still interested in considering it for publication, and would like to have it examined by any additional readers, outside your institution, I hope you will be kind enough to get in touch with me before you make your choice. I am raising here a delicate point: Most of my material is new, i.e. based on my own individual research; as you may notice, I am extremely critical of many workers in the same field (e.g., the Yarmolinski-Deutsch translation); and I also take to task various commentators, in this country and abroad, who approach literature from a social-economical angle, etc.

It is essential for me to have my book published soon. If your interest endures after you get acquainted with the present material, I shall send you the next chapters and commentaries in the course of this summer. On the other hand, I would be extremely grateful if you could give me your reaction to the first part of the book at your earliest convenience.

With best regards,

Sincerely yours,
Vladimir Nabokov

* under separate cover

1. Of the Bolligen Foundation.

TO: MAURICE GIRODIAS

CC, 2 pp.
Ithaca, N.Y.

August 3, 1957

Dear Mr. Girodias,

Many thanks for your kind letter. I was interested to learn about your negotiations with British editors. I had asked Mr. Knittel of Jonathan Cape to get in touch with you. If he did not it may mean they, too, were frightened away by the risks. In June, I have been approached by Bodley Head. They want a long-term option, but they offer an advance which they would be willing to forfeit if they did not publish within the delay. If you are willing to discuss this offer, I shall ask them to get in touch with you. Please let me know your reaction for I must answer them. They asked for a delay of "two or three" years, and therefore would probably agree to make it two years.

I do not think you are quite right about Doubleday and about the whole question of option and delay of publication. The situation here is extremely delicate. Doubleday have chosen the passages from LOLITA for the Anchor Review with the help of their lawyers, who in two instances made them change their choice of text. These lawyers have now been consulted as to the prospects of a complete edition; they have advised against it for the present. As you probably know, the Supreme Court has just handed down some very disappointing decisions. Although the cases judged were far removed from LOLITA's case, the important thing is that the Court did not bother with the definition of the term "obscenity", and did not take any measures against local censorship. This means that any small-town postmaster can set in motion the machine of censorship, starting the case on its way from Court to Court, until it reached the Supreme Court, which probably (though by no means certainly) would exonerate my book.

I assure you that in spite of it Doubleday's interest is very real. The reason they want an option is to be prepared to publish the moment a favorable break in the situation allows it. Of this I am certain. I agree with you that *some* delay should be established. I also believe that a more substantial advance than the one they offered should be asked. On the other hand, there is no doubt, unfortunately, that no publisher, who is big enough to handle the matter properly, will consider acceptable the terms you suggested to Doubleday. Incidentally, I think you are wrong in your assumption that Doubleday would not be prepared to defend the book. It was mentioned (and I am convinced that a clause to this purpose should be included in any agreement with either an American or a British publisher) that they would have to assume an obligation to defend the book before the Courts, carrying the proceedings, if need be, all the way to the Supreme Court. An important consideration is, too, that Doubleday think of me as of one of "their" authors. They have acquired two more books from me, and will do more than any other publisher to "push" LOLITA, which would be as much to your advantage as to mine (or theirs). For all these reasons I am sorry that you so resolutely rejected their offer.

I was sorry to learn that your lawsuit was postponed. On the other hand, if Gallimard publishes the French translation in the early fall, it may help the outcome. So let us hope for the best.

Please, do keep in touch with me. I am positive that LOLITA is the best thing I have written so far; I shall be always grateful to you for having published it. It would be an awful shame if some false move prevented you and me from enjoying some profit from it.

Sincerely yours,
Vladimir Nabokov

TO: **IVAN OBOLENSKY**                                   cc, 1 p.

Goldwin Smith Hall
Cornell University
Ithaca, NY.
August 7, 1957

Dear Prince Obolensky,

If you are still interested in LOLITA would you care to get in touch with Olympia?

VLADIMIR NABOKOV

Here is the situation. Olympia has the English-language rights (no licensing right, so I would have to approve the final arrangements). Mr. M. Girodias, Olympia's owner, is a difficult person. I suggest (provided, of course, that you still want to publish the book in this country) that you make it clear to him from the start that you are prepared to defend the book in the American Courts, the Supreme Court included, and that you would publish immediately.

I would be delighted if you could come to terms with the man. His address is 8, rue de Nesle, Paris VI. Of late he has been writing me from 7, rue St. Severin. Paris V, so maybe this is the one to use.

I was sorry to miss your party. I thank you for sending me your two books. They are very handsomely presented. I hope to find time soon to read THE END OF PITY.[1] The other one I know from having read it in MS.

Sincerely,
Vladimir Nabokov

1. Robie Macauley, *The End of Pity and Other Stories* (New York: McDowell, Obolensky, 1957).

FROM: **WALTER J. MINTON**[1] TLS, 1 p.

August 30, 1957

Dear Mr. Nabokov:

Being a rather backward example of that rather backward species, the American publisher, it was only recently that I began to hear about a book called LOLITA. Since then we have heard much and read much. Briefly, I am wondering if the book is available for publication and if, as I have heard, the Olympia Press controls all English rights, we have your blessing to negotiate with them. I realize that there are distinct obligations to Doubleday and I would not wish to intrude on already established relationships.

Sincerely,
Walter J. Minton

1. President of G. P. Putnam's Sons. According to "The *Lolita* Case," *Time* (17 November 1958), Minton learned about *Lolita* from "onetime Latin Quarter showgirl" Rosemary Ridgewell. Her finder's fee was "the equivalent of 10% of the author's royalties for the first year, plus 10% of the publisher's share of the subsidiary rights for two years."

TO: **WALTER J. MINTON**                                        CC, I p.

Goldwin Smith Hall
Cornell University
Ithaca, N.Y.
Sept. 7, 1957

Dear Mr. Minton,

Thanks for your nice letter. There is nothing to prevent you from negotiating with Olympia. They control the English rights, you are right. I might add that my contract with them does not contain a clause on licensing, so, as I see it, I would have to give my approval to the final arrangements.

Mr. Girodias, the owner of Olympia, is a rather difficult person. I shall be delighted if you come to terms with him.

Sincerely yours,
Vladimir Nabokov

TO: **ELENA SIKORSKI**                    ALS, 2 pp. Elena Sikorski.
                                          Ithaca, N. Y.

14 September 1957

My dear Elenochka,

After Olga's letter yours was, in a certain sense, a relief. Yes, of
course you did the right thing. When a new vacuum forms,[1] the recollections immediately rush in, and one senses with increased intensity
the eternal oppression of the past. Only recently I had still hoped to
see our poor E.K. again—over here our American oldsters live to
be 97, and walk five miles a day with a pedometer. I recall every detail
of her first summer with us, the postman for whom she would wait
by the "mill" escarpment behind the oldest lilacs of the garden, so
she could bring Mother a letter of Father's as quickly as possible, and
how Aunt Katya was jealous, and then, immediately after, came the
Crimea, London, Berlin, Prague....

As far as help for Olga is concerned, I shall do whatever you think
necessary; as for Rostislav (unless he intends to study something in
particular a little more), he must select an office job or some other
kind of work and try to hold on to it. In my opinion the theatre (if
one has acting talent, of course) is no worse that any other career,
especially since in Soviet circumstances that is one of the ways to retain a semblance of independence; and, since the first two or three
years may be unremunerative and difficult, wouldn't it be advisable
to give him a little help in the beginning? Let me know what you
think about it, and to what degree his theatrical inclinations are serious.

With regard to Sonia[2]—we weren't certain until the end whether
she would make it to Switzerland and when, and exactly where. Véra
and I are very glad you got together. She wrote us about all of you:
she fell in love with Zhikochka and the way he speaks Russian. She
described your apartment, his arsenal, and much else. It was all very
interesting for us.

Mityusha comes home from his Army service fairly often, usually
by airplane, and the first time he walked in with his elegant uniform
I remembered Yurik.[3] He went through eight weeks of basic training

with flying colors, crawled beneath real machine-gun fire, commanded a platoon,[4] led it on nighttime maneuvers in the woods, etc. As a reward he got a soft berth in New York—twice a week he meets military transports at the pier.

My *Lolita* has come out in Danish and in Swedish. I hope that I can finally, finally finish my monstrous Pushkin. After the notes about Eug. Onegin in *Noviy Zhurnal* there will be further ones in *Opïtï*. I am tired of this "bookish exploit", as my patient used to put it. Véra embraces you and commiserates deeply.

Keep well, my dearest, give our regards to your husband and a kiss to your son.

V.[5]

1. Evgeniya Konstantinovna Hofeld had just died.
2. Sonia Slonim, Véra Nabokov's sister.
3. Baron Yuriy E. Rausch von Traubenberg, VN's cousin.
4. DN was a squad leader.
5. Translated from Russian by DN.

TO: **WALTER J. MINTON**                                        cc, 1 p.

Goldwin Smith Hall
Cornell University
Ithaca, N.Y.
September 19, 1957

Dear Mr. Minton,

The fall term at Cornell is about to begin and my husband asks me to answer your letter for him, since he could not do it himself right now.

At the time Olympia Press published LOLITA, there was no choice for my husband but to accept their conditions: 10% for the first 10.000 copies, 12% after 10.000. Mr. Girodias being of a somewhat ogreish disposition, there is but slight chance of bettering this unfortunate agreement. So my husband would like to leave it to you to see what you can do.

He says it would be unethical for him not to warn you that he knows Mr. Girodias is at the moment in touch with one or two American publishers. He hopes this will not discourage you.

Sincerely,
(Mrs. Vladimir Nabokov)

TO: **MAURICE GIRODIAS**                    CC, I p.
Ithaca, N.Y.

October 5, 1957
*Registered Airmail*

Dear Mr. Girodias,

In view of your failure to submit your statement and to pay me as required by paragraph 9 of our Agreement, I regret to inform you that I am now invoking paragraph 8 of said Agreement and am exercising my right to declare the Agreement between us null and void, and that all rights granted under the Agreement revert to me.[1]

Yours truly,
Vladimir Nabokov

1. Girodias replied on 9 October that the royalties had been paid to VN's Paris agent.

TO: **CARL BJÖRKMAN**[1]                    CC, I p.

Goldwin Smith Hall
Cornell University
Ithaca, NY., USA
October 8, 1957

Dear Mr. Björkman,

I was glad to see from your letter that you have ordered a complete, unabridged translation of LOLITA to be prepared and were going to recall all the unsold copies of the first edition. These, of course, must be immediately destroyed.

I note with satisfaction that the new translation will be submitted to me for approval before publication.

I am afraid you are mistaken in your evaluation of the cuts and contractions your translator made in LOLITA. The size of the pages is non-essential. You can easily see this if you compare the number of pages in the two parts of the original with that of the two parts of the translation.

I must again voice my strongest objection to any attempts at "adjustments". There are no "recapitulations" in the second part and I must insist that in such cases the author is the best judge. I trust I may assume now that we are agreed LOLITA is to be published in Swedish in an exact, complete translation, without any rearrangements, additions or paraphrases whatsoever.

I hope you are now in a position to tell me that the original Swedish edition *has* been withdrawn from circulation.

Yours truly,
Vladimir Nabokov

PS. I would like to assume that the above provisions will be also applied by you to the translation of PNIN. If you have not yet committed yourself, perhaps you might want to entrust this translation to Mme Ellen Rydelius, if she still occupies herself with translations. She made a very satisfactory translation of a novel of mine,[2] published by Bonniers in 1936 under the title HAN SOM SPELADE SCHACK MED LIVET.

1. Of Swedish publishers Wahlström & Widstrand. The 1957 Swedish edition was withdrawn because the translation was unacceptable to VN; a second Wahlström & Widstrand translation was also withdrawn.
2. *The Defense.*

TO: **JASON EPSTEIN**                                                    CC, 1 p.
                                                           Ithaca, N.Y.

Oct. 13, 1957

Dear Jason,

The cover copy[1] is all right with the exception of the end of the middle paragraph. I am enclosing a copy of your copy with that sentence slightly revised.

Many thanks for your kind invitation. We shall be in New York on Friday and Saturday, and shall drive back to Ithaca on Sunday the 3rd.

Obolensky offered a flat rate of 15% and found some way to satisfy Girodias besides as to his outlay. You know that I would have preferred you to publish LOLITA, but your negotiations with Girodias were definitely suspended. Simon and Shuster notified me that their lawyers had advised them against publishing LOLITA. Putnams never came through with the offer they had announced they would make. The only standing offer was that of Obolensky, and he managed, moreover, to subdue Girodias. So there was no choice but accept.

How are the sales of the ANCHOR REVIEW? Has the landmark of 50.000 been reached?

Have you been hearing from Heinemann? I hope they will send you the reviews.[2] Did Lady Avebury finally write her essay? And finally, could you remind them to send their advance which was due on publication?

I would like to ask for a short delay with the collection of stories. I shall send them to you sometime in the course of November, if this is all right.

Love to both of you.

As ever,
Vladimir Nabokov

1. For *A Hero of Our Time*. (New York: Doubleday, 1958).
2. Heinemann had published *Pnin* in England.

Goldwin Smith Hall
Cornell University
Ithaca, N.Y.
November 5, 1957

Dear Prince Obolensky,

My wife and I enjoyed very much seeing you again and meeting Mr. McDowell. It was most kind of you to make twice the trip to Poughkeepsie to get us and to bring us back. The whole visit was a pleasure.

I cannot get the man here to make a photostat of the letters fast enough, so we have prepared a copy of the pertinent passages. Passage 2 from Mr. G.'s letter and the excerpt from my own letter refer to the matter of the deferred statement. Passage 1 from G.'s letter mentions the sale of "a few hundred" copies, whereas his statement has only 170 copies sold during April-June (and only 19 copies for the period January-April!) But then he also mentions that he had to buy back copies on which he had already paid a royalty. In other words, he creates a certain confusion making it impossible to control his declarations.

Another odd detail is that there is a considerable discrepancy between the prices of Frs. 2.400 and $7.50, and my royalty is computed on the basis of the Frs. 2.400. The agreement says that the royalty is to be computed from "the published price". But that was (originally) Frs. 1.800 (the two vols.); yet the royalty is computed from the price of 2.400. Olympia thus recognizes that I am entitled to get my share of their new price. However, the $7.50 certainly is not equivalent to Frs. 2.400.

All this is an awful nuisance. Still, my friends whom I consulted in New York advise me against a lawsuit, unless a perfectly clear case can be derived from the very wording of the agreement (the clause concerning the annullment of the contract). They are even more definitely convinced that under no circumstances should I allow myself to be involved in "arbitration", the reasons being the same that Mr. McDowell mentioned during our discussion. Finally, I am told on all sides that time is of the essence and that if much more time is allowed to pass before LOLITA is published, the interest of "the reading public" may wane. This is why I am rushing the enclosed material to you; I hope you too will send it at once to your advisers' office in Paris.

I wish to mention one further circumstance: my agent writes me that G. threatens to go back to his original scheme and publish the book here under his own imprint. I am telling her that I am not intimidated since it would not be difficult to stop the sales here if he published without my consent after I had notified him that I considered my agreement with Olympia void.

And finally: the situation being what it is I did not raise any questions which would arise if publication of LOLITA became imminent. I would like nevertheless to mention that while I consider the royalty you offer as very generous, I would want a rather more substantial advance than the one you offered to Mr. G. I prefer to say this now since I would not want you to undertake any steps in behalf of LOLITA under the impression that we were agreed on this point.

With best wishes,

Sincerely yours,
Vladimir Nabokov

то: CARL BJÖRKMAN                                          CC, 2 pp.

Goldwin Smith Hall
Cornell University
Ithaca, NY., USA.
November 11, 1957

Dear Mr. Björkman,

I have received your new version of LOLITA, Part II, and am returning it to you under separate cover.

While I appreciate your effort to improve the translation and note that many passages omitted in your first edition have been restored, I am distressed to say that the translation remains a sorry mess. In its present condition it would take weeks to correct it and there is hardly any sense in my pointing out to you its innumerable errors, blunders, mistranslations—and, alas, remaining omissions. Here are a few, just to give you an idea of the thing.

p.2. madamic is rendered in Swedish as torgmadammmiga. Actually, a "madam" means a woman who runs a brothel.

p.12. an orchestra of zootsuiters with trumpets is rendered as an "evinnerliga orkester". If the translator was incapable of finding some equivalent he could at least have said a "jazz band".

p.23. tender pale areolas are rendered as "sidenglänsande omgivingen". What terrible nonsense! Areolas means here the colored area around the nipples.

p.24. The "Kingdom by the Sea" is an allusion to Edgar Poe's "Annabel Lee". Your translator omits the Kingdom by the Sea thus depriving the "angels" in the next sentence and "Dolores Lee" at the end of the paragraph of any sense whatsoever.

p.3. "Miranda", omitted on p.3, comes from Hilaire Belloc's poem ("Do you remember an inn, Miranda" etc.), while "Mirana" on page 12 is the name of the Riviera Hotel which had belonged to Humbert's father and is described in the beginning of Part I. Your translator after omitting "Miranda", turns "Mirana" into "Miranda".

p.82 A football cheerleader, in this case of course a *female* one, to which Lolita is compared, has become "a football-playing boy"—not only a meaningless, but also an idiotic comparison.

Sampling the translation here and there (and finding it hopeless everywhere) I have discovered a considerable number of omissions, ranging from one-word pictures (as, for instance, "non-Laodicean" quality of the water, meaning that it was not lukewarm and referring to the famous passage in the Gospels (Rev. III, 14–16), on p.2, to whole passages of which I have marked only a few—pp. 3 and 6, for instance).

Page 6 also has a perfectly unwarranted, and rather nasty, insertion or transposition by the translator, which I have marked in the typescript.

I mention only in passing the swarm of errors or misprints in the English text of my poem on pp. 106–107 of the typescript, a poem which was merely transcribed from my book.

All in all, you certainly could not call this "an authorized" translation, or even a "translation approved by the author". I emphatically disapprove of it. I probably cannot prevent you from publishing it— under the express condition that *all* the omissions are reinstated, in this second volume as well as in the first volume, where a whole chapter is missing° and innumerable passages and paragraphs are omitted; e.g., the opening paragraph of my Chapter 31 (your Chapter 30). Fortunately I do have the right to insist on the complete reinstatement of the entire English text.

Frankly, I fail to understand why a first-rate publishing house, after acquiring a work they obviously consider worth translating and publishing, would want to bring out a mutilated and worthless version of it. If I were in your place I certainly would not settle for the abominable version your translator has prepared for you. In any case I must insist that PNIN's translation into Swedish be made by another translator, someone who knows English and can be trusted to respect the text of the original. I was sorry to hear of Mme Rydelius' death. There is another lady who is supposed to be an honest translator, Mme Karin de Laval. I am not familiar with her work but you might want to ask her to make a sample translation of one chapter or less.

I had better finish this letter now. The perusal of Mr. Kjellström's mistranslation of my poor book has plunged me in despair.

Yours truly,
Vladimir Nabokov


PS. I am convinced that Mr. Kjellström cannot be trusted to reinstate all his omissions since in many cases he appears incapable of understanding the text. Your best chance of improving your version would be to have an American Swede or a Swedish American go carefully over the whole book.

*due to a combination of condensation and omission in chapters 12 and 13.

TO: **IVAN OBOLENSKY**           CC, 1 p.

Goldwin Smith Hall
Cornell University
Ithaca, N.Y.
November 20, 1957

Dear Obolensky,

I have just received a registered letter from Girodias in which he says: "I inform you that we are proceeding with the printing of a special edition of 'Lolita' for sale in the United States since it seems improbable that we will arrive at an agreement for a reprint by another publisher."

I know, however, from my agent that he has received an offer from yet another American publisher so that I am inclined to deem his letter a mere threat. Nevertheless all this worries me extremely. I am no businessman.

I thank you for your letter of November 13. May I assume that the papers have already gone to Paris? Could you speed up the proceedings so as to obtain a clear answer from your Paris lawyer within a week? I am afraid that unless I can write Girodias a determined and final letter soon, he may take the initiative and involve me into difficulties. I wish to avoid a legal fight at all cost.

With the greatest pleasure I have read "A Death in the Family".[1] It is full of delightful images. I am now beginning the splendid-looking "Andersonville".[2]

My best regards to Mr. McDowell. Do write me very soon.

Sincerely,
Vladimir Nabokov

1. By James Agee.
2. By Mackinlay Kantor.

TO: **IVAN OBOLENSKY**                                        CC, I p.

Goldwin Smith Hall
Cornell University
Ithaca, NY.
November 29, 1957

Dear Prince Obolensky,

I hear from Mr. Minton of Putnam's that he had a talk about LOLITA either with you or with Mr. McDowell.

I would like to avoid any kind of misunderstanding, so let me remind you that, as has already been mentioned, I cannot enter into an agreement before a clarification of my relations with OLYMPIA has been achieved. I also mentioned to you that, much as I would desire a break with Mr. Girodias, I would not undertake litigation, since this would involve a loss of time (a most essential consideration) and, probably, considerable expenses.

It is important for me to establish my legal position with regard to OLYMPIA in the shortest possible time and I would be most interested to know the conclusions to which your legal adviser has arrived. I also expect to receive shortly a legal opinion direct from Paris which it might be interesting to compare to the one you may obtain.

Sincerely yours,
Vladimir Nabokov

TO: **WALTER J. MINTON**                                      CC, I p.

Goldwin Smith Hall
Cornell University
Ithaca, N.Y.
November 29, 1957

Dear Mr. Minton,

It was nice of you to telephone. I would like to repeat that, although McDowell, Obolensky did make an offer for LOLITA, no agreement has been signed, nor am I under any definite commitment, either to them or to any other publisher.

I would welcome a formal offer from you. My wife forgot to mention one important consideration. Can I assume that if you publish LOLITA you would be prepared to defend it in the Courts, going all the way to the Supreme Court, should such a necessity arise; and that this could be made part of the agreement?[1]

Sincerely yours,
Vladimir Nabokov

1. On 3 December Minton wrote VN: "I rather doubt that any publisher will make the blanket guarantee you suggest, or at least make it in terms which are actually effective. . . . I can therefore only say to your request that we will do our best to make LOLITA the success it deserves and will do everything practical to prevent its being prosecuted."

TO: **WALTER J. MINTON**                                      CC, 1 p.

Goldwin Smith Hall
Ithaca, NY.
December 23, 1957

Dear Mr. Minton,

Please find enclosed a photostat of my agreement with Olympia and copy of some passages from a letter, referring to the question of copyright.

Incidentally, it might interest you to know that Obolensky had the legal situation analyzed by his lawyers whose opinion was that an arbitration would probably be necessary to make the abrogation of the agreement with Olympia "stick", and that such litigation might or might not be successful. I wish to avoid litigation if at all possible, although I believe my case is actually stronger now than when Obolensky's lawyers looked into it. Mr. Girodias's statement which he has now elaborated by stating that of the copies he allegedly sold between April and June 30, which he puts at 170, only 8 copies were sold in the USA, appears to me as a fraudulent statement.

Here is a first paragraph from a letter of Dec. 10 that I received from Barney Rosset of Grove Press: "Recently I received a letter from Maurice Girodias asking me if I would be interested in publishing LOLITA in this country. I certainly am interested and wrote back to him to that effect, suggesting that we make an arrangement whereby I would pay you a royalty of 7½ per cent on the first 10,000 copies and 10 per cent thereafter. A separate royalty of 5 per cent would go to M. Girodias."

Finally, I wish to thank you for the beautiful bird book. The illustrations are splendid, and to-night I am going to plunge into the text.

Sincerely yours,
Vladimir Nabokov

Encl.


COURSE DESCRIPTION                                              1958

Prof. Vladimir Nabokov, Cornell University
Lit 312. Course description. (Spring semester). Masters of European Fiction. 3 hrs. MoWeFr 12–12.50

Starting with a comparative study of three fantasies: Stevenson's *Dr. Jekyll and Mr. Hyde*, Gogol's *The Carrick* and Kafka's *The Metamorphosis*, and going on to a close analysis of three novels: Tolstoy's *Anna Karenin*, Proust's *In Quest of Lost Time* (first volume only; in English translation) and Joyce's *Ulysses*. All these works are studied from the point of view of structure and style with great attention given to technical details and factual, specific features.

Lit 326. Course description. (Spring semester). Russian literature in Translation. 3 hrs. MoWeFr 11–11.50

The same approach holds good for this course which covers *A Hero of Our Time* (Lermontov, in my translation); literal translations of poems by Lermontov, Tyutchev, Nekrasov, Fet and Blok; Turgenev's *Fathers and Sons* (Guerney's translation); Dostoevski's *Memoirs from under the Floor* (Guerney's translation); Tolstoy's *Anna Karenin* (students enrolled in both courses substitute *Hadji Murad* and *Death of Ivan Ilich*); and Chehov's *The Ravine* and *The Lady with the Small Dog*.

TO: **RICHARD SCHICKEL**[1]                                            CC, I p.

Goldwin Smith Hall
Ithaca, NY.
January 1, 1958

Dear Mr. Schickel,

For many years (1941–1949) I looked after the lepidoptera in the Museum of Comparative Zoology at Harvard. I have been collecting leps during more than fifty summers in many remote regions. I have worked out several taxonomic problems. I have discovered several new American butterflies, one of which is pleasingly called by lepidopterists "Nabokov's Wood Nymph" (a feral cousin of our common friend). Although I do not teach biology at Cornell, I am in touch with the admirable entomological museum here. Moreover, I discuss in detail beetles and their parasites every year around April, when in my literature course, I get to Kafka's "Metamorphosis", after which, in May, I annually attempt to identify the noctuid moth that circles around a lamp in the brothel scene of Joyce's "Ulysses". And there are three butterflies in "Madame Bovary", black, yellow, and white, respectively. So you see that your making me a professor of biology was not only very much to the point, but warmed a cockle which no success in comparative literature can so exquisitely prick.

I never write to critics—and therewith have hurt friends and disappointed foes. In the present case, however, I confess to having found it very difficult not to write to you when I read your article in "The Reporter", which was the most intelligent and most artistic appreciation which has appeared so far in regard to my nymphet.[2]

I trust LOLITA will be published soon in this country. It has appeared in Danish and Swedish, and is being translated into Italian, German, Dutch and French. I am in the very act of revising the French translation, and have spent several hours trying to explain to the French reader the meaning of "majorette".

I wish you a very happy New Year.

Sincerely,
Vladimir Nabokov

1. Literary critic.
2. "A Review of a Novel You Can't Buy" (14 November 1957); Schickel wrote VN on 26 December 1957 apologizing for identifying him as a biology professor.

TO: **PROF. MEYER ABRAMS**[1]

cc, 4 pp.
Ithaca, N.Y.

January 6, 1958

Dear Mike,

I have greatly enjoyed "A Glossary of Literary Terms".[2] It is a neat, clear, precise, and scholarly piece of work. Many thanks for the book and for the nice inscription. The critical remarks I have jotted down are of slight importance in comparison to the worth of your work—but here they are, anyway:

p.1 Grishkin is nice. . . .[3]

I object to this example for three reasons: a) the student of today is not obliged to recognize a mediocre poem by a minor poet of yesterday; b) there can be nothing "concrete" about a name ("Grishkin") which is either an impossible derivation from "Grisha" (in that case, it should have been "Grishin") or a yiddish comedy name, or simply a vulgar allusion (rather typical of Tom's vulgar mind) to "griskin", which means "pork chop" in Tom's high-tea England; and c) it happens to represent a prosodic variation (inversion of accent or my "tilt", see further) which is not accounted for under "Meter", pp. 50–52.

**p.3 Assonance**

The Kubla Khan example illustrates at best an "eye assonance" since all these "a" (and "u") sounds are pronounced differently. It does not illustrate the "ear assonance" to which the unqualified "assonance" refers. Moreover, one might note that the term "assonance" is also used for a certain type of inexact rhyme and for internal instrumentation, such as

When *vapours* to their swimming brains advance
And *double tapers* on the *table* dance

or                       (Dryden)

......and with a store
Of indis*tinguishable* sympathies
*Mingl*ing most earnest *wishes* for the day

(Wordsworth)

**p.13 Cliché**

Pope's satiric comment which you quote pertains not to Clichés in general but specifically to the Expected Rhyme, a term which should be listed, I think.

p. 39 The "chanson innocent", by another Grishkin,[4] should be, of course, "chanson innocente".

p.50 "Wrenched accent" has been also applied by prosodists to what I call "tilting" (see further).

**p.51 Spondaic**

No spondaic words can be said to exist in English—unless a very special pause is made between the syllables, or the compound mouthed with a good deal of didactic rumination and slow jaw work. The word "heartbreak" is a trochee at heart. True spondees (⸚) do not occur in English metrical verse but can be imitated in cadential or pausative verse:

Gone is Livia, love is gone:
Strong wing, soft breast, bluish plume;
In the juniper tree moaning at dawn:
Doom, doom.

**p.51 Scansion**

I am prejudiced against these little crosses and darts (instead of dimples and dashes) and am handicapped in analyzing this section because of my own work on prosody, unpublished but to appear soon, I hope. If you do not accent "into", it is illogical to accent "-ness". The scansion dart-cross of "full of" is meaningless since it is obviously not a trochee. Let me briefly explain my point of view:

An ordinary iambic foot (i.e., one not affected by certain contractional and rhymal variations) consists of two semeia, the first semeion being called a depression (∪ or ∪́) and the second, an ictus (⸓ or -). Any such foot belongs to one of the following types (where the basic metrical stress is marked thus – , and the variable word accent thus´):

1. Regular foot, ∪⸓ (Unaccented non-stress followed by accented stress), e.g. *"Appeáse my griéf, and deádly páin"* (Surrey)

2. Scudded foot (or False Pyrrhic), ∪- (Unaccented non-stress followed by unaccented stress), e.g. *"In expectátion of* a guést" (Tennyson) or "In lóve*liness* of pérfect déeds" (*id.*)

3. Tilt (or Inversion), ∪́- (Accented non-stress followed by unaccented stress), e.g. *"Sense of* intólerable wróng" (Coleridge), or *"Vaster* than Émpires, and more slów" (Marvell), or *"Perfect*ly púre and góod: I foúnd" (Browning)

4. False Spondee, ∪́⸓ (Accented non-stress and accented stress), e.g. *"Twice hó*ly wás the Sábbath-béll" (Keats)

p.60 Proust, Mann, Joyce

I violently object to Mann's intrusion here. What on earth is this ponderous conventionalist, this tower of triteness, doing between two sacred names? His fame has been puffed up by German professors. Why should we continue to mislead students by teaching them that Mann, Galsworthy, Faulkner, Tagore and Sartre are "great craftsmen"?

Finally, let me list a few additional terms that readers might like to find explained:

Anacreontic sonnet
Aphorism, aphoristic
Autograph
Canto
Code
Copy, fair

Digression
Draft, rough
Editio optima, editio princeps
Elegiac quatrain
Elision, liaison
Epigraph
Flourished
Gallicism
Gloss
*Ibid.*
Ictus and depression
Instrumentation
Inversion; 1) phrase, 2) accent
*L.c.*
Metaphrase
Meter: add amphibrachic
Motto
Octosyllable
Parallel passages
Paraphrase
Plagiary
Poetaster (e.g. Mr. Auden)
Pyrrhic ⏑⏑ (part of ternary measures, ⏑⏑́; etc.)
Recension
Recto, verso
Reminiscence
Reported speech
Scholium, —ia, —iast
Semeion, semeia
*Sic*
Stave
Tautology
Transition, the art of
Ultima
Very cordially yours,
Vladimir Nabokov[5]

1. Department of English, Cornell University
2. Abrams, *A Glossary of Literary Terms* (New York: Holt, Rinehart & Winston, 1957).
3. From "Whispers of Immortality" by T. S. Eliot.
4. E. E. Cummings
5. Abrams did not act on VN's advice and corrections in subsequent editions.

TO: **WALTER J. MINTON**           CC, 1 p.

Goldwin Smith Hall
Ithaca, N.Y.
January 12, 1958

Dear Mr. Minton,

Many thanks for your letter.

I do not think I would go to court for the sake of the foreign-language rights: they represent a minor matter, not worth the effort or the expense.

Nor would I under any circumstances go to a French court. I would rather follow a course which might prompt Mr. Girodias to serve action on me, and do it in this country.

Your offer of the additional royalty for me is a considerable inducement. I still believe that Mr. Girodias should (and will) back down somewhat. I regret very much that you showed him all your cards, and all my cards, when you first approached him. One of these days I am going to write him again and make him a take-it-or-leave-it offer. But I think we should first know the verdict in his court suit. The suit was to be judged on January 7th. The verdict might make a great difference in the entire situation.

Incidentally, you do not tell me what advance I would get under the arrangement you discuss in your letter.

Sincerely,
Vladimir Nabokov

TO: **WALTER J. MINTON** CC, I p.

Goldwin Smith Hall
Ithaca, NY.
January 14, 1958

Dear Mr. Minton,

My husband asks me to acknowledge your kind letter of Jan. 10.

Please do not worry about his warning to Mr. G.: Mr. G. in his letters tries to establish as a fact that my husband has agreed to negotiate on the basis of the original agreement and moreover, is willing to modify the terms of this agreement to Mr. G.'s advantage. My husband thinks (and so do I) that it is essential for the time being to insist that 1. the old contract is non-existent and 2. any agreement, if arrived at, would be an entirely new matter.

The three solutions[1] you suggest seem to sum up the situation, except that my husband is convinced that Mr. G. will accept a lesser royalty. He was in a most conciliatory mood in November, changed his attitude entirely when Putnams entered the picture, and, if left alone for a fortnight or so, will probably come back to his senses.

His letter of Jan. 7 contains a curious sentence: "Our trial against the French Home Secretary takes place this afternoon". This letter was mailed on the 8th. Does not it strike you as strange that he says nothing about the verdict? The agent (whom we do not consider entirely trustworthy) has not written us about it either. An adverse decision of the Court might prove very much to my husband's advantage since there seems to be a provision in the French law releasing the author if the publisher cannot continue to publish his book. We shall try to find out about the verdict. You may find it easier to do than it will be for us under the present circumstances. Please let us know in any case what you think of these suggestions.

Sincerely,
(Mrs. Vladimir Nabokov)

1. Minton had suggested to VN three courses of action: 1) VN to file suit to abrogate the contract in Paris; 2) VN to sign a contract with an American publisher providing for division of the royalty with Girodias; 3) VN to sign a contract with an American publisher and ignore the dispute with Girodias.

TO: **DMITRI NABOKOV**

MS, 1 p.<br>Ithaca, N.Y.

*The Corsair's Lied*
To D. N.

*I have on deck my rebec,*
*And zwiebacks from a wreck,*
*And zephyrs waft my xebec*
*From Lübeck to Quebec.*

Vladimir Nabokov<br>Jan. 14, 1958

1. Father and I were discussing the rhymability of "xebec," and he made up this little poem for me, which contains not only a proper rhyme for it but also a pair of iambic rhymes on the same sound, plus two internal nuggets. DN.

TO: **MAURICE GIRODIAS**

CC, 1 p.

Goldwin Smith Hall<br>Cornell University<br>Ithaca, NY., USA<br>January 16, 1958

Dear Mr. Girodias,

I was glad to hear that the ban on LOLITA was lifted. Many thanks for your wire.

This new situation raises a new question. I don't think you quite understand my position: as far as I am concerned the original agreement between Olympia and me is null and void. In order to sell your edition you need a new agreement.

I would be willing to consider a reasonable offer from you for such a new agreement, provided that it took care of all the aspects of the matter, including the American, British and foreign-language rights (the latter item being the least important of the four). Such an agreement would have to be a three-way contract: 1) Between you and Putnams, and 2) Between me and Putnams, regarding an American edition; and 3) between Olympia and me, regarding the other matters.

The thing has been dragging on too long. I would prefer to arrive at an out-of-court settlement, but one way or another I am resolved to have the whole matter settled now.

I suggest that you think matters over once again and see if you can suggest a reasonable settlement. I shall not accept a 50/50 division of the American royalty.

I wish to repeat that all the suggestions in this letter are made by me on a voluntary basis, that I consider myself under no obligations, and that these suggestions will in no way prejudice any rights or privileges that are mine in consequence of the abrogation of my agreement with Olympia Press.

May I hear from you within ten days? If no agreement can be reached I shall consider myself obliged to obtain an injunction against the sales of your original edition of LOLITA.[1]

Sincerely yours,
Vladimir Nabokov

1. On 16 January VN wrote to Walter J. Minton: "Here is a copy of my letter to Girodias, mailed today. If this does not do it, I shall admit to defeat."

TO: **WALTER J. MINTON**                    CC, 1 p.

Goldwin Smith Hall
Ithaca, N.Y.
January 25, 1958

Dear Mr. Minton,

Here is a copy of a letter I have just received from Mr. G. in reply to the one I wrote him (of which you have a copy).

I do not know why he thought that I "had long ago abandoned the claim."[1] Nor do I know what he is driving at now. I am inclined to assume that his suggesting that my lawyer get in touch with his lawyer means that Girodias is ready to discuss matters and settle out of court. Do you agree with me that it might be worth trying to ask a lawyer to do so? And, in that case, would you suggest a lawyer whom I could engage—someone versed in literary litigation, but not likely to charge me more than I can pay?

On the other hand, if you feel sure that all this is but another Olympia trick, and that nothing can be gained by going along with Mr. G.'s suggestion, I would be prepared to ask you to write him a letter on the following lines:

1. That though I was very eager to take the matter to court, you prevailed upon me to give up the idea;

2. Time being of the essence, you convinced me to accept the arrangement you had worked out with him, with the provision however, that he take 7% and I get 8% (if only because I have to pay the agent's fee).

Before you write such a letter, please let me hear from you once more. I would also like to know what would be the largest advance I could expect under this arrangement.

Sincerely,
Vladimir Nabokov

---

1. VN's holograph note in the margin: "if you re-read my letter of Jan. 16 to him, you will see that this is unfounded"

TO: **PASCAL COVICI**                                   CC, I p.

> Goldwin Smith Hall
> Itnaca, N.Y.
> February 3, 1958

Dear Mr. Covici,

My husband asks me to thank you for sending him the Stanislaus Joyce book.[1] He found in it some very interesting information and is very happy to possess it in his library.

He thanks you, too, for THE LEOPARD.[2] To my regret, I am to tell you that he did not think much of it. In his opinion it belongs essentially to "juvenile literature" with its ready-made types, emotions and situations.

With best wishes,

> Sincerely yours,
> (Mrs. Vladimir Nabokov)

1. *My Brother's Keeper* (New York: Viking, 1958).
2. By Giuseppe di Lampedusa.

TO: **WALTER J. MINTON**                                CC, I p.

> Goldwin Smith Hall
> Ithaca, NY
> March 1, 1958

Dear Mr. Minton,

Thanks for the agreements, one of which I am returning to you, signed and witnessed.

I have almost finished checking the published text of LOLITA for misprints etc., and shall mail it to you, together with the Anchor article, on Wednesday.

Please find enclosed two scrapbooks with clippings on LOLITA— one multilingual, the other sent me by my Swedish publisher. I have sold the following rights: French (Gallimard), German (Rowohlt), Italian (Mondadori), Swedish (Wahlström & Widstrand), Danish (Reitzel), Dutch (Oisterwijk). Is there anything else you would like to have or to know? List of publications? Curriculum vitae? If you want to know more about me and my background, you can look it up in CONCLUSIVE EVIDENCE (Harper). Do you need a photograph?

What about the jacket? After thinking it over, I would rather not involve butterflies. Do you think it could be possible to find today in New York an artist who would not be influenced in his work by the general cartoonesque and primitivist style jacket illustration? Who would be capable of creating a romantic, delicately drawn, non-Freudian and non-juvenile, picture for LOLITA (a dissolving remoteness, a soft American landscape, a nostalgic highway—that sort of thing)? There is one subject which I am emphatically opposed to: any kind of representation of a little girl.

Coming back to the contract, I regret we did not delete paragraph 11. If taken literally, it would mean that I could never offer you another book. Perhaps you can still find a way of expunging it.

Sincerely,
Vladimir Nabokov

Encl.


TO: **W J. MINTON**                      cc, 1 p.

Goldwin Smith Hall
Ithaca, NY.
March 7, 1958

Dear Mr. Minton,

Thanks for your letters and the check.

Yes, I quite see your point and agree with you that the inclusion of the article might add an extraneous element to the book. I would be delighted to have it re-published in the form you suggest,—with Doubleday's consent.

I am sending you herewith a copy of LOLITA which we have checked for misprints and errors. I would not like to change the paragraphic division, and would like to be consulted on any questions of punctuation that may arise. A number of words are not in Webster, but will be in its later editions.

Jason Epstein has just sent me an amusing trifle: page 5 of the Sunday Times magazine (March 2), with the picture of a Lord & Taylor's blond model standing near a table on which one can clearly distinguish volume 2 of the Olympia Press LOLITA.

Sincerely yours,
Vladimir Nabokov

TO: PETER RUSSEL[1]                                    CC, I p.
                                                    Ithaca, N.Y.

March 12, 1958

Dear Sir,

My husband had hoped to answer your letter himself but the pressure of work keeps interfering with his plans. He therefore asks me to write you for him.

In the first place he wants me to thank you for your very nice letter, for the copy of NINE and for your catalogues.

LOLITA does not exist in Russian. The ban on the Parisian edition has been lifted now. There will be an American edition of the novel, published by Putnams early next fall. Gallimard will do it in French as soon as the translation is completed. Further translations, either already published or to come out soon, are the Swedish, Danish, Dutch, Italian and German ones.

My husband further wants me to say that he shares your admiration for Osip Mandelshtam, but not for Ezra Pound. He wishes you every success with your Russian issue of NINE. As to his own translations from Pushkin, Lermontov and Tyutchev, he does not want to reprint them. His approach to the problems of translating has changed since he published his THREE RUSSIAN POETS. He does not believe in verse translations any more. He thinks that a translation's merit is determined by its literalness alone, and that, since a verse translation is inevitably a compromise, it cannot claim to be a "translation", but is, at best, an imitation or (at its worst) a mutilation of the original. In this spirit of absolute literalness, my husband has just completed the translation of EUGENE ONEGIN. Pushkin's stanzas are rendered in iambic lines of varying length; but rhyme has been sacrificed to reason. If you are interested, he could give you a few stanzas for your Russian issue. He regrets that lack of time makes it impossible for him to advise you on the choice of your material.

Of my husband's other works, you could probably obtain THE REAL LIFE OF SEBASTIAN KNIGHT (New Directions), SPEAK, MEMORY (Victor Gollancz) and PNIN (Heinemann). SPEAK, MEMORY is the English equivalent of the American CONCLUSIVE EVIDENCE. My husband's Russian books (with the exception of the three you have) can be only obtained from second-hand dealers.

I hope I have answered your questions.

Sincerely yours,
(Mrs. Vladimir Nabokov)

1. Editor of the English literary journal, *Nine*.

TO: **REV. LOUIS M. HIRSHSON**[1]

cc, 1 p.
Ithaca, N.Y.

March 13, 1958

Dear Sir,

I thank you for your invitation to attend the lecture to be given at your Colleges by Mr. Ustinov of the Soviet Embassy, and the reception that will follow.

I never have attended, nor ever will attend, any function to which Soviet agents are invited.

Very truly yours,
Vladimir Nabokov

1. President of Hobart and William Smith Colleges.

TO: **CALDER WILLINGHAM**                                     CC, 1 p.

Goldwin Smith Hall
Ithaca, NY.
March 30, 1958

Dear Mr. Willingham,

I had started to read a library copy of TO EAT A PEACH when I received your sumptuous gift for which I thank you very warmly. I thought Daddy and the Bowel Expert came out marvelously well; but I am not quite sure of the artistic validity and necessity of the intercourse scene at the end. I then turned to NATURAL CHILD and came into closer contact with your magnificent talent. The structure of the whole thing is very striking and original. I admired greatly such things as the repeated modulations in pages 126 and 131. Wonderful, too, is the Beethoven record booming suddenly in that terrible pansy apartment—and the spices, the spices! In 1954 my wife and I, when trying to establish convenient headquarters for our butterfly-hunting expedition in New Mexico, made the dreadful mistake of renting sight unseen an adobe house in dreadful trite Taos,— and that house belonged to a (less opulent) Mariss, with a carriage-lamp on a pole just inside the entrance hall, and fancy danglers, and spices.

I also want to thank you for your amiable letter. I informed my publisher of your kind suggestion and also of your advice regarding the False Lolita.[1] And of course the Coney Island episode is a master-piece.

Yours sincerely,
Vladimir Nabokov

1. Novelist Willingham had informed VN that Mary Chase was writing a play entitled *Lolita*.

TO: **JOHN E. SIMMONS**[1]

CC, 2 pp.
Ithaca, N.Y.

April 8, 1958

Dear Mr. Simmons,

I am sending you eleven folders (further called "volumes") containing my translation of Pushkin's "Eugene Onegin" and a copious Commentary to it. You will find a table of contents at the beginning of vol.1.

This typescript is a precious one (I have only one other copy) in view of the tremendous amount of research involved. There does not exist any other literal and complete English translation of this greatest masterpiece of Russian literature. Nor is there in any language, including Russian, the kind of thorough commentary I have appended to it.

It is of the utmost importance that whoever reads this typescript should bear in mind that it is based on individual research and contains many new interpretations and discoveries. Both in Russia and in this country a number of scholars are working in the same general field (Pushkiniana),—I might mention in passing that political issues play some part—and this calls for a very careful choice of publisher's reader. I have taken to task a number of inept commentators and have trodden on many toes.

I am giving you the names of three Russian scholars well qualified to examine the book. My personal contacts with them have been very limited, but I know them to be honest scholars. I am definitely opposed to the book's going to anybody connected with either Columbia or Harvard. I must have your assurance that, should you desire to have the book read by anyone (outside of your office) other than the persons I mentioned, you will discuss your choice with me.

My permanent address is: Goldwin Smith Hall, Cornell. My telephone number (residence) to the end of May is Ithaca 3–2015. I am *not* connected in any way with the Russian Dept. in Merrill Hall.

Sincerely yours,
Vladimir Nabokov

1. Prof. Albert Parry, Russian Literature Department, Colgate University

2. Prof. Ekaterina Wolkonsky, Department of Russian, Vassar College

3. Prof. George Ivask, Germanic and Slavic Department, University of Kansas, Lawrence, Kansas.

1. Of Cornell University Press.

TO: **RANDALL JARRELL**[1]                                    cc, 1 p.

Goldwin Smith Hall
Cornell University
Ithaca, NY.
April 12, 1958

Dear Mr. Jarrell,

I wish to thank you for your charming letter. I shall be delighted to avail myself of the invitation to deposit some of my manuscripts at The Library of Congress.

During the last ten years I have been moving from one furnished house to another, and my manuscripts and papers are stored in a rather haphazard way, mostly at my office at Cornell. It will take a little time to unearth them and sort them out. By the way, would you be interested in the Mss. of my earlier works (Russian-language novels)?

Sincerely yours,
Vladimir Nabokov

1. At the time Consultant in Poetry at the Library of Congress.

TO: **WALTER J. MINTON**
CC, 1 p.
Ithaca, N.Y.

April 23, 1958

Dear Mr. Minton,

I have just received the five designs and I quite agree with you that none of them is satisfactory. I have looked up in *The Reporter* the picture you mention but find it to be in the primitivistic wobbly style which I dislike.

I want pure colors, melting clouds, accurately drawn details, a sunburst above a receding road with the light reflected in furrows and ruts, after rain. And no girls.

If we cannot find that kind of artistic and virile painting, let us settle for an immaculate white jacket (rough texture paper instead of the usual glossy kind), with LOLITA in bold black lettering.

Just to make sure: I assume that the photostatic copies, the questionnaire, the second photograph and the PNIN clippings have all reached you safely.

Sincerely,
Vladimir Nabokov

TO: **PROF. HARRY LEVIN**                                    CC, I p.
                                                        Ithaca, N.Y.

                                                        April 28, 1958

Dear Harry,

It was most kind of you to send me THE POWER OF BLACK-
NESS.[1] I delayed this acknowledgement because I wanted to read the
book before thanking you for it, but I am invaded by galleys of
LOLITA in various languages, including English, and have only had
time to glance through it, so far.

I enjoyed your treatment of Poe. Not only did he not visualize the
death's-head moth, but he was also under the completely erroneous
impression that it occurs in America. In Kafka's case the reader sees
the brown domed beetle quite clearly.

We often think of our pleasant Cambridge visits and wonder when
we shall see you all again. In the meantime Véra joins me in sending
all three of your our very best wishes.

                                                        Sincerely,

1. A critical book by Levin.

FROM: **WALTER J. MINTON**                              TELEGRAM
                                             3:46 p.m., 18 August 1958

EVERYBODY TALKING OF LOLITA ON PUBLICATION DAY
YESTERDAYS REVIEWS MAGNIFICENT AND NEW YORK
TIMES BLAST THIS MORNING[1] PROVIDED NECESSARY
FUEL TO FLAME 300 REORDERS THIS MORNING AND
BOOK STORES REPORT EXCELLENT DEMAND CON-
GRATULATIONS ON PUBLICATION DAY

                                             WALTER J MINTON

1. Orville Prescott, "Books of the Times": "To describe such a perversion with the pervert's enthusiasm without being disgusting is impossible. If Mr. Nabokov tried to do so he failed." On 21 August, Minton reported reorders for the first week: Monday, 1,943; Tuesday, 2,789; Wednesday, 670; Thursday, 1,375.

to: **WALTER J. MINTON**                                                    cc, 1 p.

Goldwin Smith Hall
Ithaca, NY.
August 29, 1958

Dear Walter,

I am writing you separately about INVITATION TO A BE-HEADING. Two things the translator must be: 1) male, 2) American-born or English. He must also have a sound and scholarly knowledge of Russian. I do not know anyone who would meet these requirements except my son—but he is unfortunately much too busy and has already had to refuse to translate a book for Doubleday.

You might be able to find an intelligent Russian-speaking English-writing man in New York. Or perhaps England is a better place to look for such a translator? In any case, I would have to control his work throughout and, moreover, would want to see a sample of it before you engage him. For reasons which would be tedious to explain in a letter I would certainly not want Guerney. For different reasons I would not want Magarshack whose work is very poor.

Elek speaks in his letter of having "reliable" Russian translators. Could he be of some help? (But the translator *must not* be a Russian-born lady).

Regards.

Sincerely,
Vladimir Nabokov

TO: **ELENA SIKORSKI**    ALS, 1 p. Elena Sikorski.
Ithaca, N. Y.

6 Sept. 1958

My dear Elenochka,

I am sending you the Prague money for November.

Thanks for the heart-rending snapshot.[1] Those lindens, of course, were not there before, and everything is grayer than the artwork of memory, but it is all very detailed and recognizable.

*Lolita* is having an unbelievable success—but all this ought to have happened thirty years ago. I don't think I shall need to teach any more, yet I am sorry to abandon my idyllic Cornell. I have not yet made any decisions, but now there will be nothing to prevent us from visiting Europe in American fashion. In the meantime I am preparing E.O. for publication and finishing my Engl. translation of *The Song of Igor's Campaign.*

Our heartfelt thoughts[2] are with you and Zhikochka, be cheerful, be well, I embrace you.

V.[3]

1. A photograph of the Nabokovs' St. Petersburg house, Bol'shaya Morskaya 47 (now Herzen Street).
2. Elena Sikorski's husband was seriously ill.
3. Translated from Russian by DN.

TO: **VICTOR REYNOLDS**[1]    CC, 1 p.
Ithaca, N.Y.

September 7, 1958

Dear Mr. Reynolds,

I cannot conceal my disappointment at not getting any royalty from your edition of my "Onegin". However, I do understand your reluctance to pay royalties since you expect to sell only 975 copies over a period of several years. I have a hunch that it will sell much better than that. Let us say, then, that I shall get no royalties for your first edition of 975 copies.

On the other hand, the more I ponder the less I can see how a trade edition (less than 200 pages, comprising only the translation itself and a few footnotes) can interfere with the big book which I am offering you, and which is especially and uniquely important because of the exhaustive commentaries that will not appear in the trade edition.

Granted that, as you say, your edition would be purchased by libraries and some private collectors, I suggest that none of these would replace it by the kind of utilitarian trade edition mentioned above.

I would like you therefore to meet me halfway in this matter by allowing me to bring out the aforesaid trade edition (i.e., about one tenth of the whole book) in January 1961—although I actually see no reason why it should not appear simultaneously with the big opus.

I would very much appreciate if you could let me know what you think of this in the course of this week.

Sincerely yours,
Vladimir Nabokov

1. Director, Cornell University Press.

TO: **WALTER J. MINTON**

cc, 1 p.<br>Ithaca, N.Y.

September 8, 1958

Dear Walter,

I spent two delightful days with Paul O'Neil [1] who pumped me very delicately with great skill and acumen.

I am not very happy about the Goulden offer.[2] It does not strike me as very promising in view of his having changed his terms between the letter he wrote me and the conversation he had with you: in his letter, of which I sent you a copy, he offers definitely: 12½% on first 3,000 copies; 15% on 3,000 to 10,000; 17½% on 10,000 to

15,000; 20% thereafter. You seem to have difficulties in reaching the 20% mark—though it is true that the initial royalty he offers you is higher. If you think you could postpone clinching this business with him until you see him in London—so much the better. But if you think no time should be lost, I shall be willing to sign now.

I am sending you the copy of an offer from Lewis Allen (Producers Theatre, Inc.). I am telling him that you are handling the movie rights. His offer does not appeal to me at all. For one thing, my supreme, and in fact only, interest in these motion picture contracts is money. I don't give a damn for what they call "art". Moreover, I would veto the use of a real child. Let them find a dwarfess. I am also sending you a copy of a new letter from Chambrun [3] who says he has "a lead". But I know you do not want to deal with him.

I don't know what to think of the Canadian ban, though I am sure Prince Philip has managed to get a copy. By the way I would like to have one or two copies of this Canadian edition.

I don't know if I mentioned that the N.Y.Times mag. asked me for an essay on pornography and that I refused.

Another matter begins to bother me. I am a poor man and if all the LOLITA revenues are lumped together into one income-tax year, there will be very little left for me. I am told that some precautions can be taken when contracts are written. Should I get in touch with a lawyer? Could you suggest one—who would not be too expensive? I have been referred to a man called Max Chopnik, 9 East 40 Street— have you ever heard of him?

Finally, would you be so very kind and have the Russian copy of INVITATION TO A BEHEADING which I mailed you, sent to my son?

Very cordially,
Vladimir Nabokov

1. "'Lolita' and the Lepidopterist: Author Nabokov Is Awed by Sensation he Created," *Life International* (13 April 1959).
2. Mark Goulden of W. H. Allen.
3. Jacques Chambrun, agent who wanted to handle the *Lolita* movie rights.

TO: VICTOR C. THALLER[1]                                         CC, 1 p.

Goldwin Smith Hall
Ithaca, NY.
September 17, 1958

Dear Mr. Thaller,

When you are ready to sign the motion picture agreement with Kubrick-Harris,[2] could you try and have them pay for the rights, say, 50% in cash and 50% in so many government bonds or other safe stock? You would then undertake to pay me $12.500 a year plus so many shares or bonds. I wonder if such an agreement is feasible. I am not interested in the dividends accruing while you hold the shares. I would merely like to be protected against inflation or devaluation.

I may seem overcautious to you—but I am a European who went through two disastrous inflations, and I would feel very much easier if the matter could be worked out the way I suggest. I mentioned it to Mr. Minton, and he said it could not be done, but I am not sure that I made myself clear.

Sincerely yours,
Vladimir Nabokov

1. Treasurer of G. P. Putnam's Sons.
2. Stanley Kubrick and James Harris.

TO: PROF. JEAN-JACQUES DEMOREST[1]                              CC, 2 pp.
Ithaca, N.Y.

September 30, 1958

Dear Professor Demorest,

As you know, the prerequisite for enrollment in my course 315–316 is "qualification in Russian". By "qualification" I understand the ability to read and write, a knowledge of grammar and as much of a vocabulary as, say, is needed for the understanding, with my assistance, of Pushkin's text. This fall three students, all of them bright talented boys whom it would have been a pleasure to teach, wished to enroll in Russian Literature 315. All three had taken Russian 101–102 in the University's Modern Languages Department. That course, I am told, is designed to give "proficiency in Russian". I examined the three students asking them to 1. translate a simple Russian poem of 12 lines into English; 2. to perform a few simple exercises in declension and conjugation; and 3. to replace the blanks in a few sentences as given in the seventeenth lesson of a "Beginner's Manual" ("Conversational Russian"). After a brief spell of stunned contemplation, all three students declared that the task was utterly hopeless, that they did not understand the words and that they were absolutely unprepared for that type of work.

I should have found this situation inexplicable had I not been aware of the farce taking place year after year in the Russian Dept. at Morrill Hall. At the root of the evil there is one simple fact: the head of the Russian Language Dept., Prof. G. Fairbanks,[2] does not have any Russian. He cannot speak it, he cannot write it. I believe he can teach the linguistics of any language, including Armenian, Korean, Hungarian and what not, — but that is all he can do. So that our students are taught not the Russian language itself but the method of teaching others to teach that method.

On the other hand, since Dr. Fairbanks knows no Russian, he has no means to ascertain whether or not the instructors he appoints have sufficient Russian for the task assigned to them. The result is that the young instructors (mostly graduate students appointed by him) are likewise incapable of reading and writing Russian.

When I joined the Cornell faculty in 1948, three Russian ladies with excellent knowledge of the language and teaching were in charge of the Russian language courses. Two of them have long left, to be replaced by ludicrously incompetent young instructors whose major field frequently lies outside the Russian Language Dept. The only courses in Russian language that still have value are those given by Mrs. Jaryc. It is plain that one excellent instructor cannot outbalance the disastrous nonsense going on in the other classes.

The situation at the Russian Language Dept. has been steadily deteriorating over a number of years and now it has really reached a point at which continued silence on my part would be disloyal to the University.

Moreover, at a time when the country desperately needs Russian-language experts, it is distressing to think what havoc Mr. Fairbank's MA's and PhD's are bringing into the work of the State Department and of other agencies which require not phonemes, but able translators, and who engage Cornell alumni on the false assumption that a Cornell diploma is still a guarantee of scholarship.

Linguistics may be all right. But I want to repeat again that it is madness to have a person not knowing a given language direct the teaching of that language.

Sincerely yours,
Vladimir Nabokov

1. Dept. of Romance Literature, Cornell U.
2. Gordon Fairbanks, Division of Modern Languages.

TO: **DWIGHT MACDONALD**[1]                                          CC, I p.

Goldwin Smith Hall
Ithaca, NY.
October 3, 1958

Dear Mr. Macdonald,

This is just a short note between lecture and library to thank you for your delightful and stimulating letter.

My wife and I remember with pleasure your brief—too brief—visit.

Had not *Zhivago* and I been on the same ladder[2] (I feel his grip on my ankles), I would have been glad to demolish that trashy, melodramatic, false and inept book, which neither landscaping nor politics can save from *my* waste paper basket.

I hope to visit the New Yorker offices on the 20th or the 27th of October and hope to see you there. Thanks for your nice invitation.

Sincerely,
Vladimir Nabokov

It was good of you to put in a kind word for *Lolita* in Hollywood. Hedda Hopper is waging a spirited anti-*Lolita* campaign—on moral grounds, I understand.

1. Literary critic.
2. The best-sellers list.

TO: **ANITA LOOS**[1]                                          CC, 1 p.

Goldwin Smith Hall
Ithaca, NY.
October 3, 1958

Dear Miss Loos,
My husband asks me to tell you that he was glad to autograph *Lolita* for you.
What comes now is a little embarrassing: he has been autographing *Lolita* only for personal friends and the very few writers whose work he admires. He has refused his autograph to so many of his own students and to so many of his acquaintances that it would be impossible for him to make an exception in the case of young MacArthur.[2] He hopes you will excuse him, especially as you must have often been in the same situation.

Sincerely yours,
(Mrs. Vladimir Nabokov)

Both books are being mailed to you today.

1. The author of *Gentlemen Prefer Blondes* wrote VN on 25 September: "I have enjoyed 'Lolita' more than any book since 'Huckleberry Finn' and am endlessly grateful to you."
2. James MacArthur, the son of Helen Hayes and Charles MacArthur.

TO: **GRAHAM GREENE AND MAX REINHARDT**        TELEGRAM
Ithaca, N.Y.

LT Graham Greene and Max Reinhardt
Bodleian Westcent London

Delighted[1]

Vladimir Nabokov

October 11, 1958

1. On 10 October Greene and Reinhardt cabled VN that Bodley Head had made an offer to Putnam for British rights to *Lolita*. The offer was not accepted.

TO: *CORNELL DAILY SUN*        PRINTED LETTER
Ithaca, NY.

To the Editor:

I wish to correct two misstatements in Mr. Metcalf's article "Learning the Russian Language" (The SUN, Oct. 15):

The "one genuine Russian literature course" (Russian 317) is not offered this term[2] because of "lack of interest" but because of lack of grammar. The three bright and intelligent candidates who enrolled in this course after a year of Morrill Hall could not pass a simple test I gave them—proving that they had not been taught the most elementary rules of Russian.

I am not on the staff of the language and linguistics department as implied by the last paragraph of Mr. Metcalf's article. My courses in Russian literature (315–16 and 317–18) are given under the jurisdiction of the Department of Romance Literature and my course in

Russian literature (325–326) under that of the Division of Literature. In other words I am strictly a Goldwin Smith man.[3]

—Prof. Vladimir Nabokov

1. Published 20 October 1958.
2. The published text omitted *not* after *term*.
3. Goldwin Smith Hall housed the Department of Romance Languages and Literatures.

TO: **WALTER J. MINTON**                                    CC, 1 p.

Goldwin Smith Hall
Ithaca, NY.
December 2, 1958

Dear Walter,

Véra and I had a wonderful time with you and your charming wife and the Thallers. The TV trialogue, in a colorful setting with books, chrysenthemums and coffee cups with brandy, was a great success.

The more I think about Miss Chase's *Lolita*, the more I dislike the coincidence. I think the matter is far graver than poor Warren's faux pas. The point is that the name Lolita is constantly used by the people writing about similar situations and little girls, and if the Chase play is a success it will create an undesirable confusion. Moreover, complications would be bound to arise when or if my *Lolita* is staged. This thing worries me. Have you seen her vulgar agent again?

I wrote to the out–of–season Diana,[1] the trespassing Mexican huntress as you suggested, and got a shock in return. They wrote back in righteous wrath saying that they wanted to buy the Spanish–language rights, that they had sent an offer via Putnams on October 16th, and were told by your office to get in touch with Olympia! All rights except the English are mine, and mine only. Neither Olympia nor Girodias has any say in the matter. I am sure there is some mistake and would like you to make a note that all inquiries about translations should go to me.

Incidentally, I am about to sell *Lolita* to Japan and to Israel, which practically spans the globe.

Look up a very nice article by Richard Schickel in the November *Progressive.*[2]

Yours cordially,
Vladimir Nabokov

1. Mexican publishing house Editorial Diana.
2. "Nabokov's Artistry" (November 1958).

TO: **FRANCIS E. MINEKA**[1]

cc, 2 pp.
Ithaca, N.Y.

December 7, 1958

Dear Dean Mineka,

I have been in touch with several friends at different universities and colleges, and the two names I submitted to you are those of two teachers who seem to me to be best suited to substitute for me in the coming term.

Miss Helen Muchnic of Smith is a professor of comparative literature and of Russian literature. She has been at Smith for a number of years, has written at least one book that received excellent notices. Miss Muchnic, as I mentioned to you, could come to Cornell only for the second half of the week and would have to commute between Northampton and Ithaca. I realize that it might be difficult to have my two courses rescheduled for the last three days of the week, but you thought you might be able to arrange it.

Mr. H. Gold, the other prospect, is even better qualified to continue my courses, since he is not only a teacher but also an author. I do not know him personally but he is well recommended by reliable people. He was first mentioned to me by a friend, Miss Aileen Ward, who taught for several years at Wellesley and Vassar and has now temporarily given up teaching to finish a book of her own (on a grant). Mr. Gold seems to be quite at home in both fields (European and Russian literatures) in which my courses belong. He has other excellent recommendations. He would be able, moreover, to settle down in Ithaca for the semester and thus continue both courses at their regularly scheduled hours.[2]

I believe this should solve the problem of a replacement for me for the spring term. My own situation at this time is such that I am compelled to re–apply for a leave of absence beginning February. I would have hesitated to do it even now were I not convinced that I can be adequately replaced. However, the time is running out. I must give an answer to my two candidates since either of them would have to have time to make their own arrangements if asked to give the courses at Cornell. I would therefore be most grateful if the question could be settled in the course of this week.

Sincerely yours,
Vladimir Nabokov

PS. I would like to submit yet a third name for your consideration, that of Charles Norman. He is a professional writer, author of two novels, four volumes of verse, and biographies of Marlowe, Shakespeare, Johnson, Rochester and E.E. Cummings, as well as of a little book on Ezra Pound. He is interested in teaching the novel from a point of view close to my own. He has some Russian background. He has taught, I am told, at the N.Y.U. and the New School (Shakespeare and writing courses) and has recommendations from both. His address is 47 Perry Street, New York 14, NY.

1. Dean, College of Arts and Sciences, Cornell University.
2. Herbert Gold received the appointment.

TO: **PYKE JOHNSON, JR.**[1]    cc, 1 p.

Goldwin Smith Hall
Ithaca, N.Y.
December 16, 1958

Dear Mr. Johnson,

You are bringing out a collection of stories by a dear friend of mine, Sylvia Berkman ("Blackberry Wilderness"). I think very highly of her talent, of the delicate brilliancy of her writing and am keenly interested in the success of her book. I would very much appreciate if you could keep a sympathetic eye upon it. Please let me know when it is coming out. If Miss Berkman had not written about "Nabokov's Dozen" in the Times Book Review, I would have recommended it publicly in one way or another—but now my wings are tied.

May I ask you to have ten copies of the "Dozen"[2] shipped to me, charging them against my account? It is the ideal Christmas present. I am frankly distressed by your not advertising it.

I notice that I do not have in my files a copy of the Spanish contract regarding PNIN. I would appreciate if you could send me one.

My wife joins me in wishing you a merry Christmas.

Sincerely,
Vladimir Nabokov

1. Editor at Doubleday.
2. *Nabokov's Dozen*.

TO: **DAVID C. MEARNS**[1]    cc, 1 p.

Goldwin Smith Hall
Ithaca, N.Y.
December 10, 1958

Dear Mr. Mearns,

Tomorrow I shall ship to you by Railway Express a box of manuscripts, some Russian, some English; I am enclosing a list with this letter.

I am particularly happy to deposit in the Library of Congress the manuscripts of my early Russian novels and stories. They represent my early years, those when I was developing as a writer. They have had a tempestuous history: left in the care of a friend in 1940, when I was migrating to this country, they were scattered and partly destroyed by the invading Nazis, who assassinated my friend.[2] What could be rescued by his niece lay then for years, pell–mell, in her cellar, next to a coal heap. I eventually regained possession of what was left, at considerable cost and effort.

I have become much more careless of late as regards my recent manuscripts. *Pnin* may be lying at the bottom of a chest. *Lolita*, however, was written on index cards, and I am still using the files for some work in progress. These I shall, if I may, ship to you when I have finished using them.

I would also like to deposit with you gradually some family correspondence and papers; correspondence exchanged with publishers some fifteen years ago; correspondence exchanged with fellow writers etc.—if I may do so gradually, as I can find time to unpack, sort them out and get them ready for shipping.[3]

I would like to retain the copyright in all the material I am sending you now or may send in the future. I think that fifty years of restricted access would make me happier than a shorter period; during this period the collection would be made available only by my permission or that of my heirs.

I am notifying today the Exchange and Gift Division of the Library that my box of manuscripts is on its way by Railway Express.

Sincerely yours,
Vladimir Nabokov

1. Of Manuscripts Division, Library of Congress.
2. Ilya Fondaminsky.
3. A large number of manuscripts and practically all the correspondence and other papers referred to remain in the Nabokov Archive that was subsequently organized in Montreux. DN.

TO: VICTOR REYNOLDS                                     CC, I p.
                                                  Ithaca, N.Y.


                                          January 8, 1958 [1959]
Dear Mr. Reynolds,

   I am not sure that I made it quite clear that the right to publish
a trade edition of the translation and a limited number of notes is
of the utmost importance to me. I may have been mistaken but it
was my impression that this was understood between us from the
start of our discussions. As you may remember, I found it difficult
to agree that there should be no royalties from your first printing
of 975 copies, but no objections had ever been raised by you against
*my* bringing out a trade edition one year after publication of the entire text by you.

   As you know, it would please me very much to have the book (the
complete translation and commentaries) published by the Cornell
Press. To make things easier for you I agreed (very much against
my better judgment since in my opinion it detracts from the value
of the book) to take out the two appendixes. But I would be extremely
sorry if you insisted on sharing in the trade edition for this would
make it impossible for me to sign an agreement with the Press.


                                          Sincerely yours,
                                          Vladimir Nabokov




TO: GEORGE WEIDENFELD[1]                                 CC, 2 pp.


                                          Goldwin Smith Hall
                                          Ithaca, NY., USA.
                                          January 12, 1958 [1959]
Dear Mr. Weidenfeld,

   Many thanks for your kind letter and the interesting clippings. I
note gratefully that you have made the necessary arrangements with

a clippings agency; and it is good to learn that you are in touch with my cousin Peter.[2]

I am looking forward very much to the "full account" of the "Battle for LOLITA".

As I have already told you, your idea of gradually bringing out my other works is most appealing. I would suggest that you begin with BEND SINISTER which was published by Henry Holt here in 1947. It is out of print now and if you cannot obtain a copy I shall gladly send you one. Next, THE REAL LIFE OF SEBASTIAN KNIGHT. Then a volume of short stories (corresponding more or less to NABOKOV'S DOZEN, Doubleday 1958, with some omissions and additions) and SPEAK, MEMORY (Gollancz, 1951; corresponding to CONCLUSIVE EVIDENCE, Harper, 1951). After that I would have for you an English translation of my three best Russian novels: LUZHIN'S DEFENCE (the story of a demented chess player), THE GIFT (a novel of love and literature) and INVITATION TO A BEHEADING (a grim fantasy which at this moment is being translated into English by my son Dmitri Nabokov for Putnam). There are other novels besides as well as scholarly works such as a huge study of Pushkin's EUGENE ONEGIN (complete translation and copious commentaries), but of this later. This eliminates for the time being the troublesome problem of translation.

Now, the following little matter may seem to you trivial but it bothers me. I suspect the phrase "Mr. Nabokov is a second Pasternak" is a reporter's distortion. It might be correct to say, perhaps, as some have been doing that Pasternak is the best Soviet poet, and that Nabokov is the best Russian prose writer but there the parallel ends; so just to prevent any well-meaning publicity from taking the wrong turn, I would like to voice my objection to DOCTOR ZHIVAGO— which may brim with human interest but is wretched art and platitudinous thought. Its political aspects do not interest me; I can only be concerned with the artistic character of this or that novel. From this point of view ZHIVAGO is a sorry thing, clumsy, melodramatic, with stock situations and trite characters. Here and there a landscape or metaphor recalls Pasternak the gifted poet but that is not sufficient to save the novel from the provincial banality, so typical of Soviet literature during the past forty years. The novel's historical background is muddled and frequently quite false to fact (thus his ignoring the liberal revolution and its Western–European ideals in the sequence of events leading to the Bolshevik coup–d'état is quite in keeping with the Communist party line)—but again I am not concerned with any but the artistic aspects of the book.

In mid–February my leave of absence from Cornell will start its pleasant cycle. I would like to try and plan my movements so as to be in New York when you are there. Do let me know your schedule when it is established. I am very eager to meet you.

Sincerely yours,<br>
Vladimir Nabokov

PS. Perhaps it is too early to discuss this matter but before you decide on the binding and jacket of LOLITA may I suggest that you take a look at the pictures on jacket and cover of the Dutch edition. They are perfectly and enchantingly right. On the other hand, the Swedish edition has a horrible young whore instead of my nymphet.

1. Chairman of Weidenfeld & Nicolson.
2. Peter de Peterson, the son of VN's aunt Natalya Nabokov de Peterson.

TO: **JASON EPSTEIN**                                                CC, 1 p.

Goldwin Smith Hall<br>
Ithaca, NY.<br>
January 18, 1959

Dear Jason,

Vladimir has withdrawn his Pushkin MS from the Cornell Press. Ever since LOLITA's financial success they have been trying in various ways to extract money from him. It had been clearly established from the beginning of the negotiations that he was to keep the right to publish a trade edition of the main text and some notes. When time came to sign the agreement, the Press suddenly claimed those rights for itself. Vladimir got furious and took back the MS.

As a matter of principle he would have nothing against partly subsidising the edition. Can you think of some way of publishing the big book and then partly financing it from the proceeds from the little book? The Cornell Press (or rather its director) likes to produce "beautiful" books. Therefore the budget was to run higher than $12.000. This, too, annoyed Vladimir when they tried to make him pay for the luxury. What he would like is publish the complete text, no matter how modestly presented, even as a paperback, just so that it would be in print. Could you be kind enough to explore these possibilities? The Bollinger Foundation seems hopeless unless one has a formidable "pull" (or is a mystic or a crackpot), but what about Columbia? Or Yale? Indiana Univ. Press might do it, but they would want both the big and the trade edition. Do think of it and let us know.

Vladimir has very nearly finished the commentaries to his translation of the Igor epic and has collected a considerable number of Russian poems done by him into English, a few with notes. This collection will comprise three short dramas by Pushkin and poems from Lomonosov (XVIII century), through Zhukovski, Batyushkov, Tyutchev, Pushkin, Lermontov, Fet, to Blok.[1]

Love from us both to you and Barbara.

1. This collection of translations was not published.

TO: **WALTER J. MINTON**                                   CC, I p.

Goldwin Smith Hall
Ithaca, NY.
January 20, 1958 [1959]

Dear Walter,

Thank you for your two letters. Yes, you are right, the agreement about INVITATION should better be signed between you and me, and I should be the one to hire Dmitri.[1] I accept your terms. I would like to keep the agreement separate from the LOLITA affairs, in other words I would like to receive the advance on signature of the contract.

Something which has been bothering me. The title I originally suggested for PRIGLASHENIE NA KAZN' (INVITATION TO A BEHEADING) can be improved upon by the shorter: WELCOME TO THE BLOCK with its splendidly gruesome double entendre. The very good French translation which Gallimard has purchased is entitled INVITATION AU SUPPLICE.

I have been granted one year's leave of absence from Cornell. As you know the university's attitude toward the LOLITA matter has been above reproach. Yesterday I delivered my two last lectures to which some glamour was added by the fact that a reporter–photographer from the Swedish *Vecko journalen* (Bonnier's publications) kept snapping pictures throughout the proceedings.

I was glad to see that your beautiful ad is paying off in reorders.

The Bureau Clairouin is working on the Steimatzky agreement.[2] I was at first against it but gave in. Thanks for explaining about agent fees. I got a long letter from Girodias summarizing the past with a bizarre slant and offering me the leaf of a thorny palm.

I don't mind signing the Warren[3] agreement but let us first clear it with the Harris–Kubrick people—just in case.

Cordially,
Vladimir Nabokov

276

1. As translator.
2. Refers to an illegally authorized edition of *Lolita* for sale in Israel under the Olympia Press imprint.
3. Harry Warren, songwriter who had been approached about writing the song "Lolita."


TO: **MAURICE GIRODIAS**                           CC, 1 p.
                                                    Ithaca, N.Y.


                                                    January 26, 1959

Dear Mr. Girodias,

I have received your letter of January 14th. I am sorry that lack of time prevents my commenting upon it in detail. On several occasions in my letters to you and to Mme Ergaz I have already listed most of my reasons. I never resented my connection with your firm. What a ridiculous thing to say.

The American Customs were admitting the book anyway. No publisher has a right to share motion picture profits with the author. My consent to give you part of the proceeds from some of the foreign rights was a concession on my part, not a recognition of a "natural claim". And so on.

*I* wrote LOLITA.

                                                    Yours truly,
                                                    Vladimir Nabokov


TO: **MAX REINHARDT**                              CC, 1 p.
                                                    Ithaca, N.Y.


                                                    January 26, 1959

Dear Mr. Reinhardt,

I am very much moved by Mr. Graham Greene's attitude toward my book. Will you please convey to him my deepest gratitude.

Under no circumstances whatsoever would I consent to a bowdlerization of LOLITA.[1] In the Putnam–Olympia–Weidenfeld agreement there is a special clause to the effect that the London edition of LOLITA must be an exact replica of the Putnam edition (including my afterpiece). So far the question of abridgement has not arisen.

I wish to thank you for your continued interest in my book. As you know, I greatly appreciated your offer but the final decision was not in my hands.

With best wishes,

Sincerely yours,
Vladimir Nabokov

1. On 19 January Reinhardt wrote VN conveying Graham Greene's concern that a cut version of *Lolita* was to be published in England and repeated the Bodley Head offer to publish the complete text.

FROM: **GEORGE WEIDENFELD**                                        TLS, 2 pp.

28th January, 1959.

Dear Mr. Nabokov,

I have just returned from a trip to Holland and France and hasten to write to you and give you the latest news.

The battle for LOLITA goes on and I hope that both the press cuttings and also your cousin will have kept you up to date with developments. I look forward to seeing Mr. de Peterson again next week and discussing the strategy of publication with him.

The Times letter was obviously very helpful, although today's rejoinder by Douglas Woodruff, the editor of the Catholic paper The Tablet, is the first seriously argued thrust of counter attack.

The salient problem is one of timing. As you know the Obscene Publications Bill has now had its formal second reading and will reach the crucial committee stage at the end of February and should we are reliably informed become law in May or June. Our legal advisers and indeed our literary friends are strongly of the opinion that we should not publish before this new bill has become effective. The reason for this is that under the present law the literary quality of the book in question is held to be entirely irrelevant and one is not allowed to call any witnesses to testify to the book's merits. Under the new bill not only will literary merit be taken into account in deciding the fate of the book but the defence will be able to call witnesses to testify to the book's merits. I need not explain to you how enormously the chances of victory, in the event of prosecution would be increased if we could produce in court as witnesses the formidable array of literary personalities who signed the letter to The Times.[1]

I cabled you on Monday last as I did not want you to gain a false impression from the report of Nigel Nicolson's[2] meeting at Bournemouth on Saturday. He was reported in The Times as saying that we were not considering publication of LOLITA. It is almost impossible to know exactly what was said in the heat of an angry political meeting and he may well have inadvertently used this phrase. This of course does not represent our policy and we are going ahead with our plans to bring out the book as soon as possible. However the position changes from day to day and all I can do at the moment is to keep you in touch with events.

We are most anxious to lose no time in re–publishing your past works. The scheme you suggest regarding the chronology of this reissue seems to me admirable. I would, however, like to propose that we start off with THE REAL LIFE OF SEBASTIAN KNIGHT, followed by the short stories and your Russian novels. BEND SINISTER could be sandwiched in between the first and second Russian novels. If we could agree on this programme, we would like to publish THE REAL LIFE OF SEBASTIAN KNIGHT at the earliest opportunity—perhaps in June or July regardless of the publication date of LOLITA. My whole point is to impress on critics, the book trade and the public alike that we are bent on publishing your whole opus, which we wish to have in print as soon as possible. I am most anxious to have your permission to go ahead and I would appreciate an intimation from you as to whom we should approach regarding terms. If you could give me your approval in principle, then we could discuss outstanding details when we meet. At the moment I plan to leave London on February 20th, but it is possible that my departure may be delayed for a few days. I wonder therefore if there is any chance of our meeting in New York during the following weekend on Saturday 28th or Sunday 1st March. We could perhaps have dinner and spend the evening together. Needless to say I look forward immensely to the pleasure of meeting you.

With best wishes,

Yours sincerely,
George Weidenfeld

1. 23 January 1959. List of signers: J. R. Ackerley; Walter Allen; A. Alvarez; Isaiah Berlin; C. M. Bowra; Storm Jameson; Frank Kermode; Allen Lane; Margaret Lane; Rosamund Lehmann; Compton Mackenzie; Iris Murdoch; William Plomer; V. S. Pritchett; Alan Price Jones; Peter Quennell; Herbert Read; Stephen Spender; Philip Toynbee; Bernard Wall; Angus Wilson.
2. Partner in Weidenfeld & Nicolson and Member of Parliament.

TO: **VAUN GILLMOR**
cc, 2 pp.

Goldwin Smith Hall
Ithaca, N.Y., USA.
February 3, 1959

Dear Miss Gillmor,

I am sending you today, by Railway Express, my translation of EUGENE ONEGIN, with commentaries—eleven folders, or volumes, in all. You will find a Table of Contents at the beginning of vol.1. The Index, now in three shoe boxes, is not quite ready; it and a brief bibliography (explaining some abbreviations in my text) will be added later.[1]

I realize that a number of pages are smudgy and messy, but they are legible, and I did not want to delay matters by having them transcribed for the third or fourth time. You will also note that the first three chapters of the translation, the Introduction in vol.1, and the first hundred pages of the Chapter One Commentary have been edited (by a very able person at the Cornell University Press, before I withdrew the thing from them).

The bibliographical descriptions at the end of the Introduction will be carefully rechecked at the Houghton Library where all three first editions are represented. I also see that I shall have to repeat in vol.3, p. 160, the text of all Pushkin's own notes to E.O., which are distributed throughout my Commentary, at the lines to which they refer.

In vol. 4, disregard the red and green underscorings (my Index-maker's checks, now transferred to my second copy).

A few remarks: I use square brackets [] for my own additions within texts, and broken brackets <> to frame Pushkin's deletions in his drafts.

In the course of his work, he indiscriminately uses the terms Canto and Chapter but settles for Chapter in the published form; I have followed him. My notes are referred to by the Chapter, Stanza and Line (e.g., One, I, 1) to which they apply. When quoting verses in the original (transcription), I use accent marks; but this is done solely to help foreign readers in the matter of stress and scanning; no such accents are used by Russians in Russian script or print, and I generally omit them if the word is not part of a poem. I use capitals at the beginning of lines when giving a transcription of the original poem, or when retaining its rhythm and rhyme in translation; otherwise—no (my translation of E. O. does not render its rhymes).

I would like, if possible, to have my copious commentaries appear as footnotes (even if they do rise above sea level; the text can swim).

The *Partisan Review* is bringing out Chapter One (with a minimum of notes—about one page or so).[2]

I hope that the random observations in this letter will be of assistance to your editor, and I will readily comply with any special preferences your Press may have in the matter of punctuation, capitalization, italization and so forth.

I am absolutely delighted that you have decided to publish my book. I shall be in dithers until you tell me that the MS has safely arrived. May I ask you to acknowledge its receipt? I understand that your decision is final and am looking forward to the signing of an agreement.

It was so pleasant to talk to you on the phone.

With best wishes,

Very truly yours,
Vladimir Nabokov

1. See William McGuire, *Bollingen: An Adventure in Collecting the Past* (Princeton: Bollingen Series/Princeton University Press, 1982). See also *The Nabokov-Wilson Letters*, ed. Simon Karlinsky (New York: Harper & Row, 1979) for background on this project.
2. Not published.

TO: **WALTER J. MINTON**                                                      cc, 1 p.

Goldwin Smith Hall
Ithaca, N.Y.
February 6, 1959

Dear Walter,

I have just thought of an interesting little scheme.

As I explained in my essay appended to your edition of LOLITA, I had written a kind of pre–LOLITA novella in the autumn of 1939 in Paris. I was sure I had destroyed it long ago but today, as Véra and I were collecting some additional material to give to the Library of Congress, a single copy of the story turned up. My first movement was to deposit it (and a batch of index cards with unused American LOLITA material) at the L. of C., but then something else occurred to me.

The thing is a story of 55 typewritten pages in Russian, entitled *Volshebnik* ("The Enchanter"). Now that my creative connection with LOLITA is broken, I have re–read *Volshebnik* with considerably more pleasure than I experienced when recalling it as a dead scrap during my work on LOLITA. It is a beautiful piece of Russian prose, precise and lucid, and with a little care could be done into English by the Nabokovs. Therefore I wonder if you would be interested in publishing THE ENCHANTER somewhen, at a favorable moment—perhaps in a limited numbered edition at a rather steep price (but that would be for you to decide).[1]

Tell me how does this idea strikes you.

Sincerely,
Vladimir Nabokov

1. *The Enchanter*, trans. DN (New York: Putnam, 1986).

TO: **F. J. PIOTROW**[1]                                                        cc, 1 p.

c/o Putnam's Sons
210 Madison Ave.
New York 16, NY.
March 5, 1959

Dear Mr. Piotrow,

Your letter of February 24 has been forwarded to me in New York where I am spending a fortnight before leaving for the west. In reply to your inquiry I would like to suggest the following sources:

Russian newspapers and reviews of the period immediately following March 28, 1922 – such as *Rul, Posledniya Novosti, Russkaya Mïsl', Sovremennïya Zapiski* etc.

The new (unfinished) *Brokhaus–Efron Encyclopedia* of 1914, which has a short biography of my father.

His own articles in *Rech'* (especially those on the pogrom of Kishinev (1909), the Beilis case) and in *Pravo*.

His own description (published as a pamphlet) of his confinement in the Krestï prison (1908).

His description of a mission to England in which he took part in 1914.

My memoir *Speak, Memory* (Victor Gollancz, 1953, I believe).

I hope this may be of help to you.

Sincerely yours,
Vladimir Nabokov

1. Oxford scholar who had asked for information about VN's father.

TO: **PYKE JOHNSON, JR.**                                     CC, 1 p.

Hotel Windermere
666 West End Ave.
New York 25, NY.
March 15, 1959

Dear Mr. Johnson,

Many thanks for sending me the designs for jacket and title page of the Collected Poems.[1]

I like the two colored butterflies on the jacket but they have the bodies of ants, and no stylization can excuse a simple mistake. To stylize adequately one must have complete knowledge of the thing. I would be the laughing stock of my entomological colleagues if they happened to see these impossible hybrids. I also want to draw your attention to the fact that nowadays butterflies are being displayed on birthday cards, lampshades, frocks, curtains, candy boxes, wrapping paper and all kinds of ads.

Anyway, the body should look as in the sketch I am enclosing, and not the way they look in your artist's drawing, and the wings should be attached not to the abdomen but to the thorax. I like the texture and tints of these two insects, and the lettering is admirable.

Now, turning to the title–page butterfly, its head is that of a small tortoise, and its pattern is that of a common Cabbage White butterfly (whereas the insect in my poem is clearly described as belonging to a group of small blue butterflies with dotted undersides), which is as meaningless in the present case as would be a picture of a tuna fish on the jacket of *Moby Dick*. I want to be quite clear and frank: I have nothing against stylization but I do object to stylized ignorance.

I suggest therefore either of two courses: 1) Not to have any butterflies, or any pictures, at all or 2) To provide the insects depicted with butterfly bodies and butterfly heads and (in the case of the title–page butterfly) with a different pattern.

If you look up my correspondence with Jason regarding the *Pnin* jacket, you will note into what hideous trouble the otherwise excellent artist got in his first sketch. I think there were some fourteen mistakes.

Sincerely,

PS. I am enclosing your two sketches and my explanations of structures and patterns.

1. *Poems* (Garden City, NY: Doubleday, 1959).

TO: *ENCOUNTER*                                   PRINTED LETTER[1]
New York

Vladimir Nabokov (*who congratulates* ENCOUNTER'S *first five code–crackers, listed below*) *writes*:
"The first letters of the last paragraph of *The Vane Sisters* (ENCOUNTER, March, p. 10) form a phrase if read consecutively. Here is how it works:
I Could Isolate, Consciously, Little. Everything Seemed Blurred, Yellow–Clouded, Yielding Nothing Tangible. Her Inept Acrostics,

Maudlin Evasions, Theopathies—Every Recollection Formed Rip-
ples Of Mysterious Meaning. Everything Seemed Yellowly Blurred,
Illusive, Lost.
The coded message is:

ICICLES BY CYNTHIA. METER FROM ME, SYBIL.

"The implication is that the ghost of Cynthia, who had been such
a good painter of frost and thaw, (see p. 6, end of section 3) supplied
the brilliant icicles which the narrator saw on the first page of the
story, just before he learned that Cynthia was dead. On the same Sunday, a little later, he noticed the strange ruddy umbra cast upon the
snow by a parking meter; this came from dead Sybil.

"Unless the acrostic is as accidental as ATOM in Shakespeare's sonnet (p. 9), Cynthia has proved the correctness of her theory (described
on p. 6). My difficulty was to smuggle in the acrostic without the
narrator's being aware that it was there, inspired to him by the phan-
toms. Nothing of this kind has ever been attempted by any author. . . ."

A prize of one guinea each is being sent to Philip Gabriel
(Tadworth), Alan R. Smith (London), L. F. T. Smith (Cambridge),
Mrs. T. M. Schmoller (West Drayton), and The Rev. M. B. Sewell
(Llandeilo).

1. Published April 1959.

TO: *LIFE INTERNATIONAL*                              CC, 1 p.
                                                    New York

                                                  April 2, 1959
Dear Sir,

May I ask you to print this letter in the next issue of *Life
International*?

There are two little errors in your fascinating account of me and
*Lolita*.[1] In the photograph (p.64) showing my brother and me in boyhood he is on the *left* and I am on the *right*, and not vice versa as
the caption says. And on p.68 I am described as being "startled . . . and

indignant" when my Parisian agent informed me that the Olympia Press wanted "to add Lolita to its list": I certainly was neither "startled" nor "indignant" since I was only interested in having the book published —no matter by whom.[2]

Yours faithfully,
Vladimir Nabokov

1. "*Lolita* and the Lepidopterist," 13 April 1959.
2. An altered text of this letter was published in the 6 July 1959 issue of *Life International* along with a letter from Maurice Girodias.

TO: **PYKE JOHNSON, JR.**                                   cc, 1 p.

Hotel Windermere
666 West End Avenue
New York 25
April 15, 1959

Dear Mr. Johnson,

Thanks for sending me the designs. The title–page butterfly is now charming—a very natural and stylish little lep in comfortable surroundings. The binding–design swallowtail lacks antennae but otherwise is presentable. The jacket is well drawn but the choice of models (two popular European insects, the Galatea Marbled White and the Machaon Swallowtail) is not apt, and the whole arrangement looks like the jacket of some popular insect book for young collectors. I beg you to give up the idea of a lepidopterological jacket. Let us have it quite plain, with no drawings at all, or perhaps just a duplicate of the title–page lep.

I also thank you for your letters received this morning. I am glad the unfortunate W. & W. business is about to be settled.[1]

As to the division of foreign–rights royalties I must confess that I was under the impression that our agreements reserved 25% to

Doubleday for acting as my agents or representatives. I am very much surprised that additional agents and agent fees are involved.

Sincerely yours,
Vladimir Nabokov

PS. Now is the time to run a big ad of PNIN and the DOZEN together.

1. Wahlström & Widstrand published an abridged Swedish translation of *Pnin*. Doubleday arranged for the edition to be destroyed.

TO: **PROF. GLEB STRUVE**[1]                       TL, 1 p. Hoover Institution.

General Delivery
Sedona, Arizona
3 June 1959

Dear Gleb Petrovich,

My unconditional thanks for sending your interesting and very clearly constructed article. "First of all and before anything else" (as Lenin used to put it) I would like to clear away some obstructions and snow–covered potholes between my world and yours. I cannot understand how you, with your taste and experience, could have been carried away by the turbid Sovietophile torrent bearing the corpselike, mediocre, false, and completely anti–liberal *Doctor Zhivago*. *Ceci dit*, let me say that I valued very highly your remarks about the Russian language of our dear Edmund.[2] At present my wife and I are in a charming canyon near Flagstaff, where I am collecting butterflies. I have also completed my translation of *The Song of Igor's Campaign*, with comments, to be published by Random House (without the collaboration of the unacceptable Roman Jakobson), and have edited *Invitation to a Beheading* in my son's English translation. (This splendid book has, of course, nothing in common with Kafka.)[3]

288

There is something else I wanted to tell you some time ago, but somehow never got around to. I read somewhere once your account of Ivanov's[4] attack on me in *Chisla*. In your capacity of literary historian you may be interested in knowing that the only grounds for this attack were the following: Madame Odoevtsev[5] had sent me her book (I don't recollect its title—*Winged Love? Wing of Love? Love of a Wing?*), with the inscription "Thank you for *King, Queen, Knave*" (i.e., thank you for having written *KQK*, since, of course, I had not sent her anything). I panned that novel of hers in *Rul'*. That demolition provoked Ivanov's revenge. *Voilà tout.* Apart from this, I assume he had gotten wind of an epigram I had written for Khodasevich's album:

> *"You could not find in all of Grub Street*
> *a rogue to match him vile enough!"*
> *"Whom do you mean—Petrov? Ivanov?*
> *No matter ... Wait, though—who's Petrov?"*

I was really flabbergasted by Shmelyov's[6] letter (either in *Mostï* or *Opïtï*), demanding mention in print of the fact that he had been visited by Foma Mann.[7]

Gleb Petrovich, why don't you write a scholarly analysis of the incredibly rubbishy Pasternak "translations" of Shakespeare (my hands are itching, but we still hang together on the golden trapeze of the bestseller list)?[8]

While we were in New York we had a visit from Feltrinelli bearing a bunch of roses.

From here we shall go on to California. I hope to see you there.

> With cordial greetings to you and yours,
> V. Nabokov[9]

---

1. The acquaintance between VN and Gleb Petrovich Struve went far back, to the emigration and the university years (Nabokov and Struve had met while the former was at Cambridge and the latter at Oxford, and they had become friends in Berlin soon thereafter).

Struve had a distinguished career as a scholar, teacher, and critic of literature, and, for a long period, was professor of Slavic Literatures at the University of California at Berkeley. He is not to be confused with Prof. Nikita Struve, who vigorously propounded the lame hypothesis that VN was the real author of "Agheyev's" *Novel with Cocaine*. (It has since been established that the book was the work of Mark Levi.) DN.
2. Edmund Wilson.
3. Reference to the assertions of certain proponents of "schools" and "influences." DN.
4. Georgy Ivanov, émigré poet.
5. Irina Odoevtsev, poet and novelist; Ivanov's wife.
6. Ivan Sergeyevich Shmelyov, novelist and short–story writer.
7. The Russian form of "Thomas."
8. VN did not want his appraisal misconstrued as petty rivalry. DN.
9. Translated from Russian by Véra Nabokov and DN.

TO: **PETER MROSOVSKY**[1]

cc, 1 p.
Sedona, Ariz.

June 6, 1959

Dear Peter,

It was good to hear from you again. Your letter was forwarded to this canyon in Arizona where my wife and I are collecting butterflies. We spent some time in the Big Bend National Park, Texas which I think is not far from a former stamping ground of yours. It was interesting to read about your large family. We have only one son who is 25 now and just under 6'5". He finished Harvard with honors in 1955 and has been since then preparing for a singing career: he has an admirable bass voice. He is also a successful mountaineer, skier and translator. Some years ago he and I published a translation of Lermontov's A Hero of our Time, and this year he translated one of my Russian novels (Priglashenie na Kazn'), which Putnam will bring out as Invitation to a Beheading in September. It is very amusing that you mentioned poems because I do have a little volume of verse which Doubleday is publishing this month. By another pleasant coincidence, we intend to go to Italy, Véra, Dmitri and I, sometime in the fall. We shall also visit Paris and London. Dmitri plans a year of studies in Milan.

For the last ten years I have been lecturing every spring on Joyce's *Ulysses* which you were the first to bring to my attention forty years ago.

Best regards. Let's meet soon.

Yours,

1. Cambridge University friend.

TO: **JASON EPSTEIN**                                            CC, I p.

General Delivery
Sedona, Arizona
June 6, 1959

Dear Jasŏn,

My Song of Igor's Campaign is now finished—neatly typed out and ready to be mailed. However, before sending it to you I would like to say this:

The work consists of a foreword (18 pp. typescript) explaining the discovery of the *Slovo* and describing its structure. This is followed by an Index of the princes, a genealogical chart and a map. Next comes The Song itself (the pagination of The Song in print should correspond exactly to the pages of the typescript, 44 pp.). This is followed by a Commentary including notes to the Foreword and notes to The Song, in all 74 pp.

The further the work advanced the clearer it became that it is a book in itself which cannot be combined with that kind of second half that we had planned. That second half, the translation of the short poems of Pushkin, Tyutchev and others, would throw the book completely out of balance because it would necessarily lack the copious notes the first half has.

Seeing that the second half was supposed to cover the entire century of Russia's renaissance in poetry the commentary should have taken at least twice as many pages as that on The Song.

Since I cannot think of doing it now, and since the now completed book has turned out to be different from the "anthology" you and I envisaged, you are free, of course, to say you do not want it, and in that case I shall immediately return the advance.[1]

I hope all is well with you and Barbara. We shall stay here for another fortnight (see address given above). This is a beautiful green and cool canyon where we have a comfortable little chalet.

Véra joins her greetings to mine.

Sincerely,

PS. I hope Jackie liked the Smokies bear.

---

1. *The Song of Igor's Campaign* was published in the Vintage paperback series by Random House in 1960.

---

TO: *SATURDAY REVIEW*                            TLS, 1 p.
                                                 Sedona, Ariz.

June 19, 1959

*Re*: Belles–Lettres, S.R. of June 20th, 1959, p.20.

Sir,

If Mr. Robert Payne could compare Mr. Boris Paternak's "translations" from Shakespeare with the original text, he would discover for himself (what Sovietophile propaganda has obscured) that these are as vulgar, inept, and full of howlers, as any of the versions from Tolstoevski concocted by Victorian hacks. One cannot help doubting, however, that Mr. Payne is qualified to discuss these matters since he still does not know the difference between *mir* (мирЪ), "peace", and *mir* (мiръ), "world". I wonder if he also confuses "piece" and "whirled".[1]

Yours truly,<br>
Vladimir Nabokov

1. This letter was not mailed.

TO: **WALTER J. MINTON** CC, 1 p.

Till July 15:<br>
Gen. Delivery<br>
Sedona, Arizona<br>
July 3, 1959

Dear Walter,

Many thanks for your wire. Here is another copy of INVITATION.

Many thanks, too, for your kindness in obtaining for us the addresses of the Paris lawyers. Grasset seems to want a settlement, but I am not sure of what may come of it.

Here is something I would like to ask you: please do not ask Edmund Wilson for any endorsement of this or any other of my books. Personally, I am against all endorsements—especially the ones that come from old friends. In this case, however, I am prompted to say what I say by my utter disgust with Edmund's symbolico-social criticism and phoney erudition in regard to DOCTOR ZHIVAGO.

There is a funny LOLITA cartoon in the July *Playboy*.[1]

Regards.

As ever,<br>
Vladimir Nabokov

1. The cartoon by John Dempsey depicts a middle-aged man attempting to check into a motel with a very young girl. He is saying to proprietors, one of whom is holding a copy of *Lolita*: "Dammit, what's the matter with you people? She's my *daughter*, I tell you!"

TO: **HARRY LEVIN**                                            CC, 1 p.

General Delivery
Sedona, Arizona
July 10, 1959

Dear Harry,

I am writing you from the depths of a marvelous, green and red, well watered Arizona canyon where the mingling of deciduous trees with desertic elements of flora forms a fascinating ecological paradox.

Where are you spending your summer? We were so sorry not to have been in Ithaca when you were there. Did they show you Herbert Gold, my talented substitute?

I am hearing all kinds of good things about your Shakespeare book.

My Pushkin opus is in the process of being published by the Bollingen people, and I have two other books coming out soon: a volume of poems and a translation, with commentaries, of The Song of Igor (without Jakobson's participation). Putnams will publish in September Dmitri's translation of a Russian novel of mine, Invitation to a Beheading. Our LOLITA is doing well in France and Italy.

I cannot believe that Poggioli[1] really believes that Pasternak, whose version of HAMLET is a farce, is capable of translating Shakespeare. I can imagine how amused you were by the success of the wretched and mediocre ZHIVAGO.

Have you read two really great novels, gems of our time, Robbe-Grillet's[2] LE VOYEUR and JALOUSIE?

I am getting some wonderful butterflies here. The beautiful place where we are staying has been inhabited by Max Ernst and Cholishchev in the past, but we got here by pure chance. If you ever

Nabokov at Domaine de Beaulieu,
France, 1923

Vladimir Nabokov's mother in her
twelfth year of exile, Prague, 1931

The Nabokov family in Salt Lake
City, 1943

Father and son, Berlin, 1936 (*photo by
Véra Nabokov*)

Vladimir Nabokov teaching at Wellesley College, 1943 (*Wellesley Alumnae Magazine*)

Nabokov at the Harvard Museum of Comparative Zoology, 1947 (*Life*)

Nabokov at Cornell University, ca. 1947 (*photo by Louise Boyle*)

Ithaca, mid-1950s (*photo by McLean Dameron*)

Vladimir Nabokov with his brother Kirill and sister Elena, in Switzerland, 1959

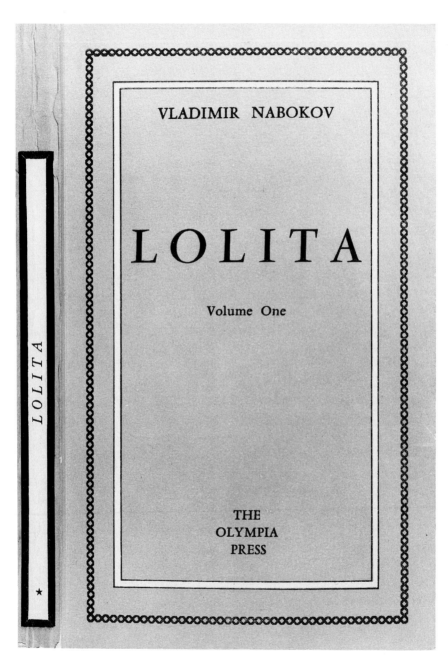

Front and spine of the first edition of *Lolita* (Paris, 1955)

*The New York Times Book Review,* 24 August 1958 (ad for *Lolita*)

Nabokov's sketch of the view from his balcony in Montreux

Nabokov in his apartment at the Palace Hotel, Montreux, with the lectern at which he wrote (*photo by Horst Tappe*)

Switzerland, July 1963 (*photo by Max Fleissel*)

The Nabokovs at Dmitri's 1961 Milan debut as Don Basilio in *The Barber of Seville*

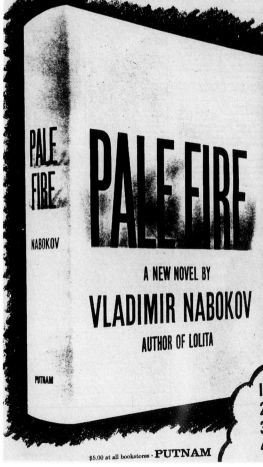

*The New York Times Book Review,* 3 June 1962 (ad for *Pale Fire*)

FIFTY CENTS *          MAY 23, 1969

TIME

THE NOVEL IS ALIVE
and Living in Antiterra

VLADIMIR
NABOKOV

Publication of *Ada or Ardor* occasioned a cover story in *Time;* the portrait is of
Nabokov's mother.

PUSHKIN
*painted by Orest Kiprenski in 1827*

*Eugene Onegin*

A NOVEL IN VERSE BY Aleksandr Pushkin
TRANSLATED FROM THE RUSSIAN, WITH
A COMMENTARY, BY Vladimir Nabokov

IN FOUR VOLUMES

1

Translator's Introduction
*Eugene Onegin* · The Translation

Bollingen Series LXXII  *Pantheon Books*

Frontispiece and title page of Nabokov's 1964 translation, on which he worked more than ten years.

The Master in his seventies

Véra and Vladimir Nabokov, Montreux, ca. 1970

Switzerland, mid-1970s (*photo by Gertrude Fehr*)

Montreux, 1970s (*photo by Horst Tappe*)

visit the west I highly recommend this resort (Forest Houses, Oak Creek Canyon).

Regards to the whole family.

Yours,

1. Renato Poggioli, Harvard professor.
2. French novelist Alain Robbe-Grillet.

---

TO: **PROF. GLEB STRUVE**          TL, 1 p. Hoover Institution.

General Delivery
Sedona, Arizona
14 July 1959

Dear Gleb Petrovich,

I wish I knew what idiot could have told you that I found "antisemitism" in *Doctor Zhivago*: I am not concerned with the "ideas" in a bad provincial novel, but how members of the Russian "intelligentsia" can avoid being jarred by the complete dismissal of the February Revolution and by the overblown treatment of the October one (what, exactly, caused Zhivago to rejoice while reading, beneath that theatrical snow, of the Soviet victory in that newspaper sheet?). And how could you, orthodox believer that you are, not be nauseated by the cheap, churchy-sugary reek? "The winter was a particularly snowy one. A frost hit on St. Pafnuty's Day" (I quote from memory). The other Boris (Zaytsev) made a better go of it. And the good doctor's poems![1] "To be a woman is a gigantic step. . . ."

Sad. Sometimes I feel as if I had disappeared behind some remote dove-gray horizon while my former compatriots are still sipping cranberry drinks at a seaside stall.

Yours,
Vladimir Nabokov[2]

1. As opposed to Pasternak's own early poems, some of which VN had praised highly. DN.
2. Translated from Russian by Véra Nabokov and DN.

TO: **JAMES HARRIS**[1]                                        CC, 1 p.

Brockway Hotel
Brockway, California
August 12, 1959

Dear Mr. Harris,

My husband asks me to write you a few lines to explain why he decided against undertaking the writing of the script for LOLITA. The day Mr. Kubrick and you came to talk things over with him he felt quite enthusiastic about the approach to the script-writing which had been evolved in that conversation. But as the negotiations dragged on, somehow the pattern became upset, and he began to feel more and more that the thing could not be managed (at least, in so far as he was concerned) along the lines that had been suggested. A particular stumbling block became to him the idea of having the two main protagonists married with an adult relative's blessing.

He hoped that a few days of quiet thought devoted to the matter amidst the Sierra pines, in complete solitude, might trigger his imagination into finding an artistic solution which would help him to harmonize your needs with his own vision of the book. But unfortunately nothing came of it.

We both enjoyed very much meeting Mr. Kubrick and seeing you again. My husband was very pleasantly impressed by the way you two had read, and saw, the book, and has no doubts that the picture you eventually make of LOLITA will be artistic and excellent in every respect.

We both send you our best regards.

Sincerely,
(Mrs. Vladimir Nabokov)

1. Co-producer of *Lolita* movie; partner in Harris-Kubrick Pictures.

то: **PYKE JOHNSON, JR.**                                        cc, 1 p.

Brockway Hotel
Brockway, California
August 16, 1959

Dear Mr. Johnson,

I have decided to postpone indefinitely the writing of PALE FIRE.[1] The work has not been advancing and I have come to the conclusion that the very existence of the contractual obligation has been interfering with the free development of the novel. I am not sure I shall ever write it; but if I do it will not be in the near future. Therefore, I would like to be released from all the obligations presupposed by that contract. I shall be in New York early in September and shall arrange then for the return of the advance of $2500 which I received from you under the contract for PALE FIRE, dated April 8, 1957.

I think my wife already wrote you that I am delighted with the book of poems. It is very pretty and quite substantial despite the limited number of pieces, and the butterfly, as finally evolved, is right lepidopterologically.

We are going to leave Lake Tahoe tomorrow by car. Because of a necessary sidetrip, we shall arrive in New York around the 1st of September. I shall be in touch with you upon our arrival there.

With best wishes,

Sincerely,
Vladimir Nabokov

1. New York: Putnam, 1962.

TO: **DMITRI NABOKOV**                                          ALS, 1 p.

1959                                                            Los Angeles

My dear Ragazer,[1]

My congratulations[2] and my love to you. I think in two or three
months we'll see each other—if not here, then in your European
haunts, else the razluka [separation, parting] will grow unbearably
tedious; how is the translation of my poor *Dar* coming along?

We await details of your success in the concert. I ask you quite
seriously: write! A longish letter should be sent to Anyuta[3] too. And
to Davidova.[4]

I am struggling with the script[5]—it is all very difficult and exhausting.

I embrace you
P. [for Pápa][6]

1. Word play on *ragazzo* ("boy" in Italian) and *rîtsar'* ("knight" in Russian).
2. Presumably in response to DN's cable that his Italian concert debut had gone well.
3. Véra Nabokov's cousin Anna Feigin, a close family friend.
4. Lucia Davidova, pioneer aviatrix, a close family friend.
5. For *Lolita*.
6. Translated from Russian by DN.

TO: **PRES. DEAN W. MALOTT**[1]                cc, 1 p. Cornell University.

c/o Putnam's Sons
210 Madison Avenue
New York 16, N.Y.
September 23, 1959

Dear President Malott,

Last February I was granted a leave of absence for one year. After
considerable deliberation I have now decided to ask Cornell University to release me from my duties there for good. With one thing
and another I feel a sovereign urge to devote myself entirely to literary

work. I have been very happy at the University and the pang of parting with it is most keen, but the burden of age is not be be discounted, and I feel that I can no longer combine the pleasures of teaching with the toil of creative writing as I have been doing for many years.

I am sure you and the Faculty will understand.

Yours faithfully,
Vladimir Nabokov

1. Of Cornell University.

TO: **GEORGE WEIDENFELD**

CC, 1 p.
New York

September 25, 1959

Dear Mr. Weidenfeld,

I am glad everything is going well with the printing of LOLITA. Please do not forget to show me the proofs—unless you are absolutely certain that no misprints could occur. I shall be in Geneva not later than October 10th and can be reached there c/o my sister, Mme Hélène Sikorski, Palais des Nations, Bibliothèque, Genève, Switzerland. I shall spend there a fortnight at least.

Your news from India is indeed disturbing. I wonder if the guilty Pandit[1] is any relation of Mme Pandit who invited me to visit her in London (we know her daughter).

Now about that Cambridge lecture. I have not heard from Mr. Annan except in an indirect way: Professor Elizabeth Hill in the letter you forwarded says "the Provost tells me that he will offer you hospitality for the night." The date (Nov. 4) would have been all right but frankly I was surprised to find myself invited by the Slavonic Department. My understanding was that I was to come as an American writer and not as a Russian professor. A lecture sponsored by the Department of English might conceivably serve your purpose in regard to the launching of LOLITA. I do not think that this purpose would be served by my appearing under the second-rate auspices of a fringe department.

Since lecturing is for me a great strain, I believe that the present arrangement would hardly justify a trip to chilly Cambridge. I suggest therefore that we drop the lecture, and that I limit my activities to being around in London when LOLITA comes out.

Let me mention in passing that ordinarily I am a very expensive lecturer though I had agreed to disregard this point for once when I envisaged my Cambridge appearance as part of your campaign rather than as an educational venture. I have retired from Cornell and am not going back.

Sincerely yours,
Vladimir Nabokov

1. R. V. Pandit, publisher of an unauthorized edition of *Lolita* in India.

TO: **MORRIS AND ALISON BISHOP**     TLS, 1 p. Mrs. Morris Bishop.
Hotel Beau-Rivage, Geneva

October 12, 1959

Dear Morris and Alison,

Your charming letter met us on the *Liberté*. The timing was perfect, and we were deeply touched.

We had a very pleasant crossing. The diet of Bonamino and Russian caviar was just right. The captain, cautiously but insistently, wanted to know just *why* V. had chosen the subject he had chosen (he was rather *calé* on Freud; he had not read *Lolita*). The head of Bobbs-Merrill, lodged in an adjacent cabin, did his best to lure V. away from Putnams (no "sale"). He said he had succeeded in luring Boyington.[1] The boat seemed to be crawling with V.'s readers and admirers (female and male, the first predominating).

Paris was undergoing a new occupation, by le Salon de l'Auto, in this case. Not a single room in any hotel, anywhere. Crowds of roomless American tourists discussing the situation at every corner and mobbing the Express. Rather than accept a room "a few miles out of Paris" we took the night train for Geneva.

It is delightful here. We are staying till the 20th, then Paris and London. We shall be in Milan by the middle of November, we think. If Alison happens to come to Italy, Mondadori of Milan, Via Bianca di Savoia 20, will have our address. But since our plans can still change (e.g. should V. find himself in the Old Bailey), it might be safer to write us in care of V.'s sister, Mme Hélène Sikorski, Palais des Nations, Bibliothèque, Genève. Is there any chance of Morris's joining Alisons later?

It was nice of you to think of the Retirement Fund matter. We have written Mineka.

We hope to see Alison in the near future, and preferably both of you.

Love from us both to you both.

V. and V.

1. Presumably Gregory Boyington, whose novel *Tonya* was published by Bobbs-Merrill in 1960.

TO: **GEORGE WEIDENFELD**                    CC, 1 p.
                                        Taormina, Italy

November 26, 1959

Dear Mr. Weidenfeld,

I thank you very much for the amusing clippings Miss Cheminais was kind enough to mail to me to Rome. They have been forwarded to Taormina.

Miss Cheminais also asks me if I wanted the subscription with Romeike & Curtice renewed. In this connection I would like to draw to your attention that my publishers in other countries take care of this sort of thing for me. This seems to be customary. If I asked you to take out a subscription at my charge this was because at that time it was still uncertain whether you would be able to publish the book, and it seemed unfair to ask you to assume any expenses before you could be sure of publishing it. Moreover, two other books of mine were then about to be published by Heinemann. Since henceforth you are to be my only publisher in England, I would consider it fair that you take care of the clippings service for me. I hope you will agree.

There is something else I would like to mention. The papers recently announced that you have commissioned Aragon[1] to write a history of Soviet Russia. You know of course without my telling you that the Soviet historians have made up a history of Soviet Russia which has nothing in common with the actual sequences of events (in fact, they rewrote it several times in accordance with the newly developed "party line"), and that Aragon, being a communist, will follow the Soviet version (especially, since Khrushchyov is supposed to give his blessing to the project when it has been completed). It is a sad and disappointing thing that this wonderful opportunity of setting the record straight should be missed and the Soviet lie get support from a scholarly work published in England. In saying this I am not taking it upon me to give you any advice. My only object is to put this on record, since you discussed the matter with me in New York and Geneva and asked me to suggest historians suitable for the job. I would like, however, to submit one suggestion: It might be a good idea to have the "history" written by Aragon annotated by some real scholar (not a political propagandist) who would be allowed to comment freely on the historical myth created in Moscow.

We are leaving for Genoa tomorrow morning. We shall be on Saturday at the Hotel Colombia-Excelsior, Genoa.

Sincerely,
Vladimir Nabokov

1. Louis Aragon of *Le Nouvel Observateur*.

TO: **MORRIS BISHOP**               TLS, 1 p. Mrs. Morris Bishop.

Genoa
December 7, 1959

Dear Morris,

It was so sweet of you to write. Vladimir was delighted that you liked INVITATION. Poor Dmitri did not get enough credit from the papers, it is quite true. For reasons of copyright, this translation had to be described as done "in collaboration with the author". With the next one it will be different.

Christmas is nearing and we wonder if you are not planning to join the Alisons in Europe. If you do, we hope to see all of you. If you are not, and Alison alone may plan to visit Italy, we hope she will get in touch with us. Our best address for the time being is that of V.'s Italian publisher: c/o Mondadori, Via Bianca di Savoia 20, Milano.

Our Italian is definitely poor. We tried the other day to find out something about the "*actualités*" given in a movie here and were given in return elaborate explanations how to get to the "tualette". Sad.

While in Paris we met there (by design) the greatest French writer of the day (V's opinion backed by Véra's humble one), Robbe-Grillet. Here is a man who should be persuaded to come to the States—if only he would agree! Do read his books, especially "Jalousie" though "Le Voyeur" and his latest, "Dans le labyrinthe", are marvelous too. He is strictly original, in writing and in speaking, and this explains why the literary prize juries did not even consider him while admiring such puffed-up nonentities as Schwarz-Bart or Butor.[1]

We are leaving Genoa (which is lovely) for a few days in Lugano, then Milan (where Dmitri will join us), then for some quiet *nook* where V. could go on with his new *book*.

We are sending you our warmest Christmas greetings and wishes.

Sincerely,
V. and V.

1. André Schwarz-Bart and Michel Butor, French novelists.

TO: **STANLEY KUBRICK**[1]

cc, 2 pp.

San Remo, Italy

December 31, 1959

Dear Mr. Kubrick,

We have just received your letter of December 21, addressed to Milan. In the meanwhile Mr. Lazar[2] has been in touch with you and with us. We are now waiting for his call but my husband welcomes this opportunity to sum up the situation in a letter from us to you.

Ever since his interview with you in Hollywood, he kept reverting in thought to the cinematic possibilities of LOLITA. The solution of the problem that had eluded him in Beverly Hills came to him in an esthetically satisfying form during our stay at Taormina. At the present time he would therefore be definitely interested in writing a script for LOLITA.

There are, however, the following considerations:

1. The financial terms, which must be discussed and settled between you and Mr. Lazar, must be such as to make the undertaking of this big task worth while for the author.

2. For the sake of a LOLITA script he is willing to lay aside and postpone a new work that he has commenced, but he is afraid that the present creative impulse pertaining to the screenplay might weaken during the course of protracted negotiations.

3. The composing of the screenplay as he now sees it would necessitate a considerable amount of freedom and non-interference. Would you be prepared to allow him this creative latitude? This means, would you be prepared to leave him to his own devices while he is writing the first draft? He could write it either in Hollywood (where we could come around mid-March), or he could start work on it immediately upon reaching a definite agreement with you, and then bring it to Hollywood in March in a half-finished condition, to finish

this first job there. At the end of this first creative stage, he would be glad to discuss the thing with you, step by step, making such changes as you deem necessary, etc.

In view of all this, my husband now suggests that you make him now in writing the best final offer you can, which would be either accepted or rejected by him. In case he does not find it satisfactory, you will be immediately notified, and will be free to engage another scriptwriter. In case he accepts it, he will ask his lawyers and Mr. Lazar to see to the details of the agreements, while he himself will either start at once writing the script or (if you prefer) will postpone the writing of the script until his arrival in Hollywood and will devote the interim period to the work now in progress.

We think we have found a house here that we would like to rent in case we are not going to Hollywood, and there is this additional consideration that we would not like to lose this house if we decide to stay on in Europe. Otherwise we could be in Hollywood, as I have already said, in mid-March or so.

As to my husband's "queries" you mention in the last paragraph of your letter, they refer to the several pictures which are being prepared by various French and Italian producers, ostensibly based on LOLITA. There is in particular the case of the Italian producer, a Mr. Alberto Lattuada, whose picture will be called "The Little Nymph" and who tells reporters that it is an "adaptation of Vladimir Nabokov's novel". The report appeared in several French papers (i.e. in the *Figaro*). The German paper *Hannoversche Allgemeine Zeitung* of Dec. 12th reports that "Nabokov's controversial novel LOLITA will, as it has been decided now, be filmed in Italy," by Alberto Lattuada etc.

Please address your letter to us, at the Hotel Excelsior-Bellevue, San Remo, Italy, mailing a carbon to Mr. Lazar, at his Hollywood address. He is flying home on Jan. 2, I believe. With best wishes for a happy New Year from both of us.

Sincerely yours,
(Mrs. Vladimir Nabokov)

In my husband's opinion a denial of this report should be sent to the papers which published it, or a general denial, strongly worded, should be given to the press.

1. Director and co-producer of the *Lolita* movie.
2. Agent Irving ("Swifty") Lazar.

TO: **STANLEY KUBRICK**                                      cc, 1 p.

> Hotel Astoria
> Avenue Carnot
> Menton, France
> January 15, 1960

Dear Mr. Kubrick,

I am replying to your letter of January 7th.[1] I think I did not convey to you my husband's suggestions with sufficient clarity. He is quite willing to start the work on the basis you suggest. In his opinion it might have been more practical to begin discussions between you, Mr. Harris and him on the basis of a short written draft. But you can have it your way.

More about Lattuada. One paper reports his script as dealing with a teenager who becomes frightened of an affair with a coeval, looks for a "cure" in an affair with a man of forty, gets "cured" of whatever inhibitions she had, and, tired of her aged lover, goes back, this time happily, to the original (or a different) teenager. Unless the middle part of the story bears too much resemblance to LOLITA, there is nothing to worry about except the title (*Le Ninfette*) and Mr. Lattuada's own declarations to the press that he is adapting LOLITA. In Italy, my husband was continuously asked if he knew that his novel was being filmed by Lattuada. And there are other movies, on similar lines, in preparation both in Italy and France.

My husband was very much interested to know that fine actors are interested in Humbert's part.

We are reserving passages on the *United States*, sailing on Feb. 19th. It will be a pleasure to see you and Mr. Harris.

> Sincerely yours,
> (Mrs. Vladimir Nabokov)

1. Kubrick had expressed concern about VN's stipulation that he be allowed to write the first draft of the screenplay without the participation of Kubrick and Harris.

TO: **IRVING P. LAZAR**                                       cc, 2 pp.

> Hotel Astoria
> Avenue Carnot
> Menton, France
> January 16, 1960

Dear Mr. Lazar,

My husband received your cable which read "HAVE CONCLUDED NEGOTIATIONS WHEREBY NABO-KOV IS REQUIRED TO BE IN HOLLYWOOD ON OR BEFORE MARCH FIRST AND NABOKOV RECEIVES THE SUM OF FORTY THOUSAND DOLLARS TO BE PAID AS FOLLOWS TWENTY THOUSAND DOLLARS PRO RATA OVER A PER-IOD OF TWENTYSIX WEEKS OR ACCELERATED IF NABO-KOV FINISHES SOONER AND THE OTHER TWENTY THOUSAND DOLLARS TO BE PAID UPON COMMENCE-MENT OF PRINCIPLE PHOTOGRAPHY BUT IN ANY EVENT NOT LATER THAN JULY FIRST 1960 PLUS AN AD-DITIONAL THIRTYFIVE THOUSAND DOLLARS BONUS IF IT IS A SOLO SCREEN PLAY PLUS WEEKLY EXPENSES OF THREE HUNDRED DOLLARS FOR 1960 EACH WEEK IN CALIFORNIA PLUS FIFTEEN HUNDRED DOLLARS ROUND TRIP TRANSPORTATION STOP PLEASE ADVISE ME IF ALL THIS IS SATISFACTORY AND WHEN YOU ARE

ARRIVING STOP WE WILL MAKE RESERVATIONS TEMPO-
RARILY AT A HOTEL AND SUBSEQUENTLY GET YOU A
FLAT OR HOUSE STOP HARRIS AND KUBRICK ARE PRO-
CEEDING WITH LAUGHTER IN THE DARK AND IT IS IM-
POSSIBLE TO IGNORE THE COMMITMENT WE MADE
SINCE IT MIGHT INVOLVE A LAWSUIT AND MORE
ABOUT THIS WHEN I SEE YOU BEST."

and replied:

"I ACCEPT HARRIS KUBRICK OFFER REGARDING MY
WRITING LOLITA SCRIPT AS STATED IN YOUR CABLE
NUMBER 131 OF JANUARY 13 STOP BOOKING PASSAGES
FEBRUARY NINETEENTH MANY THANKS."

My husband wants me to say again that he appreciated very much
your efforts on his behalf and is very pleased with the results. Our
reservations on the *United States*, sailing on the 19th of February from
Le Havre have been confirmed by Cook's. We shall stop for a couple
of days in New York so as to arrive in Hollywood on March 1st. It
would be very kind if you could reserve for us living quarters at the
Beverly Hills hotel. If you think that we shall be able to find a house
or flat within a day or two, one large room with two beds would
suffice; if this takes more time, we would like to have a bungalow,
though smaller than the very large one we had last time, but still having bedroom and livingroom.

We have written Mr. Sidney L. Posel, of Paul, Weiss, Rifkind,
Wharton & Garrison, 575 Madison Ave., NYC, and asked him to
write the contract. They will be in touch with you or perhaps you
could get in touch with them. We have asked Messrs. Posel and
Iseman to see if the contract can be written not between my husband
and Kubrick-Harris but rather between the trust my husband has
set up in New York last year and H.-K., in such a way that the
$40.000 and the less certain $35.000 would go to the trust while the
expense and traveling money would go to the author.

LAUGHTER IN THE DARK. This contract, too, would have to
be signed between the trust and H.-K. or whoever buys the rights.
It might be unwise to quarrel with H.-K. about this matter while

collaborating with them on the script for LOLITA, but otherwise, I mean, legally, they do not have "a leg to stand on". They wanted an option on condition of paying for it; they never paid, and thus can hardly claim to have acquired the option. They might, at least, agree to match the Lewis Allen offer, don't you think? But, as you suggest, this can be discussed when we have a chance to talk.

With best wishes,

Sincerely yours,
(Mrs. Vladimir Nabokov)

TO: **MORRIS BISHOP**        TLS, 1 p. Mrs. Morris Bishop.

Hotel Astoria
Menton (A.M.)
January 28, 1960

Dear Morris,

Many thanks for your letter, and welcome home!—to both Alisons.

We are coming back next month: my producers want me to come to Hollywood and write there the script for LOLITA. As you know, I had refused to write it last summer. But ever since then I regretted it because a pleasing and elegant solution of the problems involved suddenly dawned upon me in the gardens of Taormina. And then the offer was repeated (in more sonorous terms), and was accepted— especially since I am dreadfully homesick for the States.

We shall stay at Hollywood (Beverly Hills Hotel, at first; then, probably, a house) about half a year, and perhaps join Dmitri next autumn in Europe. Europe is not a hit with me. I feel bored and dejected, despite LOLITA's noisy triumphs. Time has tampered with the places I knew, and those I visited now for the first time did not promise any memories worth storing. Moreover, there are too many motorcycles.

We are sorry we missed your radio talk.

Dmitri has commenced his studies in Milan with a first-rate teacher who thinks highly of D.'s voice. Dmitri delights both in his singing master and in the Sestriere skiing slopes. And, of course, in his Triumph sport car in which he travelled from Southampton to Milan. We spent together with him some time in Milan and in San Remo.

We both send our love to all three of you.

Yours ever,

V

Vladimir Nabokov

TO: **GLENWAY WESCOTT**[1]    cc, 1 p.

Hotel Astoria

Menton (A.M.)

France

February 7, 1960

Dear Mr. Wescott,

This is a difficult letter to write. I have to choose between bad manners and the betrayal of principle. Sadly, but without hesitation, I choose the first. Believe me, I am deeply touched and feel greatly honored by the distinction you propose to confer upon me, and the little rosette is perfectly charming but, alas, I must return it.

I could not imagine belonging to an organization without being active in it—yet, in my case, any organizational activity is utterly out of the question. Socially, I am a cripple. Therefore all my thinking life I have declined to "belong". I have never joined any union or club (not even a faculty club), have never served on any committees, taken part in faculty meetings, or been a member of any organization whatsoever. I have gratefully accepted grants from organizations I respected—but would never accept a honorary degree from a university no matter how much I respected it. What should I do, what could

I do, as member of your Department of Literature? Even making a speech at a public ceremony is as impossible for me as saying grace is for a good atheist. In consequence, my name on your distinguished list would be meaningless.

So let me repeat again that I fully appreciate the Institute's kindness in electing me but must decline that honor.

Very truly yours,<br>
Vladimir Nabokov

1. Novelist and officer of the National Institute of Arts and Letters.

TO: **STANLEY KUBRICK** cc, 1 p.

2088 Mandeville Canyon Rd.<br>
Los Angeles 49, Calif.<br>
March 23, 1960

Dear Mr. Kubrick,

Here is Act One of "Lolita". I shall now climb on to the next two acts, and then do the prologue (the view will be clearer from the pass).

This Act One is, of course, still very rough and incomplete. But structurally it does hang together rather neatly. You will note the seeds I have planted and followed up (the dog, the gun, etc.). You will also note that some scenes are sketched in greater detail than others, and that I still have to write in many things relating to action, gestures, scenery, etc.

Do please ring me up as soon as you have a chance to read this.

Sincerely yours,<br>
Vladimir Nabokov

TO: JAMES HARRIS                                                  CC, I p.

2088 Mandeville Canyon Rd.
Los Angeles 49, California
April 20, 1960
*Airmail, Special Delivery*

Dear Mr. Harris,

I am informed that a French motion picture company is about to make a picture entitled *"The Nymphets"* (*"Les Nymphettes"*). The use of this title is an infringement of my rights since this term was invented by me for the main character in my novel *Lolita* and has now become completely synonymous with Lolita in the minds of readers throughout the world.

In other words, any title with the term "nymphet" in it would naturally and inevitably suggest Lolita, whether she is named or not.

Could you please find out the exact name and address of the French company in question. It is my intention to sue them without delay.

Sincerely yours,
Vladimir Nabokov

TO: *NEW YORK TIMES BOOK REVIEW*                              CC, I p.[1]

2088 Mandeville Canyon Road
Los Angeles 49, Calif.
April 22, 1960

Sir,

Mr. Popkin, in his recent article on Monsieur Girodias,[2] the first publisher of my *Lolita*, says that I "did some rewriting at Girodias' request". I wish to correct this absurd misstatement. The only alterations Girodias very diffidently suggested concerned a few trivial French phrases in the English text, such as *bon, c'est moi, mais comment* etc., which he thought might just as well be translated into English, and this I agreed to do.

> Yours truly,
> Vladimir Nabokov

1. Published 15 May 1960.
2. Henry Popkin, "The Famous and Infamous Wares of Monsieur Girodias," *New York Times Book Review* (17 April 1960).

TO: **STANLEY KUBRICK**                    cc, 1 p.

> 2088 Mandeville Canyon Rd.
> Los Angeles 49, Calif.
> April 25, 1960

Dear Mr. Kubrick,

I am sending you Act Two of the LOLITA screenplay. The concatenation of scenes proved to be very troublesome and I don't know how many times I rewrote the motel sequence. I think that it now makes some structural sense.

When you have studied the act, please give me a ring.

> Sincerely yours,
> Vladimir Nabokov

TO: **STANLEY KUBRICK**                                   CC, 1 p.

2088 Mandeville Canyon Rd.
Los Angeles 49, Calif.
June 7, 1960

Dear Mr. Kubrick,

I am sending you four new scenes, two for Act One, and two for Act Two.

*In Act One*; page 60 a (beginning of honeymoon sequence), and pp. 85 a— 89 a (the Jack Beale scene), which should go at the end of the act to replace pp. 85–86 (I think we should retain pp. 83–84).

*In Act Two*: four new pages, 14–17 (scene of the dresses) should follow old page 13; then, after new 14–17, the *old* 14 becomes new 18, and so on, to old p. 24 which is now p. 28. After this there are two *new* pages, 29–30 (scene of her telling about Charlie). From there on the pagination must be changed to the end of the act (old 26 is now 31, and so on).

I am now working on the prologue. This is more complicated than it might seem because the murder sequence must be related to still unwritten scenes in Act Three.

Sincerely yours,
Vladimir Nabokov

Encl.: 12 pp. screenplay

TO: **STANLEY KUBRICK**                                   CC, 1 p.

2088 Mandeville Canyon Rd.
Los Angeles 49, Cal.
June 17, 1960

Dear Mr. Kubrick,

I am sending you the Prologue, a batch of 25 pages. You will find therein certain allusions, as for instance to the mask, which will be cleared up in my Third Act. The whole play with the mask can, of course, be omitted if you are quite convinced you want the audience to see Humbert's face in the prologue. You will also note that several scenes pertaining to Humbert's European past can be expanded if necessary.

After considerable thought, I am leaving out, at least for the time being, the scene we discussed in which Humbert was to be engaged in some amusing job. To be amusing it would have to present various colorful details and *new* characters which, of course, I could invent, but I have come to the conclusion that artistically it would be all wrong because it would tend to bulge out and upset the unity and symmetry of the whole play as it is planned now.

I am now going to tackle the Third Act.

I am attaching a page from the Spring issue of *The Partisan Review* which you may have already seen.[1]

Sincerely yours,
Vladimir Nabokov

Encl.

1. Dwight Macdonald's "Masscult and Midcult" quotes Kubrick on p. 230.

TO: **STANLEY KUBRICK**                                          cc, 1 p.

2088 Mandeville Canyon Rd.
Los Angeles 49, Cal.
June 25, 1960

Dear Mr. Kubrick,

I am sending you fourteen new pages to replace or amplify certain scenes in the prologue. Pages 14 a to 21 a should replace the old pages 14 to 16 so that the old pages 17 to 23 become now 22 a to 28 a, after which come the new pages 29 a to 34 a.

As you will see, I have let Humbert talk about his first love but no matter how I fussed with it in my own mind I could not get him to discuss his marriage without encroaching upon the tone of his scenes with Charlotte. Therefore I have had Dr. Ray take over again (p. 20 a) after Humbert has finished with Annabel. It seems to me that it is very trim this way but if you still object to Ray's handling the Valeria scenes, we can have another discussion and try to find another way.

We shall leave on Monday, 27th, and return soon after 5th of July. The address will be: Glacier Lodge, Big Pine, Calif.; there is no phone at the lodge but messages can be left at Big Pine 351.

Sincerely yours,
Vladimir Nabokov

Encl.

TO: **STANLEY KUBRICK**                                        cc, 1 p.

2088 Mandeville Canyon Rd.
Los Angeles 49, Calif.
July 9, 1960

Dear Mr. Kubrick,

I am sending you the Third Act of the LOLITA screenplay. As you will see, I have several scenes between Quilty and the nymphet since otherwise he would have remained a ghostly, uncharacterized and implausible figure.

The act is probably too long but can be easily cut.

I was not sure whether you would want some of the scenes at the end, and so have left them in descriptive quotes.

I hope I have won you over to my vision of the last act, but if not, I am ready to discuss alternate renderings.

Sincerely yours,
Vladimir Nabokov

TO: **STANLEY KUBRICK** cc, 1 p.

2088 Mandeville Can. Rd.
July 21, 1960

Dear Mr. Kubrick,

I am sending you a new beginning of Act Three (new pages 1–40 to replace old pages 1–30) incorporating your suggestions. In the Quilty telephone scene (which follows old p. 30, now p. 40) a few details should be deleted, in keeping with the alterations (such as Humbert's long speech on old p. 35) but that is simple. I would like to go on to the corrections in the second part of the act, and then prune what has to be pruned in earlier scenes.

Sincerely yours,
Vladimir Nabokov

TO: **STANLEY KUBRICK** cc, 1 p.

2088 Mandeville Canyon Rd.
Los Angeles 49, Calif.
August 11, 1960

Dear Mr. Kubrick,

I am sending you the following new sequences (making in all 37 pp.) for Act Three.

Four consecutive scenes (pursuit, highway, service station, moving car) on new pages 47 A to 50 A (to replace old pages 47–48), after which come the picnic and trailer scenes (old pp. 49–51) which should now become pages 51 A to 53 A.

Nine consecutive scenes (Wace supermarket, street, dress store window, highway, turnout, motor court, hospital room, motel room, hospital vestibule) on new pages 54 A to 74 A (to replace the old pp. 51, 52 etc.) after which come the Grantchester scenes and the Psychiatrist, now to be numbered 75 A to 78 A.

And five consecutive scenes (continuation of Psychiatrist, Detective, class room, Humbert's office, Humbert's room, university post office) to replace the first Clemmburg scenes and to be numbered now 79 A to 91 A, so that the pagination from Examination Hall to End of Act should now become 92 A to 111 A.

Please let me know whether you now consider that the screenplay is completed or if there is any more work on it that you would like me to do.

Sincerely yours,
Vladimir Nabokov


TO: JAMES HARRIS AND STANLEY KUBRICK                    cc, 1 p.

2088 Mandeville Can. Rd.
Los Angeles 49, Calif.
August 19, 1960

Dear Messrs. Harris and Kubrick,

I have been very busy trying out tentative cuts of the screenplay to meet the time requirements. I would like to remind you that you promised to send me shortly your own suggestions in this matter. I would like to receive them from you as soon as possible so that I can conciliate the cuts with your wishes rather than do the whole work twice.

May I also repeat that I feel I could do some important improvements in the dialogue if you were able to show me screentests of the two main protagonists, or, should this still not be possible, to arrange for a ten-minute interview with each or both simultaneously (the latter would be preferable).

Sincerely yours,<br>
Vladimir Nabokov

I am enclosing two pictures that came in today's mail with a letter in Italian, explaining that this young girl is acting (or studying) under Sofia Loren's husband and that she would like to play either the main or a secondary part in LOLITA. As on previous occasions of this kind, I am informing her that I have nothing to do with the casting.

TO: **STANLEY KUBRICK**                                                  CC, I p.

2088 Mandeville Canyon Rd.<br>
Los Angeles 49, Calif.<br>
August 26, 1960

Dear Mr. Kubrick,

This is the situation: I think I have brought the script down to a reasonable number of minutes—Prologue, 10; Act One, 40; Act Two, 30; Act Three, 50—and I indicate a few additional omissions or reinstatements here and there, for you to decide. Furthermore: In a number of scenes I have trimmed down speeches and have devised new bridges where scenes are left out. And there have been some other readjustments. Now the whole play is a physical mess and has to be retyped, and I am wondering if you might have a typist familiar with this kind of work. I would have to talk to her to explain my signs on the script.

I need the weekend to finish giving the material a typable form and, once the typing is done, I shall have to go through it (on my own time).

If you would prefer to go with me over the new version of the script before it is retyped, perhaps we could get together on Monday. Please, give me a ring at your earliest convenience.

Sincerely,
Vladimir Nabokov

TO: **IRVING P. LAZAR**                                              CC, I p.

2088 Mandeville Canyon Rd.
Los Angeles 49, Calif.
August 29, 1960

Dear Mr. Lazar,

I was so busy with the screenplay that it was only this Sunday that I could give the new version of the contract the attention it deserves. It had been my impression that, after you had taken my wife to Mr. Blau's office, a satisfactory settlement of matter of publication rights had been reached. A letter I received yesterday from Mr. Davidson makes it quite clear that according to the new version of the contract, the "publishing rights still belong to the Producer and Mr. Nabokov still has a very limited right to publish the screenplay" etc. and "nothing in this agreement prevents Harris-Kubrick from publishing a screenplay based on the novel. On the contrary, publication rights in the screenplay are expressly granted."

To this I cannot agree. Since we have reached a blind alley, I wish to make one last suggestion. Let us say on the subject of publication merely this: "Neither the Producer nor the Author may publish, fictionalize or dramatize any version of the screenplay or of the motion picture based on the novel LOLITA without the written consent of the other party; the only exception to this provision shall be that the Producer may exercise those rights which are given to him by his Agreement with Putnam of _____ 1958." This implies, of course, that "publication" and "dramatization" will have to be deleted in line 14 of Par. (9) on p. 7, and the rest of the contract be made to comply with the meaning of this condition. I am not a lawyer and the wording will have to be approved by Mr. Davidson, but my meaning, I trust, is quite obvious. I would like to assume that in the present light Mr. Blau may see his way to find a plain and unequivocal wording to state this matter.

I wish to make it quite clear that this last concession is as far as I am prepared to go, or shall go at any time. This is a very big concession on my part since I am convinced that publication rights should always be left with the author.[1] In compensation for this concession I shall expect Mr. Blau to comply with my lawyer's demands in the two remaining controversial paragraphs, namely the elimination of paragraphs 13 and 29. With regard to the latter one, there is no objection on my part against the application of the laws of the State of California in case of litigation. But I do object, on my lawyer's advice, against the other implications of this paragraph, termed "harsh and unusual" by my lawyer, which would make me subject to the jurisdiction of the California courts no matter where I might be living.

I repeat with all possible emphasis that I shall not go beyond the concession I am making today. We shall be leaving Los Angeles for New York on Sept. 15th, and shall sail for Europe on Oct. 5. It would be preferable to sign this contract before Sept. 15th; otherwise it might still be signed in New York.

Sincerely yours,
Vladimir Nabokov

1. *Lolita: A Screenplay by Vladimir Nabokov* was published in 1974 by McGraw-Hill.

TO: **DMITRI NABOKOV**     HOLOGRAPH PS to Véra Nabokov letter.

2088 Mandeville Canyon Rd.
Los Angeles 49, California
4 Sept. 1960

It is very unhealthy for us to worry like this (we are 120 years old), and we simply cannot understand why you don't understand this.

P.[1]

1. Translated from Russian by DN.

TO: **STANLEY KUBRICK**     CC, 1 p.

2088 Mandeville Canyon Rd.
Los Angeles 49, Calif.
September 8, 1960

Dear Mr. Kubrick,

I am sending you an abridged and corrected copy of my screenplay LOLITA. You will observe that I have not only eliminated several long scenes but have also introduced considerable alterations in the remaining dialogue, changing a number of phrases and spanning with new bridges the gaps between sundered parts.

You have thus a practically new version of the play.

It is up to you, of course, to re-introduce, if you wish, any of the deleted scenes—you have them all in your copy of the old versions. I still feel painful twinges in my torn ligaments (the elimination of the marvelously moodful motel dialogue in Act Two hurt most), but I do think that the play has now gained in unity and neatness.

Sincerely yours,
Vladimir Nabokov

TO: **DMITRI NABOKOV**                                                    TLS, 1 p.

2088 Mandeville Canyon Rd.
Los Angeles 49, Calif.
October 7, 1960

My dear,

Today I sent you a telegram asking you to stop the "Lolita publicity"[1] and would like to say the following to you.

This publicity is in very bad taste. It can only harm you in the eyes of those who take music seriously. It has already harmed me: because of it I cannot come to Italy since the reporters would immediately pounce on me there, and I would have to deny categorically everything that you or your agent have been saying.

Here I have resolutely kept my distance from the search for an actress and from all casting matters. This was in the interest of my reputation, and also in that of the producer. I cannot tell you how unpleasant, repugnant even, I find the reports in the Italian press linking you with a presumed search for an actress (who has, incidentally, long since been found by Kubrick and Harris).

No less important is that this unhealthy ruckus can only dilute your young fame.

We are leaving here on Wednesday, 12 October, for New York, where we shall stay at the Hampshire House Hotel, Central Park South. On 2 November we shall sail on the *Queen Elizabeth* for Cherbourg. From there we shall head for Geneva, and arrive on Tuesday, 8 November. You please come there too.

Your recordings will probably be completed by then. Arrange your schedule so as to arrive on Tuesday or, if that is impossible, at the end of the week, for as many days as you can. Fly if you want.

Mother will soon write you at which hotel we shall stop in Geneva.

I embrace you
Pápa

Hotel rooms must be reserved in Geneva. I would like your reply to this letter, confirming that you will be in Geneva on 8 November (or the tenth if you prefer), to be waiting for me at the New York hotel.[2]

1. DN had yielded to the various temptations of a project to arrange a "Lolita" contest at DN's Milan apartment. For two days those lodgings were invaded by decidedly postpubescent aspiring nymphets, some with provincial mothers in tow. The jury was composed of DN's opera colleagues—Anna Moffo, Giulio Fioravanti, and others—as well as friends prominent in other fields. The Italian press and newsreels gave the event considerable coverage. VN's assessment of this puerile stunt was perfectly accurate. DN.
2. Typed in Russian on English-language keyboard. Translated by DN.

TO: **DMITRI NABOKOV**          HOLOGRAPH PS to Véra Nabokov letter.

Nice, France

Jan. 16, 1961

I have interrupted my literary labors to compose this instructive little jingle:

In Italy, for his own good,

A wolf must wear a Riding Hood[1]

Please, bear this in mind.

Love,
Father

1. DN's parents were concerned about the possible consequences of his amorous adventures. DN.

TO: **RUST HILLS**[1]          cc, 2 pp.

57, Promenade des Anglais
Nice (A.M.)
February 11, 1961

Dear Mr. Hills,

Many thanks for your letter. I am not annoyed with you, and, in fact, may have some curious material for you very soon. And had you not raised the point yourself, I would not have bothered to bring to your attention what follows.

Helen Lawrenson's article[2] in your issue of August 1960 contains some absurd misstatements:

1. ". . . said Mrs. Nabokov calmly, '. . . when we were very poor in Paris I supported him by working as a milliner, and he has always been so grateful that he never gets angry at me.' "

My wife never worked as a milliner, nor in any other shop, and anyway could not have made that trite and silly remark.

2. Her father was not "the former owner of the largest and most important publishing house in Russia." He was an industrialist, and a jurist by education.

3. "In the opinion of some of his colleagues" [on the Cornell University faculty] "if the book had not been such a success, he would probably have been fired."

The book, published in 1955 by the Olympia Press of Paris, did not become "a success" until published by Putnam in 1958. There was ample time in which to fire me. Actually, however, during the years my book was banned in France, prohibited in England, and vilified by vulgarians, and up to 1959, when I deliberately and regretfully left Cornell, administration, faculty and students showed me nothing but sympathy, respect and understanding.

4. Finally, let me quote this incredible passage: "He . . . of course, feels that in the good old days of the Czar, a freedom-loving Russian had more freedom than under Lenin, without, however, specifying whether he meant freedom-loving aristocrats or freedom-loving serfs."

Irony, of course, is all right, but when starved by ignorance it chokes on its own tail; for surely any schoolgirl should know that no serfs existed in Russia since 1861, one year before the liberation of slaves in this country, and all lovers of freedom certainly realize that it was Lenin who restored serfdom in Russia.

I do not intend to continue though there are some other less piquant items I might list. None of these blunders was inevitable: all you had to do was send me your article to check the factual points before publishing it. Let me repeat, I would not have written this letter, but you asked for it. I have no objection to your publishing it, and indeed would welcome your correcting those errors as soon as possible. We should not allow future commentators to make fools of themselves by relying on fancy articles.[3]

With best wishes,

Sincerely yours,
Vladimir Nabokov

1. Fiction editor at *Esquire*.
2. "The Man Who Scandalized the World," *Esquire* (August 1960).
3. *Esquire* published corrections in the June 1961 issue with a cartoon.

TO: *THE INTERNATIONAL HERALD TRIBUNE*                CC, 1 p.

57, Promenade des Anglais
Nice (A.M.)
Feb. 25, 1961

Sir,

I am about to start a devastating war against genteel mistranslators. This, however, is an incidental foray. In your issue of February 25–26, 1961, Mr. Thomas Quinn Curtiss quotes a passage from what he calls "the best to my knowledge" translation of "Uncle Vanya" in English (by Rose Caylor). Does his knowledge include some familiarity with the original text? I am asking this because one of the glaring errors in that passage is the corny "We shall see Heaven in all its radiant glory" instead of the literal "We shall see the whole sky bediamonded" or, paraphrased, "ablaze with stars".

Yours truly,
Vladimir Nabokov

1. Not mailed.

TO: *THE NEW STATESMAN*                                         CC, 1 p.

> 57, Promenade des Anglais
> Nice (A.M.)
> February 25, 1961

Sir,

If, as I suspect, it is a robot that has composed the Associated Television Limited "Russian" advertisement in your issue of February 17, 1961, page 253, he, or it, should be scrapped at once. There are thirteen incredible blunders in those ten lines (my favorite is *"Tot ugorov"* instead of *"Etot dogovor"*). Or was it the company's object to provide the Muscovites with an example of British humour?[1]

> Yours truly,
> . Vladimir Nabokov

1. Unpublished.

TO: **ROBERT C. CRANE**[1]                                      CC, 1 p.

> 57, Promenade des Anglais
> Nice (A.M.), France
> March 15, 1961

Dear Sir,

I am in receipt of your letter of February 17th.

As a novelist, I have, I think, imagined some of my characters driving through New Jersey. As a lepidopterist, I see maps and visualize regions in terms of the butterflies found in this or that place; and New Jersey is for me the State from which have been described certain exciting butterflies, such as Hessel's Hairstreak (type locality: Lakehurst) or Aaron's Skipper (type locality: Cape May).

> Yours truly,
> Vladimir Nabokov

1. Chairman of the State of New Jersey Tercentenary Commission; he had asked VN for a "New Jersey experience."

TO: **GEORGE WEIDENFELD**      CC, I p.

57, Prom. des Anglais, Nice (A.M.)
March 18, 1961

Dear George,

I am writing to advise you that Vladimir has started proceedings against Olympia Press in the French courts.

Olympia has failed to pay on the two last statements. Nor have they paid within a delay of eight days given them by a "mise en demeure" executed by Vladimir's lawyer (in Paris).

It may be that Olympia is short of money. Anyway, here is Vladimir's chance to break this impossible connection (I could not begin to tell you all the unpleasantness of it, especially since the time M. Girodias began to make pronouncements in favor of pornography; he has also consistently used LOLITA as a kind of shield for his list of publications some of which are absolutely devoid of any artistic value and extremely repulsive).

Vladimir would like to repeat his request that you do not make any payments to The Olympia Press, either now or later, until the suit has been decided by the courts. Olympia may apply pressure to make you pay. Vladimir would be grateful if you could resist it as long as you possibly can. Perhaps depositing any sums that may be due to Olympia in escrow (I think this is the correct English term) might solve the problem. Anyway, if you paid anything now to Olympia, you would jeopardise V.'s chances to obtain a resiliation of his contract with Olympia.

By way of information, Vladimir wants me to add that his object is not to deprive Olympia of any money (he had offered Olympia to buy back from them the rights in LOLITA but Olympia was not agreeable). V.'s purpose is to sever once and for all a connection which, with the passage of years, proved immeasurably more obnoxious than he had ever expected it to be, both because of Olympia's publications list and because of the character of its owner.

We shall be away from Nice for a few days the week before Easter (probably returning just after Easter) and shall then stay on at the above address until about April 27th.

With kind regards,

Sincerely,
(Mrs. Vladimir Nabokov)

TO: **RUST HILLS**                                                    cc, 1 p.

57, Prom. des Anglais, Nice
March 23, 1961

Dear Mr. Hills,

I was delighted to receive your kind letter of March 2 which took exactly three weeks to reach me. Yes, I do have that material for you, and since you are brave you might like to consider it. It is a narrative poem of 999 lines in four cantos supposed to be written by an American poet and scholar, one of the characters in my new novel,[1] where it will be reproduced and annotated by a madman. The parenthesis I have added for magazine publication at the end of the last canto explains briefly, but I think sufficiently, what the pre-novel reader should know. If you want this poem despite its being rather racy and tricky, and unpleasant, and bizarre, I must ask you to publish all four cantos. The novel is going to take several more months to finish, and there might be some showable parts later on.

Thanks for your fairness in the matter of the Lawrenson article. Yes, I should have howled earlier; my general policy is never to argue with anything written about me but your letter prompted an answer.

I shall be out of town for a few days but my address remains the same till April 25.

Sincerely yours,
Vladimir Nabokov

*Poem enclosed.*

1. *Pale Fire. Esquire* declined VN's offer because of its policy against publishing poetry.


TO: **JACQUELINE STEPHENS**[1]    cc, 1 p.
Nice, France

September 15, 1961

Dear Miss Stephens,
    My husband asks me to tell you, in reply to your kind letter of Aug. 22, that he is fairly indifferent to gastronomic matters. However, he detests 1) underdone meat, 2) all inner organs, such as kidneys, brains, liver, tongue, sweetbread, etc., 3) sea food other than fish.

Sincerely yours,
(Mrs. Vladimir Nabokov)

1. Compiler of a projected book of celebrity recipes.


TO: **MORRIS AND ALISON BISHOP**    TLS, 2 pp. Mrs. Morris Bishop.

Palace Hotel, Montreux
November 4, 1961

Dear Alison and Morris,
    We had hoped to hear from you before, or during, or after your Italian trip—we had also hoped to see you on that occasion. Have you been to Italy? Did you have a happy and successful trip? Did

Morris find those impressions he was after with regard to his Petrarca book? Has he finished the HISTORY?

We have settled down for the winter in Montreux. The weather here, though mild, is no match for that on the Riviera, but there is much less traffic noise, and also we have found a much more comfortable place to live. Vladimir has been writing steadily, with very few interruptions, since December 1960, a book which he had started several years ago. It is almost finished now—and is not like anything either he or anyone else has ever written before. It is absolutely fascinating, I wish I were permitted to say more about it.[1]

Between Nice and Montreux we spent two months in Italy and two more in the Swiss mountains. But we did not move much around because as soon as we got anywhere Vladimir settled down to write and there was no point in interrupting his writing again. We have a rented Peugeot 404, which took us to Reggio, to Dmitri's debut (which was wonderful), to Modena (where one of his performances took place), then to Stresa, etc. Dmitri sang again in a concert in Milan (Rubinstein's "Demon"), then in Perugia (where we did not go), and again in Milan in September, twice in the Barbiere, where he used Shalyapin's[2] make-up and was tremendously acclaimed by the public.

Our plans for the future are a little vague. We extended our return passages till the fall 1962—so I suppose this is when we shall be going back. I shall hate to give up all the comforts of European life, but Vladimir misses the States very much, the language, the general atmosphere, everything, including the American lepidoptera. However, there are certain things right now that make it necessary for him to be in Europe.[3]

The film LOLITA (everyone tells us it is a "marvellous" picture but we have not yet seen it) has passed the British censorship, so it will certainly be shown in England, Germany, the Scandinavian countries and Italy, and—? This is something that remains to be seen.

The mountains around the lake are covered with snow, but we still were playing tennis last week. The lake is a delight to look at, all kinds of water fowl are arriving for the winter, replacing happily the tourists who are leaving, leaving, have almost all left. We like it here very much.

Please write soon and tell us all about you. What is little Alison doing this year? Will you be much in Ithaca? Has Alison ("big" Alison) painted much, and what? We would love to hear from you.

Much love from us both to you all.

As ever,
V. and V. Nabokov

1. *Pale Fire* (New York: Putnam, 1962).
2. Feodor Shalyapin (Chaliapin), great Russian basso.
3. Vladimir and Véra Nabokov did not return to America, except for isolated visits for professional or personal reasons.

TO: **JENNINGS WOOD**[1]                                                       cc, 1 p.

Palace Hotel
Montreux
December 7, 1961

Dear Mr. Wood,

I am sending you tomorrow the manuscript of a novel, entitled PALE FIRE, which I have just completed, and the typescript of which is being mailed to my publisher in New York.

The manuscript is written in pencil on index cards of which there are about 1075. The book consists of:

Foreword (cards I–XLVII); A narrative poem in four cantos (cards 1–88); A commentary (cards 89–925); And an Index (cards 926–1029).

The commentary *is* the novel.

The material has been divided into three packages which are being mailed to you by registered airmail, as "commercial papers".

I assume that this material will be treated in the same confidential manner as the papers and manuscripts I sent you before.

I would appreciate if you could let me know that the three batches have safely arrived.

Sincerely yours,
Vladimir Nabokov

1. Of The Library of Congress.

TO: **STANLEY KUBRICK**                CC, 1 p.
Montreux, Switzerland

December 17, 1961

Dear Mr. Kubrick,

Please believe that I have never held you responsible for my not having been shown the picture.

Since you have been so kind to send me that wire, I shall now confess that not only have I been disappointed not to have been the first to see the film, but also not to be kept informed of the general developments. I would have liked to know the tentative date of the general release; whether or not it has received the seal of approval in the US (I know it did in England); who will distribute it in the various countries. It was my plan to attend the premieres in the US[1] and in some of the European countries (where, my publishers tell me, this might help the sales of the book of which several new editions are planned); any additional information would have been welcome—and also some stills.

Since I am entitled to a percentage of the profits I would have thought that that kind of information would be sent me as a matter of course. I apologize for putting all this griping in your lap but it is the only lap available to me.

I take this not unpleasant opportunity to wish you and your family, as well as Mr. Harris, a merry Christmas and a happy New Year, and my wife joins her wishes to mine.

Sincerely yours,
Vladimir Nabokov

PS. Please do not forget to return the clippings I sent you from here.[2]

1. The three Nabokovs accepted an invitation to attend the *Lolita* premiere in New York on 3 June 1962.
2. Articles in European newspapers about *Lolita*.

TO: **MORRIS BISHOP**                    TLS, 1 p. Mrs. Morris Bishop.

Montreux, March 5, 1962
Palace Hotel

Dear Morris,

I have had a busy time but now the yellow-beaked alpine choughs that have been haunting our balconies are getting ready to return to their summer quarters high up in the mountains, and Putnam is getting ready to publish my new novel. And I am able to relax a little.

I have greatly enjoyed your review of Ciardi's *Dante*,[1] and the subsequent exchange of letters. I wonder which will come out first— Cornell Press with your *History*[2] or Bollingen with my *Onegin*. I am in the act of correcting the last proofs. Have you reached that stage? I shall never forget Reynolds'[3] huge and absolutely uninhabited desk.

Is the Muse being kind to you? (as my Commentator says in *Pale Fire*). I saw a wonderful sample in the *Saturday Review*.

I hope Arthur Mizener[4] did not really mean what *The New York Post* made him say.

We are living very quietly in this hotel. Our apartment is under that of Peter Ustinov, whose tread I know well by now. The *Lolita* film will soon be released, as the saying goes, but I have not seen it yet. Dmitri's carreer is developing well but the poor boy had a bad case of food-poisoning and had to spend a month in a hospital. As soon as he got out he felt entitled to do some skiing in Gstaad.

How are you all? Our love to all three of you.

As Ever,
Vladimir Nabokov

1. *New York Times Book Review* (24 December 1961).
2. *A History of Cornell* (Ithaca: Cornell University Press, 1962).
3. Victor Reynolds, director of Cornell University Press.
4. Cornell colleague.

TO: **A. C. SPECTORSKY**[1]                                         CC, I p.

Montreux, May 9, 1962
Palace Hotel

Dear Mr. Spectorsky,

My husband thanks you for your kind letter of April 18 (which, incidentally, came by surface mail).

My husband asks me to say that he is flattered by your confidence in his versatility, but that he has never seen Brigitte Bardot either on the screen or in life, and that the entire project has no interest for him.[2]

He sends you his kindest regards.

Sincerely yours,
(Mrs. Vladimir Nabokov)

1. Associate publisher and editorial director of *Playboy*.
2. Spectorsky had invited VN to "undertake a study of Brigitte Bardot."

TO: **JASON EPSTEIN**                                              CC, I p.

Montreux, May 9, 1962
Palace Hotel

Dear Jason,

First of all let me thank you, or not thank you, for Harry Matthews' THE CONVERSIONS. It is a shapeless little heap of pretentious nonsense. When I used to teach Creative Writing, there would always be at least one student who would reel out this kind of automatic stuff. Sorry.

Véra and I look very much forward to seeing you and Barbara in your high-ceiled abode in the beginning of June.

As ever,
Vladimir Nabokov

TO: *THE LONDON TIMES*                    PRINTED LETTER[1]

Sir.—I find my name listed in the programme of the Edinburgh International Festival among those of writers invited to take part in its Writers' Conference. In the same list I find several writers whom I respect but also some others—such as Ilya Ehrenburg, Bertrand Russell, and J.-P. Sartre—with whom I would not consent to participate in any festival or conference whatsoever. Needless to say that I am supremely indifferent to the "problems of a writer and the future of the novel" that are to be discussed at the conference.

I would have preferred to bring this to the notice of the Festival Committee in a more private way had I received an invitation to the conference before my name appeared on its programme.

Yours truly,
VLADIMIR NABOKOV.

Palace Hotel, Montreux, May 26

1. Published 30 May 1962.

TO: **MELVIN J. LASKY**[1]                                        CC, 1 p.

Zermatt, July 20, 1962
Hotel Mt. Cervin

Dear Mr. Lasky,[1]

My husband asks me to thank you for your note marked "July 20" to which was attached copy of a letter you received from Mr. Dwight Macdonald.[2] We both hope that you will visit Montreux at a time when we shall be there. To the end of July we shall stay at Zermatt, and *may* go to Cannes for August.

With regard to Mr. Macdonald's letter my husband asks me to transmit to you the following comment from him:

"Sirs,

Criticism is valid only when illustrated with examples. Mr. Dwight Macdonald offers none. Hence his criticism can apply only to a delusion (especially since he conjures up an "unknown graduate student"—who would have been the redemption and glory of my years of professorship, had that student ever existed).

Vladimir Nabokov

In case you publish Mr. Macdonald's letter, you may also publish the foregoing comment (provided it is used in the exact wording given above).[3]

With best wishes,

Sincerely yours,
(Mrs. Vladimir Nabokov)

1. Editor of *Encounter*.
2. Macdonald had written to *Encounter* (September 1962) attacking VN's "Pushkin and Gannibal" (July 1962) and asking if the magazine would have published it if the author had been "an unknown graduate student."
3. Published in the September 1962 issue of *Encounter*.

TO: **PETER AND JOAN DE PETERSON**     TLS, 2 pp. Glenn Horowitz.

Zermatt, July 24, 1962
Hotel Mt. Cervin

Dear Joan and Peter,

We feel terrible to find that Joan's letter of many weeks ago was not answered sooner. We had hoped for a while that the LOLITA premiere might take place in London, but no, it was New York, and Vladimir naturally wanted to attend. We sailed on the *Queen Elizabeth* on May 31 and came back on its next trip. This allowed us exactly two very busy, very amusing, very tiring weeks in New York plus exactly two weeks going from Montreux to New York and back. Dmitri flew over for only eleven days, but we all three attended the opening night of the film. Vladimir had been worrying about the picture but already after the preview they arranged for us before the premiere he felt completely reassured. The picture might have been somewhat different had he made it himself but it certainly was excellent anyway and contained nothing whatsoever that he could find offensive, false or in bad taste. He liked the performance of all the four actors[1] and even found some of the deviations from his script were very fortunate. The English premiere will be in September (we do not know the exact date yet). We hope to come over to London for that occasion. Especially since PALE FIRE will be published by George Weidenfled at about the same time. We are very much looking forward to seeing you again if this trip materializes.

In the meantime we are spending a month in Zermatt and shall probably go to a small place just above Cannes for August. Do you both or any one of you have any plans of visiting Europe in August? If yes, could we arrange a meeting somewhere?

Our permanent headquarters is Montreux (Palace Hotel). They will forward mail throughout the summer. We shall go back there some time in September and stay until spring when we may go back to the US.

Vladimir was very pleased that Joan found PALE FIRE amusing. Unexpectedly and amazingly, it has been for two weeks now on the bestsellers list (at the very bottom of the list, but nevertheless there).

We do not expect it to stay there for long. It is indeed a very funny book, and only few reviewers realized what it was really about. The best article was by Mary McCarthy in *The New Republic*[2] but literally scores upon scores of enthusiastic reviews appeared throughout the US. A notable exception was the NY Times and its Book Review.

Zermatt is charming. One of its nicer features is a complete absence of automobiles. If you have to drive you must hire a horse and buggy. This is very upsetting to Elena's citified dog who thinks that horses (he has never seen one in Geneva) are some kind of monsters from which it is his sacred duty to protect his mistress. Zhika plans a trip to Greece in the fall. Dmitri will come to stay with us in Cannes.

Last week a team of very brilliant young television men who put on "The Bookman" show for the BBC came over for a televised interview with Vladimir. Since they brought a kind of girl Friday with them from London and a three-man team of technicians from Zurich, and since the six of them with all their photographic and soundtrack equipment followed Vladimir for two days all over Zermatt, mostly in cabs, unpacking, putting up cameras and mikes, repacking, moving to another location, and all the time shooting pictures of V. catching butterflies or talking, this occasion, I am afraid, became for many tourists the highlight of their stay here. They followed in droves! And one little old lady (not this one) did her best trying to get into the picture. Altogether we had a marvelous time, and the BBC men felt confident they had a magnificent picture. It will be run in the fall and we shall try to advise you of the exact date and hour.

Do write us soon. We hope we may have an opportunity to get together before too long.

Love to both of you from us both.

V. and V.[3]

1. James Mason, Sue Lyon, Peter Sellers, and Shelley Winters.
2. "A Bolt from the Blue," *New Republic* (4 June 1962).
3. Butterfly drawing beneath signature.

TO: **BARLEY ALISON**[1]                                                      CC, I p.

Zermatt, July 24, 1962
Hotel Mt. Cervin

Dear Miss Alison,

I am sorry to say that I find the jacket design for PALE FIRE with the mauve beatnik horrible, disgusting and tasteless. If I have any say in the matter I would like to insist that it be as plain as possible, with no pictorial effects, and in the same style as the American edition. The lettering is hideous. It should be large, simple, and very black.

I am rushing this letter express. It arrived only today having been addressed to Saas-Fee. Please cancel the Saas-Fee address and use the one in Zermatt till the 28th, after which it will be best to write to Montreux whence my mail will be forwarded. We are planning to spend August at a place near Cannes.

With regard to your request for autographs for the Cheltenham Festival, I regret to say that I never give autographs and cannot make an exception that would automatically involve me in more and more autographing.

Very sincerely yours,
Vladimir Nabokov

1. Of Weidenfeld & Nicolson.

TO: **GEORGE WEIDENFELD**                                                    CC, I p.

Montreux, September 25, 1962
Palace Hotel

Dear George,

We are back in Montreux. I notice with dismay that another London publisher has published somebody's novel under the title of BEND SINISTER.[1]

I read with pleasure your remarks on PALE FIRE. On the other hand I am perturbed by the fact that you published that vicious Soviet stooge Aragon's History of Russian Revolution, falsified with the gleeful aid of the Soviets themselves.

I want to ask a favor of you: clippings. I am buying regularly Observer, S. Times, S. Telegraph, S. Express, D. Express, D. Mail, N. Statesman, Spectator, Punch and Encounter. I wonder if you could supply me with cuttings from the rest?

The weather here is blue and silver, and we have a charming new flat here at this hotel.

Best regards,
Vladimir Nabokov

1. Juliet Dymoke, *Bend Sinister* (Jarrolds)—an historical novel that used VN title, apparently innocently.


to: **WILLIAM McGUIRE**[1]     TLS (XEROX), 1 p.
Montreux, Switzerland

January 15, 1963

Dear Mr. McGuire,

Many thanks for your kind letter of January 11 and the delightful Epiphany gift of page proofs vol. 3 right through Ap. 2. I also thank you for agreeing to do a separatum of that Appendix. I am enclosing the prefatory note with the proposed title-page.

I would by no means object to your selling or sending out copies of the Notes on Prosody.[2] Would you be so kind as to send copies to the following:

University Libraries (Cornell, Harvard, Berkeley, Wellesley, Columbia, Stanford, Oxford, Cambridge and London), NYL, BM, BN (any others?); periodicals: The New Yorker, New Republic, Encounter, Times Lit. Suppl. (no others); people (if this is not asking too much): Harry T. Levin (14 Kirkland Pl., Cambridge), Morris Bishop,

903 Wyckoff Rd., Ithaca, NY, Edmund Wilson, c/o The New Yorker, 25 W. 43, NYC.

For myself I would be happy to have 20–25 copies.

I have practically finished reading the page proofs of vol. 1 (with prelims) and vol. 2, and they will be in BW's[3] hands next week. Alas, the inevitable has happened. That little virgin has been left too long with the shipwrecked sailor on Christmas Island, and in result the beautiful and once intact page proofs of my translation of the poem have undergone a number of changes. Not only have I now achieved almost total literalism, but I have managed to match every recurrent epithet of Pushkin's with a recurrent English one (except in such cases of course where another shade of sense in the hard-working Russian word required a different English epithet). If possible I would like to check the revised page proofs of the translation (only).

Upon BW's advice I bought a repulsive-looking stamping machine and used it to number the 5000 cards of my Index; it had a very sick six, it made a thunderous thump, and at the start of every new century it would muff the last three digits. Two hefty chaps from Kramer Brothers[4] came for the three boxes, and since January 3 a girl has been taking pictures of sets of four cards. Every other day I have been dropping in to inquire if l'Index n'a pas froid, etc., but the people here don't understand jokes. The photostats will be ready and cut up after tomorrow.

My wife joins me in wishing you, BW and EO a very happy New Year.

As ever,
Vladimir Nabokov

1. Of the Bollingen Foundation
2. Princeton: Bollingen, 1964.
3. Bart Winer, Bollingen editor.
4. Montreux stationery store with copying service.

TO: **PASCAL COVICI**                                         CC, 1 p.

Montreux, Switzerland

February 23, 1963

Dear Pat,

I liked very much NOTES FROM A BOTTLE FOUND ON A
BEACH AT CARMEL. It is an elegant blend of inspiration and
information. But while it is a pleasure to express my admiration, I
am obliged to warn you that what I have just said about Mr. Connell's
book is not for quotation.[1] I am emphatically against blurbs penned
by friendly fellow-writers. I have been often asked to contribute quot-
able lines and have always refused, and of course I cannot make an
exception in this case. Incidentally, my latest books are as free of these
ornaments as were my very first ones.

Yours very cordially,
Vladimir Nabokov

1. Novelist Evan S. Connell, Jr.

TO: **GEORGE WEIDENFELD**                                    CC, 1 p.

Montreux, Switzerland
March 30, 1963

Dear George,

I have your letter of March 28th (to Véra) and the books. Since
you are so eager about it I shall certainly sign a copy of the paperback
LAUGHTER IN THE DARK for Sir Allen Lane.[1] I want to put
on record, however, that I find the cover design of this edition atrocious, disgusting and badly drawn besides having nothing to do whatever with the contents of the book. I would appreciate if you would
use your influence and have them substitute a pretty dark-haired girl,
or a palmtree, or a winding road, or anything else for this tasteless
abomination. In any case, please show them this letter. And please
do put it in your future contracts with them that I have to be con-

sulted about cover designs. The one they put on NABOKOV'S DOZEN was pretty bad and insulting, but this one is the limit.

Cordially yours,
Vladimir Nabokov

1. Founder of Penguin Books.

TO: **GERMANO FACETTI**[1]                                cc, 1 p.

Montreux, April 13, 1963
Palace Hotel

Dear Sir,

Thank you for the opportunity you gave me of seeing the proposed cover for INVITATION TO A BEHEADING.

I think a cover should have some aesthetic appeal. Mr. André François' macrocephalic homunculus has none. Moreover, I object to the style he has chosen with its, by now academic, simplifications and distortions. I am returning your sketch and am sending you another one.[2] It is in the spirit of the book and translates some of its poetical quality (which is absent from the pseudochildish drawing you sent me). I would be happy if you could use it as it is. If there exists some technical reason against using it, then at least you will have a clear idea of what I want for this book.

Yours truly,
Vladimir Nabokov

1. Of Penguin Books.
2. By DN; it was used for the 1963 Penguin paperback.

344

TO: **WILLIAM MCGUIRE**                    TLS (XEROX), 1 p.

Montreux, May 26, 1963

Dear Mr. McGuire,

I have nothing against Edmund Wilson's immersing himself, as you say, in the final revised, or revised final, page proofs of my EO; but he should not be made to immerse himself in one puddle at a time. He should have the whole torrent at his disposal.

Any reader of the Commentary (vol. 2 and vol. 3) must have before him vol. 1 (Introduction and Translation) and vol. 4 (Appendixes, Original Text and Index). A work of this kind cannot be studied piecemeal, and a critic of Wilson's kind should not be deprived of the task and pleasure of comparing the translation with the 1837 text (which he does not have in his library) or of consulting the index (without which he could not track down certain short poems mentioned in the commentary).

I do not want to exert undue pressure on you but I am convinced that for a serious study a reviewer must have the entire text on his desk before him. I therefore suggest that we wait until we can supply Edmund Wilson with the final version of the complete text, and only in case of an insuperable craving give him at least vol. 1 (complete and revised), vol. 2 (ditto) and the 1837 Russian text in page proof, *all in one batch*. You do not have my blessing for this course but only my very reluctant agreement.

I would like to add that I do not believe that a distinguished critic's review (or indeed any review) helps to sell a book. Readers are not sheep, and not every pen (pun) tempts them. Some of my best flops had been ushered in by extravagant (albeit well deserved) praise from eminent critics. The only thing that is of some help to the commercial success of a book (apart from topicality or sexuality) is a sustained advertising campaign, lots of ads everywhere.

This leads me to another consideration. During the last years publishers have been steadily sending me novels (mainly powerful ones with dirty dialogue) for endorsements, and these I have steadily refused to give. In some cases I notice with dismay that the authors had endorsed my own books in the past. So a couple of years ago

I wrote Walter Minton of a great decision I had taken, in consequence of which the jackets of PALE FIRE and THE GIFT are without endorsements. I am afraid I must also ask you not to quote any friendly opinions in the jacket of my EO.

Yours ever,
Vladimir Nabokov

Could you make me a present? I would love to possess Huntington Cairns' critical anthology THE LIMITS OF ART.[1]

1. New York: Pantheon, 1949.

TO: **WILLIAM MCGUIRE**　　　　　　　　　TLS (XEROX), 1 p.
Montreux, Switzerland

June 14, 1963

Dear Mr. McGuire,

I am worried by the reference to "aspersions" in your letter of June 10. I do not have my text here but whatever "aspersions" I cast on the Deutsch-Elton-Radin-Spalding versions, they should *not* be diluted. Please, send me *my* text of the "aspersions". As far as I remember that passage, it was a very important one, and it should remain *tel quel*. Why on earth should I spare the feelings of Babette, Dorothea, Oliver and the gallant Henry S.—or of their publishers?

I also object to my being "grateful for permission to quote" them and Edmund Wilson. Why can't I quote if I like? Please explain this to me. It sounds awfully mawkish. To *whom* am I "grateful"? "Grateful" is a big word. And anyway, if unavoidable, all these acknowledgements should be made by my publishers and not by me.

In answer to your other suggestions:

Acknowledgement to Houghton.[1] OK.

Credit BW[2] for his work: In the Vol. 1 foreword (and I, too, should receive some credit for the Index).

"A photographic reproduction," etc.—OK.
But my aspersions should be treasured, not "diluted".

> Yours ever,
> Vladimir Nabokov

Copy to Mrs. Warren

Yes, I would like to see the "brilliant" translation of Walter Arndt[3]—whoever that is—but will not mention his work—whatever its worth.

1. The Houghton Library, Harvard University.
2. Bart Winer.
3. Recipient of the Bollingen Prize for poetry translation in 1963.

TO: **BART WINER**                                          cc, 2 pp.

> Palace Hotel
> Montreux, Suisse
> August 21st, 1963

Dear Mr. Winer,

I have just received your kind letter of Aug. 19, 1963. Sorry—I emphatically object to deleting most of the epithets you list. This is a matter of principle. Omitting them would mean admitting censorship—and censorship is the villain of my book. If a paraphrase is ridiculous and if an illustration is monstrous, I will say so. I will not give in. I will summon Pushkin's ghost to fight Elton's poltergeist. Indeed, I regret very much having allowed some of my kittens to be altered during the copy preparation; in a few cases the stylistic considerations suggested to me were valid and these prevailed—since the moral strictures were safely tucked up elsewhere.

Taking up the matter specifically, I wish, first, to establish that the dead cannot take legal action against the quick. Spalding, Elton, and

Brodski are no more with us. This eliminates five of the fifteen quibbles (Elton's triteness, [2]463; his being inimitable [3]4; Spalding's inability to write poetry [3]185; the character of Elton's versification [3]187; and Brodski's political servility; [3]363). Secondly: since nobody took legal action several years ago when the passages in question first appeared in print, i.e. in the articles I published in American and Russo-American literary reviews, it is highly unlikely that any action would be, or could be, taken now. This eliminates three more of the remaining ten quibbles (Foreword, p. 3, "unfortunately": see my article on Problems of Translation, Part. Rev. 1956, p. 506; Miss Deutsch's incredible coyness, [2]463: see P.R. 1956, p. 509; and [3]7 Penguin's execrable *Candide*: see the notes to my Servile Path in Brower's collection.[1] We have seven left. The two items [2]112 and [2]424 (asking for the omission of "ridiculous" and "ludicrously" would, if agreed to, make my text absurd; and item [3]234 ("grotesque achievement") has already been pruned once and should not be pruned any more. My criticism of the infamous EO illustrations in [3]353 is so dear to me that I would prefer giving up the publication of my entire work rather than surrendering that passage. This leaves us with three, and only three items, and these may be modified if really desirable, namely [2]186 (substituting "misleading" for "atrocious") [2]285 (omitting "unbelievable nonsense"), and [2]286 (omitting "and hideously").

Your—or rather Bollingen's—letter is very upsetting. I would like those lawyers of theirs to give me a single instance when a literary critic's describing a translator's mistake as "ridiculous" or "atrocious" or "nonsensical" ever lead to legal action on the part of that translator or of his publisher, or of their associated shades.

You should have received the rest of the index by now.

Thanks for the Note of Acknowledgement and the Headnote, but please delete the word "perhaps" which is ambiguous and superfluous. The Note heading the Commentary is OK.

My wife is in Zurich (Plaza Hotel) but I hope that she will be back here in a couple of days. We would be delighted to spend an evening at the Montreux-Palace with Miss Gillmor and Mr. Barrett.

I regret very much that I cannot come to London. I have cancelled my television engagement there; but thanks all the same.

> Yours ever,
> Vladimir Adamant Nabokov

Copy to William McGuire

1. *On Translation*, ed. Reuben Brower.

TO: *THE SUNDAY TELEGRAPH*                                    CC, I p.

> Montreux, August 24, 1963
> Palace Hotel

Sir,

I cannot resist correcting a cruel misprint in your caption (August 18, 1963, page 3) under the photograph of King George V, Tsar Nicolas II, and his son, the Tsarevich. The inadvertent substitution of "Tovarich" for the last word is especially distressing in view of the fact that it was indeed a *tovarishch* ("comrade" in the Bolshevist sense) who a few years later was to murder the poor little boy.

> Yours truly,
> Vladimir Nabokov

TO: **AL LEVIN**[1]                                          CC, I p.

> Montreux, September 13, 1963
> Palace Hotel

Dear Mr. Levin,

My husband asks me to thank you for your letter of September 9. He has not seen the article in *Nugget*, which makes it difficult for him to answer your letter. At the time he was writing LOLITA he studied a considerable number of case histories ("real" stories) many of which have more affinities with the LOLITA plot than the one mentioned by Mr. Welding. The latter is mentioned also in the book LOLITA. It did not inspire the book. My husband wonders what importance could possibly be attached to the existence in "real" life of "actual rape abductions" when explaining the existence of an "invented" book. He is particularly curious as regards the meaning of Mr. Welding's statement about "a shrewd maneuver to provide himself legal protection." Legal protection against what?

Had he read Mr. Welding's article, my husband might have been able to give you more pertinent comment although he fails to see what importance that article could possibly have.

Sincerely yours,
(Mrs. Vladimir Nabokov)

1. Of *The New York Post*. Levin had called VN's attention to an article by Peter Welding claiming that *Lolita* was based on the abduction of eleven-year-old Sally Ann Horner by Frank LaSalle.

TO: **JACK DALTON**[1]  TLS (XEROX), 1 p.
Montreux, Switzerland

October 15, 1963

Dear Mr. Dalton,

In answer to your kind letter of September 21, my husband asks me to say that he thinks ULYSSES by far the greatest English novel of the century but detests FINNEGANS WAKE "whose obscenities when deciphered are not justified by the commonplace myths and silly anecdotes they laboriously mask."

He very much regrets that the amount of work already lined up for the next year or two does not allow him to undertake the writing of an article on this subject.

Sincerely yours,
(Mrs. Vladimir Nabokov)

1. James Joyce scholar.

TO: **STANLEY EDGAR HYMAN**[1]                          CC, 1 p.
Montreux, Switzerland

December 15, 1963

Dear Mr. Hyman,

My husband asks me to thank you for your letter of Nov. 19 and for sending him a copy of your review in The New Leader.[2]

He also thanks you for inviting him to speak or read at Bennington College. To his great regret he cannot accept it because he plans only a very short stay in the East.

Regarding your kind and admirable review: We do not think we have much chance of convincing you that my husband has no Oedipus complex; that Fyodor's mother is not his mother; that Zina has no resemblance to me; or that my husband has enough good taste never to put his wife, or his courtship, in his novels. After all, it would only be our word against Freud's. But one thing my husband would like to ask you. Who was your "consultant in Russian literature"? We strongly suspect that this person was pulling your leg—if he or she exists. It is a matter of historic record (and even Freud could do nothing about it) that my husband never signed any poems or indeed anything else with the name "Godunov-Cherdyntsev". (Are you sure your consultant did not confuse this name with that of a minor poet Golenishtshev-Kutuzov?). And it is of course absurd to equate Koncheev with Khodasevich, a much older man whose reputation had been well established before the Revolution.

Sincerly yours,
(Mrs. Vladimir Nabokov)

1. Literary critic.
2. "Nabokov's Gift" (14 October 1963); review of *The Gift*.


TO: **BYRON DOBELL**                                    CC, 1 p.
                                          Montreux, Switzerland

                                               January 8, 1964

Dear Mr. Dobell,

   I have given much thought to the highly attractive and flattering
offer (in your letter of Dec. 27) to take the place of Miss Dorothy
Parker whose admiring reader I have been for many years.[1]

   Very reluctantly, I must decline it. I am a painfully slow writer:
it would take me ten days at least to write my column, and I could
not possibly fit this regularly into my crowded schedule. I am not
getting any older but neither is my present season that of blooming
and energetic youth.

   It is, of course, not a matter of pay which I consider quite adequate
but purely one of non-elastic time.

   With best regards,


                                          Sincerely yours,
                                          Vladimir Nabokov


1. Dobell, an *Esquire* editor, had invited VN to take over the magazine's book-review column.


TO: **ERNEST KAY**[1]                                   CC, 1 p.
                                          Montreux, Switzerland

                                               March 3, 1964

Dear Sir,

   My husband asks me to send you his answers to your questions
of December 27th:

   1. Pencil
   2. Anyhow

3. Anywhere

4. It finds me

He has also a question for you: Why do you spell his name with two "a"s?

Yours truly,
(Mrs. Vladimir Nabokov)

1. Of the London publication *Time and Tide*; he had asked VN how he wrote, when he wrote, where he wrote, and how he found inspiration.

to: DMITRI NABOKOV      HOLOGRAPH PS to Véra Nabokov letter.

Hampshire House
One Fifty Central Park South
New York 19, N.Y.
11 April 1964

In his short opening speech Levin mentioned that the writer's son had climbed the walls within which his father was lecturing.[1] Your father embraces you, my dearest. I am writing standing up; that is why the handwriting is so *nabokiy* [lopsided].

I love you. My dearest! Keep well!

Pápa[2]

1. VN had given readings at Harvard, where he was introduced by Prof. Harry Levin. DN and a fellow-student had climbed Memorial Hall at Harvard while his father was a visiting lecturer, but not during VN's lecture. DN.
2. Translated from Russian by DN.

TO: *NEW YORK REVIEW OF BOOKS*                PRINTED LETTER[1]
                                              Montreux, Switzerland

I have often been asked to allow the reprinting of my old verse translations (such as the three stanzas in the *Russian Review*. 1945, mentioned by Mr. Arndt) and have always refused since they are exactly what Mr. Arndt says—lame paraphrases of Pushkin's text. They may be a little closer to it than Mr. Arndt's effort but still have nothing in common with the literal translation I have prepared now.

—Vladimir Nabokov

1. VN's response published with Walter Arndt, "A Reply to Vladimir Nabokov: Goading the Pony" (30 April 1964).

TO: **GILBERTE NABOKOV**[1]                ALS, 1 p. Elena Sikorski.

                                              Montreux-Palace
                                              Montreux
                                              May 5, 1964

My dear Gilberte,

I understand what you are experiencing too well to try to send condolences. Believe me when I say that Véra's thoughts and mine are with you in the profoundest sense. The shock of losing my poor brother was a great one. I regretted very deeply not being able to come to Brussels;[2] on the other hand, I know that, with that keen, charming sense of humor that made him such an original being, he would only have been grateful that I was absent, and would have cast no more than a smile on his own funeral. It is a very meager consolation, I know, but one truth is undeniable: the only thing the death of a beloved person cannot take away from us is the living, colored image of him which remains with us like a benediction and a promise.

Affectionately,
Vladimir[3]

1. The Belgian wife of Nabokov's brother Kirill. The latter had lived in Brussels and died of a heart attack while employed by Radio Liberty in Munich on 16 April 1964. His widow, whom VN knew only very slightly, was to perish not long afterwards in a Brussels department-store fire set by an arsonist. DN.
2. Nabokov was in the U.S. at the time of his brother's death, and was prevented by speaking engagements from returning in time for the funeral. This letter was written shortly after his arrival in Montreux.
3. Translated from French by DN.

TO: **WILLIAM McGUIRE**                                      TLS (XEROX), 2 pp.

Montreux, August 18, 1964
Palace Hotel

Dear Bill,

I am returning Miss Volochov's Index to Notes on Prosody to you (not to BW) as I think the thing should be retyped taking into account my drastic corrections—the deletion of all non-names, and then forwarded to BW. Yes, I would like to see the galley proofs.

The essay is so short, and the Table of Contents so informative, that the inclusion of "scuds", "tilts" etc. in its index is completely unnecessary. I am quite sure of this, and have deleted all references to them in Miss Volochov's Index. On the other hand, I think that all the titles cross-referred to author *should be* included.

I have answered your main queries in the corrected Volochov

Index. The mistranslation is "Copper" (Edmund Wilson's blunder in his tribute to Pushkin). The correct translation is "Bronze". Thus the slight change in the main Index should be: "Bronze [mistranslated Copper] Horseman"; but in the present index "Bronze Horseman" is enough.

I have taken note of the errors in the general Index listed by Miss Volochov except "Poltava" which despite her strange assertion *is* indexed both as "Poltava" and under P.'s works!) and the two last (which are for you to settle). I have now completed a list of some thirty errors (all trivial) in the four volumes. I am saving them for later, as you suggest, but the question is should they not be corrected in the British edition or given there under *Errata* at the end?

Incidentally, I wonder if it would not be worth while to add a footnote on p. 492 of vol. 3 (to "monosyllabic adjectives"): "Not counting, of course, the monosyllabic predicative forms—adverbish mongrels, really—of disyllabic adjectives, such as *glup*, "is stupid", from *glupïy*, or *bel*, "is white", from *belïy*." I would also like to insert a cautious "most" between "as" and "nonmasculine" on p. 491 of the same volume. Question: Should we include these two corrections in the new edition of Prosody so as to thwart the pounce of purists?

You say you hope I have been as pleased as you about the good press. The only good of it is that some of its banal compliments might be useful for commercial purposes, and this is why I repeat it would be wise to include these pearls of publicity in a full-page advertisement now or in the early fall. It seems to me frivolous, after spending so much money on the production of my work, to let it float away on a random ripple. Otherwise, I have no illusions about these articles. None of the reviewers is really competent. Poor Simmons[1] (whose book on Pushkin, teeming with mistranslations and other errors, I generously omitted from my commentary) is no scholar, and his knowledge of Russian has always been very patchy. Lydia Pasternak Slater's translations of her brother's poems are almost as bad as her brother's translations of Shakespeare's plays. Stephen Nichols, Jr., is no doubt a disciple of one of my victims. Salisbury[2] is a well-meaning journalist. And so on. I have not seen Barkham's[3] review but I do get the S.R. which takes only a fortnight to reach me—much faster than the Santa Maria.

Yes, I have heard from the British publisher about the publication date.[4]

I hope your boys will arrive in excellent shape. I am sure you will have a splendid year together.

As ever,

V

Vladimir Nabokov

PS. Yes, apostrophization, of course, on p. 32 (orig. 477).

PPS. Please give Miss Oldham my thanks for her letter of August 11.

1. Ernest J. Simmons, *Pushkin* (1937).
2. Harrison Salisbury of the *New York Times*.
3. John Barkham of *Saturday Review*.
4. London: Routledge & Kegan Paul, 1964.

TO: **WILLIAM MCGUIRE**
cc, 1 p.
Montreux, Switzerland

August 27, 1964

Dear Bill,

I have decided not to insert an errata slip in the British edition.

Thank you for trying to include one of the corrections in the Prosody separatum.

The "Koenig, Dame, Bube" is "King, Queen, Knave", as translated by Dmitri from my Russian, and will be published by Putnam in due time, and "Das Bastardzeichen" is my "Bend Sinister" (about to be republished by Time, Inc. for their reading circle).

Yes, I did intend to delete the entire "rhyme" entry.

I am glad you like my little discourse on reviewers. Good

Pushkinists among the expatriates who followed the Russian muse abroad, such as Hodasevich and Gofman,[1] are long dead. In Soviet Russia political considerations must taint any mention of my work. The Foundation keeps looking forward to the Edmund Wilson article; but as I have mentioned before his Russian is primitive, and his knowledge of Russian literature gappy and grotesque. (He is a very old friend of mine, and I do hope our quarter-of-a-century correspondence in the course of which I attempted not quite successfully to explain to him such matters as the mechanism of Russian—and English—verse, will be published some day).[2]

We enjoyed the visit here of Miss Gillmor and Mr. Barrett.

Véra and I send you our kindest regards.

As ever,<br>
Vladimir Nabokov

1. Vladislav Hodasevich and M. L. Gofman.
2. *The Nabokov-Wilson Letters 940–97*, ed. Simon Karlinsky (1979).

TO: **WILLIAM MAXWELL**[1]        TLS, 1 p. Harvard University.

Montreux, October 5, 1964

Dear Bill,

In recent years I have been increasingly hampered by a resolution I took at the very start of my literary career five decades ago never to react either to friendly or adverse reviews of my books. Updike's article on *The Defense* in an issue of *The New Republic*[2] that I have been shown today is so charming, intelligent, witty and splendidly phrased that I find it very hard not to respond directly. The fact that just before his review's appearance (about which, of course, I knew nothing at the time) I naively chanced to praise his work in a letter to you, is a really diabolical—but otherwise rather satisfying—coincidence, which is the chief reason for my writing this note.

Yours ever,

V

Vladimir Nabokov

1. Editor at *The New Yorker*.
2. "Grandmother Nabokov" (26 September 1964).

TO: **JANE HOWARD**[1]                                              CC, 1 p.

Montreux, October 5, 1964
Palace Hotel

Dear Miss Howard,

Thanks for letting me see your jottings.[2] I am returning them with my notes and deletions. I do hope you won't find the latter too discouraging. You have done your job extremely well, but I didn't. Much of what I said was idle talk, mainly and lamely meant to entertain you and Mr. Grossman[3] in between business.

I am a poor *causeur*, and this is why I prepare my answers to interviewers in writing; and since this method takes up time, I very seldom grant interviews. Several things that I said, and that you took down, are quite unfit for publication. I cannot discuss my obesity in public. I do not want to embarrass a heroic, and now ailing, cosmonaut by recalling a fishy television program. I find it unseemly to speak of my pedigree or of the butterflies bearing my name. I cannot be made to criticize contemporary writers. I have sufficiently worried poor Zhivago. The Gogol bit has already appeared in my book on Gogol, and the Tolstoy bit, referring to his having been infected by a complaisant Swiss chambermaid, should not be mentioned in this kind of discussion. My remarks about British vulgarity are also not for print in this form. And I would rather not mention the odious *Fact*[4] at all. Finally, the history of *Lolita* has been aired many times and is old hat, and I have said what I wanted about the film in my written answer.

Let me repeat that it was a great pleasure to talk to you. We all three enjoyed your and Henry Grossman's visit tremendously. Please, do not resent my fastidious and fussy alterations. I did take a lot of trouble with the written answers I sent you.

We hope you had a marvelous stay at Ercoli.

Kindest regards,
Vladimir Nabokov

1. Free-lance interviewer for *Life*.
2. "The Master of Versatility—Vladimir Nabokov: Lolita, Languages, Lepidoptera," *Life* (20 November 1964).
3. Photographer.
4. Magazine published by Ralph Ginzburg.

TO: **GEORGE WEIDENFELD**                                   CC, 1 p.

Montreux, October 27, 1964
Palace Hotel

Dear George,

Vladimir has now heard indirectly from you (via Dmitri) and from Mr. Thompson (via Walter Minton) that the British Museum has informed you they have available about 50% of Vladimir's butterfly list. He considers this good news. But he has been waiting in vain to hear from your office *which* are the species on his list that are represented in the BM collection. Of those subspecies they don't have, some could be replaced by others, and many might be found in the Museum d'Histoire Naturelle in Paris. He would like to be put now in direct touch with the person who did the research for you at the BM. He would then also get in touch with the French museum.[1]

It has now been more than a year since you first mentioned this project. As you know, Vladimir is very much interested. On the other hand, he has been putting off many other things because of it (things that by now would have been accomplished), and the delays and silences are keeping him, he says, "in a constant state of perplexity and irritation." He thinks that if you still intend to go on with the project, some schedule ought to be worked out *now*. For instance, he finds it rather odd that more than a fortnight has elapsed since Minton told him of your having received the BM report without his having received a copy of it.

There is another small matter I must mention—that of the statements. My letters to your bookkeeping department have so far elicited, piecemeal, all but the PALE FIRE statement (which was due at the end of September, and now October is almost gone). I wonder if you could think of some way to organize this more efficiently, some way that would spare me the necessity of writing so many letters on this subject?

Finally, Vladimir asks me to add that he has received the copies of your charming edition of THE DEFENSE but "has not the vaguest idea when it is coming out."

Besides and beyond those tiresome matters, we are sending you our cordial greetings, and are still hoping that your peregrinations may some day touch Montreux.

Sincerely,
(Mrs. Vladimir Nabokov)

---

1. In 1962 VN and Weidenfeld began discussing the possibility of a complete and fully illustrated catalogue of European butterflies, including photographs of all species and major subspecies. Unfortunately Weidenfeld saw fit to abandon the project. DN.

FROM: **ALFRED HITCHCOCK**　　　　　　　　　　　TLS, 3 pp.

November 19, 1964

Dear Mr. Nabokov:
Further to our conversation on the telephone regarding future

projects I have in mind and for which I require stories, I would like to give you a rough outline of two of them with the hope perhaps that one or the other might interest you to develop into a story.

If perhaps you would become interested, I would like to point out that I do not require any rights except motion picture and television. Any literary rights would belong to you.

Now the first idea I have been thinking about for some time is based upon a question that I do not think I have seen dealt with in motion pictures or, as far as I know, in literature. It is the problem of the woman who is associated, either by marriage or engagement, to a defector.

I think in the case of the married woman, there is very little question that she sides with her husband. We have, for example, the case of Burgess and MacLean, where Mrs. MacLean eventually followed her husband behind the Iron Curtain, and obviously Mrs. MacLean had no other loyalties. The question I'm really interested in is what would be the attitude of a young woman, perhaps in love with, or engaged to, a scientist who could be a defector.

To give you a crude example, let's imagine that Von Braun's son is as brilliant as his father and has been working on very secret projects. He has become very American and, to all outward appearances, completely removed from any of his father's background. But suddenly one day, he wants to go on a vacation and visit his father's relatives—the old folks.

To the security people this excursion could be interpreted in a way that casts doubt upon his true intentions. In other words, they wonder perhaps whether he's going to defect (naturally there could be other circumstances that would give them this idea).

The young man's fiancee is the daughter of a senator and she was to accompany him on his excursion. The security people, having their doubts about the young man, endeavor to enlist her help.

The motion picture line for this story would develop into the journey behind the Iron Curtain and expressed in terms of action and movement, but within it all, would be the basic problem faced by the girl. Who knows? Maybe she goes over to the side of her fiance. It would depend upon how her character is drawn. It is also possible if she did this, she might be making a terrible mistake—especially if her fiance, after all, turned out to be a double agent.

The feasibility of a man posing as a defector, but in reality is an agent for the government, could arise entirely out of the close security methods within the government. We have seen examples of how the FBI is ignorant of what the CIA is doing, and sometimes the CIA is not always aware of what some higher-ups are doing in these intelligence jobs.

Anyway, Mr. Nabokov, the type of story I'm looking for is an emotional, psychological one, expressed in terms of action and movement and, naturally, one that would give me the opportunity to indulge in the customary Hitchcock suspense.

Now this next idea I'm not sure will really appeal to you but, on the other hand, it might.

Many years ago I started to work on an idea for the English company to which I was under contract. The idea was never completed because I left to come to America. I wondered what would happen if a young girl, having spent her life in a convent in Switzerland due to the fact that she had no home to go to and only had a widowed father, was suddenly released from college at the end of her term. She would be returned to her father, who would be the general manager of a large international hotel (at the time I imagined it would be the Savoy in London). This general manager, the father of our young heroine, has a brother who is the concierge, another brother who is the cashier, another brother one of the chefs in the kitchen, a sister who is the housekeeper, and a bedridden mother living in a penthouse in the hotel. The mother is about 80 years of age, a matriarch.

The whole of this family are a gang of crooks, using the hotel as a base of operations. Now into this setting comes our young 19-year-old girl. As you will see, the hotel setting—especially the "backstage" part—would be extremely colorful, especially when the bulk of the story would take place, not only backstage, but in the public rooms and even to the night club section. In other words, I was looking for a film that would give us the details of a big hotel and not merely a film played in hotel rooms.

Arnold Bennett, the famous English novelist, had quite a fascination for hotels. He wrote two books, one "Grand Babylon Hotel" and another, "Imperial Palace". This latter book contained enormous detail about the Savoy Hotel, London, although it was actually a work of fiction.

Well there it is, Mr. Nabokov. I sincerely hope you could be interested in one or the other. Naturally I have just indicated the crudest conception of these ideas. I haven't bothered to go into such details as characterizations or the psychological aspects of these stories. For example, in the hotel story I have in the original material, the development of the situation whereby the father of the young girl, having achieved the position of general manager, has no more interest in the unlawful pursuits of the rest of his family; and it is the advent of his daughter that makes his problem so much greater.

As I indicated to you on the telephone, screenplay writers are not the type of people to take such ideas as these and develop them into responsible story material. They are usually people who adapt other people's work. That is why I am by-passing them and coming direct to you—a story-teller.

Kindest regards.

Sincerely,
Alfred J. Hitchcock[1]

1. Published by permission of Pat Hitchcock O'Connell.

TO: **ALFRED HITCHCOCK**                                    cc, 2 pp.

Montreux, November 28, 1964
Palace Hotel

Dear Mr. Hitchcock,

Many thanks for your letter. I find both your ideas very interesting. The first would present many difficulties for me because I do not know enough about American security matters and methods, or how the several intelligence bureaus work, separately and together.

Your second idea is quite acceptable to me. Given a complete freedom (as I assume you intend to give me) I think I could turn it into a screenplay. But there would be the matter of time. What delays did you have in mind? I am at the present very busy winding up several things at once. I could devote some thought to the screenplay this summer but could hardly settle down to work on it yet. Please let me know what are your ideas about this.[1]

In the meantime I, too, would like to give you a short resume of two ideas of my own. You will find them, very baldly jotted down, on the separate sheet attached to this letter. Please let me know what you think of them. If you like them, we might discuss their development.

It was good talking to you on the telephone.
With best wishes,

Sincerely yours,
Vladimir Nabokov

I.

A girl, a rising star of not quite the first magnitude, is courted by a budding astronaut. She is slightly condescending to him; has an affair with him but may have other lovers, or lover, at the same time. One day he is sent on the first expedition to a distant star; goes there and makes a successful return. Their positions have now changed. He is the most famous man in the country while her starrise has come to a stop at a moderate level. She is only too glad to have him now, but soon she realizes that he is not the same as he was before his flight. She cannot make out what the change is. Time goes, and she becomes concerned, then frightened, then panicky. I have more than one interesting denouement for this plot.[2]

### 2.

While ignorant of the workings of the American intelligence, I have gathered considerable information regarding those of the Soviets.

For some time now I have been thinking of writing the story of a defector from behind the Iron Curtain to the United States. The constant danger he is in, the constant necessity to hide and be on the lookout for agents from his native land bent on kidnapping or killing him.

I would have this man meet a benevolent American couple who would offer him the security of their western ranch. But these would turn out to belong to certain pro-Soviet organizations and would betray him to his pursuers. I have in mind some marvellous scenes at the ranch and a very tragic ending.[3]

1. Hitchcock answered on 3 December that "My needs are immediate and urgent."
2. Hitchcock replied that this idea was not in his genre.
3. Hitchcock responded that this idea had been used for *The Iron Curtain* (1948).

TO: **RAYMOND WALTERS, JR.**[1]         TELEGRAM, I p.
Montreux, Switzerland

NEAT LITTLE THINGS

VLADIMIR NABOKOV

Vladimir Nabokov
   Le 8 decembre 1964

1. Walters, of the *New York Times Book Review,* had asked VN for a 150-word statement on what paperbacks had done for him. VN's reply was published on p. 4 of the 10 January 1965 issue with responses from other authors.

TO: *NEW STATESMAN*                                   PRINTED LETTER[1]

Sir,—Such opportunities are too precious to be missed. The letter of a puzzled reader in your issue of 15 January[2] reflects in an inkdrop a world of misconception—alas, far too common—in regard to the true purpose of translation. I cannot resist pointing out that the passages M. M. Carlin quotes represent in one case a paraphrase and in the other a faithful rendering of certain lines written by the Russian poet A. S. Pushkin, and that paraphrases (e.g. Miss Deutsch's "the rose, romantic flower") are apt to be more pleasing to ladies and gentlemen than a plain literal translation (e.g. 'romantic roses' for *romanticheskie rozy*).

VLADIMIR NABOKOV

Palace Hotel
    Montreux
        Switzerland

1. Published 22 January 1965, p. 112.
2. "Deutsch and Nabokov," letter to the *New Statesman* from M. M. Carlin expressing preference for Babette Deutsch's translation of *Eugene Onegin*.

TO: **WILLIAM H. HOWE**                                   CC, 2 pp.

Montreux, Jan. 25, 1965

Dear Mr. Howe,

I thank you very much for sending me a copy of your *Our Butterflies and Moths*.[1]

As an illustrator of lepidoptera you reveal a rare and splendid talent. Although some of the subjects of the watercolor paintings are strongly stylized, there is always a smiling brightness about them, and in certain cases the stylization brings out nicely an otherwise inconspicuous detail. Most of the black-and-white wash drawings of butterflies and moths in various stages are equally delightful (my only criticism here would be that in the settled butterflies the position of the legs in profile is not always correct). On the other hand, the drawings of non-entomological objects—and especially those deliberately "comic-strip" little people—are banal and irritating.

My two main objections to the book are: The higgledy-piggledy arrangement of specimens and the enormous preponderance of common, showy species, sometimes repeated, among the North-American butterflies. The worthwhile youngster, the passionate novice (for whom your work is presumably meant) will demand first of all some kind of classification and comparison, and good pictures, of rare, drab, small, precious bugs. He cannot be expected to chase *Papilio glaucus* for very long. It is curious how authors and publishers of so-called "popular" butterfly books never seem to realize that the only reader who matters—the bright, eager, gifted boy (generally called "a sissy" by his schoolmates) will toss aside with bored disgust the book in which he cannot find that bizarre little thing he has just caught in a Vermont beechwood, or any of the *Colias, Boloria* and *Plebeius* that he sees in the willow bog of his Wyoming home. Why not figure for a change only the *less known* North-American butterflies?

I refrain from dwelling on the text of your work; it is not on the level of the paintings. Your genuine enthusiasm seldom finds the right word, and your science errs not infrequently. I also cannot imagine what or who induced you to insert all those stale anecdotes, pseudo-Indian legends and samples of third-rate poetry (in this respect, old Dr. Holland[2] was a notorious offender).

Let me add in conclusion that instead of doing the rather bleak-sounding portfolio you plan—depicting feeding habits and migrations—your gifts entitle you to concentrate on something where art and science can really meet, such as an illustrated monograph on *Polygonia* or on the various races (both sexes and undersides) of

*Papilio indra* (for a real thrill you should go one day to hunt the Grand Canyon subspecies).

Sincerely yours,
Vladimir Nabokov

PS. I have no special connection with the NY Times Book Review, but if they ask me, I can send them a copy of this letter, provided this is what you would like.

1. William H. Howe, *Our Butterflies and Moths: A True-to-Life Adventure into the Wonderland of the Butterfly World and its Related Insect Kingdom as Seen Through Fact and Fancy, Fable and Folklore.* North Kansas City, Mo.: True Color Publishing, 1963.
2. W. J. Holland, *The Butterfly Book.* Garden City, N.Y.: Doubleday, Doran, 1931.

TO: **PROF. ROBERT C. WILLIAMS**[1]                CC, I p.
Montreux, Switzerland

February 23, 1965

Dear Mr. Williams,

On my husband's request I acknowledge your letter of Feb. 6. My husband's heavy working schedule does not allow him to write any letters. Moreover, the range of your questions is so extensive that answering them would call for a very long letter indeed.

The two questions in your paragraph one, for instance, cannot be answered in a few lines. The Russian emigrants in Berlin were divided into numerous discrete groups, and your questions would have to be answered for each of these groups separately.

I can answer your question why the Nabokov family moved to Berlin from London. My husband's father was offered by two friends (A. Kaminka and J. Hessen) the editorship of "Rul". This meant to him both a forum on which to continue his struggle against bolshevism and a means of providing for his family. "Rul" was printed in the printing shop of Ullstein. It is more than probable that Ullstein lent also other support to the paper, but my husband has no precise information on this. Of the Ullstein group, Mr. Ross was closest to

"Rul" and its publishers and editors. As far as we know, there was no link with the Mosse group ("Berliner Tageblatt").

Personally, my husband had no contacts with any Germans at all and never learned, or tried to learn, the German language. For this he had reasons of his own. His books were offered to the Ullsteinverlag by his Russian language publishers ("Slovo"). His first two novels were published by Ullstein who had also been responsible for their prepublication in the "Vossische Zeitung". Some of his short stories were translated by various translators who had them published in various publications. Of these I remember "Berliner Tageblatt" and "Koelnische Zeitung". My husband had never any contacts with Gorkiy, the "Scythians", the "Smenovehovtsï", "Molodaya Rossiya" etc. The best Russian émigré review, from the moment of its inception and until it finally folded because of the war, was of course "Sovremennïye Zapiski" (I am sure you know this).

Finally, Berlin was for several years the center of émigré literary (and political) activity for the simple reason that its Russian population at that time approached 200,000, the largest anywhere in Europe. Later, the center moved to Paris.

I am sorry I cannot tell you more. I hope the above helps a little.

Sincerely yours,
(Mrs. Vladimir Nabokov)

1. Of the Russian Research Center, Harvard University.

TO: **BYRON DOBELL**                                                    CC, 1 p.

Montreux, April 9, 1965
Palace Hotel

Dear Mr. Dobell,

I would be very grateful to you if you published the following little "Letter to the Editor" in your nearest issue:

Sir,

Miss Meeske (Memoirs of a Female Pornographer, Esquire, April 1965, p.113), in describing the atmosphere of the Olympia Press office in Paris, remarks "I am sure Nabokov had to pass the wine cellar and climb up those rotting steps through the musty air." This is a gratuitous and grotesque assumption. I never climbed those rotting steps, I never visited the Olympia Press office, and I never met Mr. Girodias (several years ago, in Playboy magazine, April 1961, I had the opportunity to deal with his contention that I had spoken to him once at a cocktail party).[1]

Vladimir Nabokov

Montreux, Switzerland

With best wishes,

Sincerely yours,
Vladimir Nabokov

1. *Esquire* did not publish this letter.

to: *NEW STATESMAN*                    cc, 1 p.[1]

Montreux, April 11, 1965
Palace Hotel

Sir,

I am sorry to continue this correspondence but I really have to clear up another misunderstanding. Judging by her letter in the *New Statesman* (April 9, 1965), I assume that Miss Deutsch has not read either my work on "Eugene Onegin" (and especially vol.2, pp. 491–2, where the very lines she quotes are discussed) or my reply to M.M. Carlin's letter. In that reply I was concerned with Pushkin's, not Miss Deutsch's, poetry.

Now here is the text Miss Deutsch paraphrases in her letter:

*Zima!... Krest'yanin, torzhestvuya,*
*Na drovnyah obnovlyaet put';*
*Ego loshadka, sneg pochuya,*
*Pletyotsya rïs'yu kak-nibud'.*

The lexical translation is: "Winter!... Peasant, celebrating [the first snowfall], on *drovni* [low sleigh without carriage body] inaugurates track; his little horse [of either sex; caressive diminutive; hence "naggy", which Miss Deutsch will find in Webster, unabridged, 1950, and elsewhere], snow having sensed [*chuyat'* applies to more senses than that of smell], shambles at trot any old way."

This Miss Deutsch renders as:

Here's winter ... The exultant peasant
Upon his sledge tries out the road;
His mare scents snow upon the pleasant
Keen air, and trots without a goad.

I will maintain on rack and block, with a saint's patience and a pedant's passion, that "pleasant keen air" and "without a goad" are not in Pushkin; that a Russian peasant does not prod his horse with a pointed stick; and that "exultant" and "mare" are common mistranslations. Let me add—since Miss Deutsch has seen fit to pun on my lame "naggy"—that I can also pun on her "mare". Paraphrases are related to the original text as dreams are to reality, and Miss Deutsch's version is little more than a nightmare.

Yours truly,
Vladimir Nabokov

1. Published in the 23 April 1965 issue of *New Statesman*.

TO: **A. C. SPECTORSKY**                                    cc, 1 p.

St. Moritz, July 4, 1965
Suvretta House

Dear Mr. Spectorsky,

Your letter of June 25 has just arrived. My husband asks me to say that he is very happy that you are publishing DESPAIR, and that you like it so well.[1]

You certainly may refer to the work as a "novel". This is exactly what my husband considers it to be.

You could hardly call it "new". But my husband did revise the translation sentence for sentence, introduced many improvements and included a passage which was never published before. If you can think of some formula that would give you the most satisfaction while staying close to the actual facts, please tell us. My husband will do his best to accommodate you.

It was indeed the first of my husband's novels that he himself translated, although LAUGHTER IN THE DARK that he translated immediately afterwards had already been published in the US in 1938 (Bobbs-Merrill). DESPAIR, however, came out in England in 1937 (John Long).

Finally: the title. The idea of changing it does not appeal to my husband very much. But he understands your problem. Do you have some title in mind that would make PLAYBOY feel happier?)*

Please note the new address at which we shall stay for several weeks. Letters mailed to Montreux will be forwarded and will also reach us.

With best wishes,

Sincerely,
(Mrs. Vladimir Nabokov)


*After giving a little more thought to the matter, my husband suggests a switch to "A Beastly Mess". This would fit into the passage at the end where the narrator hits upon the right title.

1. Published as "Despair"; December 1965, January-February 1966.

TO: **BARBARA EPSTEIN** CC, 1 p.

St. Moritz, July 8, 1965
Suvretta House

Dear Barbara,

I wired you yesterday "Please reserve space in next issue for my thunder." Here it is.[1] For reasons I explain, I have limited my reply to refuting the "Russian" part of Edmund Wilson's article. Its offensive tone compels me to be quite ruthless in regard to his linguistic incompetence. On the other hand, though well aware of the real reason behind this attack, I consider this reason far too sad and private to be aired in print.

I must beg you to publish my reply in full. Since you were not too shocked by some of Edmund's epithets, you ought not to be shocked by mine; and anyway I rely on your journal's spirit of freedom and fair play.

I would certainly like to see the proofs but if there is no time to shuttle them across, then I would prefer a very careful proofreader's checking them against my text to any postponement of its publication. But do try to get them to me—there are lots of pitfalls.[2]

Cordially yours,
Vladimir Nabokov

1. Wilson's "The Strange Case of Pushkin and Nabokov," *New York Review of Books* (15 July). VN's letter was printed in the 26 August 1965 issue of the *New York Review of Books*. Wilson attacked VN's translation of *Eugene Onegin* as awkward; he protested the use of rare words as well as VN's "errors" in Russian and English.
2. The last sentence is in holograph.

TO: ***NEW YORK REVIEW OF BOOKS*** PRINTED LETTER.[1]

*To the Editors:*

As Mr. Wilson so justly proclaims in the beginning of "The Strange Case of Pushkin and Nabokov," we are indeed old friends.

I fully share "the warm affection sometimes chilled by exasperation" that he says he feels for me. In the 1940s, during my first decade in America, he was most kind to me in various matters, not necessarily pertaining to his profession. I have always been grateful to him for the tact he showed in refraining from reviewing any of my novels. We have had many exhilarating talks, have exchanged many frank letters. A patient confidant of his long and hopeless infatuation with the Russian language, I have always done my best to explain to him his mistakes of pronunciation, grammar, and interpretation. As late as 1957, at one of our last meetings, we both realized with amused dismay that despite my frequent comments on Russian prosody, he still could not scan Russian verse. Upon being challenged to read *Eugene Onegin* aloud, he started to do this with great gusto, garbling every second word and turning Pushkin's iambic line into a kind of spastic anapest with a lot of jaw-twisting haws and rather endearing little barks that utterly jumbled the rhythm and soon had us both in stitches.

In the present case, however, things have gone a little too far. I greatly regret that Mr. Wilson did not consult me about his perplexities (as he used to do in the past) instead of lurching into print in such a state of glossological disarray. Some time later I plan to publish a complete account of the bizarre views on the art of translation which have been expressed by some critics of my work on Pushkin. Mr. Wilson's article in *The New York Review of Books* of July 15, 1965, will then receive all the friendly attention it deserves. The main object of this preliminary note is to undeceive credulous readers who might assume that Mr. Wilson is an expert in Russian linguistics. Here are some of the ghastly blunders he makes in his piece.

1. "Why," asks Mr. Wilson, "should [Nabokov] call the word *netu* 'an old-fashioned and dialect form' of *net*. It is in constant colloquial use and what I find one usually gets for an answer when one asks for some book in the Soviet bookstore in New York."

Mr. Wilson mistakes the common colloquial *netu*, which means "there is not," "we do not have it," etc., for the obsolete *netu* which he has never heard and which, as I explain in my note, is a form of *net* in the sense of "not so" (the opposite of "yes"). If Mr. Wilson had continued "All right, but can you get me that book?" and if the shopman had replied *"netu"* instead of *net*, only then would my friend's attempt to enlighten me be not as ludicrous as it is now.

2. "The character ... called and pronounced *yo*—but more like 'yaw' than as [N.] says like the *'yo'* in 'yonder'...."

I do not think Mr. Wilson should try to teach me how to pronounce this or any other Russian vowel. The "yaw" sound he suggests is grotesque and quite wrong. It might render, perhaps, the German-Swiss affirmative ("yaw-yaw") but has nothing to do with the Russian "yo" pronounced, I repeat, as in "yonder." I can hear Mr. Wilson (whose accent in Russian I know so well) asking that bookseller for *Myawrtvïe Dushi* instead of the correct *Myortvïe Dushi* (*Dead Souls*).

3. "*Vse* and *vsyo*, the former of which is 'all' applied to people and the latter 'all' applied to things."

This is a meaningless pronouncement. *Vse* is merely the plural of *ves'* (masculine), *vsya* (feminine) and *vsyo* (neuter). Examples: *vse veshchi*, "all things," *vse lyudi*, "all men," *vsyo naselenie*, "all the population"; *vse hlopayut*, "all applaud," *vsyo hlopaet*, "all the audience applauds." *Eto vse ego oshibki?* "Are these all his mistakes?" *Net, ne vse*, "No, not all."

4. "Pushkin is always shifting these stresses [i.e., "the main stresses in the often so long Russian words"]."

Pushkin does nothing of the kind. We have in Russian a few words that can be, or could be in Pushkin's day, accented in two different ways, but this has nothing to do with prosody. The "always shifting" is a pathetic, but quite nonsensical, grumble.

5. "What does [N.] mean when he speaks of Pushkin's 'addiction to stuss'? This is not an English word, and if he means the Hebrew word for nonsense which has been absorbed into German, it ought to be italicized and capitalized. But even on this assumption it hardly makes sense...."

This is Mr. Wilson's nonsense, not mine. "Stuss" is the English name of a card game which I discuss at length in my notes on Pushkin's addiction to gambling. Mr. Wilson should have consulted my notes (and Webster's dictionary) more carefully.

6. "His poor horse sniffing the snow, attempting a trot, plods through it."

This is Mr. Wilson showing me how to translate properly *ego loshadka, sneg pochuya, pletyotsya rïs'yu kak-nibud'* (which in my correct literal rendering goes "his naggy, having sensed the snow, shambles at something like a trot"). Mr. Wilson's version, besides being a gross mistranslation, is an example of careless English. If, however, we resist the unfair temptation of imagining the horse plodding through its own trot (which is rather what Mr. Wilson is trying to do here), and have it plod through the snow, we obtain the inept picture of an unfortunate beast of burden laboriously working its way through that snow, whereas in reality Pushkin's lines celebrate relief, not effort! The new snow under the sleigh facilitates the horse's progress and is especially welcome after a long snowless autumn of muddy ruts and reluctant cartwheels.

7. "That [i.e. N.'s translation 'having sensed'] would be *pochuyav*, not *pochuya* [which Mr. Wilson thinks should then be 'sensing']. Where is our [i.e., N.'s] scrupulous literalness?"

Right here. Mr. Wilson is unaware that despite the different endings, *pochuyav* and *pochuya* happen to be interchangeable, both being past gerunds and both meaning exactly the same thing ("having sensed"). Compare *zametiv* and *zametya*, which both mean "having noticed," or *uvidev* and *uvidya*, which both mean "upon seeing."

Let me stop here. I suggest that Mr. Wilson's didactic purpose is defeated by the presence of such errors (and there are many more to be listed later), as it is also by the strange tone of his article. Its mixture of pompous aplomb and peevish ignorance is certainly not conducive to a sensible discussion of Pushkin's language and mine.

Vladimir Nabokov

Montreux, Switzerland

1. Published as "The Strange Case of Nabokov and Wilson" with a reply from Wilson on 26 August 1965.

TO: **PROF. GLEB STRUVE**

TL, 1 p.
Hoover Institution.

Montreux, October 4, 1965

Dear Gleb Petrovich,

My wife and I thank you for Mandelshtam's[1] poems. The poems are marvelous and heartrending, and I am happy to have this most precious volume on my bedside shelf.

As to Field,[2] the errors of his that you mention are monstrous, of course, but not any worse than the "symbols" that Wilson (and a recent Briton) discover in *Zhivago*.

Besides, Field's book[3] will, for the most part, be about my English writings.

I shake your hand,
Vladimir Nabokov[4]

1. Osip Mandelshtam, *Collected Works*, ed. Struve and B. A. Filipoff (Washington: Inter-Language Literary Associates, 1964–1966).
2. Struve had written VN on 22 September 1965 warning him that "a certain Andrew Field, has embarked on a book about you (and a 'definitive' one at that). I want to caution you: this Field is a total ignoramus when it comes to Russian."
3. Andrew Field, *Nabokov: His Life in Art* (Boston: Little, Brown, 1967).
4. Translated from Russian by Véra Nabokov and DN.

TO: **LYNDON B. JOHNSON**              TELEGRAM

WISHING YOU A PERFECT RECOVERY AND A SPEEDY RETURN TO THE ADMIRABLE WORK YOU ARE ACCOMPLISHING[1]

VLADIMIR NABOKOV

V. Nabokov, Palace Hotel, Montreux
Le 9 octobre 1965

1. The President had undergone surgery.

TO: **SAUL STEINBERG**[1]                                     CC, I p.

Montreux, October 18, 1965
Palace Hotel

Dear Mr. Steinberg,

We have just received your magic ledger "The New World."[2] Everything in it is a delight—the curlicues of genius, the patch on the C of "Etc" in the lower queue, the wonderful balancing acts of fractions, the performance of trained numerals, St. George spearing the Mis-sum or attacking the attackers of his prey, the dreamlife of wayward cubes and circles, chairs and dogs, the peacock arrows, the activities of speech balloons and question marks, the lepidopterist tiptoeing toward the unknown species, the gentleman doffing his Steinberg to Pi, the animated volutes, cornucopias, alphabets, labyrinths, the museum barrier between the master and his future masterpiece, the catman teaching refridgeometry; and his garden of vignettes.

My wife joins me in gratitude and admiration.

Yours ever,

PS. Please, do come and see us when you are again in Europe.

1. Artist whose work often appeared in *The New Yorker*.
2. Steinberg had sent a copy of his book *The New World* (New York: Harpers, 1965) to VN.

TO: **BARBARA EPSTEIN**                                           cc, 1 p.

October 30, 1965
Montreux, Palace Hotel

Dear Barbara,

I notice that you continue to print the letters of ignorant nincompoops who cuddle up to Edmund Wilson.

I am completing an article of about the Wilson article's length dealing exhaustively with his carps and quibbles as well as with various items connected with it. I think it is important that it should be printed in the same place and reach the same readers as the previous detractions.

I am not sure I could mail it in time for the next issue (vol. 5, No. 7) but you will certainly get it in time for your vol. 5, No. 8. Please let me know if you can save for me the necessary space in that issue, since I consider it essential to get rid of the matter as soon as possible.

Love from us both to you all.

Yours ever,
Vladimir Nabokov

TO: **BARBARA EPSTEIN**                                           cc, 1 p.

Montreux, Nov. 8, 1965
Palace Hotel

Dear Barbara,

Many thanks for your very kind telegram.

I am now sending you a copy of my article (entitled Appendix 3) dealing with the various reviews of my EO, and especially with Edmund Wilson's.

I have marked with a wavy line in the margin (so as not to mess up the main copy) the passages which appeared in the preliminary rejoinder you published and which need not be repeated in your journal.

The article (including those passages) will also appear in a British periodical. In this connection, I would like you to tell me if you have any preferences as to dates—synchronized? later? earlier?

I have written the damn thing rather rapidly—am sick of the whole business and want to get it off my chest as soon as possible.

The bit about Magarshack's English I could not check, see if you have it in your tall library, and if he is the offender, please stet the sentence ("Magarshack's English, I believe") that I have crossed out.

It is of course quite essential that I should see the galleys.

Love from us both.

Vladimir Nabokov

TO: **ROBERT HUGHES**[1]                                    CC, 1 p.

Montreux, Nov. 9, 1965
Palace Hotel

Dear Mr. Hughes,

Thanks for the copy of the transcript which I am mailing back with my deletions. Please return this copy to me after use.

Pages 1–9 are wonderful (the passage about the critics can be retained), and that takes care of at least twenty minutes of talk. Pages 52–54 are also good, and, with the action, they provide at least ten more minutes. The rest (pp.10–51) is pretty awful, and a lot must be deleted.

I am greatly distressed and disgusted by my unprepared answers—by the appalling style, slipshod vocabulary, offensive, embarrasing statements and muddled facts. These answers are dull, flat, repetitive, vulgarly phrased and in every way shockingly different from the style of my written prose, and thus from the "card" part of the interview. I always knew I was an abominably bad speaker, I now deeply regret my rashness, and in fact must apologize for yielding so foolishly to the mellow atmosphere of your Glion terrace. I have kept what I managed to stomach of this spontaneous rot, but shall be grateful to you if you make still heavier cuts in that section. A number of answers had to be obliterated entirely. In some cases it seemed a pity because I would have expressed it so well, so concisely, if I had written it down beforehand. But that does not matter much now—you have plenty of material without the deleted pages.[2]

I am enclosing a copy of the bibliography.

I am terribly sorry if my extensive cuts are causing you any disappointment, but I am sure you will understand that after all I am almost exclusively a writer, and my style is all I have.

With best regards from my wife and me.

Sincerely,
Vladimir Nabokov

1. Of National Educational Television.
2. Excerpts from this television interview were published in *The New York Times* on 30 January 1966 as "Why Nabokov Detests Freud."


TO: **BARBARA EPSTEIN**                        TELEGRAM
Montreux, Switzerland

Terribly sorry must withdraw article was without news three weeks stop too late now greetings[1]

Nabokov

Vladimir Nabokov
    1-er decembre 1965

1. After the *New York Review of Books* held VN's article without scheduling publication, VN withdrew and published it in *Encounter* (February 1966).

TO: *NEW YORK REVIEW OF BOOKS*[1]                                    CC, 1 p.

In a recent issue a correspondent alludes to the French rhyme:

*Cet animal est très méchant:*
*Quand on l'attaque, il se défend.*[2]

For the benefit of my learned friends, I have devised 1. a para-phrase in English, 2. a fairly close English version, and 3. a very close Russian translation:

1.

This animal is very wicked:
Just see what happens if you kick it.

2.

This beast is very mean: in fact
It will fight back, when it's attacked.

3.

*Zhivótnoe sié—prezlóe sushchestvó:*
*Oboronyáetsya, kol' trógayut evó.*

Vladimir Nabokov
Montreux

1. Published 20 January 1966, p. 30.
2. 11 November 1965, p. 38.

TO: **BUD MACLENNAN**[1]                                    CC, 1 p.

Montreux, February 8, 1966
Palace Hotel

Dear Miss MacLennan,

I thank you for your two letters, both of February 4.

*Dial Press*: My husband would appreciate your giving them the permission to use the quotations they ask for in Page Stegner's book ESCAPE INTO AESTHETICS: THE ART OF VLADIMIR NA-

BOKOV, for the British Commonwealth, gratis. The American rights have already been granted.

Paperback rights DESPAIR and THE EYE: My husband agrees to Panther's offer with regard to THE EYE but he rather thinks it too early to dispose of the paperback rights of DESPAIR since this work has not even appeared in full in the *Playboy* yet. He would prefer to wait until publication.

THE GIFT, jacket design: This is one of the things on which my husband makes his own decisions. In the present case he asks me to say the following:

"The design for the jacket seems to me tasteless in the extreme. The only symbol a broken butterfly is of is a broken butterfly. Moreover, there is a grotesque clash between that particular peacock butterfly (which does not occur in the St. Petersburg region) and the Petersburg spring poem, while, on the other hand, in regard to the explorer father the peacock butterfly is pretty meaningless because it is one of the commonest butterflies in Asia, and there would have been no point in rigging up an expedition to capture it. The girl does not look like Zina Mertz at all. The entire conception is artistically preposterous, wrong and crude, and I cannot understand why they are not using the subtle and intelligent sketch I sent them, with the keys on the floor of the hall."[2]

I am sorry that he should feel so strongly about this, but he does.

Sincerely yours,
(Mrs. Vladimir Nabokov)

PS. My husband reminds me that I forgot to say the quotations for the back cover are O.K. with the exception of the line on *Doctor Zhivago*, a book which he considers wholly without literary merit.

---

1. Subsidiary rights director, Weidenfeld & Nicolson.
2. This design, by DN, was used for the Panther paperback.

TO: **MELVIN J. LASKY**                                              CC, I p.

Montreux, Feb. 11, 1966
Palace Hotel

Dear Mr. Lasky,

My husband thanks you for the opportunity offered to answer Edmund Wilson's letter.[1] He does not think that pitiful little letter rates a rejoinder.

He thanks you again for the hospitality of your columns.

Sincerely yours,
(Mrs. Vladimir Nabokov)

1. Not published.

TO: *ENCOUNTER*                                                      CC, I p.
Montreux, Switzerland

February 18, 1966

The couplets Mr. Lowell[1] refers to are not at the end but at the beginning of PALE FIRE. This is exactly the kind of lousy ignorance that one might expect from the mutilator of his betters— Mandelshtam, Rimbaud and others.

Vladimir Nabokov

1. *Encounter* had sent VN a copy of Robert Lowell's letter; neither letter was published.

TO: **MELVIN J. LASKY**                                        CC, 1 p.

Montreux, February 22, 1966
Palace Hotel

Dear Mr. Lasky,

If it is not too late, disregard please my reply to Lowell's drunken lunge and insert the following lines instead:

To the Editor:

I do not mind Mr. Lowell's disliking my books, but I wish he would stop mutilating his betters—Mandelshtam, Rimbaud, and others. I regret not having entitled my article "Rhyme and Punishment."

Vladimir Nabokov[1]
Greetings.

1. Not published by *Encounter*.

TO: **L. QUINCY MUMFORD**[1]                                 CC, 1 p.

Montreux, March 3, 1966
Palace Hotel

Dear Mr. Mumford,

I wish to tell you first of all how deeply honored I feel by the invitation in your letter of February 21 to serve as Honorary Consultant in American Letters.

With reluctance and regret, I must decline this honor. I lack the necessary energy and aptitude to be of any practical use to the Library. I would not be able to acquit myself properly even of the very limited duties you outline; and my conscience forbids me to accept your offer while knowing that I should not be able to force myself to write a single letter or read a single book beyond those that nature compels me to write or read. Let me add that I lead a very secluded life and have very little contact with either American or foreign writers.

Thank you again for having thought of me.

Very sincerely yours,
Vladimir Nabokov

1. Librarian of Congress.

TO: **MELVIN J. LASKY**                                   cc, 1 p.

Montreux, March 3, 1966
Palace Hotel

Dear Mr. Lasky,

Many thanks for letting me see Lowell's second version. This is great fun. I suppose he has now realized how dangerous my reaction to the vulgar and irrelevant remarks in his first letter might have been. I now append my third, and final, reply.

Cordially yours,
Vladimir Nabokov

To the Editor:

Mr. Lowell's intuitional (but hardly commonsensical) arithmetic cannot interest me since he does not know Pushkin's language and is not equipped to tackle the special problems of translation discussed in my article. I wish though (as intimated therein) that he would stop mutilating defenceless dead poets—Mandelshtam, Rimbaud, and others.

Vladimir Nabokov[1]

1. *Encounter* (May 1966); published with Robert Lowell's letter claiming that "both common-sense and intuition tell us that Edmund Wilson must be nine-tenths unanswerable and right in his criticism of Nabokov."

TO: **MELVIN J. LASKY**                                        CC, 1 p.

Montreux, March 3, 1966
Palace Hotel

Dear Mr. Lasky,

I sent you today my third version of a reply to Lowell's second version. The present letter refers to a totally different matter.

Some time ago, in the *Olympia Reader* and in the *Evergreen* review, Maurice Girodias made a number of misstatements in his account of our "strained relations." I have prepared an article of eleven type-written pages, "Lolita and Mr. Girodias" in which I put matters straight. My lawyer has approved it. Please let me know if you would consider publishing it in *Encounter*.[1]

Cordially yours,
Vladimir Nabokov

1. VN withdrew this article on 10 March, explaining to Lasky that he preferred to publish it in New York for "legal reasons." After the article was declined by the *New York Review of Books* on advice of counsel, VN resubmitted it to *Encounter*; but Lasky also declined it on advice of counsel. It was published as "'Lolita' and Mr. Girodias" in *Evergreen Review* (February 1976).

TO: **MELVIN J. LASKY**                                        CC, 1 p.

Montreux, April 4, 1966
Palace Hotel

Dear Mr. Lasky,

Legate, I come to you in tears:

My cohorts ordered home!
I've lived in England forty years
What shall I do in Rome?

This Kipling bit that I loved in my boyhood is to introduce the account of a rather silly situation I find myself in. The *Lolita and Girodias* article had been cleared by my lawyers in New York (Joseph S. Iseman of Paul, Weiss, etc.) and my lawyer in Paris (Maître Schirman). Nevertheless, Barbara Epstein tells me today that she is afraid to publish it. So, in tears, I come back to you.

I shall eagerly await your answer.

Sincerely,
Vladimir Nabokov

I enclose the article.

TO: **MELVIN J. LASKY**                                                    CC, I p.

Amalfi, May 10, 1966
Hotel Cappuccini Convento
(Italy)

Dear Mr. Lasky,

My husband asks me to thank you for the May issue which has followed him to Amalfi.

He was amused by Robert Graves' article[1] in which Graves reproaches Vladimir for using "pal" in writing of Eugene's girl friend (which he never did, of course) and "youthen" (which does not occur in the translation). How absurd that people should write authoritatively of things with which they have not taken the trouble to acquaint themselves. However, Vladimir does not plan to bother you with another "Reply".

He is worried about not having your reaction to his Girodias-

Lolita article. It is extremely important for him to have this article published. In fact, it is extremely important for him to have it published as soon as possible. He would consider it a personal favor if you would do this. Girodias is all over the place nowadays, and his anthology with his mendacious article on *Lolita* is about to be published in England (or has been published).

I believe Vladimir wrote you that the article was examined by two lawyers, one in Paris, the other in New York (Joseph Iseman), that both lawyers pointed out one and the same passage as possibly objectionable, that this passage has been removed accordingly, and that therefore he cannot see why Barbara was afraid to publish it anyway.

We shall stay at the above address for three weeks or so. Please treat this address as confidential.

Sincerely yours,
(Mrs. Vladimir Nabokov)

1. "Language Levels," *Encounter* (May 1966).

TO: **PROF. CARL R. PROFFER**[1]                    CC, I p.

September 26, 1966
Montreux, Palace Hotel

Dear Mr. Proffer,

I have read with great pleasure your witty *Keys* to *Lolita*,[2] and here are some little corrections and explanations that occurred to me on the way:

Page 3 The "favorite author" is not Chateaubriand but Delalande mentioned in *Invitation to a Beheading* and *The Gift*, who survived Chateaubriand by one year. The quotations, and Delalande himself, are, of course, invented.

Page 11 The abbreviation after "the Nouveau Petit Larousse"

stands for "Illustré", not only for "Illinois." The "Little Russian" is nonsense—an impossible pun in French since *"rousse"* is pronounced quite differently from *"russe"*.

Same page. "Forbeson" is a stock character of old Italian comedy.

Page 15 "Quelquepart Island" is another name for "Quelpart Island", N.E. Canada.

Page 19 "Ormonde" refers to Ormond Bar in *Ulysses*—you should have caught that.

Page 20 The allusion to Valeriy Bryusov is nonsense.

Page 29 "Hop-hop-hop" comes from *Lenore*, Bürger's famous ballad.

Page 52 "Vivian Darkbloom" is an anagram of "Vladimir Nabokov" planted at a time (1954) when I toyed with the idea of publishing *Lolita* anonymously but wished to affirm my authorship in code.

Page 59–60 "Miss Empereur". A similarly named lady is Emma Bovary's music teacher in a similar incident, and "Gustave" is an obvious allusion to Gustave Flaubert. I was surprised you did not see this.

Page 69 Also note that the "waterproof" passage at the end of Ch.20 occurs just before John happens to interrupt the indecent story (about Clare Quilty, the dentist's nephew) that Jean is about to tell. In another passage, *she* interrupts John when he is about to make an antisemitic remark.

Page 72 A considerable part of what Mr. Nabokov thinks has been thought up by his critics and commentators, including Mr. Proffer, for whose thinking he is not responsible. Many of the delightful combinations and clues, though quite acceptable, never entered my head or are the result of an author's intuition and inspiration, not calculation and craft. Otherwise why bother at all—in your case as well as mine.[3]

Sincerely yours,
Vladimir Nabokov
(Vivian Bloodmark)

1. Department of Slavic Languages, Indiana University.
2. Bloomington: Indiana University Press, 1968.
3. Last sentence added in Russian holograph.

to: **Barbara Epstein**                                    cc, 1 p.

October 13, 1966
Palace Hotel, Montreux

Dear Barbara,

Thanks for letting me see Enright's article.[1]

You say that it distresses you very much and that you would be awfully glad if I replied.

I never reply in print to scurrilities of this kind, nor can I sympathize with anybody, however "distressed", who would want to publish them.

Sincerely yours,
Vladimir Nabokov

1. D. J. Enright, "Nabokov's Way," *New York Review of Books* (3 November 1966). This review of *The Waltz Invention, The Eye, Despair, Speak, Memory*, and Page Stegner's *Escape into Aesthetics* discusses VN's alleged inhumanity and absence of moral substance.

to: **Prof. Page Stegner**[1]                              cc, 1 p.
Montreux, Switzerland

October 14, 1966

Dear Mr. Stegner

Many thanks for your charming letter of Oct. 5 and a copy of ESCAPE,[2] which was followed in a little cascade by three other copies from other sources. I read it with considerable interest. It is well written and well constructed (except for the bumpy last run). Had

I been shown the MS, it might have been possible to eliminate a few errors of fact (with errors of judgment I am not concerned). I never was the shockheaded, tippling, monarchistic, inferior chessplayer P.P. Rechnoy, married to a dressmaker with a farcical patronymic. Not Kinbote, but his uncle, an irresponsible paraphrast, mistranslates Shakespeare. "Cincinnatus C.'s affinity with Rodion and Monsieur Pierre" is a monstrous idea which if true would have destroyed the entire novel. You should have been warned that Mrs. Butler's article is pretentious nonsense from beginning to end.[3] Uncle Ruka did *not* exercise "an abiding influence on Vladimir". There is nothing remotely "absurd" in Dr. Kozlov's titles (they are, in fact, very much like those of my own scientific papers—which is the point of the passage). You have a perfect right to quote Edmund Wilson on my contempt for ignoramuses but your readers might have liked to be told that (in my *Encounter* article) I *proved* him to be one. You refer twice to some mysterious faults of mine so "evident" and "obvious" as to be not worth naming: obvious to whom for goodness sake? (my Audience? my Maker? my Tailor?). Such errors do not detract seriously from the essential value of an excellent book whose subject may be alone to notice them, but if ever a second edition loomed and you wished to correct slips of that sort, I would be glad to list them all for you.

My wife and son join me in sending you and your people our very cordial regards.

Vladimir Nabokov

1. Member of the English Department at Ohio State University.
2. *Escape into Aesthetics* (New York: Dial Press, 1966).
3. Diana Butler, "*Lolita* Lepidoptera," *New World Writing* (Philadelphia: Lippincott, 1960).

TO: **PROF. PAGE STEGNER**                         CC, 1 p.

Montreux, Switzerland

October 21, 1966

My husband asks me to add that he will be
glad to discuss the inclusion of Pnin (Ch 5)
in your anthology.[1]

Dear Mr. Stegner,

My husband thanks you for your good letter. My husband asks me
to list some other little errors we have noticed in your book.

p. 7      "Shaversky" should be "Shabelsky"

p. 11     All Russian émigré books came out in paper covers, the
          same as most French books

p. 12     "Oxford University Press" should be "Henry Holt"

p. 26–29  My husband wants to repeat that there is no connection
          whatsoever, either in his work or in his mind, between
          entomology and humbertology. He says "Good thing
          Diana Butler did not know that there is a butterfly called
          (long before Lo) 'Nabokov's Nymph'. There is a famous
          American butterfly called 'Diana', and there was a cele-
          brated British lepidopterist called Butler."

p. 36     "Luchin" should be "Luzhin"

p. 57     "interneutral" should "interneural"

p. 67     There are no chess allusions here, either in Virginia or
          Roquebrune

p. 84     Quist is not a Negro

p. 86     "cypress" should be "cypresses"

p. 94     Lisa's new lover is not a poet

p. 104    The Ramsdale dentist is Quilty's uncle, not brother

p. 107    Again, the Diana butterfly

p. 111    My husband says that "coitus interruptus" is hardly the
          right term here

p. 113    He has never read Poe's "Imps of the Perverse"

p. 121    "how far to go" should be "how far up to go"

p. 130    Why could not there be an amusement park outside a se-
          cluded cabin?

My husband wants me to confirm that he *is* supremely indifferent to hostile criticism and advises you to adopt the same attitude when you come to read reviews of your book in The NYRB and The NYBK. He sends you his warm greetings, and so do I. I shall certainly ask Dmitri about that movie. I remember the two of you striding away together.

(Mrs. Vladimir Nabokov)

1. Added in holograph. The anthology was published as *Nabokov's Congeries* and as *The Portable Nabokov* (New York: Viking, 1968).

TO: **ALLENE TALMEY**[1]                                            CC, I p.

Montreux, November 29, 1966
Palace Hotel

Dear Miss Talmey,

I have received your sumptuous Christmas issue with the delightful Orion and Nabokov.[2]

I know how easily a careless babbler's reported remarks can acquire a look of inane vulgarity in merciless print or be flawed by some slip between lip and script. Therefore I had asked Mrs. Gilliatt to send me the typescript of the interview before it went to the printers. I received it in mid-September. It was on the whole a brilliant piece of work but I strongly objected to the beginning which looked remarkably tasteless in print as well as to the entire Pasternak bit which was off-key in matters of literary detail ("scarf" should have been "shawl", etc.), and moreover happened to impinge on some other work of mine.

I considered that themes that had casually bobbed up and down in the chitchat at the Tarasp Kurhaus should be drastically revised for print or omitted altogether. On September 16, immediately after reading the piece, I telephoned Mrs. Gilliatt's office and carefully dictated my revisions to her secretary. In the correspondence that followed I was assured by Mrs. Gilliatt that they would be taken into account.

I have now received the review and am appalled to discover that my wishes have been ignored.

The passages I objected to completely spoil the article for me and cannot be redeemed by the splendid pictures. However, they are splendid, and the essay is full of talent, and I wish you a happy Christmas.

Sincerely yours,
Vladimir Nabokov

Could you send me a second copy please for my files?

1. Associate Editor at *Vogue*.
2. This issue published an interview with VN by Penelope Gilliatt.

TO: *LONDON SUNDAY TIMES*                    PRINTED LETTER[1]

Sir—I strongly object to the remark in "The Red Letter Forgers" (December 18, 1966) about my father who, according to your four investigators, was shot by a monarchist because "he was suspected of being too Left-wing." This nonsense is distasteful to me for several reasons: it is remarkably similar to the glib data distorting truth in Soviet sources; it implies that the chieftains of the Russian emigration were bandits; and the reason it gives for the murder is false.

My father had been one of the leaders of the Constitutional-Democratic Party in Russia long before the revolution, and his articles in the émigré Rul—the only influential Russian-language daily in Berlin—merely continued the strain of West European liberalism, in the large sense, that had marked his life since at least 1904.

Although there could be found a number of decent elderly persons among the Russian monarchists in Berlin and Paris, there were no original minds or influential personalities among them. The stauncher reactionaries, Black Hundred groups, votaries of new and better dictatorships, shady journalists who claimed that Kerenski's real name was Kirschbaum, budding Nazis, blooming Fascists, pogromystics and *agents provocateurs*, remained on the lurid fringe of Russian expatriation and were not representative in any way of the liberal intelligentsia, which was the backbone and marrow of émigré culture, a fact deliberately played down by Soviet historians; and no wonder: it was that liberal cultural core, and certainly not the crude and ambiguous activities of extreme rightists, that formed a genuine anti-Bolshevist opposition (still working today), and it was people like my father who pronounced the first and final verdict on the Soviet police state.

The two sinister ruffians who attacked P. N. Milyukov at a public lecture in Berlin on March 28, 1922, had planned to assassinate him, not my father; but it was my father who shielded his old friend from their pistol bullets and, while vigorously knocking down one of the assailants, was fatally shot by the other.

I wish to submit that at a time when in so many Eastern countries history has become a joke, this precise beam of light upon a precious detail may be of some help to the next investigator.

Vladimir Nabokov
Montreux, Switzerland

1. Published 1 January 1967.


TO: **STEPHEN FAY**[1]                                          CC, 1 p.

Montreux, January 1, 1967
Palace Hotel

Dear Mr. Fay,

Many thanks for your letter of December 23, 1966. It was awfully nice of you to telephone, and I am very pleased that my letter has been displayed so prominently and faithfully in today's issue of The Sunday Times.

I would be delighted to talk to you about émigré politics and society. As I told you I am not particularly interested in politics and history, and everything I wanted to say about my own émigré impressions in the twenty years between 1919 and 1940 (after which I migrated to America) has been expressed in the first two sections of Chapter Fourteen of my *Speak, Memory*, a revised edition of which is about to appear in London and New York. Moreover, in the same work, section 1 of Chapter Nine contains a concise biography of my father.

I could not supply from memory exact data and details of events that took place so many years ago; anyway, I would welcome your telling me beforehand what questions you would like to discuss with me. I shall look forward to meeting you.

Sincerely yours,
Vladimir Nabokov

1. Of the London *Sunday Times*.

TO: **HUGH M. HEFNER**[1] **AND**
    **A. C. SPECTORSKY**                            cc, 1 p.

Montreux, January 14, 1967
Palace Hotel

Dear Mr. Hefner and Mr. Spectorsky,

I want to thank you warmly for the many kindnesses—the good wishes, the beautiful cigarette box, the album in which I was pleased to find myself represented, and the 500 doll. bonus. I apologize for being so late with my thanks and my own New Year wishes of happiness and prosperity for yourselves and for *Playboy*. I was submerged in work some of which had to be finished by Christmas but was not.

I always enjoy reading *Playboy*, and the latest issue was especially entertaining and informative.

Cordially yours,
Vladimir Nabokov

1. Publisher of *Playboy*.

TO: **HUGH M. HEFNER**                       CC, 1 p.

Montreux, Palace Hotel
January 27, 1967

Dear Mr. Hefner,

After receiving your bonus I now receive your prize.[1] I want to tell you how very much touched I am.

This is the first time that any magazine—or in fact any kind of publication—has awarded me a prize. But then Playboy can be always depended upon to provide brilliant surprises.

Cordially,
Vladimir Nabokov

1. The editors of *Playboy* had awarded the $1,000 Best Fiction Award for 1966 to *Despair*. The second paragraph of this letter was published in *Playboy*'s May issue.

TO: *ENCOUNTER*                                    PRINTED LETTER[1]

I welcome Freud's "Woodrow Wilson" not only because of its comic appeal, which is great, but because that surely must be the last rusty nail in the Viennese Quack's coffin.

Vladimir Nabokov

*Montreux,*
*Switzerland*

1. February 1967, p. 91.
2. Sigmund Freud and W. C. Bullitt, "Woodrow Wilson," *Encounter* (January and February 1967).

TO: **MORRIS BISHOP**                    TLS, 1 p. Mrs. Morris Bishop.

Montreux, February 7, 1967
Palace Hotel

Dear Morris,

I am reading and admiring your and Alison's LETTERS FROM PETRARCH[1] in your magnificently limpid style. Many thanks for your kind letter. *Passio et morbo aureliana* occurs in the work of an old aurelian (chrysalid lover), and thus is stamped in my mind. I tried to turn it into your better Latin in the British edition of my book but it resulted in a hideous misprint. Jézabel was Athalie's mother whose messy remains were disputed by devouring dogs *entre eux*— poor ribby beasts that did not expect such a sumptuous feast.

One of my young biographers has visited you in Ithaca—lucky fellow! He saw my *Papilio waterclosetensis*![2]

Véra joins me in sending you and Alison our warmest love.

V[3]

What is little Alison's address in Cambridge?


1. Translated by Bishop (Bloomington: Indiana University Press, 1966).
2. Sentence added in holograph; a jocular reference to a butterfly drawn by VN in a bathroom in Bishop's home. DN.
3. With butterfly drawing.


TO: **WALLACE STEGNER**[1]                                        cc, 1 p.

Montreux, February 18, 1967
Palace Hotel

Dear Mr. Stegner,

If I started to list all the enchanting, heartrending, and eminently *enviable* things in *Wolf Willow* (such as the splendid rhythms in the bronze boot paragraph or in the geometry of sky one; the green cow manure fights, the gopher in the cyclone, or bottoming out—the little hero!—and the flood, and the flies, and the cactus spine), I would only stop because, after all, you know them perfectly well yourself.

Many passages I read with nostalgic exceitement: I have had some unforgettable butterfly collecting in the Glacier Park region (we rented a cabin near Babb, and later in Waterton) and at many points between Browning and the Dakotas—which is not far from *your* collecting localities, and I think I smelled your *Shepherdia* (henceforth to be known as *Stegneria*), though not there but on a lake in Oregon. I was also happy to meet in your book our good old Russian "yellow acacia", caragana (to which I devoted some space in my book on *Eugene Onegin*, vol.3, p.12)

Grateful greetings.


1. Father of Page Stegner; novelist and professor of English at Stanford University; author of *Wolf Willow* (New York: Viking, 1962). Wallace Stegner and VN had met at a writers' conference at the University of Utah in July 1949.

TO: **ALEXANDER FRATER**[1]                                        CC, I p.

Montreux, February 18, 1967
Palace Hotel

Dear Sir

I have received your kind letter offering me to interview Mr. Stravinsky in Marrakesh.

I am afraid there must be some misunderstanding. I hardly know him. I do not care for music in any form. I never interview anybody anywhere.

Yours sincerely,
Vladimir Nabokov

1. Editor of weekend edition of the *London Telegraph*.

TO: **PROF. PAGE STEGNER**                                        CC, 2 pp.

Montreux, February 20, 1967
Palace Hotel

Dear Page,

Here are my husband's considerations regarding your list of contents for a *Portable Nabokov*:

Novel: He agrees that an entire novel should be included, and his preference goes to PNIN, as does yours.

Poems: He agrees with the following choices: "An Evening of Russian Poetry"; "On Translating EO" (but the last line should be changed to "Dove droppings on your monument"); "A Discovery"; "The Refrigerator Awakes"; "Ballad of Longwood Glen"; and "Restoration".

He does not agree with "Exile", "Softest of Tongues" and "Dream" and suggests instead:

"Rain"; "Ode to a Model"; and "Lines from Oregon."

Memoirs: He agrees to your selections from Chapters 1, 2, 4, 9, 11, 14, and 15. But Chapter 6 should not be cut. He would like you to include it in its entirety, possibly instead of "Mademoiselle" (which you are listing under Short Stories, and of which more below)

Essays and Criticism: Chichikov (yes, but there are some indispensable revisions that V.N. would make); "On a Book entitled LOLITA" (yes); "Foreword to BEND SINISTER" (yes).

V.N. is against the inclusion of "Problems of Translation" and "Art of Translation".

"Reply to My Critics", published in *Encounter*, Feb. 1966. The inclusion of this piece V.N. considers very important because Mr. Wilson furtively continues his personal attacks; and any part or parts of the Commentary to Eugene Onegin (f.i. the big bit on Romanticism or the one on Duels)

Short Stories: "Spring in Fialta", "Signs and Symbols", "First Love", "That in Aleppo Once", "Mademoiselle" and "Vane Sisters" have V.N.'s approval ("First Love", Ch.7 of "Speak, Memory", and "Mademoiselle", Ch.5, should be printed from the new revised edition, Putnam 1966; you can include them under Short Stories, if you so prefer, but "Mademoiselle"—not "Mademoiselle O"—in its final form has been shorn of its fictional wool, says V.N., and should be used only as it appears in the final 1966 ed.)

He does not agree with the inclusion of "Lik", "The Aurelian", and "Conversation Piece".

Instead, he suggests: "Lance", "Assistant Producer", "Scenes from the Life of a Double Monster"; and "Cloud, Castle, Lake".

For balancing the "Essays & Criticism" section, V.N. suggests that you include his Foreword to Dmitri's translation of "A Hero of Our Time" by Lermontov.

He would also like you to include part of an Onegin chapter as a sample of translation. If you want to include it, he will supply the text. Let me know if you have any preference as to the passage (V.N.

thinks part of Ch. One would be best), and how long a bit you want.

V.N. would want to check all the texts very carefully. He may want to make changes in the proofs or a final typescript of the book. Revisions may be also needed because of misprints existing in the published texts.

Should you want any further changes in the contents of the volume VN will be glad to consider and discuss them.

Kind regards from us both (Dmitri is away in Italy).

Sincerely,
(Mrs. Vladimir Nabokov)

TO: *SATURDAY EVENING POST*                    PRINTED LETTER[1]
                                          Montreux, Switzerland
**Vladimir Nabokov writes**
*In the Feb. issue of the* Post, *in a profile of Vladimir Nabokov entitled THE ARTIST IN PURSUIT OF BUTTERFLIES, Herbert Gold quoted the novelist as having said about a mutual friend:*
'*Of course, he is a very nice fellow.*
*Of course, do not lend him any money.*
*Of course, he is completely untalented.*
*Of course, he is a liar and a hypocrite.*
*Of course, he is a pederast.*
*Of course, isn't that good you know him,*
*he's a very nice fellow.*'
*As a result of the article, the following correspondence ensued. We believe it has a peculiar documentary interest.*

—THE EDITORS.

To the editor of *The Saturday Evening Post:*

January 21
Sir,
There are many excellent things in Mr. Gold's article, but it is most unfair of him to have quoted a converesation he and I had about a

404

common friend. That friend was, and is (for he is still very much alive—and very much upset) no other than Sam Fortuni, the poet. Sam tells me that he has seen Mr. Gold only once, forty years ago, and would have never dreamed of asking him for a loan. I may add that—in refutation of the statements attributed to me—Sam does have some talent, loves women, always tells the truth, is not a particularly nice fellow, and does not exist.

This is one of the reasons I invariably beg interviewers either to stick to the script which I supply in the form of written answers to their written questions, or else, if they prefer their own impressions to my expressions, to let me check the article for factual slips before publication.

Despite his promise to do so, Mr. Gold has not complied with my request. I could not have dreaded the German TV team's impending visit which was to include my admirable translator Dieter Zimmer whom I was very keen to meet. The Montreux Palace Hotel does not consist of "cuckoo-clock carved wood." Cornell's "deans and administrators" would certainly confirm that I never "tormented" them. There are other embarrassing inaccuracies in the article but these will suffice as examples. I hope Mr. Gold, who seems to like anagrams, will take a good look at the name of our poor old furious poet.

VLADIMIR NABOKOV<br>
Montreux

February 3

Dear Mr. Nabokov,

Thank you for your letter of January 21. We are ready to publish it in our Letters column, as you requested, but I must confess that I am puzzled by the question of "Sam Fortuni." If such a person exists, it would be clearly libelous to identify him as the subject of the comments quoted in the article. This would be true even if there is a Sam Fortuni somewhere whom you have never met. On the other hand, assuming your last sentence to mean that the name is an anagram, we have struggled in vain to decipher it, and there is even one student of Nabokoviana who argues that the hint of an anagram means that it isn't an anagram.

What I suggest is that the letter be cut and edited to delete all reference to Fortuni, as in the attached copy. If this is satisfactory, please let me know.

Very truly yours,
OTTO FRIEDRICH
*Managing Editor*

February 11

Dear Mr. Friedrich,

I am in receipt of your letter of February 3—with your version of mine of January 21.

Sorry—the Letters to Editors that I write now and then are never edited. The reason is plain. If A writes to B, and B revises A's letter, the correspondence is no longer between them but between AB and B—which does not make sense and has no value.

I am afraid I must ask you to print my letter, in full, and not your abridged version of it. If you do not care to do so, please send me back my typescript. If you want it after all, it might be wise to send me the galley so as to avoid misprints—such as the accidental omission of my reference to the German TV, a major point in my letter.

Since I state in my letter that "Sam Fortuni" is my invention, and his name my riddle, it cannot be true that there is anything libelous in my comments, even if an old poet of that name could dig himself up and stomp, very drunk, into your office. An elderly woman in Colorado called Lolita Haze pestered me at one time with cranky protests but neither she nor the namesakes of any of my other characters have ever found a lawyer to champion their cause.

The very simple recombination SAM-FORTUNI=12345678910=35178942106=MOST UNFAIR (a phrase actually used in my letter) might be unscrambled, if you like, in an editorial footnote for the benefit of inexperienced Nabokovians.

Yours truly,
Vladimir Nabokov

1. Published in the 25 March 1967 issue.

TO: **PROF. ALFRED APPEL, JR.**[1]                                        CC, 1 p.

Montreux, March 28, 1967
Palace Hotel

Dear Mr. Appel,

Minton showed me your notes to page 252. Theoretically, the idea is splendid but specifically it is a great pity that the three first notes of this display batch are wrong.

*Note* a) "Quelquepart" means "somewhere" in French and that was Quilty's *only* reason in using it. There is no harm (except that it is quite irrelevant) in adding that "There is a Quelpart (*sic*) Island off Korea," but the rest of the note is misleading and must go.

b) "few known Asian specimens"(!) A great number of Asian specimens of various forms of *Lycaeides* are preserved in English, German, and Japanese museums.

c) "bears Nabokov's name." An improper phrase. Although a genus (*Nabokovia* Hemming) and several new species (e.g., *Eupithecia nabokovi* McDunnough) do bear my name, no *Lycaeides* species or subspecies happens to be named after me. I have described, however, several new members of that genus, and my name is *appended* to the names I have given them (e.g., *L. sublivens* Nabokov) in the same way as that of the great Canadian lepidopterist is appended to the name of a moth I discovered (see above).

I am quite sure that in the present case items (b) and (c) are unnecessary, but these taxonomic niceties may come handy elsewhere.

*Note 2.* "An undine is a nixie"—okay, but the main point is that "undinist" is a person (generally male) who is erotically excited by another person's (generally female) making water (H. Ellis[2] was an "undinist", or "fountainist," and so was Bloom[3]).

*Note 3.* "Arsène Lupin" has no connection whatever with Edgar Poe's story in my story, or the name of a common weed (the foodplant of a huge number of Lycaenids). Arsène Lupin is a detective character (created by Leblanc or Blanc, check) as famous in France as Sherlock Holmes is in England. The phrase about the entomologist's standing by the host plant is meaningless since it is the caterpillar and not the adult insect that feeds upon it.

I shall check all your notes but please do leave out all reference to lepidoptera, a tricky subject (which led the unfortunate Diana so dreadfully astray). There are a couple of passages where lep notes are quite necessary but these I shall supply myself.

Very cordially,
(VN)

1. A member of the Stanford University English Department (and a former student of VN's at Cornell), Appel was compiling *The Annotated Lolita* (New York: McGraw-Hill, 1970).
2. Havelock Ellis, English literary critic; author of *Studies in the Psychology of Sex*.
3. Leopold Bloom in James Joyce's *Ulysses*.

TO: **PROF. ALFRED APPEL, JR.**                                           CC, 2 pp.

Montreux, Palace Hotel, April 2, 1967
Dear Mr. Appel,

I see that in my copy of Putnam's hardcover I have corrected one misprint (p.6, there should be a full stop after "sophomore") and the following author's errors:

p. 6 September-October (instead of "September")

p. 8 There should be a date after the John Ray signature: August 5, 1955

p. 266 Late in September (instead of "early")

and p. 232 flashlight (instead of "torch light")

I have corrected in my Russian translation a curious dream-distortion on p. 305. Q. could not be trudging from room to room since H. H. had locked their doors, but this is okay on second thought and need not be corrected in your edition.

Thanks for your delightful letter of March 28. Here are my answers to your questions:

*Note* "Dr. Blue" does not have the slightest connection either with my Blues (Lycaenids), or with Blue, Kubrick's formidable lawyer.

"Strange Mushroom." Somewhere, in some collection of "cases,"

I found a little girl who referred to her uncle's organ as "his mushroom."

"The Lady who loved Lightning." Yes, this is the play they go to in Wace; but I do not think it has much to do with H.'s mother's being killed by lightning—though the connection is cozy and tempting.

"Dark Age." Yes, italics everywhere.

Neither the "Girl in Green" nor "I was dreaming of you" contains any allusion.

*Note 2* No allusions in these titles. The slip of the pen on p. 34, 3rd line, is "disappeared" (i.e. referring to Dolores Haze) replacing the obvious "appeared" (in the plays Miss Quine appeared in).

*Note 3* Mirana: a heat-shimmer blend of "mirage", "*se mirer*", "Mirabella" and "fata morgana".

*Note 4* That poet was evidently Lepping who used to go lepping (i.e. lepidoptera hunting) but that's about all anybody knows about him.

*Note 5* Yes, Mona Dahl. Vindictive Hum!

*Note* Widworth—non-allusive.

*Note 7* This is Bürger's "Lenore", not Poe's!

*Und hurre, hurre, hop, hop, hop!* See my Onegin Commentary, vol.3, p.154, where you will also find the irresistible line "*Und aussen, horch! ging's trap, trap, trap*"

*Note 8* Thomas the Apostle, a believer in the tactile sense. The other Tom had nothing.

*Note 9* OTTO OTTO. A magical name that does not change in the looking glass.

The late tennis player Bill Tilden who, in the twenties, incurred Wimbledon's wrath by consorting with ball boys, wrote fiction under the pen name of Ned Litam. He now plays with those balls on Elysian turf. Shall we spare his shade?

Cordial greetings
Vladimir Nabokov

TO: **PROF. ALFRED APPEL, JR.**                                   CC, 1 p.

Montreux, April 3, 1967

Dear Mr. Appel,

You say you don't understand the mistakes of tricksters but they would not be tricksters if they did not profit by their own tricky mistakes. I have been shown an atrocious one in my commentary, vol. 3, p.202, where I did not realize that "Red Rover" was by Fenimore Cooper, and had evolved a wonderful but quite incorrect theory instead.

*Re* Reds and Blues. I protest vehemently against the lycaenization of my common use of the epithet "blue". In the p. 265 passage, what Rita does not understand is that a white surface, the chalk of that hotel, does look blue in a wash of light and shade on a vivid fall day, amid red foliage. H. H. is merely paying a tribute to French impressionist painters. He notes an optical miracle as E. B. White does somewhere when referring to the divine combination of "red barn and blue snow." It is the shock of color, not an intellectual blueprint or the shadow of a hobby. H. H. knows nothing about lepidoptera. In fact, I went out of my way to indicate (p. 112 and p. 159) that he cannot distinguish a butterfly from a moth, and that he confuses the hawkmoths visiting flowers at dusk with "gray hummingbirds". But on the other hand, I confess that Miss Phalen's name attracted me because *phalène* means moth in French.

*Re* French. Ormonde is a Joycean double-bottomed pun for it not only alludes to his bar but also means, in comic translation, "out-of-this-world" (*hors [de ce] monde*). The Dubliner's rainbow of children on p. 223 would have been a meaningless muddying of metaphors had I tried to smuggle in a Pierid of the Southern States and a European moth. My only purpose here was to render a prismatic effect. May I point out (at the risk of being pretentious) that I do not see the colors of lepidoptera as I do those of less familiar things—girls, gardens, garbage (similarly, a chessplayer does not see white and black as white and black) and that, for instance, if I use "morpho blue" I am thinking not of one of the many species of variously blue

*Morpho* butterflies of South America, but of the ornaments made of bits of the showy wings of the commoner species. When a lepidopterist uses "Blues", a slangy but handy term, for a certain group of Lycaenids, he does not see that word in any color connection because he knows that the diagnostic undersides of their wings are not blue but dun, tan, grayish etc., and that many Blues, especially in the female, are brown, not blue. In my case, the differentiation in artistic and scientific vision is particularly strong because I was really born a landscape painter, not a landless escape novelist as some think.

We are going to Italy tomorrow, to Camogli, Hotel Cenobio dei Dogi for several weeks.

My wife joins me in sending you our warmest regards.

> Cordially,
> Vladimir Nabokov

TO: JASON EPSTEIN                                    CC, 1 p.

> Camogli (Genova), Italy
> Cenobio dei Dogi
> May 19, 1967

Dear Jason,

I would like to submit to you certain considerations in answer to your kind letter of May 10.

*Bollingen.* The right to publish a paperback edition of my translation of EO, plus a limited critical apparatus, is provided in my contract with Bollingen. In the foreword I shall supply for your edition[1] I shall formulate the necessary credit in a footnote which will also mention that "a second edition of the complete text is in preparation." All this you can check any time you want by calling Bill McGuire at the Foundation. Incidentally, if you publish the paperback it would be in our common interest to have Barton Winer for editor.

*Text.* What you are going to publish is not an ordinary paperback reprint of the original edition but something that will require a good deal of work on my part. First of all, the version you will publish will be a new one. Moreover, you will be the first to publish the Lexicon. And last but not least, I shall have to supply the footnotes. This is why I consider that I should be paid separately for the extra work.

*Royalty rate.* 7½% will not do. Since it is going to be an "expensive" paperback, the rate should be at least 10% at the start, and should go up after a certain number of copies sold. On the other hand, I would accept an advance of $2.500 (instead of the $3000 you suggest) if you agreed to pay me $1,000 for my work described above, and this thousand should not come out of the royalties.

I do hope that you can see my point and that we can arrive at an agreement.

We are staying at a charming place (address above) where we shall remain till June 15th. A new novel[2] I am writing takes a good deal of my time but I manage to walk up to 15 kilometers daily on the steep paths in search of butterflies.

Véra joins me in sending you and Barbara our most cordial regards.

Vladimir Nabokov

1. Random House did not publish this paperback edition of *Eugene Onegin*.
2. *Ada*.

TO: **PROF. ALFRED APPEL, JR.**                                     cc, 2 pp.

Camogli (Genova), Italy
Cenobio dei Dogi
May 23, 1967

Dear Mr. Appel,

Here are the answers to the questions in your letter of May 6.

p. 33, "Dillingham" has no significance. *A Murder is Announced* on the next page, of course. A Percy Elphinstone did write *A Vaga-bond in Italy* which I found in a hospital library, the nearest thing to a prison library. The "Elph-in-stone" is wrong. It is my own random recollection of Percy, a happier vagabond than my man. But it is worth noting that the fairy tale LOLITA ends in Elph's Stone and begins in Pixie.

p. 48. Pisky is another form of pixy (fairy, elf) and also means "moth" in rural England. Maturin's Melmoth the Wanderer is O.K. It was also Wilde's alias after prison. Melmoth may come from Mellonella Moth (which breeds in beehives) or, more likely, from Meal Moth (which breeds in grain).

p. 253. John Randall of Ramble was a real person, I think (as was in the book also Cecilia Dalrymple Ramble, p. 254). Catagela is a town invented by Aristophanes in one of his plays. James Mavor Morell is one of the main characters in Shaw's CANDIDA, and Hoxton is a place-name therein.

p. 260–65. False. If Rita is a "pun" (what a dreadful one!) on "reader" then we may as well see in "Lolita" another bad pun on Low Litter (especially in view of a phrase on p. 302). I suspect you were pulling my leg with the "Rita-Reader."

Counting "Phalen" (Fr. *phalène*, moth), "Melmoth" and "Pisky", I can glean only eleven lep references in LOLITA (less than there are references to dogs or birds). I may have forgotten two or three, but there are certainly not fifty references!

p. 54. Falter (German for "butterfly"), one of Lo's schoolmates.

p. 112. I think I have given you earlier this "moth-or-butterfly" example of Humbert's complete incapacity to differentiate between Rhopalocera and Heterocera.

p. 123. The "powdered bugs" wheeling around the lamps are noctuids and other moths which look floury on the wing (hence "millers", which, however, may also come from the verb) as they mill in the electric light against the damp night's blackground. Bugs is an Americanism for *any* insect. In England, it means generally bedbugs.

p. 158. The insects that poor Humbert mistakes for "creeping white flies" are the biologically fascinating little moths of the genus *Pronuba* whose amiable and indispensable females transport the pollen that fertilizes the yucca flowers (see, what Humbert failed to do, "Yucca Moth" in any good encyclopedia).

p. 159. The gray hummingbirds at dusk etc. are, as I have mentioned in an earlier communication, not birds but hawkmoths which do move exactly like hummingbirds (which are neither gray nor nocturnal).

p. 191. When naming incidental characters I like to give them some mnemonic handle, a private tag: thus "Avis Chapman" which I mentally attached to the South-European butterfly *Callophrys avis* Chapman (where Chapman, of course, is the non-italicizable name of that butterfly's original describer).

p. 213. This "patient bug" is not necessarily a moth—it could be some clumsy big fly or miserable beetle.

p. 236. Butterflies are indeed inquisitive, and the dipping motion is characteristic of a number of genera.

p. 252 & 303. "Schmetterling" (German "butterfly") blended with the author of L'Oiseau Bleu.

p. 294. Moths like derelict snowflakes.

p. 260. Under the sign of the Tigermoth (an Arctid).

p. 261. Rita's phrase "Going round and round like a mulberry moth" combines rather pleasingly the "round and round the mulberry tree" of the maypole song and the silk moth of China which breeds on mulberry.

p. 318. Footnote to *lycaeides sublivens* Nabokov.

This Coloradan member of the subgenus *Lycaeides* (which I now place in the genus *Plebejus*, a grouping corresponding exactly in scope to my former concept of *Plebejinae*) was described by me as a subspecies of Tutt's *"argyrognomon"* (now known as *idas* L.), but is, in my present opinion, a distinct species. V.N.

In answer to your last question: ADA will take me another year and a half to finish, and I'll start revising my son's translation of THE EXPLOIT only when I am quite through with her.

I have not yet received The Wisconsin Studies.[1] If it is a bulky package they may not forward it from Montreux which means that I shall not see it till August when I return to my hotel.

> Cordially,
> Vladimir Nabokov

---

1. *Nabokov: The Man and His Work*, ed. L.S. Dembo (Madison: University of Wisconsin Press, 1967).

TO: **ROBIE MACAULEY**[1]                                         CC, 1 p.

June 10, 1967

Dear Mr. Macauley,

I thank you for your letter of June 6 with which were enclosed chapters 8 and 12 of my KING, QUEEN, KNAVE.

Your suggestion that I make a new story using the elements of these chapters is amusing but completely unacceptable.

Will you kindly return the rest of the typescript to me at the following address:

Cita Grand Hotel
Limone Piemonte (Cuneo)
Italy.

> Sincerely yours,
> Vladimir Nabokov

---

1. *Playboy* fiction editor.

TO: *INTERNATIONAL HERALD TRIBUNE*                    CC, I p.

Montreux, Switzerland
Montreux Palace Hotel
November 11, 1967

Dear Paper,

For obvious reasons I refuse to tell you, in answer to your questionnaire, what brand of cigarettes my cousin smokes, nor can I divulge
my "choice of shipping methods", or the price of my wristwatch.
However: I like you very much, and here are four suggested improvements that would increase my affection.

1. Splash U.S. successes with a little more enthusiasm.

2. Reestablish the Monday stock exchange tables for the past week.

3. Consign, at once and for keeps, Mrs. Sawyer[1] to a mental asylum
(this will give everybody more elbow room).

4. Cut out the pop art (Chag *et al*) and replace it by a Book Review
page once a week.

Faithfully yours,
Old Reader
Vladimir Nabokov

---

1. Character in the comic strip *Buz Sawyer*; she suffered from amnesia.

TO: *NEW STATESMAN*                              PRINTED LETTER[1]

*Sir*, Mr Pritchett (NS, 27 Oct)[2] says he would have liked Mr
Magarshack to tell him in what language Pushkin read Byron and
other English authors. I do not know Mr. Magarshack's work or
works, but I do know that since neither he, nor anybody else, could
answer Mr. Pritchett without dipping into me, a vicious spiral is
formed with an additional coy little coil supplied by Mr Pritchett's
alluding to the 'diverting' article I published in *Encounter* (Feb. 1966).

If, however, your reviewer would care to combine the diverting with the instructive I suggest he consult the pages (enumerated in the index to my work on *Eugene Onegin* under Pushkiniana, English) wherein I explain, quite clearly, that most Russians of Pushkin's time, including Pushkin himself, read English authors in French versions.

By a pleasing coincidence the same issue of your journal contains another item worth straightening out. Mr Desmond Mac Namara, writing on a New Zealand novel, thinks that there should be coined a male equivalent of 'nymphet' in the sense I gave it. He is welcome to my 'faunlet' first mentioned in 1955 (*Lolita*, chapter 5). 1955! How time flies! How attention flags!

Vladimir Nabokov
*Montreux*

1. Published 17 November 1967.
2. V. S. Pritchett, "The Trapped Bear."

TO: **ELENA SIKORSKI**        HOLOGRAPH MEMO, 1 p. Elena Sikorski.

*Daily schedule*[1]

(26.XI–3.XII.1967)
6:30–10:30 VN drinks juices, writes, first in bed, then at lectern. Intervals: 7:45 shaving; 8:00–8:30 breakfast, perusal of mail, silence, J[ournal] de Genève for El[ena].
8:30 return to lectern. 10:30–11:15 stool, bath, dressing. 11:00 Mme. Furrer comes to "cuire." 11:30 Aida and manservant clean. VN and El. go out for a walk (chats with shopkeepers etc.).
12:15 Mme. F. serves lunch. Bordeaux. 1:00–3:00 siesta. 3:00–6:00 VN drinks vin de Vial,[2] writes at lectern or in armchair. Intervals for perusal of mail that has accumulated since 2:00. First beer. 5:30 Mme. F. arrives quietly.

6:00–9:00 games (Scrabble), exch[anges] of impr[essions]. 7:00 Mme. F. serves dinner. Second beer.

End of interesting day. VN reads in bed until 10:30. Intervals dictated by age—tr[ips] to mas[ter] W.C. around midnight and at dawn. 6:30–10:30 VN drinks juices, writes, etc.

I. *Obligations* of guest: neat appearance, making morn[ing] coffee (VN drinks 2 cups). Morning telephone calls to purveyors.*** Answering telephone. Example: "Here his secretary ("Elen Orska"). Vat? Gut. ⊛Aisle usk." *Knock* on VN's door. Occasionally he answers the phone. At 9:00 PM *three* doors are locked: kitchen, "living," corner room. Kitchen key is taken by guest to her room in case of nighttime hunger (cf. Privileges) and *is returned without fail early in the morning.* * Washing cups (*only*), on Sunday morning (*only*). Chk. eves. if *both* ranges trnd. off. No messes anywhere.

II. *Privileges*: use of living, where it is cosier than in the green boudoir (rm. 60). When making one's way at night to recover eyeglasses from living or get some cake in kitchen, use corr[idor] rte[route]. At other times: inter[ior] rte.—it is preferable to going demonstratively through the corridor.**** Radio to be used at low volume. (There is a TV downstairs for favorite programs.) Books may be taken from storage room or from VN. For toilet art[icles] or secret dainties it is permissible to use small table (green arrow) in guest's chamber.

III. *It is prohibited*: to burst into kitchen while Mme. F. ** is there, to give advice and "Russian" recipes, compare ailments, tell tales about *India and the lions,*[3] etc.
⊛ What? All right, I'll ask. (Eng.).
*** only in case liquor or some such thing is needed. Or if they forget to deliver something from the dairy. Tel. numbers are by T[elephone] in rm. 64.
* otherwise Mme. F. will be unable to penetrate from kitchen to *servants' toilet*, if she *has to go.*
** Mme. F. will make all purchases herself (i.e., *no* sudden "zhashet

muamems" ["j'achète moi-même" -"I'll buy it myself"] etc.) and will cook twice a day.

**** with loud footfalls (we are not alone in the hotel).

*Note*: change in gl[ass] ashtray by telephone in 64 is for tips to deliverymen, etc., and *not for guests*.

Vladimir Nabokov[4]
26-XI-1967
Montreux

1. Elena Sikorski spent a week in November-December of 1967 at the Montreux Palace when Véra Nabokov had to fly to New York to arrange for an ailing cousin to move to Switzerland. This parodic rulebook reflects a very special intellectual and ludic camaraderie that had existed between Nabokov and his sister from an early age (misinterpreters of *Ada* beware). DN.

2. A tonic syrup.

3. A reference to the impressions brought back from India by Elena Sikorski's son Vladimir, who had been there in his professional capacity of simultaneous interpreter. DN.

4. Translated from Russian by DN.

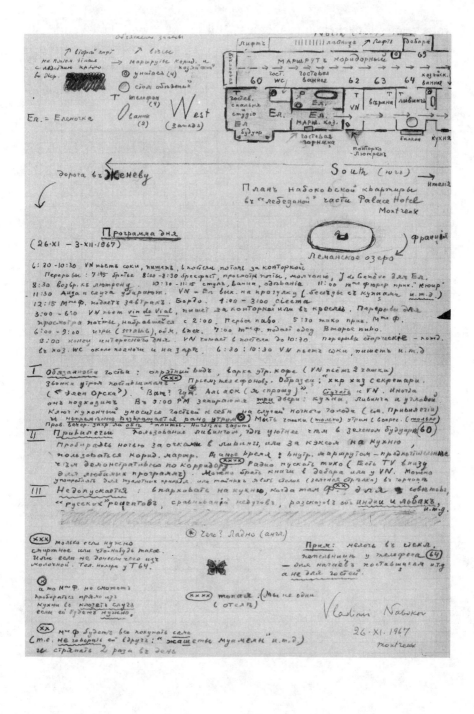

TO: **DMITRI NABOKOV**  HOLOGRAPH PS TO VÉRA NABOKOV LETTER
Montreux, Switzerland

6 December 1967

Careful with the ladies!
Your tired, very well writing, and loving

P¹

1. Translated from Russian by DN.

TO: **PROF. PAGE STEGNER**  CC, 2 pp.

Montreux Palace Hotel
Montreux, Switzerland
December 6, 1967

Dear Page,

I am returning your admirable Introduction for the *Portable Nabokov*. VN asks me to say that he enjoyed the purity of your style and the precision of your thought.

Below a few remarks:

p. 2  Not an important matter but please put an accent on "e" in my name (people are apt to read it as "Veera").

p. 4  VN suggests that you substitute "expatriates" for "displaced persons." There is very little in common between the first and the second Russian emigration, and the term "displaced persons", which came into use during the Second World War, calls to mind the new emigrants, products of almost thirty years of Soviet domination and with an ideology tainted by philistinism and marxism.

—  Is Krug the *only* hero answering your description? Is not Shade equally fixed in one spot?

p. 6  "Meaningful relationships," says VN, "is ambiguous since 'meaningful' in itself is a meaningless word, and, anyway, the phrase does not apply to many of Martin's emotions and friendships." Then, further down, you have 'meaningless', which clashes with the 'meaningful' and, moreover, is not a true assessment of Martin's 'exploit.' When he crosses the border illegally, never to be seen again, he is meeting an intolerable challenge, something he feels he must conquer, just as he met the challenge of the mountain and prevailed upon his fear of it (around the middle of the book).

p. 11 VN questions the phrase ". . . their straight man, their Lemuel Pitkin" used to characterize Pnin.

p. 13 "To get rid of a book" has no element of annihilation for VN. It means "getting rid at last of an adorable but sometimes intolerable burden."

p. 20 The pun (bottom of your page) is made by Mona in the letter, not by Humbert, who actually does not notice it.

p. 21 I believe "Any" should be "And a."

p. 25 "Little girl, not your girl," says VN.

— "*tenu*" should be "*tenue*" and p. 28, "*donné*" should be "*donnée*"

p. 29 There are two translated poems in *Gorniy Put'* (Empyrean Path), one by Byron (Sun of the Sleepless), the other from Keats (La Belle Dame sans Merci). There are no other translations either in *Gorniy Put'* or in *Grozd'* (The Cluster). But VN published fairly numerous verse translations from other poets in emigre journals and newspapers, including Baudelaire, Musset, some Shakespeare, Tennyson, some Rupert Brooke etc.

— VN suggests that you say 'poems' rather than 'verses'

p. 30 "The Wanderer" was an unfinished verse play

— At the time he translated "Alice in Wonderland" he also translated Romain Rolland's "Colas Breugnon" into Russian.

p. 31 Of the three remaining books written in Russian *The Exploit* is being translated,[1] but *King, Queen, Knave,* translated by Dmitri and edited by VN will be published in April 1968.

— Of the "eleven" books you name ten (five and five). Did you mean to say "ten" or were you going to name *The Eye* as eleventh?

— Since you give the English titles of the Russian books, it would perhaps be useful to put, after *Camera Obscura* (*Laughter in the Dark* in the English translation)?

VN very much appreciates your having let him check the factual side of the Introduction.

While I was in New York I spoke to Robert MacGregor of New Directions on the 'phone. They won't claim any permission fee for the "Government Specter."[2] I did not speak to TIME because I was not sure in what stage was the correspondence between you or Marshall Best with them.

Cordial greetings from VN and me.

1. Published as *Glory* (New York: McGraw-Hill, 1971).
2. Title of the chapter on *The Inspector General* in VN's *Nikolay Gogol*.

TO: **JOHN BOOTHE**[1]                                                    CC 1 p.

Montreux, Switzerland<br>
Montreux Palace Hotel<br>
January 10, 1968

Dear Mr. Boothe,

My husband asks me to say that he very much appreciates your kindness in allowing him to see the jacket and blurb.[2] I regret to say he cannot approve either. This is what he dictated to me:

"The picture for the jacket is misleading and embarrassing for it is apt to be taken for the author's portrait and not for that of the protagonist whose features, moreover, delicate and nervous, are quite differently described in the book." VN suggests that you use for the jacket "one, two or several eyes, nothing but eyes, no face. The eyes may vary in color and expression but the artist must read the book before proceeding."

As to the blurb, VN suggests that you omit the quotation from The Guardian since it gives a very limited and pedestrian impression of his general work.

Sincerely yours,<br>
(Mrs. Vladimir Nabokov)

May I draw your attention to the correct spelling of N a b o k o v (not "Nabakov").

I am enclosing your material with this letter.

1. Joint managing editor, Panther Books, London.
2. *The Eye.*

TO: **NEW STATESMAN**                                        PRINTED LETTER[1]

*Sir*, I do not intend to continue my chats with Mr Edmund Wilson, in private or print, but let me humbly concede before ending them, that Pushkin had almost as much English in the 1830s as Mr Edmund Wilson has Russian today. That should satisfy everybody.

Vladimir Nabokov
*Montreux*

1. Published 19 January 1968.

TO: **FRANK E. TAYLOR**[1]                                        CC 1 p.

Montreux, Switzerland
Montreux Palace Hotel
January 22, 1968

Dear Mr. Taylor,

Our letter of the 21st had not yet left when yours of January 18th arrived, and I am enclosing the letter my wife signed.

I am not very happy with the procedure you suggest for the proofreading process.[2]

If the set of galleys arrives here on Monday the 5th, it will be returned to you on the same or the following day, and reach you before the end of the week.

It is indispensible that you send me simultaneously a second set (not necessarily read by your printers if there is no time for that) to which I shall transfer my corrections and those of the printer, and keep.

In the course of half a century of proofreading I have evolved certain habits the sudden changing of which would wreck my peace of mind. In other words, I absolutely must see the page proofs. That will take me a few hours, and I can cable my response the same day either with a simple o.k., or, if there is some bad error, informing you of it; but no book of mine has ever appeared without my having checked those last proofs—except a few paperbacks, with dreadful consequences. If I don't see the page proofs, I shall never know if my corrections have been understood, and whether they match yours, and some typographical disaster is very likely to follow—something that neither you nor I surely want to happen.

An additional request: Please do not release to the English publisher (George Weidenfeld) anything but the completely corrected page proofs of the novel. In this respect, an unfortunate misunderstanding regarding LOLITA resulted in the first British edition being riddled with misprints.

With most friendly greetings,

Yours,
Vladimir Nabokov

1. McGraw-Hill editor.
2. *King, Queen, Knave,* trans. VN and DN (New York: McGraw-Hill, 1968).

TO: **EDWARD E. BOOHER**[1]                                    cc, 1 p.

Montreux, Switzerland
Montreux Palace Hotel
February 4, 1968

Dear Mr. Booher,

VN asks me to thank you for your letter of Jan. 26th which arrived only yesterday, Feb. 3, and for the clipping from *The New Republic*.

He finds it a pleasing thought that you bought his Russian translation of LOLITA for your Russian-reading child.

He would like his Russian KING, QUEEN, KNAVE to be published again.[2] We have a treasured copy of the first edition that we could lend provided it could be handled carefully by the printers. We lent our copies of INVITATION TO A BEHEADING and THE LUZHIN DEFENSE to Radio Liberty in Munich (who reproduced them for distribution in Russia, clandestine, of course). The Russian editions are also represented in the bigger American university and public libraries and could be borrowed from there (if the printers undertake to return the book undamaged). There are also a few drawbacks: The book was published more than 28 years ago and was never copyrighted. It is, of course, protected by the Bern Convention in Europe. It was written at a time when VN was stateless and a resident of an European country. The Copyright Office *may* decide that for these reasons it still could be copyrighted on publication, but this is not certain. Also: the original version was set in accordance with the rules of the "old orthography". During the revolution some of those rules were modified, three then currently used letters were scrapped (actually, five but two had not been much used anyway), certain case endings were changed, so were certain rules governing the use of prefixes. All these changes don't bother an educated Russian of the new formation but would they not put off American students? The Russian publishers who published VN's Russian books have long ceased to exist. I doubt they would have had any claims in any case since the books have been out of print for more than twenty years, and all the publishing houses had been liquidated before or during the war.

VN asks me to ask you if you would not consider taking over from Phaedra the Russian version of LOLITA? We don't know if Phaedra would agree to sell the rights but we could ask in case you were interested. (LOLITA, of course, is printed in accordance with the new orthographic rules). But LOLITA was *set* in Russian and the costs of production were high.

With best wishes from VN and me.

Sincerely
(Mrs. Vladimir Nabokov)

1. President, McGraw-Hill.
2. The 1928 Russian text of *King, Queen, Knave* was republished by McGraw-Hill in 1969.

TO: **EDWARD E. BOOHER**                                        CC, 1 p.

Montreux, Switzerland
Montreux Palace Hotel
February 23, 1968

Dear Mr. Booher,

In response to your letter of February 19th I shall mail to you on Monday under separate cover and as thoroughly registered as I can manage our copy of the Russian edition of KING, QUEEN, KNAVE.

My husband would appreciate hearing from you how long an introduction you had in mind—how long should it be to help copyright the work? He thinks he could easily manage a very short one (about one page, possibly a little longer) but would find it hard to take enough time from ADA for a longer one. He also wants me to point out to you that the following considerations might help the copyrighting: he was a stateless emigrant residing in Germany at the time he wrote the book. The laws ruling the publication and copyrighting of works by American authors may not apply in the case of the books he wrote before coming to the U.S. and being naturalized. The rules are not very clear in the case of such works. The Copyright Office was very lenient and copyrighted for him all his works which were not yet 28 years old when we applied for registration. As far as we know the rules have been more and more liberally applied in recent years.

VN would very much like to know, if you do not mind divulging it, who was it that informed you about ADA.[1] No one (but I and my typist) has read as much as one line of the work so far. In complete confidence I wish to tell you that there now exist 500 pages typed and corrected which make up the first part of the book. VN believes that the rest of the book will make up another three hundred pages.

When the TIME, INC. edition of BEND SINISTER will be in

427

your hands, I shall send you a list of a dozen misprints to be corrected in your edition.

My husband joins me in sending you our best wishes.

Sincerely,
(Mrs. Vladimir Nabokov)

PS. VN would like to know what terms you have in mind for the Russian edition of KING, QUEEN, KNAVE.

1. VN's agent Irving Lazar had told Booher about *Ada*.

TO: **PROF. PAGE STEGNER**                                   CC, 1 p.

Montreux, Switzerland
Montreux Palace Hotel
February 26, 1968

Dear Page,

Your letter of Feb. 20th arrived today. I therefore think it safer to send my answer to your new address, it would hardly reach Columbus before March 1.

Here is a suggestion for a title from VN: "A Nabokov Congeries" or "Nabokov's Congeries." He would like to have your and Viking's reaction to this "perhaps fanciful suggestion."

We hope you will be very happy in your new job and surroundings. I have seen a nice review of your book—by Granville Hicks, I believe.

With cordial greetings, from VN and from me.

Sincerely,
(Mrs. Vladimir Nabokov)

TO: **MARTIN J. ESSLIN**[1]                                           CC, 1 p.

Montreux, Switzerland
Montreux Palace Hotel
February 28, 1968

Dear Mr. Esslin,

My husband asks me to convey to you his gratitude for letting him see your article which he finds admirable, and to tell you that he likes tremendously your "elegant amalgamation of Esslinabokov."

The following are the changes which he would very much like you to accept:

p. 1. He would like you to omit the words from "after years of exile" to "America", substituting for them "temporarily from his country of adoption", or something to this effect. He does not intend to perpetuate his stay in Europe and would not like it to appear that he does. For the same reason he would like you to insert "may" after "Montreux" at the end of the same paragraph.

p. 5. He would like you to omit the parenthetical sentence "(whose society . . . . . . intellectuals)" because he does not wish to offend his American friends. For a different reason which it would take too long to explain but which has the greatest importance for him at this time, he begs you to omit the entire passage from "the name of the heroine" to "France for America in 1940. But." He suggests that you begin the following sentence with "The first book to be published by N.'s new publishers, McGraw-Hill, will be *King, Queen, Knave*, etc."

p. 6. The fact is that he published *The Gift, Invitation to a Beheading* and *Defense* without alterations, but made important changes in *Despair* (including a completely new scene).

p. 6. He begs you to delete "After a brief consultation between Nabokov and his wife it was agreed that". And so do I. It would embarrass us very much if this sentence was allowed to remain.

p. 11. He would like to have the word "peace" removed from the sentence "Cape Codpiece Peace Resistance".

This is all apart from a few misprints which we corrected from sheer habit.

We both keep a most pleasant remembrance of your visit to Montreux.

With best wishes from VN and me,

Sincerely yours,
(Mrs. Vladimir Nabokov)

1. Interviewer for the *New York Times Book Review*; the interview appeared on 12 May 1968. See *Strong Opinions*, p. 108.

TO: **PROF. SIMON KARLINSKY**[1]　　　　　　　　　CC, 1 p.
Montreux, Switzerland

February 28, 1968

Dear Mr. Karlinsky,

We are very grateful for the article you so kindly sent us. And we are delighted that you will come to Europe and visit us next year.

There is not very much chance of VN giving a lecture anywhere in the near future. He is completely absorbed in his writing. However, he thanks you very much for asking.

We wonder if you realize that, although Tsvetaeva[2] was living in great poverty she was not much worse off than most writers and especially poets of the period (Russian, of course)? In order to exist Ladinsky[3] worked as something of a handyman in Posledniya Novosti. Others drove taxis* or performed menial work. Many had no working permits and could not round out their income from writing. After the early Twenties during which émigré publications sprouted all over free Europe, and even at such places as Harbin, the opportunities of being published began to shrink. Space was at a premium. Even accepted works had to wait their turn for months. Once you take this into consideration you will see that Tsvetaeva was published more than most other poets, even by those who did not care much for her as a person. Her complaints are very much exaggerated: every reading person in emigration knew her poems, they appeared in most anthologies, some were extremely popular. And, of course, she was highly valued as a prose writer. In her letters there is a constantly recurring whining note which is not exactly endearing.

I hope you will not mind too much my saying so but we who witnessed all the stages of emigration see things from a different angle. I think Prof. Struve will concur.

Cordially,
(Mrs. Vladimir Nabokov)

*) One of those who drove a taxi for years was Korvin-Piotrovski[4]

1. Department of Slavic Languages, the University of California, Berkeley.
2. Marina Tsvetaeva, émigré poet who returned to Russia in 1939 and subsequently committed suicide.
3. Antonin Ladinsky.
4. Vladimir Korvin-Piotrovksi.

TO: **LAUREN G. LEIGHTON**[1]                     TLS (XEROX), 1 p.
                                          Montreux Switzerland

March 14, 1968

Dear Mr. Leighton,

My husband asks me to thank you for your interesting letter of Feb. 22, and also to answer it. The questions you raise are very painful and complicated. The people you write about risk very much in seeking even indirect contact with VN. But VN cannot even be sure that what they stand for is true freedom as we know it in the West, and not merely a different brand of communism (as did, f.i., Pasternak in his dreadful ZHIVAGO—so highly praised by naive libertarians in and out of Russia). Those poor young people may well be exposing themselves to dire consequences on mistaken premises. They do not even realize that every book by VN is a blow against tyranny, every form of tyranny. Until correspondence can be equally safe for both sides—and therefore may be guaranteed against any kind of

431

misunderstanding—VN has made it a rule not to enter into contact with people living beyond the iron curtain, for their sake.

Regarding the translation of his works into Russian VN is *quite* certain that the knowledge of the English language by the would-be translator is insufficient for any translation approaching his own very rigid demands. He plans gradually to translate his English novels into Russian. Some of his Russian novels have been recently reprinted and are slowly reaching some readers in Russia. He translated himself his LOLITA into Russian, and knows that at least 500 copies of it have been introduced into Russia by volunteers. He thinks that his best contact with Russians in Russia is through his books. Of course, he does not have to know of your friends' translating one or another of his English novels into Russian and circulating mimeographed copies in clandestine fashion among their friends, but he cannot bless or authorize a translation he will not be able to check and correct.

The only other thing I must add: Please be careful. No matter how careful you think you are, agents read letters, lists of dissenters are compiled, and should the Soviet regime decide to give an example of its omniscience and of its omnipotence over its wretched subjects, your friends may become the victims of such examples.

> Sincerely yours,
> Véra Nabokov
> (Mrs. Vladimir Nabokov)

1. Slavic scholar who delivered a message to VN from young Russians in Leningrad.

TO: **PROF. CARL R. PROFFER**                    TL (XEROX), 2 pp.

> Montreux, Switzerland
> Montreux Palace Hotel
> May 1, 1968

Dear Mr. Proffer,

Many thanks for both copies of your elegant book with the very cleverly stylized butterflies.[1] Ample praise should, and will, be bestowed upon your *Keys* by other readers but let me, a fellow-glossarist, contribute the following notes.

p. 28. An error. The correct allusion is to Baudelaire's "*Le crépuscule du matin*" (marred by the horrible Hugoesque line 11), the second and third verses of which may be lowelled as

It was the hour when noxious dreams in swarms
Make dark-haired adolescents writhe in dorms.

p. 30 In the autumn of 1958, when working on my Pushkin at the N.Y. Library, I glimpsed the title "Lolita", a novel by some obscure Frenchman (the name escapes me but could be easily checked in the title catalogue), wrote out my slip and gave it to an attendant. With impatient disgust (it had evidently happened before) he tore my slip in two and uttered the immortal phrase: "This is not the *Lolita* you want."

p. 33 I am not sure you realize that the Kreutzer Sonata picture is the one reproduced in the Taboo perfume ads (in The New Yorker, for instance).

p. 63 Gustave is Flaubert who has a Mlle Lempereur (I forget the exact spelling) perform similarly in *Madame Bovary*.
Nijinski (have lost page, and your index does not supply it). A reference to a famous photograph that appeared in *Life* or in some European counterpart of it and showed poor mad Nijinsky, then almost fifty, executing a pathetic *entrechat* for the reporters.

p. 143 (n. 77) In a little diary I kept in Ithaca, N.Y., in 1951 I find listed under January 6 several projects I was engaged in at the time, and among them is *The Kingdom by the Sea*, the first working title of *Lolita*, or more exactly of a fair draft on index cards of the twelve first sections plus several passages from the second part (I am, as I have often mentioned a tesselist).[2]

p. 144 Thrice misprinted French word.

p. 153 (n. 1) On p. 70 of the Putnam edition (August 1958) Humbert clearly states "...Lolita's brother, who died at two when she was four." I think that there should have been page references in Appendix B for I cannot locate my mistake about Lolita's brother but dimly recall correcting something of the kind, and other Tolstoy-time items, in my Russian translation of *Lolita* (Phaedra, 1967, New York).

Finally, and privately, Saul Bellow, a miserable mediocrity, should never have appeared on the jacket of a book about me. Is it too late to eliminate that exhaust puff?

Oh yes, two more minute flaws:

p. 12    Ponderosa is not Italian but the Latin specific name of the tree *Pinus ponderosa*; and

p. 140    *côte à côte*, and not *côté à côté*

Please let me know if you would like to use these corrections and bits of information in print. It would warm the bockles of old Boldino's bart.[3]

I am working on a tremendous new novel and send you my very best regards.

Cordially yours,
Vladimir Nabokov

1. *Keys to Lolita*.
2. tesselist: from "tesselate," to form into or adorn with mosaic. DN.
3. On the acknowledgment page of *Keys to Lolita*, Proffer used the jocular partial anagram of Nabokov's name "Mark V. Boldino." A penciled note of VN's, presumably a correction for a later edition, reads: "The incompletely anagrammatized name of the person thanked for his 'expert suggestions' (Mark V. Boldino) should have been yours truly Vivian Bloodmark." DN.

TO: **MARSHALL BEST, CHARLES NOYES, AND PETER KEMENY**[1]

cc, 1 p.
Montreux, Switzerland

October 4, 1968

Dear Sirs,

My husband was delighted with the witty cable received on

publication date of NABOKOV'S CONGERIES.[2] He almost cabled back "cannot conceal contentment nabocon", but decided it would not be quite as amusing.

I need not repeat that we are very pleased with the book. I can only add that all those who saw it thought it wonderful—both the selection and the presentation.

I take this opportunity to thank Mr. Noyes for his letter of September 4. The three packages with the author's copies sent by surface mail arrived safely on October 2.

> With VN's greetings and mine,
> Sincerely yours,
> (Mrs. Vladimir Nabokov)

1. Of Viking Press.
2. PUBDATE CONGERIES CONGENERICALLY COMMANDS CONGRATULA-
TIONS CONJUBILANT CONSENSUS CONJURES CONDIGN COURUS-
CATIONS BESTNOUSKEM.

TO: **WILLIAM MCGUIRE**                    TLS (XEROX), 1 p.

> Montreux Palace Hotel
> Montreux, Switzerland
> November 8, 1968

Dear Bill,

I do not wish to rush you in any way, but now that I have completed my 880-page *Ada* I feel singularly free and would be eager to stem the tide of another work of fiction by occupying myself with the publication of the revised EO.[1] Do you think such a plan possible? Please let me know. My seventieth birthday next year is a rather depressing smudge on my mental horizon.

We have been expecting you and Paula this summer—in vain. We hope all is well with you.

Cordially,

V

Vladimir Nabokov

1. The revised edition was published by Bollingen in 1975.

TO: **HEATHER MANSELL**[1]                                          CC, 1 p.

Montreux Palace Hotel
Montreux, Switzerland
Nov. 25, 1968

Dear Miss Mansell,

Your letter of 22 Nov. has just arrived, with the covers for the four books, and I hasten to reply.

INVITATION TO A BEHEADING: Design and blurb fully acceptable.

LAUGHTER IN THE DARK: Both design and blurb also acceptable. I have those stills.

SPEAK, MEMORY: Would like to see blurb. The butterfly part of the cover design is not acceptable. Those two *meleagers* (?) have nothing to do with the Russian background of the book since they do not occur in the north of Europe; and the female is quite incorrectly colored. Please, no butterflies at all on the cover unless you want to use the white-and-black *mnemosyne* of the Weidenfeld jacket (also facing their page 19).

NABOKOV'S DOZEN: Blurb: What on earth does "well-varnished truths" mean? Design: This is an impossible monster. Why don't you use, for instance, the CLOUD, CASTLE, LAKE idea (the picture of a lake, with a tower and cloud reflected in it)? But for Heaven's sake remove that horrible face with the crude wings.

PNIN: Blurb: Delete the absurd reference to "McCarthyism"—

436

which is not a particular phobia of mine, or of Pnin's. I also would like to replace "ludicrous progress" by "bizarre progress." Design: Completely unacceptable. This corny caricature is meaningless, badly drawn and repulsive. Pnin is an attractive and admirable person. One possibility of replacing that cartoon would be to use the very charming design on the cover of the paperback edition published by Avon Publications, Inc., 575 Madison Ave., New York, if you can acquire it from them. Or just omit picture altogether.

I would appreciate if you could tell Mr. Tony White that I have received the galleys of SPEAK, MEMORY and shall return them in good time. I must also see the LAUGHTER IN THE DARK proofs: Your 1963 edition was riddled with misprints. I assume that I shall also be given an opportunity to see the proofs of the other three works.

Thank you very much for showing me the cover material.

Sincerely yours,

1. Of Penguin Books, London.

TO: **HEATHER MANSELL**              cc, 1 p.

Montreux Palace Hotel
Montreux, Switzerland
Nov. 28, 1968

Dear Miss Mansell,

I have your telegram

"IN VIEW BUTTERFLIES ON PROPOSE SPEAK MEMORY COVER FEATURED IN PLATE OPPOSITE PAGE 228 / sic / WEIDENFELD EDITION COULD YOU RECONSIDER YOUR OBJECTION? WILL SUBMIT NEW DESIGN PNIN/ DOZEN STOP BLURB MEMORY FOLLOWS MANSELL PENGUIN BOOKS"

You are mistaken. The butterfly you figure on your cover for SPEAK, MEMORY is the one called *daphnis* by Schiffermüller and *meleager* by Esper and belongs to the subgenus called *Meleageria* by Sagarra, whilst the butterfly I figure on the plate facing p. 288 of the Weidenfeld edition of the book is the one called *cormion* by me, and belongs structurally to the subgenus called *Lysandra* by Hemming. My butterfly differs in male organ, wing shape, upperside coloration and underside pattern from your butterfly. Yours is a butterfly widely distributed throughout the southern part of central Europe and Russia; mine is an extremely rare freak, possibly a hybrid between *Meleageria daphnis* (*meleager*) and *Lysandra coridon*. The upper of your two figures is presumably a female of the *Meleageria* species (the colored photograph gives it an impossible green shade of blue and a revolting red rim); the female of my butterfly remains unknown to me (my two types are both males). And finally your butterfly is precisely one of the two, *M. daphnis* (*meleager*), from which I separate my *L. cormion* as a distinct organism!

To recapitualte: You illustrate the wrong butterfly on your cover. This adds a gratuitous pictorial muddle to an obscure and subtle taxonomic problem. I cannot reconsider my objection.

Sincerely yours,
Vladimir Nabokov

TO: **ROBIE MACAULEY**                    TL (XEROX), 1 p.

Montreux Palace Hotel
Montreux, Switzerland
December 24, 1968

Dear Mr. Macauley,

I have received your cable "Imminence book publication permits us use one section only from Ada in April we want chapters five, six, nine, fifteen, eighteen, nineteen, twenty, twenty-five total about fifteen thousand words offer ten thousand dollars please cable reply"—and have answered by cable "Delighted but would want a little more money to cope with tax. Letter follows."

The idea is that I would like fifteen thousand—to make the figure neater ("dollar per word") and to help me defray the tax which otherwise will eat up a considerable part of the plump ten thousand.

I greatly approve your choice of chapters. Please indicate the number of each chapter when you print the thing. May I be sure that there will not be any changes, cuts, or bridgings without my knowledge and consent (for instance, in Chapter Twenty, a phrase must be decoded). Should omissions be inevitable, please indicate them by means of a few dots.

Illustrations, if any, should be pleasing, elegant, lyrical, lyrotic. The material should be printed from the corrected McGraw-Hill proofs (which I am working on today between spells of enthralling TV lunar pictures.)

Merry Christmas!

Vladimir Nabokov


TO: **HUGH M. HEFNER**                                          cc, 1 p.

Montreux Palace Hotel
Montreux, Switzerland
December 28, 1968

Dear Mr. Hefner,

I wish to thank you, Mr. Spectorsky and The Playboy for your letter, charming cards and gifts and the bonus.

It pleases me very much to know that "One Summer in Ardis" (an excellent title suggested by Mr. Macauley) will appear in *Playboy*.[1]

Have you ever noticed how the head and ears of your Bunny resemble a butterfly in shape, with an eyespot on one hindwing?[2]

Happy New Year.

Yours sincerely,
Vladimir Nabokov


1. Excerpt from *Ada*.
2. The third paragraph of this letter was published with VN's rabbit-butterfly drawing in the January 1972 issue of *Playboy*, p. 18.

TO: **FRANK E. TAYLOR**                    TLS, 1 p. Lilly Library.

Montreux, Switzerland
Montreux Palace Hotel
January 6, 1969

Dear Frank,

I just got the photostat of the new jacket design for ADA, and do not like it at all. The lettering is dumpy, with apertures en cul-de-poule. The coloration of the word ADA recalls at first blush the nacrine inner layer of a dejected shellfish, and, at a closer inspection, the bleak marblings of a ledger's edge. At six paces the D of the title looks like a badly deformed O. *Please*, let us go back to the joyful, elegant, black VN and red ADA on a white ground!

I wrote you yesterday thanking you for the duplicate set. In the same letter I mentioned how I stand with the Atlantic.

We did not go to Rome after all to avoid being caught in strikes and riots.

Thanks for your good wishes. We wish you a marvelous year, too.

Cordial greetings.
V
Vladimir Nabokov

TO: **FRANK E. TAYLOR**                                    CC, 1 p.

Montreux, Switzerland
Montreux Palace Hotel
January 14, 1969

Dear Frank,

I would not like to interfere in any way with your publicity plans.
"Erotic masterpiece" sounds all right, though, as you are no doubt
aware, it has been loosely applied in the recent past to books like
*Poxus* and *Capri Corn*[1]—and also to my own *Lolita*. Prompted by your
question, I have rapidly passed in review such epithets as "fantastic,"
"iridescent," "demonic," "mysterious," "magic," "glorious," and the
like; but, let me repeat, I entirely rely upon your good taste and experience.

Incidentally "Paris Match", whose reporter I had refused to receive, has retaliated with a spatter of nonsense about me (January 9,
1969) and an idiotic bit about *Ada*, but I don't think it needs shaking
a stick at.

We shall be of course absolutely delighted to see you and your wife
here. Even if you cannot come do let me know where to get in touch
with you while you are in Europe.

Yours ever,
Vladimir Nabokov

1. Puns on titles of works by Henry Miller.

TO: **GEORGE WEIDENFELD**                                CC, 1 p.

Montreux, January 20, 1969

Dear George,

I have just seen a copy of Harold Nicolson's *Diaries and Letters,
945–92* (a Christmas present from Miss Alison). It contains a passage (p. 370) which I would like to comment upon by placing on re-

cord (and this is the purpose of my note) that the statement attributed to me ("Niggs tells me that VN said to him that all his life he had been fighting against the influence of *Some People*")[1] is terribly exaggerated. I did say to Nigel Nicolson (in 1959 in London) that I greatly admired *Some People* and I may have added that in my thirties (when writing *Sebastian Knight*) I was careful to steer clear of its hypnotic style. But the idea of "fighting all my life" against its influence on me is, of course, nonsense. You may show this note to Nigel Nicolson—just for the record.

Cordially,
Vladimir Nabokov

1. A volume of prose sketches published in 1927.

to: **FRANK E. TAYLOR**                                        cc, 1 p.

Montreux, Palace Hotel
March 9th, 1969

Dear Frank,

I was very pleased to receive your letter from New York. Thank you for sending me the three copies of the Literary Guild magazine and the Publishers Weekly with the excellent Adavertisement. It contains, however, three little errors. If you propose to repeat its text anywhere, please note that Van did *not* seduce Lucette; that the name of the émigré publishing house is not "Slava", but "Slovo;" and, most important, that there should be no "a" between "is" and "random variation" (see p. 416 of the novel: "is random variation").

I recall that at some point in the past either you, or Mr. Booher, or Mr. Kemeny mentioned that it would please McGraw-Hill to concentrate in their hands as many of my works as possible. In the light of this admirable idea I would like you to know that Phaedra (who published my THE EYE, THE WALTZ INVENTION, THE

QUARTET and my Russian translation of LOLITA) are on the brink of bankruptcy and are trying to dispose of their business. Oscar de Liso, who owns Phaedra, ran an ad to that effect.

Warm greetings from us both.

Yours ever,
Vladimir Nabokov

PS. Please do not use any of the Lit. Guild illustrations for publicity. They are well drawn artistically but otherwise quite wrong. The two little slum girls have no resemblance whatsoever to those meticulously described in my book; only in movies and cartoons do people begin a duel by standing back to back; the pistols are wrong. On the other hand, the moths (minus the delinquents), the boat on the dial and my sepia profile are very successful.

to: **FRANK E. TAYLOR**                    TELEGRAM
March 1969

LT
LOVELY FAT ADA BUT NOTHING IS PERFECT IN LIFE BAD MISPRINT IN PENULT LINE LAST PAGE OF BOOK VIEW DESCRIBED SHOULD BE VIEW DESCRIED.

NABOKOV

EXP VLADIMIR NABOKOV PALACE HOTEL MONTREUX SWITZERLAND

TO: **WILLIAM HONON**[1]  TELEGRAM

I WANT A LUMP IN HIS THROAT TO OBSTRUCT THE
WISECRACK

NABOKOV

Exp. Vladimir Nabokov, Palace Hotel, Montreux Le 13 mars 1969

1. Of *Esquire*. VN's message to *Esquire* about the first words to be spoken on the moon.
When published in "Le Mot Juste for the Moon" (July 1969), "I" was emended to "you."

TO: *PLAYBOY*  TELEGRAM

DEAR PLAYBOY ADA FRAGMENTS BEAUTIFULLY PRINT-
ED BUT GOODNESS WHAT ILLUSTRATIONS THAT IM-
PROBABLE YOUNG MAMMAL AND TWO REVOLTING
FROGS

NABOKOV

Exp. Vladimir Nabokov, Palace Hotel, Montreux March 17, 1969

TO: **FRANK E. TAYLOR**  TLS, 1 p. Lilly Library.
April 1969

Palace Hotel
Montreux, Switzerland

Dear Frank,

With your buxom Ada against my breast, my bathroom scale reck-
ons my weight at 88½ kg.; without her at 87. What a splendid, enchantingly appetizing volume! Tolstoy says about his Anna K. that

444

she "carried her *embonpoint* gracefully." How Ada would have maddened Leo!

As I cabled you yesterday, I somehow overlooked—probably in page proof—a bothersome little misprint on the last page. My MS gives the correct "view descried" (not "described"). I wonder if this could be cured in ensuing copies? Webster's condemns "described" when used in the sense of "descried."

Inspiration seems on the point of visiting me again despite my being so dreadfully drained after *Ada*.

Yours ever,

V

Vladimir Nabokov

TO: **MORRIS BISHOP**                    TLS, 1 p. Mrs. Morris Bishop

Montreux

7 April 1969

Dear Morris,

We were all set (including reservations on two Italian liners) to attend all sorts of festivities and ceremonies in NY in May but had to cancel our visit. You will receive a copy of my little *Ada* but not, alas, the invitation to a planned cocktail.

In the meantime we have, and treasure, your Middle Ages.[1] Your text is robust, colorful, tremendously talented. From notes I made while reading it I see that I chuckled enthusiastically over the "intimate" insects (p. 78). Of the two wonderful paragraphs (p. 102) dealing with education, I noticed, without much surprise, that the female child received twice as much attention as the boy did. Your marvelous unique humor crops up, God bless it, quite frequently (p. 115: ". . . apparently to include a roast peacock"; p. 116: "treasured teeth"; p. 131: "complete saint"; p. 373: "the rest of him"), and of course the best (incomparably best) translations are those on pages 303 and 312–13.

I humbly submit that Frederic II (p. 57) could not have known *anything* (Thirteenth Century!) about hummingbirds (which exist only in the New World). The illustrations are beautifully chosen but not all are satisfactorily identified (e.g.: p. 362, the tapestry weaver, one of the gems of its age).

Many thanks for this splendid gift. Véra and I send our love to both of you.

Yours ever,
V

---

1. *A Medieval Storybook* (Ithaca: Cornell University Press, 1970), drawings by Alison Mason Kingsbury.

TO: **FRANK E. TAYLOR**                TLS, 1 p. Lilly Library

Montreux-Palace Hotel
Montreux, Switzerland
April 21, 1969

Dear Frank,

In Ch. 19 of Part One, p. 120, 1.4 "Stanley" should be "Speke" (who discovered the source of the Nile and sent the famous cable). Since Van's jocular misidentification looks uncommonly like a silly lapse on my own part, it might be wise to substitute "Speke" for "Stanley" if and when a second printing is to be prepared.

Dmitri has taken to Monza my copy of Ada, so I have now stopped dipping into the book (and surfacing with a gasp) for the time being. Véra is in Geneva and may stay there for another week.

Yours ever
V
Vladimir Nabokov

TO: **BUD MACLENNAN**                    TL (XEROX), 1 p.

> Montreux-Palace Hotel
> Montreux, Switzerland
> 25 April, 1969

Dear Miss MacLennan,

Panther's Cover Design for my QUARTET is perfectly dreadful and disgusting. Why should a collection of poetical tales be degraded to the rank of a horror movie by a designer who has never read them?

I emphatically object to this monocled skull.

> Yours sincerely,
> Vladimir Nabokov

TO: **ANDREW FIELD**[1]                    TL (XEROX), 3 pp.

> Montreux-Palace Hotel
> Montreux, Switzerland
> April 25, 1969

Dear Andrew,

My wife is not well, and I have some difficulty in coping with my voluminous and complicated correspondence, but your charming letters have special precedence.

The 23 pictures[2] arrived just before my birthday and I am writing to Stephen Sternheimer (c/o of his father) to thank him for this absolutely magnificient birthday present. I am also deeply touched by the captions in an unknown Russian hand, by their text and tone, by this extraordinary link established between my childhood and old age through the sensitive minds of strangers in a fabled and sad land into which my books somehow penetrate.

Only six of the photographs would I want to appear in print. They have now been re-numbered by me from 1 to 6. The buildings that appear in the other pictures are quite unknown to me. The oak is not the one I remember. The snow adds, rather tactfully, its own white mask to the layers of change and loss.

I shall have the captions typed in the original Russian and sent to you, with my comments and corrections (for example the Vyra house was destroyed by fire long before World War Two, in the nineteen twenties, and of course neither my brother, nor I could have visited Russia with the German invaders).

Thanks for remembering my modest birthday.

Vladimir Nabokov

Photos

(o)

Photographs of the "Nabokov Lands in the St Petersburg region" (see VN's SPEAK, MEMORY, frontispiece, map sketched in 1965) which an American visitor obtained in that area ("had 23 pictures made and developed there" says his father in a letter of April 2, 1969) in the beginning of 1969, half a century after VN left Russia. The American visitor airmailed the photos to Prof. Andrew Field in Australia asking him to have the pictures sent to VN for his 70th birthday.

(oo)

An anonymous Russian has penned amazingly precise captions on the back of the pictures. It appears from those precious inscriptions that memories of the Nabokovs and knowledge of VN's books are alive and warm in his native countryside.

(1)

The Rozhestveno manor-house inherited by VN from his uncle Rukavishnikov in 1916. This is its northern façade showing its back porch. For the house's history see SPEAK, MEMORY, p. 64–65 & 72; and for more private associations, p. 233 of the same work. The road above which the house stands on its lone hill, some fifty miles south of St Petersburg (Leningrad) is now called the Kiev Highway

(formerly Warsaw Highway). The shell is intact, the inside is said to
be unrecognizable.

(2)

The crypt of the Rukavishnikovs (VN's grandfather, grandmother
and their eldest son Vladimir, who died *circa* 1890) just across the
river Oredezh, on its north bank. The logs are the church's fire-
wood.

(3)

The place (west of the sinuous Oredezh) where VN's parents'
country house (Vyra estate) once stood. Nothing remains of it except
traces of its foundation.

(4)

The main avenue of the Vyra park (greatly invaded by firs).

(5)

The road and bridge leading to Batovo, VN's paternal grandmother's estate (which belonged to the Ryleev family in the first quarter
of the nineteenth century, see p. 63 of SPEAK, MEMORY), about
two miles west of Rozhestveno.

(6)

The main avenue in the Batovo park where according to my hypothesis Pushkin had his pistol duel with Ryleev in 1820 (see
SPEAK, MEMORY, p. 62). The manorhouse was destroyed by fire
in 1922.

1. American critic, living in Australia, for whose *Nabokov: His Life in Art* (Boston & Toronto: Little, Brown, 1967) the Nabokovs had supplied much information and numerous
corrections. At the beginning of 1968 Field began a bibliography of VN's works, commissioned by VN's new publisher, McGraw-Hill. Later that year Field asked the Nabokovs
if they would countenance his writing a biography of VN. Since Field promised that
VN would have "the final word" (Field to VN, 25 August 1968), VN agreed.
2. Photos of places VN knew in Russia.

TO: *DIE PRESSE*[1]  TL, (XEROX), I p.

Montreux, 30 April 1969.

Dear editor-in-chief:

In the *Presse* of 25 April you published an article "Visite bei Vladimir Nabokov" by Werner Helwig.

I would like to make it clear that Herr Helwig did not visit me, although he claims to have done so. His "Interview" consists of sentences which he took from other, genuine interviews, from a number of his own inventions, and from three lines that my wife sent him in my behalf on the 28th of March 1969. These three lines had to do with Conrad, Gide and Mann and were in answer to the long and confused questionnaire that Herr Helwig had sent me and which I did not answer beyond that. I refused to enter into correspondence with Herr Helwig, and certainly never granted him an interview.

Sincerely,
Vladimir Nabokov

1. Vienna newspaper. Letter written in German (translated by Prof. James Hardin).

TO: **PROF. MATTHEW HODGART**[1]  TL (XEROX), I p.

Montreux-Palace Hotel
Montreux, Switzerland
May 12, 1969

Sir,

I do not really mind your introducing ridiculous errors (such as "at graze" instead of "at gaze" or the reference to Gardner—look up that passage in his book and index) all through your review of ADA, but I do object violently to your seeing in reunited Van and Ada (both rather horrible creatures) a picture of my married life.

What the hell, Sir, do you know about my married life? I expect a prompt apology from you.

Vladimir Nabokov[2]

1. Department of English, Cornell University. His review of *Ada* appeared in the 22 May 1969 *New York Review of Books*.
2. *New York Review of Books* (10 July 1969), with Hodgart's reply. Hodgart also sent VN a personal letter on 19 May, explaining that his comment on the Nabokovs "was an extrapolation from *Speak, Memory*."

TO: **JAMES LAUGHLIN**                    TLS (XEROX), 1 p.

Montreux-Palace Hotel
Montreux, Switzerland
June 6, 1969

Dear Jay,

Thanks for that handsome edition of the Italian and Russian *Mednïy Vsadnik*. ("*Mednïy*" in that sense means "bronze", not "copper", *pace* Edmund Wilson).[1]

I have always been tempted to translate it, and about a dozen other Russian classics, into English but have decided that from now on I will translate only your obedient servant

V
Vladimir Nabokov

1. Pushkin's poem "The Bronze Horseman."

TO: **FRANK E. TAYLOR**                    CC, 1 p.
10 June 1969                    Montreux, Switzerland

Dear Frank,

I wish to report to you on my literary activities for the last six months.[1]

1. Much time was devoted to the correcting and recorrecting of the ADA proofs. This went well into February.

2. Work on the preparation of a collection of my poems, Russian and English, with English translations made in meter.

3. Work on an English translation of MASHENKA—the difficult bits, while the first draft of the entire book is being prepared by a translator in England.[2]

4. Notes for a new novel.

Sincerely yours,
Vladimir Nabokov

1. VN sent progress reports to McGraw-Hill in order to comply with contractual requirements.
2. *Mary*, trans. VN and Michael Glenny (New York: McGraw-Hill, 1970).

TO: **ANDREW FIELD**                                TL (XEROX), 1 p.

Montreux, Palace Hotel, June 10th 1969

Dear Andrew,

I thank you for your FRACTIONS[1] which I read very carefully. As I think you suspect yourself they don't quite make a whole number. I am sorry to be saying that but I am sure you would prefer a frank opinion to jejune compliments. Were I a reviewer, I would put it this way: This little novel seems to be a very mediocre desert up to Ager's arrival after which it ends in a first-rate mirage. It is rather like winning a tennis match 0–6, 0–6, 19–17, 6–3, 6–0.

I am sending you enclosed a xerox copy of a list of all my stuff at the L.C. The material will not be open to inspection until fifty years after my death. However, I have recently received from Prague three thick albums containing many of my things (including plays) collected by my mother in the twenties and thirties.

We have also made definite arrangements for the transfer of all our stuff stored in Ithaca from there to Montreux in October. I wonder what Updike's reaction to some of the passages in your book will be. The albums and the material from Ithaca will be at your disposal when they will have been sorted out.

Cordial greetings from us both to you and Michele.

Vladimir Nabokov

1. A novel. London: Hodder-Fawcett, 1969.

---

TO: **KIRK POLKING**[1]                     TL (XEROX), 1 p.

Montreux-Palace Hotel
Montreux, Switzerland
June 13, 1969

Dear Mr. Polking,

My answer to your question "Does the writer have a social responsibility" is:

NO

You owe me ten cents, Sir.

Vladimir Nabokov

1. Of *Writer's Digest*. Polking had offered VN $200 for 2,000 words.

---

TO: **PHILIP OAKES**                     TELEGRAM
Montreux, Switzerland

YOU MAY CHANGE FRAUD TO MEDIOCRITY OR NON-

ENTITY BUT I EMPHATICALLY REFUSE TO HAVE THE
POUND ITEM EXCISED[1]

NABOKOV

Vladimir Nabokov
June 18th 1969

1. "Philip Oakes Talks to Vladimir Nabokov: Author as Joker," *London Sunday Times* (22 June 1969). Oakes had requested permission to delete VN's description of Ezra Pound as "a venerable fraud."

TO: **ELSIE TORRES**[1]        TL (XEROX), 1 p.

Our address is:
Montreux Palace Hotel
Montreux, Switzerland
July 5th, 1969

Dear Mrs. Torres,

My husband asks me to reply to your letter of May 14th. You ask in it in which of the two possible places in the stacks—American or Russian Literature—he would like to be if he had to choose one. His answer is that he would prefer to be in the American Literature since his best work was done in English.

Sincerely yours,
(Mrs. Vladimir Nabokov)

1. Of Wells College Library, Aurora, N.Y.

TO: **KENNETH TYNAN**[1]  TL (XEROX), I p.

Permanent address:
Montreux Palace Hotel
Montreux, Switzerland
July 12th, 1969

Dear Mr. Tynan,

I have no interest whatever in pornography and cannot imagine myself being titillated by what I write.

I have no intention to contribute to the Grove Press anthology you describe.[2] Sorry.

Sincerely yours,
Vladimir Nabokov

1. English drama critic.
2. On 23 June Tynan invited VN to contribute to a collection of pieces of erotica, "all written for the express purpose of arousing the author's own sexual impulses." This volume did not appear.

TO: *NEW YORK TIMES*  PRINTED STATEMENT[1]
Montreux, Switzerland

Treading the soil of the moon, palpating its pebbles, tasting the panic and splendor of the event, feeling in the pit of one's stomach the separation from terra . . . these form the most romantic sensation an explorer has ever known . . . . this is the only thing I can say about the matter . . . the utilitarian results do not interest me.

1. "Reactions to Man's Landing on the Moon Show Broad Variations in Opinions" (21 July 1969).

TO: **PHILIP OAKES**                                    CC, I p.

Adelboden, August 12th, 1969
Hotel Nevada

Dear Mr. Oakes,

I must apologize for being so late in thanking you for *The God Botherers*,[1] which got shipped back to Montreux by mistake and has been retrieved only now.

I greatly enjoyed your book. It is beautifully constructed and full of vivid details. I particularly liked the derelict chapel (68–69), the looted dispensary (105), the full stop of the last shot (138), Bateman the spectator, his bark of laughter, its effect on the poodles (152), and the eminently satisfying end. Everything about the boy's levitation is admirable. I would have gladly had these remarks published had I not stopped writing reviews and endorsements many years ago.

Please in the next edition change "carpet of dew" (44) so that it does not spoil the splendid "carpet of watercress" in the next paragraph, and substitute "pupa" for "cocoon" (228), which does not "split" but is thrust open at one end.

Yours cordially,
Vladimir Nabokov

1. London: Deutsch, 1969.

TO: **FRANK E. TAYLOR**                              TL (XEROX), I p.

Montreux-Palace Hotel
Montreux, Switzerland
September 5, 1969

Dear Frank,

Very soon I shall send you several pages of notes (explaining trilingual puns, literary allusions, etc.) to be published as a commentary in the paperback edition, the proof of which I must, of course, see.[1]

Please tell me when the paperback edition of ADA is scheduled to appear (the later, of course, the better), but I have to get those notes off my chest, especially because I have to send them (in typescript) to my various translators who are either floundering badly or concealing their flounderings.

I will be posting to you the English Mashenka[2] (Mariette—thus my third girl) in the course of the next three or four months. If I see that my revisions will take considerably more time than I expect now, then I shall saddle you with a rather satisfactory volume of poetry and/or a collection of literary essays.

Please, Frank, answer this letter soon.

Yours as ever,
Vladimir Nabokov

*P.S.*

We are very pleased with all that is happening to ADA. I hope you have not stopped to advertise her because this is the moment when she is clinging with her lovely fragile anterior limbs to the sixth rung of the ladder invaded by squabbling pornographers.

I am going to talk about her and me on Monday in an interview with James Mossman on the *"Review"* programme of the BBC-TV.

1. "Notes to 'Ada' by Vivian Darkbloom" was first published in the 1970 Penguin edition of the novel.
2. *Mary.*

to: **BROTHER JOSEPH CHVALA, C.S.C.**[1]          TL (XEROX), 1 p.

Montreux-Palace Hotel
Montreux, Switzerland
September 10, 1969

Dear Sir,

In reply to your letter of September 3, my husband asks me to tell you that he does not believe that an artist is responsible to society; he believes that an artist is responsible only to his own self.

> Yours truly,
> (Mrs. Vladimir Nabokov)

1. Of St. Edward High School, Cleveland, Ohio.

TO: **FRANK E. TAYLOR**                    TL (XEROX), 1 p.

> Montreux, Sept. 17th, 1969
> Palace Hotel, Switzerland

Dear Frank,

Your edition of KOROL', DAMA, VALET is perfectly enchanting and I also thank you for the safe return of the original in such glowing health.

I have finished the prodigious job of annotating ADA myself. It is twenty five typescript pages long, I shall have it xeroxed today and I shall send you a copy immediately. You will notice that I included the very few little misprints of your first edition so as to have them all together in one place.

As to Appel's wish to write a "critical biography of VN" there is a snag, we must not forget that Andrew Field was to write my biography. I don't like turning down all Appel's projects but don't see how to reconcile the two biogs.

I am looking forward to the annotated LOLITA.

What happened to the de Liso negotiations?[1]

Bill McGuire (Princeton Univ. Press) tells me that you turned down the publication of a revised edition of my ONEGIN in paperback. It was a great disappointment, especially as he thought it was the right book for your educational department.

Here is a brief report on work in progress:

1. I finished annotating ADA (the book had to be reread twice).
2. Most of the poems have been translated now.

3. I am waiting for the English translator of MASHENKA to deliver his work so that I can revise it and incorporate prepared passages.

4. I am finishing an Introduction to MASHENKA. (Did I tell you that I've decided to entitle the book MARIETTE since I can't stand the English "mash" in the transliteration of the Russian title. Both are diminutives of Mary.)

5. Notes for the new novel are accumulating slowly. But I know exactly how many pages there will be: 250.[2]

6. We are wrestling with the troubles of the Italian translator of ADA. Mondadori have the fantastic plan of publishing the book in November.

> Very cordial greetings from both of us.
> Vladimir Nabokov

---

1. Oscar de Liso of Phaedra, publishers of *Nabokov's Quartet* and *The Waltz Invention*.
2. *Transparent Things* (New York: McGraw-Hill, 1972). VN was referring to the typescript; the printed book had 104 pages of text.

TO: **PROF. ALFRED APPEL, JR.**                    TL (XEROX), 1 p.

> Montreux Palace Hotel
> October 8, 1969

Dear Alfred,

This is not the first time that our letters have telepathically crossed.

Thanks for the proofs of the verse and prose. There should be an apostrophe after *n* in *Stihotvoren'ya* and in "Clairouin" the "v" should be replaced by a "u".

The misprint "Backgrounds of A.A." is certainly delightful but I also notice some inaccuracies in your account of the Girodias business as far as it goes down that page.[1] Ergaz did not "refer" me to him: she handled the matter alone. Nabokov did not "seem" not to know etc., he simply did not know anything at all, not having been in Europe since 1940. No illustrations were ever contemplated. For obvious reasons (Girodias having his own several versions) perfect exactitude is essential for me in this affair. You will find an exact record of it in my "Lolita and Mr. Girodias" (*Evergreen*, Feb. 1967) and the relevant passages (pp. 37–38) should be quoted rather than paraphrased.

Annotated ADA will have to wait a few years because—by another telepathic coincidence—I have just completed a 25-page long list of Notes for the first paperback edition.

A couple of years ago I received some photographs from Russia. I was later informed that publication might mean disaster to someone involved. Although I am fairly sure I did not send you any pictures from that batch—they are easily identified by a winter background—I don't want to take any chances. The two snapshots I mentioned in my last letter are of course quite innocuous, and so are the nine photographs you already have.

Would you consider granting me a favor? I would like to check for factual errors *only* any articles you have accepted for the Festschrift that might contain biographical data (e.g., Mrs. Leon's contribution).[2] I know you are rather close to the deadline but I am a touchy pedant in these matters, and any misinformation would spoil all the pleasure.

Best greetings to you both and to little *Karen in Miceland*.

As ever,
Vladimir Nabokov

MASHENKA will not be published before 1970
KING, QUEEN, KNAVE: If not yet on sale, should be soon
Work in progress: Am, as usual, resurrecting old books and composing a new one.

---

1. "Backgrounds of *Lolita*," *Triquarterly* (Winter 1970). This issue was also published as *Nabokov: Criticism, Reminiscences, Translations, and Tributes*, ed. Appel and Charles Newman (Evanston, Ill.: Northwestern University Press, 1970).
2. Lucie Léon Noel, "Playback."

TO: **PROF. CARL R. PROFFER**             TL (XEROX) 1 p.

Montreux, Palace Hotel
Oct. 14, 1969

Dear Mr. Proffer,

Thank you for your letter, the two books, the Brodsky[1] poem. "It contains many attractive metaphors and eloquent rhymes," says VN, "but is flawed by incorrectly accented words, lack of verbal discipline and an overabundance of words in general. However, esthetic criticism would be unfair in view of the ghastly surroundings and suffering implied in every line of the poem."

I am particularly grateful for sending those dungarees.[2] Please tell me how much I owe you.

The two books that came back from Vienna were mailed to you a couple of days ago.

Karlinsky paid us a visit a week ago. We had interesting and amusing talks with him. He is a very brilliant and learned man, says VN.

Our very cordial greetings to you both.
(Mrs. Vladimir Nabokov)

1. Russian poet Joseph Brodsky who subsequently emigrated to America and won the Nobel Prize in 1987.
2. Proffer had delivered jeans to Brodsky in VN's name.

TO: **CHESSBOARD EDITOR, *NEW STATESMAN***[1]      TL (XEROX), 1 p.

Montreux-Palace Hotel
Montreux, Switzerland
October 31, 1969

Sir,

I am sending you for publication a little "fairy" that I dedicated to E. Znosko-Borovsky on the 25th anniversary of his chess mastership. It appeared (under my old penname "V. Sirin") in the column which Znosko conducted in the Russian *émigré* daily *Poslednie novosti* (*Dernières nouvelles*), N 3891, Nov. 17, 1932, Paris. My problem is perhaps worth disintering from the dust of that periodical, extinct thirty years ago and impossible to obtain to-day.

Yours sincerely,
Vladimir Nabokov

1. Published 12 December 1969.

TO: **CHARLES MONAGHAN**[1]                                   TLS (XEROX), I p.

Montreux-Palace Hotel
Montreux, Switzerland
October 31, 1969

Dear Mr. Monaghan,

   Mr. Vladimir Nabokov asks me to tell you that of all the books he happened to read in the course of 1969, he liked best

|   |   |
|---|---|
| Tukio Tabuchi | The Alpine Butterflies of Japan |
| Philip Oakes | The God Botherers |
| Sam Beckett | Molloy |

Yours truly,
J. C.
Secretary to Vladimir Nabokov

1. Editor, *Book World*. VN's choices were published in the 7 December 1969 issue.

TO: **OLIVER CALDECOTT**[1]                                             CC, I p.

Montreux, Palace Hotel
November 17, 1969

Dear Mr. Caldecott,

Thank you for your letter of Nov. 14th and the photocopy of your correspondence with Fawcett.

Your artist's Cyprideum looks like a ghastly vulva, and the Puss Moth caterpillar is all wrong (and, moreover, does not breed on orchids). I am emphatically against this symbolic design. I want three or four non-anatomical genuine orchids, prettily colored, garlanded around "A D A". Why don't you simply use the drawing of the three species I made for you—possibly multiplying and stylizing them (but not freudianizing those innocent blossoms)?

On the other hand, if you cannot reproduce, or don't wish to bother with, the reproduction of an elegant old-fashioned vignette for my elegant old-fashioned novel, with delicate contours and tender tints, then I would prefer you to cancel all idea of a pictorial design, and replace it with plain lettering. Just my name and ADA would be enough.

I am sorry to be so fiercely meticulous in these matters but I have been so pleased with your final choice of design for SPEAK, MEMORY that I flatter myself with a similar vision of ADA in the Penguin edition.

I am returning the two designs and plate.

Sincerely yours,
Vladimir Nabokov

1. Of Penguin Books, London.

TO: **FRANK E. TAYLOR**                    TLS, 1 p. Lilly Library.

Montreux-Palace Hotel
Montreux, Switzerland
December 9, 1969

Dear Frank,

I am airmailing separately (to-morrow) the complete typescript of
POEMS AND PROBLEMS. It consists of: 1) a Dedication to my
wife; 2) a Preface; 3) 36 poems in my English translation; 4) the 36
Russian originals; 5) notes to some of them; 6) 14 English poems of
my *New Yorker* period; 7) a Bibliography; 8) 18 Chess problems with
notes and 9) their Solutions. Weariness and various professional worries (the Penguin misprints in ADA, my ADA, are exasperating) prevent me from appending an Index. Has Velie returned to the fold?

It is for you to decide, but I am quite sure (and I implore, entreat,
and impetrate you to consider my point) that the Cyrillic weirdies
ought not to be tucked away, in diamond print, but should be boldly
displayed *en regard*.[1] This is both more scholarly *and* compendious,
since they will take *less* place in a verso position while satisfying the
*poignant* demands of pedantic purity. Surely, their presence in that
position would attract at least as many Russian readers (in New York
and in Moscow) as they might repulse monolingual flippers. Give this
a friendly thought. I note that I follow elderly predecessors in under-
lining words.

I have been generally against capitalizing lines; but the New Yorker
did not always respect my habit or I forgot to enforce it; anyway I
notice that some of the English poems, copied from capitalized texts,
should be checked and cured in that respect. And please, tell me
when you expect to bring out the thing because if there is time, I
would like to prepublish a couple of my translations.

Very cordially,
Vladimir Nabokov[2]

1. The Russian poems were printed with facing English translations.
2. Signed with a V and a drawing of an eye.

TO: **FRANK E. TAYLOR**          TLS, 2 pp. Lilly Library.

Montreux-Palace Hotel
Montreux, Switzerland
December 13, 1969

Dear Frank,

Now that *Poems & Problems* is out of the way, let us discuss the next projects and arrangements.

1) If you are publishing the abridged *Eugene Onegin* (I am still in the dusk regarding your plans), I would like that work to be part of my obligations and would wish to devote the next month or so (while waiting for *Mary*) to completing the revisions and to writing the notes (of these, I believe there will not be more than around a hundred, with none exceeding three or four lines, but they are not easy to select and rework, and I would like to know the maximum of space you allow me for them). The actual text (the eight chapters plus Pushkin's own notes, including fragments of an additional chapter) will occupy about 200 pages, with a three or four-page long preface.

2) I have seen the first pages (one chapter and a half) of the English MARY, have corrected a number of things, including a few howlers, and have written to the translator, telling him that you expect to get the book by March and that it will take me about a month to revise it properly before that deadline. (It *was* March, wasn't it?).

3) I must be given at least three weeks to check the Fawcett edition of ADA. I must also see the jacket design. Véra and I have had an awful time proofreading the Penguin edition which we have now finished checking. It contained a crop of misleading misprints—the worst kind, things that make sense to a demented printer, perhaps, but not to the author.

4) What is exactly the De Liso situation?

5) I need a year to finish *Transparent Things*.

Please, Frank, all this is important and worrisome, so do answer these queries by letter as soon as possible. I love talking to you over the ocean, but I forget half of what you tell me, and seven-eighths of what I tell you.

Thanks for the clipping. You probably know that ADA has made an additional penny on the "Playboy" sidewalk like a good girl. P. & P.'s should reach you on Monday. Dmitri is back at Monza, and we expect him to visit us soon.

Yours ever,
V
Vladimir Nabokov

P.S. In case you prefer not to make the paperback *Eugene Onegin* part of our general contract, I would not mind your publishing it under a separate agreement. The paperback rights belong to me (without any participation by Bollingen).

P.p.s. We have just heard from Godwin: Glenny promises to finish the translation of *Mary* by mid-February

Véra[1]

1. Véra Nabokov's P.p.s. is in holograph.

TO: **FRANK E. TAYLOR**　　　　　　　TLS, 1 p. Lilly Library.

Montreux, Palace Hotel
Switzerland
December 20th, 1969

Dear Frank,

I am absolutely delighted with the beautifully appetizing bound copies of ADA and KING, QUEEN, KNAVE. Chesterton says somewhere that there are colored minerals one would like to eat, and Russian generals have been eaten in Africa with all their decorations.

I saw with great satisfaction that, in a blue passage, Stanley has been replaced by Speke.

A few days ago I sent you a letter and the typescript of POEMS

AND PROBLEMS, and less than a few days ago, both were acknowledged in your absence. I am looking forward to a letter from you
upon your return answering my questions, in particular with regard
to our further schedule.

Thank you for your warm greeting of December 4.

Véra and I wish you a merry Christmas and a glorious New Year.

I do not know if I told you that the English *Problemist* has printed
some of my problems, and that the *New Statesman* has just published
one too.

As ever,
Vladimir Nabokov[1]

1. Signed with a V and a drawing of an eye.

**FORM LETTER**  PRINTED
c. 1969  Montreux, Switzerland

Vladimir Nabokov finds it impossible to answer all the kind letters
he receives from his readers. He extends his warmest thanks to the
many friends and strangers who send him their good wishes, gifts
and comments.

TO: **PROF. ALFRED APPEL, JR.**  TL (XEROX), 1 p.

Montreux-Palace Hotel
Montreux, Switzerland
February 20, 1970

Dear Alfred,

I deeply appreciate the enormous and tender trouble you took over
the splendid Festschrift,[1] both as ceremony-master and convive. I

must also extend my heartfelt thanks to Charles Newman. Most of the contributions, yours most especially, have a warmth that dissolved the crusty old cockles. The tail of my telegram which read

       great feast grateful greetings small growls

was prompted by errors of fact, that occur in three pieces, all three by ladies (Berberov, Léon, and Steiner).

The tributors are dears, and Timofey Pavlovich's letter is a masterpiece.[2]

Acting upon a casual suggestion of yours, Alfred, I intend to write a little essay on TriQuarterly, number seventeen, winter 1970, $1.95.[3] Would that journal publish it? Or the NYRB? Or NYTBR?

Véra joins me in sending Nina and you our very best regards.

Vladimir Nabokov

1. *TriQuarterly* (Winter 1970).
2. A parody of Pnin's style with which the *TriQuarterly* number concludes; it was written by Prof. W. B. Scott of Northwestern University.
3. *Anniversary Notes* by VN (sixteen-page supplement to *TriQuarterly*, Winter 1970).

TO: **DMITRI NABOKOV**     HOLOGRAPH PS TO VÉRA NABOKOV LETTER

Palace Hotel
1820 Montreux
30 May 1970

I am keeping the *Esquire* for you. Here is a Russian saying:

       gore vidal i bit bïval[1]

If you fly high over the tropical forest, you may notice what looks like shimmering little light-blue mirrors—*Morpho* butterflies flying above the trees.

I love you, no down![2]
P.[3]

1. This play on author Gore Vidal's name can be translated: "I've seen woes and suffered blows." DN.
2. Part of a Russian saying, "No down, no feathers"—roughly equivalent to the American expression "break a leg" for good luck before a performance. DN was performing in Colombia. DN.
3. Translated from Russian by DN.


TO: **PROF. ALFRED APPEL, JR.**                    TL (XEROX), I p.

Montreux, Palace Hotel, Switzerland
June 9, 1970

Dear Alfred,

*The Annotated Lolita* arrived only yesterday. Your comments form a superb additional book full of your own artistic vigor, gems and stratagems. I think it will fascinate the good reader as surely as it will distress flippant fools. How delighted I am that you undertook this task!

There are only two misprints to correct in later printings (apart from your own Errata which I have pasted in).

P. 369: acrosonic, not "acronsonic"
P. 375: verbal body to thoughts, not "verbal body to words"
        (my slip in the interview)

I have tried hard to discover mistakes in your notes and have come up with three little ones:

P. 336: family *Nymphalidae*, not "genus"
P. 380: bits of nudity, rather than "the nude"
P. 426: it is Dr. Larivière who sheds that tear and who is supposed
        to represent the author's father, Dr. Flaubert

We both send you our warmest greetings and look forward to seeing you and Nina in the early fall.

Vladimir Nabokov

TO: **PROF. GLEB STRUVE**

TLS, 1 p. Hoover Institution
Montreux Switzerland

June 14, 1970

Dear Gleb Petrovich,

I have no Russian reference books at hand but, in so far as I remember and know, the word *podachka*—even though vulgarized by
popular usage—is the only correct translation of the basic sense of
*curée*.[1] Alas, it does not extend to the metaphoric "quarry." Incidentally, I would be curious to know how, in his vulgar and illiterate
*Hamlet*, Pasternak translates the phrase "this quarry cries on havoc."
I like very much the Polish *otprava*![2] Is there any linguistic connection
between *curée* and *shkura*?[3]

Cordially yours,
V. Nabokov

PS: Your piece on Berberova is quite fair. By the way, in my article
about the *Festschrift*, I refute the precision of her feminine memory
(as, for ex., in the case of the idiotic anecdote about my "Rachmaninov" dinner jacket).[4]

VN[5]

1. Quarry, prey, booty, or spoils.
2. Noun with several meanings, including "rebuff," "compensation," "dispatch," and
   "offal," one of which, by extension, presumably corresponds to the sense of the Russian
   "podachka" that VN had in mind. DN.
3. The noun "hide."
4. *Anniversary Notes*. Sergey Rachmaninov had given VN an obsolete cutaway in 1940 to
   wear at his first summer-school lecture at Stanford University; VN returned it. At
   roughly the same time Rachmaninov also gave Dmitri Nabokov his first radio, a streamlined Philco portable; that present was lovingly used for many years. DN.
5. Translated from Russian by Véra Nabokov and DN.

Montreux, Switzerland
Palace Hotel
June 18, 1970

Dear Andrew,

You may use the following note in any way you wish:

My father felt so infinitely superior to any accusation of antisemitism (its official brand, or the even more disgusting household variety) that out of a kind of self-confidence and contempt for showcase philosemitism he used to make it a point—and go out of his way to make it—of being as plainspoken about Jew and Gentile as were his Jewish colleagues (such as Joseph Hessen and Grigory Landau) or the Christian but impeccably unprejudiced Milyukov. In the case of Nakhamkes, a well-known figure of fun and an impudent boor, the stress of the passage is obviously not on his race but on his portmanteau name so aptly blending *kham* (blackguard) and *nakhal* (jackanapes). I wish to point out that my father's publicistic style is marked by a certain bluntness and banality which he deplored himself when marvelling with me at say Aleksandr Hertsen's epithetic felicities; but the rugged phrasing in what you call the "Jewish references" proceeds less from a hasty pen than from that familiarity with which some professional divine might permit himself to speak of a martyr's quirks.

Answering your biographical queries will take me not quite as long as writing another *Speak, Memory* but very nearly so.

I hope you have received by now the photograph together with your Bibliography and some additional material.

Cordial greetings to you both from both of us.

Vladimir Nabokov

TO: **BO GUNNARSSON**

TLS (XEROX), 1 p.
Montreux, Switzerland

August 19, 1970

Sir,

Mr. Nabokov asks me to convey to you the following message:

"I have never read anything by Mr. Gerhardie,[1] I never heard of him until Lady Snow once mentioned his name to me at a cocktail-party in the late fifties, and I cannot understand whom it may benefit to spread the utter nonsense of his having had any 'influence' on me."

Yours truly,
Jacqueline Callier
Secretary to Mr. Nabokov

1. William Gerhardie, British novelist born in St. Petersburg.

TO: **ROSA MONTAGUE**[1]

TL (XEROX), 1 p.
Montreux-Palace Hotel
Montreux, Switzerland
September 9, 1970

Dear Miss Montague,

I do not wish to appear choosy, but the new cover design won't do.[2] The banal pop-arty combination of a broken chessboard inserted between Siamese twins (identical except for the forlock on one brow) is meaningless and repulsive. I do not insist on cover designs illustrating a novel realistically, but I do object to a pseudo-realism unconnected with anything in the book. It is a great pity Panther does not wish to use the 1967 cover-design, but if so, let us have some purely ornamental pattern without eyes, noses, or hands.

Sincerely yours,
Vladimir Nabokov

I am returning the jacket design.

1. Of Weidenfeld & Nicolson, London.
2. Of a 1971 paperback edition of *The Defence*.

TO: **ELENA SIKORSKI**    ALS.[1] Elena Sikorski.

To My Sister Elena,

We are distinguished by wings of black hue,
wine-iridescence, and granules of blue
following yellowish, crenulate borders.
Copses of birch are our favorite quarters.

> V. Nabokov
> September, 1970
> Montreux[2]

1. On picture postcard of Nymphalis antiopa L.
2. Translated from Russian by DN.

TO: **MICHAEL WALTER**[1]    TL (XEROX), 1 p.

> Montreux-Palace Hotel
> Montreux, Switzerland
> November 23, 1970

Dear Mr. Walter,

Many thanks for your kind letter with Dr. Higgins's[2] remarks.

No, I was not alluding to the Balkans in connection with the Twinspot Fritillary's map, but to peninsular Italy (where I have found it common in oak scrub country on the border of Tuscany and Umbria).

I still think that in his drawings of Ringlets Mr. Hardgreaves' faithfulness is handicapped by his incomplete grasp of the subject. The pointed hindwing may occur in underdeveloped individuals of some Ringlets (e.g. in small specimens of *E. pluto*) but it is neither a diagnostic nor natural feature of that round-winged genus and looks rather absurd when shown only on one side of the butterfly (p. 37, 7d; pl. 41, 2b and 3a).

As for the Norfolk Swallowtail what I had in view was precisely its resemblance to the first generation of certain Mediterranean races of the species (as noted long ago by Verity) and its striking difference from the typical single-brooded Swedish race.

I shall be grateful to you for transmitting these little clarifications to Dr. Higgins. I also wish to thank you for promising to send me a copy of the revised edition, though let me repeat that even without any revisions, it remains a marvellous and delightful book.

Sincerely yours,
Vladimir Nabokov

P.S. On p. 84 'Le Grand' should be 'La Grande', and on p. 85 the date after 'Esper' is misprinted.

1. Of Collins, London.
2. "Rebel Blue, Byrony White," VN's review (*Times Educational Supplement*, 23 October 1970) of *A Field Guide to the Butterflies of Britain and Europe*, ed. L. G. Higgins.

TO: **JOHN C. BRODERICK**[1]     TL (XEROX), I p.

Montreux-Palace Hotel
Montreux, Switzerland
December 14, 1970

Dear Mr. Broderick,

I am most grateful to you for sending the material which arrived safely, and for your good letter of November 25.

I appreciate your kind offer not to charge to me the xeroxing and mailing expenses. However, I would prefer you to bill me, and this for the following reason:

Much of the material you have does not exist in any other copy, some of it has never been in print, and parts of *that* I now plan to publish gradually. At the present time, for instance, I am thinking of assembling a collection of articles. I also need some letters and notes for the writing of my second volume of memoirs (SPEAK ON, MEMORY). Therefore I would like to beg you to send me at my expense, little by little, and in such installments as suits you best, xerox copies of my non-fiction material, namely everything except the manuscripts, notes and typescripts of all my published novels (Russian and English) and published translations (EUGENE ONEGIN, A HERO OF OUR TIME and THE SONG OF PRINCE IGOR'S CAMPAIGN). Also I do not need any of the following: short stories; transcripts of verse in my mother's hand (in thick batches of long sheets); my own mss (and typescripts) of my poems; material related to my screenplay LOLITA and to SPEAK, MEMORY ("Conclusive Evidence"); unpublished or published translations of my novels or stories.

I would, however, want the dramatic works including the tragedy in verse *The Tragedy of Mr. Morn*, all my correspondence, all articles (published or unpublished) and other non-fiction material.

I have been giving quite a bit of thought to the disposal of my remaining papers. Friends have pointed out to me that I might be disinheriting my son by not leaving to him such papers as the complete ms of my huge ADA which, I am told, may be worth a fortune some day. I shall probably put aside a few items that I shall bequeath to him, but I must wait for a convenient pause in my literary labors to sort things out. In the meantime please tell me more about the new law you mention and what and how exactly would it benefit my estate if I "deposited at" rather than "gave to" the Library more of my papers.

Best wishes.

Sincerely yours,
Vladimir Nabokov

1. Acting Chief, Manuscript Division, The Library of Congress.


TO: ARYE LEVAVI[1]                    TL (XEROX), 1 p.

Montreux-Palace Hotel
Montreux
December 31, 1970

Dear Sir,

I wish to thank you and your Government very warmly for inviting my wife and me to visit Israel. We shall be delighted to do so. Would April 1972 be an acceptable time? The reason we must wait till 1972 is that we have to go this spring on a business trip to New York for the opening of a musical made of one of my novels.

I would be happy to give one or two readings of my works, I would enjoy visiting museums, libraries and universities, and I would like to take advantage of this wonderful occasion to do some butterfly hunting.

I would be very pleased to discuss matters at your convenience, particularly if you and Mrs. Levavi happened to be again in Montreux.

Sincerely yours,
Vladimir Nabokov

1. Israeli Ambassador to Switzerland.

TO: *TIME*                                    PRINTED LETTER[1]

Sir: I find highly objectionable the title of your piece "Profit Without
Honor," [Dec. 21] on the musical adaptation of *Lolita*, as well as your
sermonet on scruples that I once happened to voice concerning its
filming. When cast in the title role of Kubrick's neither very sinful
nor very immoral picture, Miss Lyon was a well-chaperoned young
lady, and I suspect that her Broadway successor will be as old as she
was at the time. Fourteen is not twelve, 1970 is not 1958, and the
sum of $150,000 is not correct.

Vladimir Nabokov
Montreux, Switzerland

1. Published in the 18 January 1971 issue.

TO: **SAMUEL ROSOFF**[1]                      ALS (XEROX), I p.

Montreux
28 January 1971

Dear Mulya,[2]

Thanks for your nice, slightly melancholy letter and for the copy
of my thirty-four-year-old missive to you. Rereading it, I noticed that
two or three details had already vacated the cells of memory where
they had been aging, but, on the other hand, remembered with a
fresh, unexpected sensation the last name of our pleasant, curly
schoolmate, who had remained nameless in my 1937 letter: Fridman!
Thus work our strange, wondrous internal beehives.

I was saddened to hear of your wife's illness. Also by the news that you do not plan to come to Europe again. I have, however, gotten an official invitation to visit Israel from your ambassador, who called on us, so perhaps next year or so we shall see both you as a venerable old man, and your country's spring butterflies. Last year we did our hunting in Sicily.

Things are unchanged here since our Zermatt meeting nine years ago. Mityusha is singing in America. I am writing a new book. A collection of my poems (Russian and English) and chess problems is being published[3]—I'll send it. I have transmitted a copy of the letter you sent to the diligent and indefatigable Field.

> I embrace you and Véra sends greetings.
> Vladimir Nabokov[4]

1. Samuel Rosoff and VN had attended the Tenishev School in St. Petersburg together, and were good friends in boyhood. Rosoff eventually settled in Haifa. Even though circumstances made meetings rare later in their lives, and Rosoff was able to visit the Nabokovs only once in Switzerland, their warm reciprocal affection never diminished. DN.
2. Diminutive of the Russian form of "Samuel."
3. *Poems and Problems* (New York: McGraw-Hill, 1971).
4. Translated from Russian by DN.

TO: **ARTHUR CROOK**[1]                                   TL (XEROX), 1 p.

Montreux-Palace Hotel
Montreux, Switzerland
February 1, 1971

Dear Mr. Crook,

I thank you for your letter of January 21.

A deluge of work prevents me from undertaking to write the article about comparative immortality which you ask me for. Moreover I would not care to refer to living authors and even less, to list only my own books. Finally, when I think that such utter trash as

Galsworthy's is being enthusiastically resurrected, the entire matter loses even the faint flush of illusion it might have had.

Yours faithfully,
Vladimir Nabokov

1. Editor, *Times Literary Supplement*.


TO: **PROF. JOHN KENNETH SIMON**[1]                    TL (XEROX), 1 P.

Montreux-Palace Hotel
Montreux, Switzerland
February 15, 1971

Dear Mr. Simon,

Many thanks for your reprint from *Modern Language Notes*, Vol. 83, No. 4, May, 1968, with the interesting item at the foot of page 546.

I do not remember having ever read anything by Valéry Larbaud—even in my youth when I absorbed a lot of contemporaneous French stuff. The possibility of the lines you quote having somehow stuck in my brain since the late Twenties is, of course, out of the question: from my Pushkin studies I know that the most spectacular parallel readings do not always meet at the points where we find them; but Larbaud's list of Dolores diminutives ("Des prénoms féminins," *Oeuvres complètes*, 1950, pp. 189–201) certainly does resemble rather eerily the very rhythm of the passage (written in 1949) in the beginning of my *Lolita*.[2] But who, *au fond*, is your "aficionado"? Humbert? My reader?

Sincerely yours,
Vladimir Nabokov

1. University of Illinois.
2. ". . . Lolita est une petite fille; Lola est en âge de se marier; Dolores a trente ans; Doña Dolores a soixante ans."

TO: **ARYE LEVAVI**                     TL (XEROX), 1 p.

1820 Montreux, Palace Hotel
February 28, 1971

Dear Mr. Levavi,

I find it embarrassing to write this letter, especially after all the kindness and attention you showed me. I can only explain the making, remaking, and unmaking of my mind in relation to your Government's invitation by the highly complicated life I am leading. Such matters as the redeepening shadow of a business trip to America, where the LOLITA musical is undergoing awful difficulties, or the nightmare prospect of having to check the French translation of my huge ADA right at the time when I would have liked to be in your country, and various other worries, may prevent me from visiting Israel this year. I believe that my first reaction to your invitation was the correct one. This is a muddled year for me, and it is wiser that I apologize now than cancel our visit at the very last moment.

We certainly hope to come to Israel, unofficially, before I am too decrepit to chase butterflies!

Cordially yours,
Vladimir Nabokov

TO: **MICHAEL WALTER**                  TL (XEROX), 1 p.

Montreux-Palace Hotel
Montreux, Switzerland
April 14, 1971

Dear Mr. Walter,

I thank you for Barcant's *Butterflies of Trinidad and Tobago*[1] which I found here on my return from a trip to S. Portugal.

The photographs are good and, generally speaking, the book should be of considerable help to the butterfly hunter in those parts. Too much stress, however, is laid on "habitat" and "rarity" (and even "semi-rarity") of numerous strays, or chance colonies founded by strays of species that come from the mainland where those species are common. In itself Barcant's work is very amateurish, the style is trivial and redundant, and the higgledy-piggledy arrangement of the material, in the text and on the plates, is an absolute nightmare. Among obvious blunders I note : on p. 210, *P barcanti* should be *P. barcanti* Tite, not "*P barcanti* sp. nov.", and on p. 229, N. maravalica should be *N.* maravalica Seitz, not "*N. maravalica* sp. nov."

I continue to be distressed by the illiterate vogue of omitting the names of genus-describers—and this not because my own name is omitted (in the case of *Echinargus* Nabokov to which I assigned *huntingtoni*, p. 84, which I was the first to dissect and figure) but because no taxonomic term is clear and correct unless its author's name is affixed to it. One wonders what the beginner will make of the last paragraph on p. 21, implying, as it does, that Linnaeus is the author not only of the species *iphicla* but also of the genus *Adelpha*, which is wrong.

Anyway I read the book with interest and remain gratefully yours.

Vladimir Nabokov

1. By Malcolm Barcant (London: Collins, 1971).

TO: **A. C. SPECTORSKY**                                    TL (XEROX), 1 p.

Montreux-Palace Hotel
Montreux, Switzerland
April 14, 1971

Dear Mr. Spectorsky,

I am inflicting upon you some more of my stuff which I have asked Bill Maxwell to forward to you.

Though rotund and self-containing, *Solus Rex*, first published in Russian in spring 1940, in the last issue (LXX) of the émigré review *Sovremennĩya Zapiski*, Paris, is, or rather was, a chapter in a novel I never finished. The present translation, made in February 1971 by my son with my collaboration, is scrupulously faithful to the original text, including the restoration of a somewhat gamey scene that had been marked in the *Sovr. Zap.* by suspension points (and has put off a later, non-Russian, magazine). Send it back to me if you find it unsuitable, without one quaver of hesitation.[1]

Axelrod's story in your March issue is superb—up to the silly, and careless, final pages.[2]

Cordially yours,
Vladimir Nabokov

1. Deemed by *Playboy* to be beyond the capacities of its readers. Collected in *A Russian Beauty*.
2. George Axelrod, "Where Am I Now When I Need Me?"

TO: **PROF. GLEB STRUVE**    TL, 1 p. Hoover Institution.
Montreux, Switzerland

April 15, 1971

Dear Gleb Petrovich,

I read with great interest your information about my *Eugene Onegin* in Soviet Russia,[1] and shall be very grateful to you for photocopies unless it is too much trouble. I hope the translation, once again reworked (and by now ideally interlinear and unreadable),[2] will come out before the end of this year. I also hope the Soviet commentators will not scoop my new conjecture that the word *zhuchka*[3] was born below stairs of *Zhuzhu* and *Bizhu*,[4] i.e., the names of the masters' lapdogs. As to the "Queen of Spades," in the early fifties my wife obtained from Germany a microfilm copy of Lamotte's tale[5] and identified some amusing coincidences (as well as enormous discrepancies, of course) between it and Pushkin's short story.

You have either received, or will receive before the end of the month, my *Poems and Problems*, and, upon publication in the fall, my *Glory*, alias *The Exploit*, in a superb translation by Dmitri.

Oh yes, in regard to your excellent article about A. Turgenev,[6] I take the liberty of offering a tiny criticism: the nickname "Aeolian Harp" referred not to a burp but to a borborygmus in the Turgenev bowels.

I hope you are feeling better, and wish you a pleasant trip to Toronto.

Greetings to you and to your wife from me and from V.E.

I shake your hand.

Yours,
V. Nabokov[7]

1. News of the project reached Soviet scholars before publication, and the translation began to circulate in Russia long before glasnost'. DN.
2. A jocular reference to VN's explicit intention to make his translation an uncompromisingly literal "crib." DN.
3. "Small dog."
4. Joujou and Bijou.
5. Baron Friedrich La Motte Fouqué (1777–1843), author of *Undine* and of a *Pique-Dame*, which, according to VN, might well have been "known to Pushkin (in a French or Russian version) when he wrote his 'Queen of Spades.'" See VN's *Commentary* on his translation of *Eugene Onegin* (New York: Bollingen, 1964), Vol. 3, p. 97. DN.
6. "Alexander Turgenev, Ambassador of Russian Culture in *Partibus Infidelium*," *Slavic Review*, 29 (1970), 444–459.
7. Translated from Russian by Véra Nabokov and DN.

TO: **MICHAEL WALTER**                    TL (XEROX), 1 p.

Montreux-Palace Hotel
Montreux, Switzerland
April 16, 1971

Dear Mr. Walter,

Your very charming note of March 25, with a copy of Dr. Higgins' response to my correction, reached me only to-day in a batch of correspondence that had gone to look for me in Algarve and has now wandered back to Montreux.

Entomologists are the most gentle people on earth—until a taxonomic problem crops up : it then transforms them into tigers. In the present case I can only repeat that the type locality of the butterfly described as *aurelia* by Nickerl in 1850 is "Böhmen". The fact that the type locality of the same butterfly under another, much earlier but invalid name (*parthenie* Borkhausen 1788) is Erlangen, a hundred kilometers W. from the Bohemian border seems to me irrelevant. It is not a question of library but of logic. A "first reviser" may and should assign a definite locality to a species that has been given none, or only a very vague general region, in the original description; but "Böhmen" is definite enough, and if the reviser wants to pin down the locus, he stakes off his moor or mountainside in W. Czechoslovakia and not in Bavaria.

I feel that all this exciting lepidopterological correspondence passing through your kind hands will finally infect you with the aurelian madness! The best stuff for a butterfly net is marquisette.

Yours sincerely,
Vladimir Nabokov

TO: BUD MACLENNAN · · · · · · · · · · · · · · · · · · · · · · · · · · · TL (XEROX), 1 p.

Montreux, April 27, 1971
Palace Hotel

Dear Miss MacLennan,

I received today five copies of the Penguin Books Great Britain edition of ADA. Upon examining them I discovered that in only one the miserable misprint on page 257 (the "she was pregnant" of the Penguin Open Market edition) had been properly changed to the correct

he was pregnant.

In the four other copies the last line on p. 257 still remains the meaningless "she was pregnant" instead of the correct

he was pregnant.

You will remember that Penguin Books undertook to eliminate

this printer's blunder. I am greatly distressed by its still being there and am returning the four defective copies. Could you please insist that Penguin fulfill their obligation and destroy these and all other existing domestic edition copies which still harbor on p. 257 the wretched "she was pregnant" instead of the correct

he was pregnant.

Sincerely yours,
Vladimir Nabokov

TO: **PROF. RICHARD PIPES**[1]                    TL (XEROX), 1 p.

Montreux, Palace Hotel
May 11, 1971

Dear Professor Pipes,

Your splendid Introduction to my father's "The Provisional Government"[2] touched me greatly. I wish to tell you how infinitely gratifying it is to me to find in it this particular approach to Russian history at the revolutionary period. Few, indeed, are the foreign scholars who understand so penetratingly the terrible betrayal of the cause of liberty in the deepest sense of the word engendered on principle by the *earliest* Bolshevists.

I am really most happy to have your wise and sympathetic Introduction head the English translation of my father's memoir.

Yours very cordially,
Vladimir Nabokov

1. Department of History, Harvard University.
2. St. Lucia, Australia: University of Queensland Press, 1971.

Mr Nabokov

~~Listen Vladimir,~~ here's some of the things I'd like to know:

1 What are the first stories you remember in Russian? *English fairy tales* ( see Speak, memory)

2 Have they been translated into English? *Russian Tales of Puskin and English folk versions from other languages*

3 What was your earliest reading in English? *English, French and Russian ~~books~~ : mostly novels and poetry*

4 What were you reading during adolesence? *or snake folk anecdotes.*

5 What were you reading at Cambridge? *Russian and French*

6 Who is your favorite among the Russian novelists? *Dear Leo; dear Anton*

7 What is the best translation of him into English? *None of the translations of their works that I*

8 Who do you like among the French? *have seen were adequate* *etc*

9 Among the British? *Flaubert, Proust*

10 The Americans? *H.G. Wells, ~~Joyce~~*

11 How about Evelyn Waugh? *Melville. I do not discuss my contemporaries* ./.

12 Your favorite poets? *Pushkin, Blok; Shakespeare, Coleridge, Keats, a few things by Yeats; Hugo, Rimbaud*

13 Works of philosophy? }
14 Or history?        } ./.
15 Solzenhitsyn?          ./.

16 Any other post-Revolutionary Russians? *Anything I might say about them would only get them into trouble*

Nabokov's replies on a list of questions submitted by Alden Whitman in 1971.

TO: **DENNIS DONAGUE**[1]    CC, 1 p.

Montreux, Palace Hotel
May 11, 1971

Dear Mr. Donague,

I would like you to know what satisfaction and delight your English edition of my father's *The Provisional Government* gave me. Besides obvious filial feelings I also experienced deep gratification at seeing historical truth so authoritatively presented at a time when totalitarian politics are allowed to invade a great part of the globe. The worth of the publication is enhanced by its being brought out by the press of a great university.

Sincerely yours,
Vladimir Nabokov

1. Manager, University of Queensland Press.

TO: **ANDREW FIELD**    TL (XEROX), 1 p.

Montreux, Palace Hotel
11-V-71

I was acutely aware, dear Andrew, upon re-reading the Sologub[1] poems you kindly sent me how much I always admired parts of that Curate's Egg. A number of lines in the *Palach* are indeed first-rate— little musical storms blowing through this or that strophe; but there are also unacceptable *neuklyuzhesti* in many lines, and a quite hideous error of pronunciation in line 29: "scaffold" is *pomóst*, not the impossibly provincial—or simply wrong—*pómost*. It is really remarkable how many poets of our day, including Blok, Annenski, Mandelshtam, Hodasevich, Gumilyov, Shishkov, Bunin, and of course Pasternak, allowed vulgarisms and downright blunders to disfigure their best verse. One day I'll list and discuss examples.

I am leaving tomorrow for the south of France so that your suggestion about Struve cannot possibly be followed up at this moment.

I have just written Pipes and Donague.

Your appalling Kuz'min[2] has been mailed to you today by registered mail.

Cordially yours,
Vladimir Nabokov

1. Fyodor Sologub, pseudonym of Fyodor Teternikov (1863–1927), Russian poet and novelist.
2. Mikhail Kuz'min (1872–1936), Russian poet.

TO: **DMITRI NABOKOV**  HOLOGRAPH PS TO VÉRA NABOKOV LETTER
Tourtour, Var, France

31 May 1971

I, too, embrace my dear and also unique one. I walk a great deal here and write a great deal. The afternoons are always gloomy. Five stories have already been placed in magazines but the royalties will not go for boats of any kind![1] The Tourtour food is very rich.

I send you a kiss
P[2]

1. DN had expressed the intention of using his share of the income from publication of five VN stories he had translated for the acquisition of the first of what was to be a series of racing motorboats. Notwithstanding his (unheeded) warnings, VN followed DN's automobile and boat racing with keen interest, and reproached DN in 1975 for having lost an offshore powerboat race in southern Italy because of a fuel miscalculation. DN.
2. Translated from Russian by DN.

TO: **GEORGE WEIDENFELD**                    TL (XEROX), 1 p.

Montreux-Palace Hotel
Montreux, Switzerland
June 30, 1971

Dear George,

I was sorry to have been absent when you telephoned. There is something important I have been nursing. Here it is: I am not very happy, as you may have guessed, about the sales of my books in England. And the more I think of it the more convinced I become that this is in a large measure due to a lack of publicity. ADA, for instance, was practically hushed down by your advertising department. MARY, which sold sweetly in the US and is now a bestseller in Italy, was never given a fair start in England. I have asked McG-H. to show you the corrected proof of GLORY, but I must insist that it be given some glorious advertising. I want you to give some thought to this. Whether you include a publicity budget in the contract or simply list in a letter what you undertake to do for GLORY is not essential but I must know exactly where I stand. I am royally indifferent to nincompoop reviews in the British papers but am commercially sensitive to publicity supplied by my publishers.

Yours ever,
Vladimir Nabokov

TO: *TIME*                    PRINTED LETTER[1]

Sir: People writing about words should never use dictionaries that "come to hand" ("an old Webster's," or the practically useless Random House compilation), as does Mr. John Skow [June 14] in checking my "caprifole" (not "caprifoli," as absurdly quoted). Oldish (1957) unabridged Webster *does* list "caprifole" and this happens to be the only *exact* translation of Russian *zhimolost'* (the *Lonicera* of science), since the usual term honeysuckle is also applied to a number of sweet-smelling plants belonging to other genera (*Banksia, Azalea*, etc.).[2]

Vladimir Nabokov
Montreux, Switzerland

1. Published in the 5 July 1971 issue.
2. Skow's *Time* review of *Poems and Problems* challenged VN's use of "caprifole."

TO: **PROF. LAUREN G. LEIGHTON**                    TL (XEROX), 1 p.

Montreux, July 12, 1971

Dear Mr. Leighton,

My husband asks me to convey to you his warmest thanks for your letter of 17th June, with the fascinating information and enclosures, and his particular gratitude for the transparencies[1] and all the trouble you took.

He read with the greatest attention and interest your letter, and also the essay with the many quotations from a well identifiable un-named author. Once again, he is full of admiration for the essay's daring authors but worries about their security. He would be happy if you could let them know his sympathy and appreciation, provided you had an opportunity to do so without any risks for you or for them.

With cordial greetings from VN and me.

(Mrs. Vladimir Nabokov)

1. Photographs of the Nabokov home, 47 Morskaya Street, St. Petersburg.

TO: **BARBARA EPSTEIN**                                   TL (XEROX), 1 p.
                                                          Switzerland

August 29th, 1971

Dear Barbara,

Your constant kindness in regard to my little grievances in the past encourages me to ask you to publish the short review which I enclose.[1]

A Mr. Rowe, Assistant Professor of Russian at New York University, who recently visited us at Montreux (and seemed to be a responsible and civilized person) has now exuded a book about me: I have nothing much to say about its first two parts, but its third part and appendix suggest that in the course of writing his book he lost his mind.

If you agree to print my review, perhaps you could let me know by cable. And I would also like then to see the proof which I would keep only for a few minutes before cabling you my corrections or my OK. Ann Murphy of McGraw, who just called me up from New York about another matter, had not seen the book and the review, but thought immediately that The New York Review would be the proper place to send my piece.

I hope all is well with you. Véra joins me in sending you and Jason our love. We shall return to the Montreux Palace from this mountain retreat on August 31.

Yours ever,
Vladimir Nabokov

1. "Rowe's Symbols," *New York Review of Books* (7 October 1971). Review of William Woodin Rowe's *Nabokov's Deceptive World* (New York: New York University Press, 1971).

TO: **JOHN LEONARD**[1]                    TL (XEROX), I p.

> Montreux-Palace Hotel
> Montreux, Switzerland
> Septembre 29, 1971

Dear Mr. Leonard,

I wrote to you on September 13 enclosing a kind of Letter to the Editor which concerned my reaction to Edmund Wilson's *Upstate*. In that piece I was not airing a grievance but firmly stopping a flow of vulgar and fatuous invention on Wilson's part. I still do not know whether or not you agree to print my protest.[2]

Meanwhile, less than two days after airmailing my letter, I received from you in result of some telepathic process a long and amiable telegram dealing with three other matters. I am very grateful to you for promising to keep misprintless my chat with Israel Shenker[3] (who incidentally sent me a few days ago several absolutely first-rate pictures he took of me here). Thanks, too, for suggesting I write about J.D. Salinger : I do admire him very much but am struggling in a whirlpool of work which does not allow me to produce either that article or the third thing you mention—observations on the new OED edition.

Please do let me know at your earliest convenience your reaction to my protest. I would very much want to have your review publish it but if that is impossible then do return the stuff at your earliest convenience so that I might send it elsewhere.

> Cordially yours,
> Vladimir Nabokov

1. Editor, *New York Times Book Review*.
2. See following letter.
3. "The Old Magician at Home," *New York Times Book Review* (9 January 1972).

To the Editor:

I seek the shelter of your columns to help me establish the truth in the following case:

A kind correspondent Xeroxed and mailed me pages 154–162 referring to my person as imagined by Edmund Wilson in his recent work "Upstate." Since a number of statements therein wobble on the brink of libel, I must clear up some matters that might mislead trustful readers.

First of all, the "miseries, horrors and handicaps" that he assumes I was subjected to during 40 years, before we first met in New York are mostly figments of his warped fancy. He has no direct knowledge of my past. He has not even bothered to read my "Speak, Memory," the records and recollections of a happy expatriation that began practically on the day of my birth. The method he favors is gleaning from my fiction what he supposes to be actual, "real-life," impressions and then popping them back into my novels and considering my characters in that inept light—rather like the Shakespearean scholar who deduced Shakespeare's mother from the plays and then discovered allusions to her in the very passages he had twisted to manufacture the lady. What surprises me, however, is not so much Wilson's aplomb as the fact that in the diary he kept while he was my guest in Ithaca he pictures himself as nursing feelings and ideas so vindictive and fatuous that, if expressed, should have made me demand immediate departure.

A few of the ineptitudes I notice in these pages of "Upstate" are worth considering here. His conviction that my insistence on basic similarities between Russian and English verse is "a part of [my] inheritance of [my] father . . ., champion of a constitutional monarchy for Russia after the British model" is too silly to refute; and his muddleheaded and ill-informed description of Russian prosody only proves that he remains organically incapable of reading, let alone understanding, my work on the subject. Equally inconsistent with facts—and typical of his Philistine imagination—is his impression that at parties in our Ithaca house my wife "concentrated" on me and grudged "special attention to anyone else."

A particularly repulsive blend of vulgarity and naiveté is reflected in his notion that I must have suffered "a good deal of humiliation," because as the son of a liberal noble I was not "accepted [!] by strictly illiberal nobility"—where? when, good God?—and by whom exactly, by my uncles and aunts? Or by the great grim boyars haunting a plebian's fancy?

I am aware that my former friend is in poor health but in the struggle between the dictates of compassion and those of personal honor the latter wins. Indeed, the publication of those "old diaries" (doctored, I hope, to fit the present requirements of what was then the future), in which living persons are but the performing poodles of the diarist's act, should be subject to a rule or law that would require some kind of formal consent from the victims of conjecture, ignorance and invention.

Vladimir Nabokov
Montreux, Switzerland

1. Published in *New York Times Book Review* (7 November 1971) with a reply by Wilson.

TO: **MRS. PETER SEMLER**[1]                          TL (XEROX), 1 p.

Montreux-Palace Hotel
Montreux, Switzerland
October 1, 1971

Dear Mrs. Semler,

My husband asks me to say to you that he appreciated your good letter of September 26 very much. He regrets that it is not possible for him to make room for yet another interview in his already over-crowded schedule.

Incidentally, he very much regrets that "America" has such a neu-

tral a-political character. What is needed, he thinks, is vigorous political propaganda.

Sincerely yours,
(Mrs. Vladimir Nabokov)

1. Of *America*, a magazine "Published by Jesuits of the United States and Canada."

TO: **OLIVER CALDECOTT**[1]                                        cc, 1 p.

1820 Montreux, Palace Hotel
October 18, 1971

Dear Mr. Caldecott,

My husband asks me to write to you about your new editions of
PNIN and NABOKOV'S DOZEN. His first request is that I thank
you on his behalf for sending him three copies of each of the books
and tell you how much he liked their appearance.

I wish I could stop here. But he also asks me to call your attention
to the absence in PNIN of all mention of copyright. As you know,
this is a very serious matter in the United States. Such omission can
result in loss of copyright. This omission is the more surprising as
the copyright matter is properly taken care of in the other book
(NABOKOV'S DOZEN). I hope you can see your way to remedy
the situation without delay. If not the entire printing has already been
manufactured please have the copyright notice inserted where it belongs. Moreover, please try to have a slip with the copyright notice
tipped in in all the copies you still have on hand. It should read
"Copyright © 1953, 1955, 1957 by Vladimir Nabokov. All rights reserved."

Another matter that my husband finds extremely annoying. Who
and why has written in the blurb to PNIN (back cover) ". . . such
Nabokovian enemies as McCarthyism"? In point of fact VN has

495

never criticized or attacked McCarthy for the simple reason that he found anti-McCarthyists much more repulsive than McCarthy himself. Since, moreover, it does not reflect any statement occuring in PNIN, this sentence on the jacket, says VN, is absurd and must be removed.

When both above-mentioned matters have been taken care of please send us a sample copy. May we please hear from you by return mail?

Yours truly,
(Mrs. Vladimir Nabokov)

1. Of Penguin Books, London.

TO: **BENJAMIN P. LAMBERTON**[1]                    TL (XEROX), 1 p.

1820 Montreux, Switzerland
November 5, 1971

Dear Mr. Lamberton,

I don't know if I would have ever got around to acknowledge your kind and interesting letter in ordinary circumstances. However, my husband is so angry and disgusted with the Levy article in the N.Y. Times Magazine[2] that he asks me to make it quite clear to anyone who might ask that, among many other things, the bits about his sister, our life in Montreux, are false and vulgar.

Although he does not consider Solzhenitsyn a great writer, he would never have "cackled" over the misfortunes of that heroic man, as Mr. Levy insinuates. VN will probably take up the matter in a Letter to the Editor.[3]

Yours truly,
(Mrs. Vladimir Nabokov)

1. An attorney in Washington, D.C.
2. Alan Levy, "Understanding Nabokov—A Red Autumn Leaf Is a Red Autumn Leaf, Not a Deflowered Nymphet" (31 October 1971).
3. VN did not respond.

TO: **G. H. BELL**[1]               TL (XEROX), I p.

Montreux, Switzerland

January 24, 1972

Dear Sir,

My husband asks me to acknowledge your letter of January 17.

He does not believe that America, or the world, would have been better off if Germany had won the war. The great mistake was made in the peace-making period when so much power was allowed the Communists, when the Allies surrendered half of Europe to Russian control. Bad though things look to-day my husband is convinced that a Nazi control of the world would have been worse, and not only because of Hitler's mad-dog policy toward the Jews.

He asks you not to use his statements out of context which would produce a wrong impression.

Yours truly,
(Mrs. Vladimir Nabokov)

1. Bell was writing a book on Hitler.

TO: **STEWART H. SMITH**[1]          TL (XEROX), I p.

Montreux-Palace Hotel
1820 Montreux, Switzerland
February 25, 1972

Dear Mr. Smith,

*The Real Life of Sebastian Kinght* was written during the winter 1938–1939, in a little flat we rented in Paris in a street curiously named Rue de Saïgon, connecting the Avenue du Bois (alias Foch) with the Avenue de la Grande Armée.

The Russ. novel, which was to be titled *Ultima Thule*, was begun in 1939 and interrupted in May 1940, when we left for the United States. The two chapters—Solus Rex and Ultima Thule—is all that has been preserved by my husband who destroyed the rest of the material. *Ultima Thule* will soon appear in The New Yorker in an English translation. Both pieces will be included in the collection of short stories to be published by McGraw-Hill in the coming fall.[2]

The publication dates of the original Russian versions were 1942 (*Noviy Zhurnal*, I, New York) for *Ultima Thule* (Ch. One of the unfinished novel), and early 1940 (*Sovremennïya Zapiski*, LXX, Paris) for *Solus Rex* (Ch. Two).

It was very thoughtful of you not to bother my husband with idle queries. He quite appreciates that the ones you are asking are important.

Greetings from both of us.

(Mrs. Vladimir Nabokov)

1. Smith, a Ph.D. candidate at Columbia University, was writing his dissertation on VN.
2. *A Russian Beauty and Other Stories* (1973).

TO: **KATE RAND LLOYD**[1]          TL (XEROX), 1 p.

Montreux-Palace Hotel
1830 Montreux, Switzerland
April 13, 1972

Dear Miss Lloyd,

I thank you for sending me a copy of the April 15 issue of *Vogue* which arrived to-day, on the eve of our departure for the South of France.

Simona Morini's questions are admirable and my replies to them are reproduced with a rare fidelity—to which I am not accustomed in most published interviews.[2] The pictures, alas, are not as good as the text. The little one at the top corner of p. 78 is, I think, terrible, and the one of Mr. and Mrs. Nabokov relaxing in the "green salon" not only disfigures my wife and me but hypertrophies our lower limbs in a grotesque and incomprehensible manner. The façade of the hotel on p. 74 is, on the other hand, charming and somehow in elegant correspondence with my Givenchy tie on the opposite page!

With best regards,
Vladimir Nabokov

Dictated by Mr. Nabokov
but signed in his absence

1. Associate Editor, Features, *Vogue*.
2. Simona Morini, "Vladimir Nabokov Talks About his Travels" (15 April 1972); photographs by Oliviero Toscani.

TO: *NEW STATESMAN*                          PRINTED LETTER[1]
                                         Montreux, Switzerland

*Sir*, When the American edition of Edmund Wilson's *Upstate* appeared, I saw myself obliged to publish a detailed letter to the editor in *The New York Times Book Review* (7 November 1971) refuting the vulgar nonsense Mr. Wilson saw fit to spin around the bogus image of my person. Since your reviewer, Anthony Bailey (NS 7 April) has evidently not seen my letter (while casually quoting a portion of a particularly offensive passage in *Upstate*) may I point out for the benefit of English readers that the 'humiliation' ascribed to me therein is nothing but the product of conjecture, ignorance and invention on Mr. Wilson's part.

VLADIMIR NABOKOV

1. Published 5 May 1972.

TO: **WILLIAM D. FIELD**[1]                    TL (XEROX), 1 p.

Montreux-Palace Hotel
1820 Montreux, Switzerland
May 25, 1972

Dear Mr. Field,

Many thanks for your kind letter and the five splendid papers. I hasten to respond to your query about those Vienna examples of *V. atalanta*.

If it is only, or mainly, a reduction of the subapical white bar that gives those specimens an American look, and if the series is fairly short (say, three or four individuals), the narrowing of that bar might be regarded as a chance variation not uncommon in Europe (it is represented, for instance, in photographic figures of *V. atalanta* : South's Brit. Butts, pl. 47, female, and Verity's Farf. d'Italia, pl. 52, fig. 8, "*italica*"—which you have correctly sunk), for it is quite impossible to believe that such a wanderer as our Red Admirable could have evolved a stable race right in the center of its European dispersal (incidentally, all attempts to split it into several European races is doomed from the start, the Swedish type itself being but the summer offspring of May newcomers from the south). Anyway, I shall be collecting soon in a corner of Switzerland not too far from Austria and will try to take specimens of the thing here and there in chalet gardens.

I have been hunting butterflies in the Alps and the Mediterranean area every season since 1961 but everything is still papered and stored, and awaiting a favorable pause in my literary labors to get nicely set for study. I would certainly be delighted to give some of the rarer stuff to the National Museum and shall send a list for approval.[2]

I am looking forward to your Catalogue of New World Lycaenidae. It will, I trust, straighten out the unfortunate nomenclatorial confusion which has resulted from American lepidopterists' ignoring the change of two specific names in *Lycaeides* (Int. Comm. Zool. Nom, 1954). Since the time I wrote about that subgenus (see Bull. NCZ vol. 101, Feb. 1949) the name of the short-falx Holarctic species, which I and others used to call "*L. argyrognomon* (Bergstr.,

Tutt)", has been changed to "*L. idas* (L)", whilst the name "*L. argyrognomon* (Bergstr.)" has been shifted to the long-falx Palaearctic species, which I and others used to call "*L. ismenias* (Meigen)".

I have also arrived at the conclusion that my "*L. melissa samuelis*" should be treated as a distinct species—but that is another story.

Sincerely yours,
Vladimir Nabokov

1. Supervisor and Associate Curator, Division of Lepidoptera and Diptera, Department of Entomology, National Museum of Natural History, Smithsonian Institution.
2. After VN's death in 1977, his unspread and unmounted Montreux collection was given, in accordance with his wishes, to the Musée Cantonal de Zoologie, Place Riponne 6, Lausanne. More than half of it is now mounted; the remainder is still in preparation. DN.

TO: **PROF. CARL R. PROFFER**                    TL (XEROX), 2 pp.

Montreux-Palace Hotel
1820 Montreux, Switzerland
July 21, 1972

Dear Mr. Proffer,

I have been reading the *Russian Literature Triquarterly*[1] with great interest and attention, and here is a short list of some little adjustments that might be used in reprints of any of these articles :

p. 344: *About Buying a Horse* is a once famous book by Burnand, editor of *Punch*; and *The Author of Trixie* is by Caine (the lesser known Caine) and is about an archbishop (which would have provided Mr Olcott with yet another piece for his mythical chess set) who secretly writes a frivolous novel.

p. 361, p. 368 : Several points have been missed by the author of this excellent article. p. 361: Judging by their aspect and habitat the little butterflies on the sand could *only* belong to one species namely *Lycaeides samuelis* Nabokov (also known as *L. melissa samuelis* Nab.), a fact utterly beyond Pnin's and Château's ken. And p. 368: the double dream Pnin and Victor dream takes us to Zembla; and we actually meet Pnin again at the end of PALE FIRE (a much more secure Pnin).

p. 402: Zemski. The name existed long before 1861 (look up, for example, the *Zemskie sobory* of the sixteenth century). To a Russian ear it suggests rather an association with "Vyazemski" than with "an occasional sewer".

p. 405: Kurva is yet another dig at Lowell who understood Mandelshtam's phrase *Kurva Moskva* (Moscow the Whore) as "Moscow's curving avenues".

p. 407: *Mimo, chitatel' mimo* (meaning "let us not stop, reader, at those sordid details" *does* occur in Turgenev's peevish piece ("*Dovol'no,*" I think). And *hrip* is a hoarse wheeze, not a "snore" (which is *hrap*).

p. 418: "*Priehali, skazal Ivan*" comes straight from an *Onegin* variant (see my Commentary, vol. 2, p. 196, cancelled draft of One: LII:11)

p. 424: I was sorry that you—especially you—failed to recognize here the marvelously garbled echo of Okujava's moving melody: . . . "*Kogda trubach otboy sygraet* ("*Nadezhda, ya vernus' togda*").

I am listing these minor points merely in the spirit of critical assistance in which the erudite authors of all the delightful papers in RLT collaborated to enlighten and entertain the student.

Another matter—referring to an extraordinary and virtually unanswerable letter that I have just received from a noble but not overbright writer in Russia—keeps puzzling me so much that I think I shall permit myself to seek your advice by-and-by.

> Cordially yours,
> Vladimir Nabokov

1. 1972.

TO: **GORDON LISH**[1]                    TLS (XEROX), 1 p.

Palace Hotel
1820 Montreux
October 13, 1972

Dear Mr. Lish,

A kind correspondent has sent me an advertising supplement to The NY Times. Do I understand correctly that you are thinking of reprinting *The Potato Elf* in your 40th Anniversary Issue (Sep. 14, 1973)?

In preparing a collection of some of my Russian stories in English translation for McGraw-Hill I have had to retranslate entirely that Elf (first published in Russian in 1929).

The version by Serge Bertenson and Irene Kosinska in *Esquire*, Dec. 1939, is, alas, abominable, with innumerable errors, such as howlers, illiteracies, omissions, and so forth. It cannot be corrected, and must not be reprinted. My new translation, a very beautiful and faithful one, is scheduled to appear sometime next year in my publisher's collection of thirteen stories which is already in their hands. If you want the new, and lovely, Potato Elf, untouched by the Death's Head Moth of mistranslation, I would be delighted to have you prepublish it; but you should discuss the matter with McGraw-Hill. There is the question not only of dates but also of terms.[2]

Incidentally, I have not yet received the page proof (which I must absolutely see) of the xeroxed and galley bits of TRANSPARENT THINGS.[3]

I enjoyed immensely the last issue of *Esquire*. A humorous Russian friend of mine, upon being shown the cover, remarked that yes, many people nowadays contemplate their navel.[4]

Sincerely yours,
Vladimir Nabokov

1. *Esquire* editor.
2. *Esquire* (October 1973).
3. *Esquire* (December 1972).

4. The cover featured "The Impotence Boom" with the photograph of a man studying his lower torso.

TO: *NEW STATESMAN*                                    PRINTED LETTER[1]

*Sir*, I protest against the following passage in Mr. Roy Fuller's review of D. J. Enright's *Man is an Onion* (NS, 24 November 1972): 'Enright . . . is merciless about the pretentious and dishonest (see his pages on Nabokov).' I have seen them. Enright's treatment of my fiction conforms to a certain type of over-jocular criticism but contains nothing that might warrant an objection on ethical grounds. Mr. Fuller's statement, *per contra*, is a defamatory one, inasmuch as the term 'dishonest' can be construed as applying to me. Even supposing that your reviewer did not realise what he was saying, I believe, sir, that the NEW STATESMAN owes me an apology.

VLADIMIR NABOKOV

*Palace Hotel*
*Montreux*

1. Published 22 December 1972.

TO: EDMUND WHITE[1]                                    TL (XEROX), 1 p.

Montreux-Palace Hotel
1820 Montreux, Switzerland
January 11, 1973

Dear Mr. White,

Many thanks for this beautiful New Year gift![2] You have never set eyes upon me, and yet, by a flash of inspiration, you chose from the portfolio my best likeness for the cover of the SR The Arts, Jan. 1973! All the other pictures are good too but I hope you realize that the

504

one on p. 37 (Nabokov lives and works, *zhivyot i rabotaet*) mimicks marvelously a well-known formal of the author of "Aug. 14"[3] and that the picture on p. 43 (poncho plus a dream of infinity) is a no less amusing parody of the Argentine dreamer.[4] The NOM for MON is not your fault, but Snowdon's—I have a note from him apologizing for it.[5] My only regret is that my profile did not come out very clearly in the P. and G. picture nor am I sure the upper part of the gal really belongs to those alabaster nates and legs—but, anyway, it is a gallant attempt to picture one of my most ancient and best known successes.[6] As to the *Of Mandarins and Maoists, The Esthetics of Bliss, The N Factor, Upright Among Staring Fish, A Personal View of N*, and *Russian Transparencies*—I can only say that it is a rare treat for a writer to have, among fellow artists and scholars, such magnificent readers.[7] My own article has been reproduced with a precision that in itself is a soft-beaming joy not often granted by editors.

Wishing you and your four-leaf clover every sort of good luck I remain

yours cordially,<br>Vladimir Nabokov

P.S. Best regards and thanks to John Poppy for his letter of December 28 and the five copies of the issue. I shall be happy to be his co-explorer on another expedition of this kind.

1. Of *The Saturday Review of the Arts*.
2. The January 1973 issue, which included VN's essay "Inspiration," Lord Snowdon's photos of VN, and critical assessments.
3. Aleksandr Solzhenitsyn.
4. Jorge Luis Borges.
5. The negative was reversed for the photo of VN in front of the MONTREUX sign.
6. Reproduction of a painting of Pygmalion embracing his statue of Galatea.
7. Articles about VN by White, Joseph McElroy, William H. Gass, Joyce Carol Oates, and Simon Karlinsky.

TO: **KATHERINE FOX**[1]                                    TL (XEROX), 1 p.

Montreux-Palace Hotel
1820 Montreux, Switzerland
January 24, 1973

Dear Mrs. Fox,

I thank you for your letter of 19 January telling me that the Times would like to buy an extract from TRANSPARENT THINGS[2] starting at the beginning of page 3 and continuing to the end of page 19. I cannot agree, however, to the silent omission of the last sentence on p. 5 ("Let us now illustrate our difficulties") and to the dropping of Chapter Three (page 6 to 8). This Chapter Three is not only an integral part of the theme, but is the clue to the whole story. Its deletion would mean, among other things, that a reader who bought the book would skip the whole batch of 19 pages thinking that he had read them all in the Times, thus being cheated of an absolutely essential chapter.

On a similar occasion, in a different periodical, I suggested that not only suspension dots should mark the omission of a certain scene but that a note be appended saying that the suppressed passage would be sure to delight in due time the reader of the published book.

This is the only compromise I might accept.

Sincerely yours,
Vladimir Nabokov

1. Of Weidenfeld & Nicolson, London.
2. The excerpt was not published.

TO: MARVER H. BERNSTEIN[1]                    TL (XEROX), 1 p.

> Montreux-Palace Hotel
> 1820 Montreux, Switzerland
> January 26, 1973

Dear President Bernstein,

I was deeply touched by your letter of January 19 informing me that I was elected to receive an honorary degree from Brandeis University. I preserve and cherish the medal that the University awarded me in 1964.

It is embarrassing to have to decline your splendid offer. However, decline I must. Years ago I made the decision never to accept an honorary degree, i.e. a degree not earned by direct academic achievement at the university conferring it. All I have is my Cantab BA 1922, and that suffices. I know that many people, such as politicians, actors, foreign writers etc., do not apply this principle but I have been sticking to it for years and would be unable to renounce it now, even in the case of your offer, a particularly tempting one for me.

I entreat you to understand and excuse me.

> Very cordially,
> Vladimir Nabokov

1. President, Brandeis University.


TO: DAN LACY[1]                    TL (XEROX), 2 pp.

> Montreux-Palace Hotel
> 1820 Montreux, Switzerland
> January 31, 1973

Dear Mr. Lacy,

I thank you for your letter from The Caravanserai, of January 20. I hope you and Mrs. Lacy have thoroughly enjoyed your holiday.

To-day I can only try to answer the second part of your letter, pertaining to my literary plans.

The only two kinds of "butterfly books" that I could contemplate writing are: 1. a learned work with a minimum of text and a maximum of colored photographs on the 400 species (and about 1500 sub-species) of European butterflies; this, however, would take three or four years to complete (I had begun it for Weidenfeld but for various reasons the project was given up): this could hardly be a commercial success in the United States; and 2. a picture book, with notes, devoted to the evolution of butterfly painting from ancient times and through the Renaissance, to 1700, with reproductions of still-life pictures of flowers and insects by Dutch, Italian, Spanish, etc. masters. This is a fascinating, never-before attempted and not too complicated project (I have already collected more than a hundred samples) but it would mean your providing me with a photographer who could travel with me to several European picture galleries. I could probably finish the job within a couple of years.[2]

That takes care of the bugs.

A more definite plan is writing SPEAK, AMERICA a continuation of my "SPEAK, MEMORY".[3] I have already accumulated a number of notes, diaries, letters, etc., but in order to describe my American years adequately I should need money to revisit several spots in America such as New York, Boston, Ithaca, The Grand Canyon, and a few other Western localities. About fifteen months in all would be required for completing that book which is now much clearer in my mind than it had been before. I would be careful not to hurt people, so that there would be no need to wait for everybody to die safely.

Three other projects are: a third (and last) collection of thirteen short stories;[4] a revised translation of EUGENE ONEGIN, with only a few notes, in paperback for college students; a volume of my plays;[5] certain parts of my university lectures on European literature;[6] and, perhaps, an anthology of Russian poetry in my translation.

However, the principal and primary subject whose flushed cheek I am caressing to-day is a new novel,[7] of about 240 typewritten pages (i.e. at least twice as long as TRANSPARENT THINGS). I shall start the actual writing of this new novel on March 1, and, with no interruptions, could finish it by the summer of 1974. It will be as lucid in the long run as all my other novels. Incidentally, I greatly enjoyed your witty criticism of readers who do not find me limpid enough. Yes, let them keep up with me, by all means, and not vice versa!

Please, do send a copy of your suggestions to Iseman. Neither my wife nor I could arrive at a clear understanding of the intricacies in the various possibilities you suggest. We are very dumb. She joins me in sending our very cordial greetings to you and your wife.

Sincerely yours,
Vladimir Nabokov

1. Senior Vice President, McGraw-Hill.
2. No butterfly book was published. VN had written much of the book on European butterflies in the early 1960s, but for the butterflies-in-art project still had many galleries to visit before beginning to write. DN.
3. VN did not write this autobiographical work.
4. *Details of a Sunset* (New York: McGraw-Hill, 1976).
5. *The Man from the USSR and Other Plays* (New York and San Diego: Harcourt Brace Jovanovich/Bruccoli Clark, 1984).
6. *Lectures on Literature; Lectures on Russian Literature; Lectures on Don Quixote.*
7. *Look at the Harlequins!* (New York: McGraw-Hill, 1974).

TO: **IZHAK LIVNI**[1]                    TL (XEROX), I p.

Montreux-Palace Hotel
1820 Montreux, Switzerland
February 12, 1973

Dear Mr. Livni,

I don't have to tell you what ardent sympathy marks my feelings toward Israel and her 25th anniversary. I am not a public man, and the kind of article you want is completely outside my scope of ability. I can only extend my heartfelt congratulations to your young ancient great little country.

Sincerely yours,
Vladimir Nabokov

1. Editor in chief, *Bamahaneh* magazine, Yaffo, Israel

TO: **ISRAEL SHENKER**[1]                                   TL (XEROX), 1 p.

> Montreux-Palace Hotel
> 1820 Montreux, Switzerland
> February 23, 1973

Dear Mr. Shenker,

Miss Jill Krementz[2] tells me in a letter of February 18 that your new book begins with an essay on me. I hope it is not a reprint of "*The Old Magician at Home*" (NYTR, Jan 9, 1972).[3] You will remember I asked you to copyright its Q & A part in my name. In fact I am using that part in a forthcoming collection of my articles and interviews. The rest of the *Old Magician* piece contained certain inaccuracies and chit-chat items that rather upset me at the time. Here they are listed.

Bottom of first column: My wife's absence was indeed due to illness but it was not food poisoning.

Second column, top: I went alone to Anzère. Otherwise there would have been no point in my being given those two variants of one room. We would have taken two adjacent ones as we always do.

Third column: I write on 4 x 6 index cards, *not* 3 x 5.

My remarks about Solzhenitsyn and Bellow were not for print.

I was sorry you quoted me on Catholic converts, it was mere gossip, and Vidal's[4] response, in that footnote, was silly and vulgar.

If my conjecture is wrong and the essay you propose to publish is a different one, in which you do not quote me at all, then I shall be glad to oblige you and have Miss Krementz come here for a photograph session between the 5th and 19th of March.

> Yours cordially,
> Vladimir Nabokov

1. Of the *New York Times Book Review*.
2. Photographer.
3. Shenker replied on 5 March that VN had not asked him to copyright the interview. Shenker reprinted the interview in *Words and Their Masters* (Garden City, N.Y.: Doubleday, 1974). VN's first three corrections were made in the book text.
4. Gore Vidal.

TO: **ANDREW FIELD**                    TL (XEROX), 1 p.

Montreux-Palace Hotel
1820 Montreux, Switzerland
February 26, 1973

Dear Andrew,

I have finished reading the typescript of your *"Nabokov"*.[1] At present my cards with corrections are in the process of being typed; there are 250 of them, which is more than I had expected. It was a great mistake on your part not to have shown me the chapters one by one.

I shall be able to mail you the result within a fortnight. Tell me, please, where to send it.

Best greetings,
Vladimir Nabokov

1. *Nabokov: His Life in Part* (New York: Viking, 1977).

TO: **LORD SNOWDON**                    TL (XEROX), 1 p.

Montreux-Palace Hotel
1820 Montreux, Switzerland
March 22, 1973

Dear Tony,

Many thanks for the inscribed copy of your *View of Venice*.[1] Such visions as the reversed garlands of wash hanging in the reflected sky of a canal or that shaggy dachshund straining in one direction and the pigeons walking in the other are both witty and poetic.

Cordially yours,<br>
Vladimir Nabokov

1. *View of Venice* (Ivrea, Italy: Olivetti, 1972).

TO: **SAUL STEINBERG**        TL (XEROX), 1 p.

Montreux-Palace Hotel<br>
1820 Montreux, Switzerland<br>
March 22, 1973

Dear Mr. Steinberg,

My wife and I thank you warmly for your inscribed *Inspector* album.[1] One does not know what to single out for special praise—the prodigious nose-remover with nothing below the waist and no wonder; or the marvellous marchers (particularly the bunnydogs, the fat question mark, the many specimens of our old friend *Alligator steinbergi*); or the iridescent (albeit uncolored) I HAVE-AM; or the desperate DON'T (kicking an apostrophe is like kicking a kitten!); or the new girls (especially the recurrent young beauty consisting of horizontal shadings); or the frame house made so mysteriously opaque by the occlusion of N,O,P and Q; or the labyrinthiform person peering at the portrait of a fellow labyrinthian.

Your visit to Montreux was a long time ago, and we do hope that you will come again soon!

Best greetings from both of us.

Vladimir Nabokov

1. London: Thames & Hudson, 1973.

TO: **SAMUEL ROSOFF** ALS (XEROX), 1 p.

Palace Hotel
Montreux
23 March 1973

Dear Mulya,

Sorry to have delayed so long thanking you for the crate of wonderful oranges, which Véra and I enjoyed enormously, mentioning
your name daily! I am buried beneath a dull and complex task that
has already kept me busy for more than two months: on January 16,
Andrei Field, my "biographer," sent me his opus consisting of 680
typewritten pages. His version of my life has turned out to be cretin-
ous. I have had to correct or delete hundreds of passages teeming with
blunders and inventions of all kinds. He has now received my observations, or rather castigations, but has not yet replied.

Where and when [2 illegible words]? How is your family?

Keep well, dear friend. I embrace you and my wife sends greetings.

V[1]

1. Translated from Russian by DN.

TO: **WILLIAM F. BUCKLEY, JR.**[1] TL (XEROX), 1 p.

Montreux-Palace Hotel
1820 Montreux, Switzerland
March 26, 1973

Dear Bill,

It was sad to hear about the château disaster,[2] but much sadder to
know that you were terribly ill. What was exactly the matter? How
are you now? We have certainly missed you this winter.

Véra has been ill for more than two months. She had dreadful
pains in the back, finally diagnosed as two slipped discs plus damage
to a couple of other vertebrae. She is now much better.

The *National Review* has been always a joy to read, and your articles in the *Herald Tribune* counteract wonderfully the evil and trash of its general politics.

Did the copy of TRANSPARENT THINGS I sent you through my publisher reach you? I did get the sumptuous *Pound Era* which you were so kind to send me.[3] Though I detest Pound and the costume jewellery of his verse, I must say Kenner's approach is very interesting particularly when he discusses *other* writers of that era, and the real Chinese meaning of Uzura Pound's phony "Chinese."

Awaiting news from you, Véra and I send you and Pat our very best greetings.

Vladimir Nabokov

1. Editor of *The National Review*.
2. There had been a serious fire at the Buckleys' residence of Rougemont, near Gstaad.
3. Hugh Kenner, *The Pound Era* (Berkeley: University of California Press, 1971).


TO: **FREDERIC W. HILLS**[1]　　　　　　　　　　TL (XEROX), 1 p.

Montreux-Palace Hotel
1820 Montreux, Switzerland
April 13, 1973

Dear Mr. Hills,

I thank you for your charming letter of April 5.

As I told Miss Murphy, when sending the text of STRONG OPINIONS, I had indeed planned to write an Introduction after the contents of the volume were definitely settled. I am most grateful to you for indicating the repetitions and boring parts of interviews to be weeded out.

I want to finish first a little slice of my new novel while the going is good, and around Easter I shall re-examine STRONG OPINIONS in its entirety. I am pretty sure that I can accept all your excellent suggestions. I think the writing of the Introduction will be fun.

What you say about BEND SINISTER warms the rattles of my old heart. I can't remember now but you *are* including the preface I wrote for the Time Mag. edition, aren't you? (It is an important piece.) As to the "styling" conventions, yes, of course, the American style of punctuation should be used. And I quite agree with you that some recent photo, noble jowls and all, might do better than a jacket Adonis.

The first copy of A RUSSIAN BEAUTY arrived here today and I am delighted with its looks. Many thanks.

I take this opportunity to mention a change I would like to make in the title of the second collection of short stories,[2] the typescript of which is already in McGraw-Hill's hands. I want to change the order of the stories, moving *Perfection* to first place and switching *Tyrants Destroyed* to number 11, the former place of *Perfection*. The title of the entire volume would then be PERFECTION, which I think is more pleasing.

I would appreciate if you could confirm to me this exchange of titles and positions.

Cordially yours,
Vladimir Nabokov

1. Editor-in-Chief, McGraw-Hill.
2. *Tyrants Destroyed and Other Stories* (New York: McGraw-Hill, 1975).

TO: **ANDREW FIELD**                TL (XEROX), 1 p.

Montreux-Palace Hotel
1820 Montreux, Switzerland
May 25, 1973

Dear Andrew,

I thank you for your letter from good old Cambridge.

I cannot read your new version "at least quickly" because in order to arrive even at the outline of a conclusion that would be fair to both you and me I must 1) repaginate the thing to find my way, 2) consult every moment your voluminous first version and 3) check carefully your response to every objection of mine in the 200 pages of Critical Comments I sent you.

Since May 10, in between reworking some parts of my STRONG OPINIONS, reading the proof of a new BEND SINISTER edition for McGraw, correcting the Penguin proof of PALE FIRE, translating a Lermontov poem and a Pushkin poem needed in a hurry, and attending to a mass of business correspondence, I have had a moment to start renumbering the pages of your Version I and to notice that you have calmly disregarded some of my objections, or else simply added, with a flippant remark, my true version of an event to your garbled account of it so as to let an idiot reader decide which of us errs!

Therefore I must follow my initial plan. You can be assured (in case a hijacker takes me to Russia or a dancing butterfly leads me over the brink of a precipice) that your typescripts, my comments to the first version, and our entire correspondence will remain in steel-safe hands. But I really don't see how I can take all those typescripts with me. The one you suggest I mail to myself in Italy would not be enough, nor could I do it anyway, since I am not at all sure we shall like the rooms we have engaged in a hotel on the Adriatic coast. You also underestimate the length of time and risks involved in mailing papers to Italy.

Now at last my wife is feeling well enough to travel. We shall be leaving in a few days. I am divided between a sense of utter exhaustion, after all the tasks of this spring, and an intolerable impatience to work on my new novel. I can promise you that by the very first week of August I will be studying your new version. We shall also discuss then the mysterious addenda which you say are not yet in the text.

With best greetings,
Vladimir Nabokov

> Montreux-Palace Hotel
> 1820 Montreux, Switzerland
> August 8, 1973

Dear Mr. Field,

Your ignoble letter of July 9, 1973 arrived only now, upon my return to Montreux from Cortina d'Ampezzo, thus taking a month to reach me. I would attribute to the workings of a deranged mind some of its wild rubbish—such as my dreading the blood of the Tsars in my veins, or that [inexcusable mischaracterization] about a "separation" from my wife, or your comic complaint that I failed to inform you that she is "related to Marc Slonim" (she isn't—and who cares anyway?), or my telling my three-old-year son in Berlin: "Spit on those flowers that look like Hitler faces" (in our set, children were forbidden to spit); but mental derangement is one thing, and blackmail another, and blackmail is the word for your threats to publish my informal utterances on two afternoons of tape-recording, the garbled recollections of strangers, and the various rumors that fell into your unfastidious lap, if I continue to insist on your deleting from your book the errors of fact, the blunders of fancy, and [offensive misinterpretations] which still mar your "revised" version.

Since I cannot conceive what rational considerations can prompt the unfortunate author of a biographical work [peppered] with mistakes to refuse the help free of charge offered him by the only individual in the world who is able to set straight the incidents, situations and other matters . . . botched by that biographer, I shall persevere and send you my corrections, as promised, in the course of this month, and if you refuse to accept them you will take the consequences. I shall not hesitate to sue you for breach of contract, slander, libel, and deliberate attempts to damage my personal reputation.

I must remind you again that I am in possession of your written declaration of August 25, 1968, made when launching upon your task:

*"The final word as to what would be better deleted will rest in your*

hands ... *Above all I wish to try to make a book that will please you* ..."

It is on the strength of that declaration that I put you in touch with relatives and friends of mine and gave you much of my own time. If you violate my trust, you cannot use any information supplied by people who thought they were acting on my request; nor can you use excerpts from my diaries, letters, and other texts received directly from me; and, of course, those famous tapes, no matter how innocent, are also taboo.

But not all is lost! Both your typescripts, with all my copious notes to them, as well as our entire correspondence, will be ambushed, ready to appear and stop you in your tracks—if I am no longer there to demolish the travesty of my life that you might plan to publish.[1]

Vladimir Nabokov

1. See DN's review of Field's *The Life and Art of Vladimir Nabokov*: "Did He Really Call His Mum Lolita?" *London Observer* (26 April 1987).

TO: **ANDREW FIELD**                                   TL (XEROX), 1 p.

Montreux-Palace Hotel
1820 Montreux, Switzerland
September 12, 1973

Dear Mr. Field,

I have just received your note of September 6 and am airmailing enclosed my 25 typed pages of critical comments and the 178 typed pages of your second version of *Nabokov: His Life in Part* to which my notes refer.

Although you did take into account a number of the objections I made in the spring of this year when revising the first version of your NHILIP, I see that you have ignored quite a few errors of fact and tact which I had corrected. I have also found, in this second version, errors I had overlooked in the first. The style and tone of your work are beyond redemption, but if you wish to publish it at all you must accept *all the deletions and corrections in the present list*. If you prefer putting me in touch with your publisher so as to simplify the matter of final proof reading arrangements, I should be warned well ahead of dates and deadlines as I may have to leave Montreux for some time.

By the way: I hope you have obtained the permission of all concerned for the publication of Edmund Wilson's New Yorker letter.

Another thing: It was agreed, you will remember, that the tapes were not to be used without my approval. If you wish to quote from them at all I shall consider this only after you have submitted to me a copy (taped). I am rather puzzled by finding here and there in the chitchat phrases and terms neither my wife nor I ever use. (All the farcical germanic "Akhhs...!!!" with which you introduce the speeches of your Russian characters must go, of course.)

Vladimir Nabokov

TO: **PROF. STEPHEN JAN PARKER**[1]                    TL (XEROX), 1 p.

Montreux-Palace Hotel
1820 Montreux, Switzerland
September 18, 1973

Dear Mr. Parker,

Here are some hasty answers to queries in your letter of September 8:

1) VN says the exact year when he first read ALICE IN WONDERLAND was 1906. He has never seen a Russian translation of it—either before or after making his.

2) Yes, he was commissioned to translate it by the publisher and had not such prior plans. Yes, he was paid about $5. He says he worked

at it one summer, and it was easier than COLAS BREUGNON[2] which he translated more or less simultaneously.

3) No.[3]

4) He says he has not reread his translation for years. He remembers one mistake—using *"lohan"* instead of *"lohan'"* in the "Soup" poem.

5) He remembers his translation as a little stilted in dialogue but excellent in word play and poems.

6) He says there are some references to Carroll in STRONG OPINIONS.

We have seen an advance notice on Field's bibliography in the *Kirkus Reviews* of which I am enclosing a duplicate. McGraw-Hill say its publication is scheduled for November 15th.

EUGENE ONEGIN in the new edition: VN has corrected the final proof of two volumes; proof of volume 3 is promised for this month.

STRONG OPINIONS is coming out in October, and also BEND SINISTER of which we have just received the first advance copy.

With cordial greetings to you and your wife from VN and me.

(Mrs. Vladimir Nabokov)

1. Professor of Slavic Languages and Literatures, the University of Kansas; later editor of the *Nabokovian*.
2. A Russian translation of Romain Rolland's *Colas Breugnon* (1922).
3. Parker had asked if VN was aware of other Russian translations of *Alice*.

TO: **DMITRI NABOKOV**          HOLOGRAPH PS TO VÉRA NABOKOV LETTER
Montreux, Switzerland

Nov. 25, 1973

I embrace you as always, dearest! Since 25 September I have written 250 cards (fair copy) of my Harlequins,[1] which represents about a hundred printed pages, and there will be about three hundred in all. I work daily, five hours or so, and the writing is going very smoothly and merrily. I sympathize with your dental misadventures—I suffered for almost fifty years, and know.

I love you!
P[2]

1. *Look at the Harlequins!*
2. Translated from Russian by DN.

TO: **LESLIE J. SCHREYER**[1]                    TL (XEROX), 1 p.

Montreux-Palace Hotel
1820 Montreux, Switzerland
September 25, 1973

Dear Mr. Schreyer,

My husband asks me to thank you for your letter of August 17. He has some definite convictions as regards the questions raised in it. He regrets that a terrific pressure of work prevents his formulating these convictions. He asks me to convey some of them to you on his behalf.

He does not believe that the copyright of a letter or a manuscript should be ever assumed to pass from their author to anyone who receives it, or acquires it in any other way; and he does not think that anyone but the author, or his heirs, should be entitled to publish such material.[2]

He never sends his autograph to dealers, private collectors, or anyone else. Those autograph hunters pester a man with whom they are not even acquainted in their overwhelming desire to get something for nothing, and help clutter the poor author's letterbox, and obtrude themselves on his consciousness. They send books, photographs, magazine covers etc., that they expect the author not only to inscribe, but also to pack and carry to the post office (incidentally as often as not paying the postage). They are innumerable and come in all possible varieties, from a naive person in Calcutta who would like to be sent half a dozen autographed works by his "favorite author" to the far less naive individual in Grand Rapids or San Francisco who claims one year that his father dying of cancer could only be cheered by an inscribed copy of our "greatest living author"'s latest work, only to claim the following year that his son who is dying of leukemia has but one dream: to receive the latest work of our "greatest living author" inscribed by said author.

But I do not think this complaint is quite what you have in mind; my husband just wants to share this with you.

Sincerely yours,
(Mrs. Vladimir Nabokov)

1. Of Chadbourne, Parke, Whiteside, & Wolff, New York attorneys at law.
2. VN's position was in accord with American common-law copyright and has been upheld by the courts in the case involving Ian Hamilton's biography of J. D. Salinger.

TO: **ARYE LEVAVI**      TL (XEROX), 1 p.

Palace Hotel, 1820 Montreux
October 9th, 1973

Dear Mr. Levavi,

I would like to make a small contribution to Israel's defense against the Arabolshevist aggression. May I beg you to forward the enclosed check. I am leaving the name in blank because I don't know to what organization exactly it should go.

My wife and I send our cordial greetings to you and Mrs. Levavi.

Yours ever,
Vladimir Nabokov

TO: **CARL AND ELLENDEA PROFFER**       TL (XEROX), 1 p.

Montreux-Palace Hotel
1820 Montreux, Switzerland
December 3, 1973

Dear Mr. and Mrs. Proffer,

Thanks for your letter of November 20. We shall expect, then, to hear from Mr. Hills regarding the reprinting in Russian of MARY and GLORY, and, possibly, THE GIFT as well.

Please find enclosed a check for $100 which, I hope, will help brighten the Christmas holidays for a couple of dissident families in Russia. We leave it to you to decide what to give, and to whom.

To you both a good trip and a happy holiday!

Cordially,

TO: **PROF. STEPHEN JAN PARKER**       TL (XEROX), 1 p.

Montreux-Palace Hotel
1820 Montreux, Switzerland
December 12, 1973

Dear Mr. Parker,

Thank you for your letter of December 1.

In the first place: VN asks me to say that *of course* you may publish the Gstaad exchange.[1] The reason why he did not include it in STRONG OPINIONS is that after some hesitation he decided to use only published or ambiguous material in it.

Field's failing to give you proper credit for your work on the Bibliography is just like Field. Would you believe that he never once thanked VN for saving him from disgrace by catching and correcting the booboos and blunders in his translations of the poem titles (e.g. *Semya na kamne* was translated by Field "Family on a stone").[2] But that is nothing compared with the hideous trouble we are having with the Biography, which teems with factual errors, snide insinua-

523

tions and blunders that Field refuses to correct after having promised, when starting on the job, to publish nothing that VN would not approve. VN is no longer on speaking terms with Field.

Moser's article on SOPI is excellent and reads like a thriller.[3] VN says that his candidate for the SOPI forger is "Gavrila Petrovich Kamenev (1772–1803), a wonderful poet in his own right" (mentioned in VN's EO). He also says that his new novel LATH[4] has traversed the main mountain pass, and that "it will cause hacks to shy and asses to kick".

I look forward very much to your monograph on *Anya* when it is completed.

We both wish a very merry Christmas to you and your wife.

Sincerely,
(Mrs. Vladimir Nabokov)

1. Parker's interview with VN was not published.
2. The words for "seed" and "family"—spelled and pronounced differently in Russian—can both be transliterated into English as "semya," an error analogous, for instance, to translating the English expression "peace on earth" into another language as "a story [piece] about earth." DN.
3. Charles Moser, "The Problem of the Igor Tale," *Canadian-American Slavic Studies* (Summer 1973).
4. *Look at the Harlequins!*

TO: **EDWARD E. BOOHER**                    TL (XEROX), 1 p.

Montreux-Palace Hotel
1820 Montreux, Switzerland
December 26, 1973

Dear Mr. Booher,

Thanks a lot for your letter of congratulation.[1] Never before have I thought of my writing career in terms of prizes or rewards,—or even praise and flattering reviews. But I must truthfully admit that this recognition in the country that I consider my own warms my heart.

My wife and I shall be looking forward to seeing you again in the spring in New York.

Sincerely,
Vladimir Nabokov

1. VN had been awarded the National Medal for Literature.

TO: **PROF. PAUL KURT ACKERMANN**[1]          TL (XEROX), 1 p.

Montreux-Palace Hotel
1820 Montreux, Switzerland
December 26, 1973

Dear Professor Ackermann,

My husband asks me to reply to your letter of December 10, as he is too intensely occupied with the novel he is writing to be able to interrupt his work.

He thanks you for your kind offer to prepublish part of his collection of lectures in the Boston University Journal. It would be, however, premature to discuss this as he has several other projects that must be dealt with before comes the turn of the lecture collection.

Here are a few considerations on Thomas Mann that I am asked to transmit to you:

Although my husband's German is very limited he took the trouble to read some of Mann's work quite closely, using a good dictionary, and paying special attention to language and imagery. He failed to discover the special charms you mention. He finds Mann's style to be plodding and garrulous, his images, if carefully translated into English, to prove to be nothing but clichés (a more ambitious sentence often turning out to be an accumulation of several clichés), and his humour remindful of that of Max & Moritz.[2] Moreover, he finds Mann's psychology artificial and his characters made to develop so as to fit the author's teleological purpose. O.K.?

Both my husband and I wish you a happy New Year.

Sincerely yours,
(Mrs. Vladimir Nabokov)

1. Editor of the *Boston University Journal*.
2. German comic-strip characters.

TO: **JOHN UPDIKE**    TLS, 1 p. Harvard University.

Montreux-Palace Hotel
1820 Montreux, Switzerland
January 7, 1974

Dear Mr. Updike,

I was delighted to receive your charming note. As you know I love your prose; to get it in this personal form enhances the pleasure it gives me.[1]

I wish you a very happy New Year.

Cordially,
Vladimir Nabokov

1. On 30 November Updike wrote congratulating VN on *Strong Opinions*.

TO: **FREDERIC W. HILLS**      TL (XEROX), 1 p.

> Montreux-Palace Hotel
> 1820 Montreux, Switzerland
> February 11, 1974

Dear Mr. Hills,

I am a little upset by your cable of February 7 in which you ask me to provide a description of my new novel for your Fall catalogue.

In the case of ADA, the parody of a blurb, a built-in finale within the novel, took me at least a week to compose. I have not prepared a similar inset for LOOK AT THE HARLEQUINS. Believe me, to produce the description of a book which I have not finished writing is for me no less difficult than the writing about an unread book is for you. I have suffered some perilous interruptions in the course of the last three weeks, and cannot afford now to squander even one day of work. Four fifths of the book are completed; there remain some fifty pages to write, and I must be allowed to do so at my own pace. I can only say that LATH is a multiple-love story and that during a span of fifty years the scene shifts from my desk to Old Russia, from there to England, from England to France, from France to America and thence to Bolshevisia and back to this lake.

> Cordially yours,
> Vladimir Nabokov

TO: **ALEKSANDR SOLZHENITSYN**[1]      TL (XEROX), 1 p.

> Palace Hotel
> Montreux,
> Suisse
> 14.II.1974

Dear Aleksandr Isaevich,

I was happy to learn today of your passage to the free world from our dreadful homeland. I am happy as well that your children will be attending schools for humans, not for slaves.

Only now is it possible for me to thank you for your letter of 16.V.1972, with your appeal to the Swedish Academy enclosed.[2] I was keenly touched by your words. If I have not answered you until now, it is because for a long time I have made it a rule not to write to Soviet Russia, so as not to subject my benevolent correspondents to additional danger: I am, after all, some kind of scaly devil to the Bolshevik authorities—something that not everyone in Russia realizes. I doubt if even you have read my poems, articles, stories and such novels of mine as *Dar, Podvig, Priglashenie na kazn'*, and especially *Bend Sinister*, in which, ever since the vile times of Lenin, I have not ceased to mock the philistinism of Sovietized Russia and to thunder against the very kind of vicious cruelty of which you write and of which you will now write freely.

The newspapers cannot decide in which country you will settle; but if you should happen to visit Switzerland, let me know and we shall get together.

I never make official "political" statements. Privately, though, I could not refrain from welcoming you.[3]

I shake your hand
Vladimir Nabokov[4]

1. Russian novelist and Nobel laureate, now exiled.
2. Solzhenitsyn had spontaneously recommended VN for the Nobel Prize.
3. Solzhenitsyn replied warmly, saying that fate had brought them both to Switzerland, and would make it possible for them to meet. The Nabokovs invited him, but, through an odd misunderstanding, the encounter never took place. DN.
4. Translated from Russian by DN.

TO: **HARVEY SHAPIRO**[1]                    TL (XEROX), 1 p.

> Montreux-Palace Hotel
> 1820 Montreux, Switzerland
> March 1, 1974

Dear Mr. Shapiro,

My husband asks me to thank you for your cable. He regrets he cannot write a "Letter to Solzhenitsyn"—not only because he cannot interrupt work on a new novel he is writing but also because writing such a letter would interest him as little as reading it would Solzhenitsyn.

> Sincerely yours,
> (Mrs. Vladimir Nabokov)

1. Editor, *New York Times Magazine*.

TO: **JOHN C. FRANTZ**[1]                    TLS (XEROX), 1 p; with statement.

> Montreux-Palace Hotel
> 1820 Montreux, Switzerland
> March 11, 1974

Dear Mr. Frantz,

I hasten to send this letter in the wake of the one I mailed you on March 5. In a moment of reckless optimism, I had accepted the kind invitation contained in your letter of February 28. Now I have looked at the calendar, stared at the manuscript of my novel, looked at the calendar again, and am appalled by the difficulties of the situation.

The dilemma confronting me is either:

1) to spend the next three weeks here in a chaos of preparation, amidst all kinds of worries (monstrously magnified by the lens of nervous exhaustion), preceding an altogether delightful but very complicated voyage (note that I have *never* flown across the Atlantic and

that all my favourite liners have been scrapped), in which case I could not possibly carve out the piece of time and the peace of mind needed to finish my novel before leaving;

or

2) to deprive myself of the immense pleasure that the National Medal dinner on April 16 would give me and use instead the next weeks to complete the ascetic and rather grim but inly sparked task of working seven hours a day in order to finish turning by hand a roughish draft, of some 80,000 words in all, into a fair copy which would gradually make, in regular batches, over 250 typed pages of "LOOK AT THE HARLEQUINS!"

After careful consideration I choose the second course, and send you my deepest apologies.

Sincerely yours,
Vladimir Nabokov

1. Executive Chairman, National Book Committee.

A statement by Vladimir Nabokov
to be read by his son Dmitri Nabokov on April 16, 1974 at the New York Public Library for the Presentation of the 1973 National Medal for Literature.

My son, who represents me here, knows how hard it was for me to decide *not* to come to New York, *not* to leave my writing desk in Montreux, *not* to enjoy in person an honor I so highly appreciate. By some quirk of spacetime, the date of the National Medal Dinner happened to clash with the final, most demanding and dramatic lap of work on the new novel which I have been writing since the beginning of last year. The festive break might have proved a formidable interruption. The lone lamp had to be preferred to the blaze of the feast.

I am never sure how many hours, five or six, are deductable or addable when one tries to clock a coincidence of two events separated by a sprawling body of salt water. I wish you to know, however, that at the very moment you are hearing the voice of my son I am either at my desk or in bed, writing the last paragraphs of my book with a stubby but stubborn pencil.

Vladimir Nabokov
Montreux, March 15, 1974

TO: *THE OBSERVER*                                TL (XEROX), 1 p.[1]
                                                 Montreux, Switzerland

To the editor

Although I doubt that any words of mine can elicit the slightest reverberation amidst the unimaginable magistrates of the Soviet Union I feel compelled to raise my voice in response to the appeal Victor Fainberg sent you concerning the hideous plight of Vladimir Bukovski.[2] Bukovski's heroic speech to the court in defense of freedom and his five years of martyrdom in a despicable psychiatric jail will be remembered long after the torturers he defied have rotted away. But that is poor consolation for a prisoner with rheumatic carditis who has been transferred now to a Permian camp and will perish there unless a public miracle rescues him. I wish to urge all persons and organizations that have more contact with Russia than I have to do whatever can be done to help that courageous and precious man. Please publish.

Vladimir Nabokov

1. Published 26 May 1974.
2. Dissident writer who accused Soviet authorities of imprisoning dissidents in mental hospitals.

TO: **DMITRI NABOKOV**

ALS, 1 p.

Montreux, Switzerland

You can use my toilet remains and *nochnye toofli!*[1]

June 4, 1974

(Auction price of this card *circa* 2000 AD at least 5,000 roubles.)

Dmitrichko [a diminutive not used before or since]!

Here is a copy of LATH (acronym) for you to read carefully and lovingly.

Main queries: technical or idiomatic slips. Mark your queries or corrections with birdies in margin and explain them on a page of the notebook (with butterflies) provided by the author.

Easy on spelling and punctuation: there are editors for that.

... words unfamiliar (or objectionable) to you ... are likely to be in my large Webster or 13-vols OED, or else are noncewords (from 'once' not from 'nonsense') of my make.

Loving regards
*VN*[2]

1. Slippers.
2. Note accompanying proofs for *Look at the Harlequins!*. See "On Revisiting Father's Room," *Vladimir Nabokov: A Tribute*, ed. Peter Quennell (London: Weidenfeld & Nicolson, 1979).

TO: **HENRI HELL**[1]

CC, 1 p.

Hotel Mont-Cervin, Zermatt
Le 17 juillet 1974

Dear Mr. Hell,

I shall be mailing you early next week, before leaving Zermatt for Italy, a first batch of Gilles Chahine's ADA with my revisions and a separate report on his type of mistakes. The dreary difficulty of correcting his translation is increased by my having to weed out those recurrent flaws, besides dealing with the big blunders. His fear of saying *"d'Ada"* ou *"à Ada"* enmeshes him in ridiculous paraphrases. I am not Racine and neither is he.

I appreciated your kindly sending me your elegant piece on PALE FIRE—I confess, however, to being puzzled by the connection you find between my work and Borges' flimsy little fables.

Best regards from my wife and me.

Vladimir Nabokov

1. Directeur Littéraire, Librairie Arthème Fayard.

TO: **HENRI HELL**        CC, 2 pp.

Hotel Mont-Cervin
Zermatt, Suisse
July 23, 1974

Dear Mr. Hell,

I am sending you *sou pli séparé* 150 pp., Chapters I-XVIII, of the corrected typescript of Gilles Chahine's translation of ADA. Please have all my revisions taken into account. A foreigner's slip may well have occurred here and there in my French; this is easy to straighten out—but should always remain in keeping with the sense of the revision.

Many passages in Chahine's work are brilliantly translated. The flawless flow, however, is interrupted by monstrous mistakes and impossible mannerisms. I shall content myself with listing a few examples of his main verbal transgressions:

1. The dead metaphor which replaces a plain English word. "She cowered" (*elle tremblait*), p. 147, becomes *"elle souhaitait disparaître sous terre."*

2. A mess of images. On p. 103, the bird *"huppe"* (hoopoe) is rendered as *"bécasse perchante"*, a horrible dictionary translation, this *"bécasse"*—*perchante* or not—destroying the idea of the floppy motion of descent in the comparison; and the ornithological confusion

533

is immediately continued by Chahine's addressing Ada as *"mésange"* in the same passage!

3. When he tries especially hard to render what he assumes to be yet another arbitrary *jeu de mots* on the author's part, he lapses into macaronic nonsense. This is especially painful when an alliteration is involved. He should never try to copy alliterations which come naturally in English and do not stick out in awkward, irrelevant and artificial postures. A good example is his *"marmoréen marmonneur"* (!?), p. 147, for "immemorial ghost."

4. The urge to escape hiatus or repetition by such awful paraphrases for simple "Ada" as *"la mignonne," "l'adorée," "la belle enfant," "la jeune dame"* etc. Who cares if in a faithful translation *"d'Ada"* or *"à Ada"* shocks the ear! Literature is a visual, not auditive phenomenon.

5. His own unsolicited contributions and the explanatory phrases that he throws in for good measure. Examples: "Dawn's *doigts de rose*", p. 98, or the *"tilleuls et grillons,"* p. 109, or *"que la perle n'était point huitre"*, etc.

I do not speak of the numerous mistranslations, due to insufficient knowledge of English, in Chahine's work—I am there to correct them. But in the given circumstances my task seems to be unnecessarily complicated. I wonder if something could not be done about it—by an editor's checking in the remaining pages of Chahine's text the kind of errors I list above? At present one page takes me half-an-hour at least to correct and since I cannot devote more than a couple of hours per day to the revising of this translation I dare not imagine the amount of time I may need to terminate my task. I am sure you will agree with me that this is an impossible demand to place on an author.

Best regards.

Vladimir Nabokov

PS. Notez je vous prie que nous quittons Zermatt dans quelques jours pour l'Italie et que nous serons de retour à Montreux le 4 ou 5 août.

TO: **PROF. GLEB STRUVE**                          TL (XEROX), 1 p.

> Montreux-Palace Hotel
> 1820 Montreux, Switzerland
> September 13, 1974

Dear Gleb Petrovich,

Forgive me for replying in English to your Russian letter of August 15th.

VN appreciates all the errors you catch in Field's Bibliography (although he still thinks that Field produced a valuable book in which he invested a lot of labor). We don't know who is Foster.[1] It really does not matter, says V.V., what he (or she) included or left out of his (her) bibliography. But Field's was meant to cover the entire ground and every omission he allowed to occur is regrettable.

V.V. says that "Valentin Nabokov" was used by him to avoid confusion with his father's signature. He chose "Valentin" because the girl he was courting at that time (the heroine of *Mashenka*) was called "Valentina." With it he signed either *"Lunnaya Gryoza"* in *Vestnik Evropy* (Field 0407) or *"Zimnyaya Noch'"* in *Russkaya Mysl'* (Field 0408) (or both).

Thank you for the offer to send us xerox copies of the poems, but we do have the text of both.

The copy of V.V.'s new novel—LOOK AT THE HARLEQUINS!—that he asked McGraw to send you should be in your hands by now.

We hope your health has improved.

> Our cordial greetings to you and your wife.

---

1. Ludmila A. Foster, "Nabokov in Russian Émigré Criticism," *A Book of Things About Vladimir Nabokov*, ed. Carl R. Proffer (Ann Arbor, Mich.: Ardis, 1974), pp. 42–53.

TO: **FREDERIC W. HILLS**                    TL (XEROX), 2 pp.

> Montreux-Palace Hotel
> 1820 Montreux, Switzerland
> November 4, 1974

Dear Mr. Hills,

I see that I have not replied to your charming and very kind (the second especially) letters of October 8 and 11. Your two (thoughtful) sets of queries have been received, and I am awaiting the proof to deal with them—they seem pretty innocuous. Thanks for the information about *The Admiralty Spire*.[1] I was most interested in your tabletalk with Gillon Aitken and am enclosing for your information a recent letter, registered, that I airmailed to Miss Sifton of Viking a few days ago. In no circumstance, even on the way to the scaffold, will I ever use "Ms". I shall give Miss Sifton another week for a reply, after which, I think, I shall take advantage of a very sweet suggestion of yours to beg you to talk to Thomas Guinsburg, showing him my missive to Miss Sifton and asking him to examine all the material I had sent to her. If Field insists on telling the "history of bastardy and buggery" inherent in the Nabokov family, as well as publishing bits of my working notes toward a novel, and distorting information I gave him in idiotic ways (by asking strangers to check details of incidents that I alone could know), then I shall do everything to stop him in his stride, besides composing for a sympathizing periodical a special article about his dishonest behaviour and blunders.

I have spent most of October preparing our third collection of 13 stories (very temporarily entitled *A Letter to Russia*).[2] Three of them are completely ready:

> *The Return of Chorb*
> *The Passenger*
> and *A Bad Day*.

Six others are in the making. I am taking advantage of Dmitri's stay with us here. He has done a splendid translation into Italian of TRANSPARENT THINGS for Mondadori.

Miss Loo has seen no doubt the huge purple effigy of German

ADA (another excellent translation) at the Frankfurter Fair's Rowohlt stand.

I want to get rid of all translations (including the harrowing French ADA!) before settling down to a new novel that keeps adding nightly a couple of hours to my habitual insomnias. I am trying an old somnifacient whose name—Sanalepsi—, if I mentioned it in my fiction, would be at once attached by some aha!-criticule to both nympholepsy and lepidoptera.

Very cordially yours,
Vladimir Nabokov[3]

1. A story by VN.
2. *Details of a Sunset and Other Stories.*
3. The 63-word postscript has been omitted.

TO: **PROF. ALFRED APPEL, JR.**                    TL (XEROX), 1 p.

Montreux-Palace Hotel
1820 Montreux, Switzerland
November 8, 1974

Dear Alfred,

Thanks for *N.'s Dark Cinema*,[1] a brilliant and delightful book. I found the material beautifully arranged throughout—not an easy job, I suspect. The illustrations are fascinating. Your basic idea, my constantly introducing cinema themes, and cinema lore, and cinematophors (VN) into my literary compositions cannot be contested of course, but your readers may be inclined to forget that I know very little about *avant-garde* German and American pictures of the 1930's and that my wife and I have virtually not been to the cinema more than two or three times in fifteen years, nor do we have a TV at home (except when soccer competitions take place). I have not yet had time to read the whole book but the spots I dipped into are pleasant cool spots, where I enjoyed your good-natured touch and comfortable erudition. I was also tickled by your biographical forays—they will enrage Field. In due time I may add some remarks, but I already note that for the sake of an elegant generalization, you connect me, now and then, with films and actors whom I have never seen in my life. (I still do not quite know, for example, who this "James Bond" is). You and I and other Nabokovians will readily realize that stylistically you are slanting my works movieward in pursuit of your main thought; yet it would be rather unfair if less subtle people—poor, benighted sheep and so on—were to conclude I had simply lifted my characters (say, Gradus) from films which you know and I don't. These are trivial complaints, Alfred, but I am sure that our friendship and the susceptibilities of advanced age warrant my making them. Your book, I repeat, is delightful and you are most kind to me and I am going to re-enjoy it to-night and to-morrow and in between the ridges of insomnia. Thanks also for the description of your long-shoreman, he is marvelous.

Very cordially yours,
Vladimir Nabokov

1. New York: Oxford University Press, 1974.

TO: **HENRI HELL**                    TL (XEROX), 2 pp.

Montreux-Palace Hotel
1820 Montreux, Switzerland
November 30, 1974

Dear Mr. Hell,

Thanks for the XXXIV-XLIII batch of ADA, in two copies this time. I have not yet finished the XIX-XXXIII chapters the first of which had to be redone in the light of your corrections.

Other daily tasks such as the completion of a new book of stories for McGraw-Hill with a deadline in January, 75, and a business correspondence that keeps growing fantastically prevent me from devoting more than three or four morning hours (from about 6:00 A.M. till breakfast and bath) to my struggle with Chahine. There are errors of sense on every page; sometimes the search for a correct rendering takes longer than the twenty minutes which on the average I need for the revision of one typewritten page; and sometimes an entire paragraph has to be written in or rewritten; and of course there are those snatches of poetry in the composing of which Chahine is spectacularly helpless. With great luck I can manage about three typed pages per hour (around ten such pages per day corresponding to around eight pages of the McGraw edition). At best I shall need fifty days to revise the remaining pages (corresponding to a stretch of around 400 McGraw pages), which means that they cannot be ready till the last week of January 1975. Incidentally, a *Playboy* interview in mid-January is quite unthinkable (I have just refused to give one to the Associated Press); it would take me a week to prepare since I deal only in written answers. However I would be glad to get the French *Playboy* questions by the end of January and see J. P. Rey-Draillard in the beginning of February.[1]

What you call the *manuscrit définitif* will only exist when the entire monster is neatly retyped. My French may not be always impeccable; yet I know exactly what nuance I want in my French and would not care to have my corrections recorrected unless I am consulted in every case, and this also takes time.

As soon as feasible I will send you a goodish batch of chapters with red crosses in the margin here and there to mark samples of especially disastrous bits. I now enclose *à titre d'information* an *ADA* ad received from Rowohlt.

The Italian translation of the poor girl was *bâclée*, bungled, botched, in less than two months. The German one took years to ripen, with publisher and translators coming here for numerous sessions. But it is to the French *ADA* that I am giving the blood of my brain, and I will not be spurred on by anything short of a private illusion of perfection.

Cordially yours,
Vladimir Nabokov

P.S. Saturday, Dec. 7th.

I have delayed the posting of this letter for a week in the hope of sending it to you with a traveller. I am now told that the mails work again. During this week I have reached the revision of your latest batch (XXXIV-XLIII) and have finished to-day XXXV (printed p. 221 of the McGraw text).

It occurs to me that transferring the mozaic of my corrections onto the duplicate will be a tedious loss of time so I prefer photocopying the corrected batch and returning it to you in due time.

1. No VN interview appeared in the French edition of *Playboy*.

TO: **GROUP COMMITTEE OF WRITERS**[1]                    TELEGRAM

AM APPALLED TO LEARN THAT YET ANOTHER WRIT-
ER IS MARTYRED JUST FOR BEING A WRITER MARAM-
ZINS[2] IMMEDIATE RELEASE INDISPENSABLE TO PRE-
VENT AN ATROCIOUS NEW CRIME

NABOKOV

Exp. Vladimir Nabokov, Palace Hotel, 1820 Montreux
le 30 décembre 1974.

1. Leningrad Division of the Union of Writers of the USSR.
2. Vladimir Rafailovich Maramzin, writer of short fiction, was arrested in Leningrad for "anti-Soviet activity." He emigrated in 1975.

TO: **CARL AND ELLENDEA PROFFER**                    TL (XEROX), 1 p.

> Montreux-Palace Hotel
> 1820 Montreux, Switzerland
> January 2, 1975

Dear friends,

VN indeed never signs collective letters. Nor does he believe that the most emphatic or the most pathetic appeal to a man-eating tiger or shark can move its heart. However, your appeal to him did move his heart. Enclosed is a copy of the wire he sent on Monday December 30th to the address you recommended. You may publish it, disclose it or use it in any other way that you think might help Maramzin's cause. Happy New Year to you, and may it bring success to your humanitarian activities.

TO: **ALEX GRALL**[1]                    CC, 1 p.

> Montreux-Palace Hotel
> 1820 Montreux, Switzerland
> January 15, 1975

Dear Sir,

Thanks for your kind letter of January 10th. I would be delighted to continue with ADA the acquaintance we began with LOLITA. Of the dates you propose February 4th would suit me best.

Mr. Blandenier's help in deflating the translator's banalities is admirable, but I alone can step in when Chahine despairs. I am now toiling over ADA six hours a day, three before breakfast and three before dinner. It is a rather chaotic task, for I do not have the gift of gab in any language. In consulting my notes I see that my best time so far has been six pages (of the McGraw-Hill hardcover text) corrected in six hours of wrestling with Chahine. I am now on p. 412 (McG.-Hill) of my glorious hell, which means I still have 176 pages to revise before I reach the end of the book: another month's work. I don't want to Chahinate,[2] but today is January 15th and I strongly doubt that I shall finish before February 15th.

What takes up the most time is revamping a whole paragraph Chahine has botched or restoring one he has simply omitted, as well as redoing his French translations of poetry or fragments of poetry (those in Chapter 8, Part Two, for instance, just took up an entire day).

With best regards,
Vladimir Nabokov[2]

---

1. Président Directeur Général, Librairie Arthème Fayard.
2. My English equivalent of a French verb coined by VN for the occasion, referring to Chahine's difficulties with time limits. DN.
3. Translated from French by DN.

TO: **ROBERT L. KROON**[1]               TL (XEROX), 1 p.

Montreux-Palace Hotel
1820 Montreux,
February 11, 1975

Dear Mr. Kroon,

My husband asks me to thank you for the copy of "People". It is doubtlessly a deserving magazine but, as I believe you yourself remarked, hardly the kind whose readership would be particularly interested in an interview by Nabokov. VN finds Mr. Salter's questions interesting. It would take him a considerable time to answer them to his satisfaction. He does not believe that this would be justified in the present case, especially as he is so very hard-pressed for time. He suggests that you send him Mr. Salter's article *as written* for publication.[2] If VN finds the *factual* side of it o.k., he will agree to a photographic session in the near future. On the other hand, the plan of answering the questions would be dropped, at least for the time being.

Sincerely yours,
(Mrs. Vladimir Nabokov)

P.S. On the occasion of the arrest in Leningrad of the writer Maramzin my husband sent the following cable to the "Group Committee of Writers, Leningrad Division of the Union of Writers of the USSR, Voin street, Leningrad": "Am appalled to learn that yet another writer is martyred just for being a writer Maramzins immediate release indispensable to prevent an atrocious new crime. Nabokov." Palace Hotel, 1820 Montreux, December 30, 1974. Of course, that cable was not acknowledged by the addressee and thus never became public which rather defeats the purpose of trying to exercise some moral pressure in behalf of Maramzin. Do you think you could make it public with the help of TIME or in any other way?

1. Correspondent for *Time-Life*.
2. James Salter, "An Old Magician Named Nabokov Writes and Lives in Splendid Exile," *People* (17 March 1975).

TO: FREDERIC W. HILLS                    TL (XEROX), 1 p.

Montreux-Palace Hotel
1820 Montreux, Switzerland
February 21, 1975

Dear Fred,

Many thanks for your February 14th note. I am looking forward to receiving the golden TYRANTS before destruction.[1]

I also enjoyed the marvelous Duchess of Windsor and the Porcelain Pug.

I wonder if you will resolutely resurrect the publicity for LATH in the jumbo ads you are certainly planning to devote to the TY-

RANTS. I have a feeling that LATH has somehow been let down much too soon. I cannot believe that my publisher has run out of enthusiasm and *élan* after the first splendid spurt.

I hope to have the next collection of stories ready for you before summer.

Cordially yours,
Vladimir Nabokov

1. *Tyrants Destroyed* had a gold-colored dust jacket.

TO: **JOAN DALY**[1]                                    ALS (XEROX), 2 pp.

April 3, 1975
Montreux Palace
Montreux

Dear Miss Daly,

I have now finished revising Andrew Field's final typescript (further referred to as F3) of his work: *Nabokov: his Life in Part*. Enclosed, please find:

1. A list of my Corrections and Notes with the faults he has not corrected and my amendments encircled in red pencil.

2. The 104 pages of F3 [list of TS page numbers]—all referred to and commented on in my list, with the unacceptable passages, marked in red pencil, struck out or otherwise altered by me.

Among the many reasons I object to those passages the main ones are: they harp on grotesque rumors or—in numerous instances—are offensive to people whom I do not wish to hurt, or distort facts and garble episodes of which I alone can judge. There are also those unbearable coy and vulgar renderings of my Russian exchanges with my wife, and the morbid interest in financial trivialities, and various vicious little insinuations, and the constant attempts to direct his stings and nips at the veracity of my memoir *Speak, Memory*. On the other hand, I have generously overlooked many of his minor transgressions and wearily okayed some insufficiently corrected passages.

Since AF is a most [smooth] customer, I must see the evidence of his having deleted what I absolutely demand he deletes—in other words I must see the corrected page proof of the work.

I apologize for sending you this letter in xeroxed script but my secretary, Mme Callier, is seriously ill and my wife and I are over-whelmed with work.

Cordially yours,
Vladimir Nabokov

1. Of Joseph S. Iseman, law firm.


TO: FREDERIC W. HILLS                    TL (XEROX), 1 p.

Montreux-Palace Hotel
1820 Montreux, Switzerland
April 8, 1975

Dear Fred,

Thank you for your letter of March 31. I shall airmail express to you tomorrow the phantasm of an acceptance speech.[1] If it does not reach you by April 14 please cable me and instruct how to reach you personally by telex. Dan Lacy or you would be kind to substitute for me if fancy becomes fact.

Here is another matter I would like to submit to you. I think you have read Edmund White's marvelous first novel FORGETTING ELENA.[2] He has now written another one, A WOMAN. I have not yet seen it but Karlinsky of Berkeley, a fine judge of literature, has a very high opinion of it. White has some difficulty finding a pub-lisher because the book is too good. Would you agree to consider it for McG-H if he sends you a typescript? Would you read it *person-ally*?

Yes, I shall be at Montreux throughout April.

Cordially yours,
Vladimir Nabokov

1. *Look at the Harlequins!* had been short-listed for the National Book Award; the award went jointly to Robert Stone's *Dog Soldiers* and Thomas Williams's *The Hair of Harold Roux*. VN's speech has not been located.
2. New York: Random House, 1973; "A Woman Reading Pascal" was not published.

TO: **VÉRA NABOKOV**[1]                                                HOLOGRAPH
                                                        Montreux, Switzerland

Here we are at last, my darling
15.iv.1925–15.iv.1975[2]

1. VN's fiftieth-anniversary greeting to Véra Nabokov on 2″ x 4″ section cut from a checked index card, perhaps attached to a present, and illustrated with a beautiful iridescent butterfly. DN.
2. Translated from Russian by DN.

TO: **ROBERT WOOL**[1]                     TL (XEROX), 2 pp.

Montreux-Palace Hotel
1820 Montreux, Switzerland
April 18, 1975

Dear Mr. Wool,

To my great regret I shall not be able to write on Lepidoptera (at least this year) as you kindly suggest in your letter of March 27. I would be delighted however if, in reference to the recent note on Endangered Butterflies, you could print the following:

To the Editor:

By a nice coincidence the so-called "Karner Blue" illustrating Bayard Webster's note on insects needing protection (N.Y. Times, March 21) is a butterfly I classified myself. It is known as *Lycaeides melissa samuelis* Nabokov or more properly *Lycaeides samuelis* Nabokov (I considered it at first to be a race of the western *melissa* Edwards, but have concluded recently that it is a distinct species). My original description will be found in *Psyche*, Vol. I, 1943, followed by a more elaborate paper in the Bulletin of the Museum of Comparative Zoology, Harvard College, Vol. 101, 1949. It is a very local butterfly attached to extensive growths of lupine, in isolated colonies, from Michigan (probably its original habitat) to at least Albany, N.Y. Readers of my fiction may have found it settled on damp sand in a vacational scene of my novel *PNIN*.

Yours sincerely,
Vladimir Nabokov[2]

1. Of the *New York Times Magazine*.
2. *New York Times Magazine* (27 July 1975).

TO: **PROF. GLEB STRUVE**         TLS, 1 p. Hoover Institution.

Montreux-Palace Hotel
1820 Montreux, Switzerland
April 21, 1975

Dear Gleb Petrovich,

A moment of unusual respite allows me to write you a few words. *Zdrastvuyte* [Hello].

I am about to publish yet another collection of stories, *Details of a Sunset*, the last raisins and petit-beurre toes from the bottom of the barrel. The volume includes *The Return of Chorb* and *The Passenger*—in my and Dmitri's translation. I had not looked up your versions for many years and now find them not accurate enough and too far removed from my present style in English. Please, don't be cross! Time does not move, but artistic interpretation does.

I have spent a laborious winter correcting the French *traduction intégrale*, with all its interior decorations, of *ADA*, now completed and to be published on May 30. Last year, Rowohlt and a team of his translators visited us here several times for weekly sessions devoted to *their* translation of *ADA*—which is going strong in West Germany. I am now contemplating turning *ADA* into Russian—not sovjargon and not soljournalese—but romantic and precise Russian, and if I cannot find a docile assistant I will do the job all by myself, like Pushkin's Missail.[1]

I was both perplexed and amused by the nonsense somebody called Poirier wrote about the "prototype" of my Oxman[2] (not having read *The Island of Dr. Moreau*,[3] and not realizing that I never met the poet Oxsoup or Otsup in my life). Your joining the fray by introducing an innocent old Pushkinist amused me still more.

Cordially yours,
Vladimir Nabokov

1. Father erred. He meant Varlaam, the other of the pair of monks in Pushkin's *Boris Godunov*. Varlaam, who presumably cannot read, makes a supreme effort to decipher an ukase being read aloud by the fleeing Grigori (the future false Dmitri) who has volunteered

his services when it turns out that the police who have arrived in a border tavern in pursuit of him are also illiterate. Grigori substitutes Varlaam's description for his own to save his skin. Varlaam has no choice but to snatch the thing and do it himself, as VN said he would do, in extremis, with *Ada*. It is a pity he did not live to do it. DN.

2. Richard Poirier's review of *Look at the Harlequins!* (*New York Times Book Review*, 13 October 1974) speculated that the character Osip Oksman was drawn from Nicholas Otsup, a Russian émigré poet and editor in Paris. Struve's letter of correction (*New York Times Book Review*, 3 November 1974) also noted that there was a Pushkin scholar named Julian Oksman.

3. Novel by H. G. Wells, 1896.

---

TO: **ROBERT DIRIG**[1]                                      TL (XEROX), 1 p.

Montreux-Palace Hotel
1820 Montreux, Switzerland
April 23, 1975

Dear Mr. Dirig,

The story of *Lycaeides samuelis* Nabokov, which I separated in 1943 (Psyche, Vol. I) from the W. American race of another species, now known (after a nomenclatorial readjustment) as *Lycaeides idas scudderi* Edwards, is told in detail in my paper on the genus in the *Bulletin of the Museum of Comparative Zoology, Harvard College, Vol. 0, 949.*

The name I gave it alludes to Scudder's Christian name. When thirty years ago I attempted to classify *samuelis*, I regarded it as a subspecies of *melissa* Edw. on the basis of the length of its falx but now I know better. There are additional structural differences, there are larval differences (which I hope you will find and publish) and there is the crucial fact of *samuelis* and *melissa* not interbreeding at their meeting point which must surely exist already given the inexorable progression of *melissa* from Illinois eastward during the last decades.

This is why I am delighted by your project of writing about it and the celebrated Pine Barrens which I remember as a sandy and flowery little paradise the last time I visited them when commuting between Cornell and Harvard.

Yours sincerely,
Vladimir Nabokov

1. Of the Karner Blue Project, Xerces Society, Cornell University; VN was a member of the Xerces Society.

TO: **PROF. ALFRED APPEL, JR.**          TL (XEROX), 1 p.

Montreux-Palace Hotel
1820 Montreux, Switzerland
April 23, 1975

Dear Alfred,

I see I have not thanked you for the clipping about the protection of leps. In a sense I am the Endangered Species illustrating the article, for it is no other than *Lycaeides samuelis* Nabokov named by me in 1943! But what must tickle some of my best readers an iridescent pink is that it is precisely the butterfly which settles on damp sand at the feet of Pnin and Chateau!

I have had a terrible winter correcting French ADA whose debut in Paris is scheduled for May 23. I have also finished with Dmitri's help, another collection of short stories: the title is *Details of a Sunset*.[1]

Best regards from Véra and me to Nina and you,

Yours,
Vladimir Nabokov

1. Nine words deleted.

TO: **GLENN COLLINS**[1]                              TL (XEROX), 1 p.

Montreux-Palace Hotel
1820 Montreux, Switzerland
June 11, 1975

Dear Mr. Collins,

You caught me at a fortunate moment. I was fuming and free. I welcome your idea, with the following reservations:

1. I will supply a thousand words at one dollar (not fifty cents—a proletarian rate) per word.

2. The asking and the answering will take me a fortnight to formulate.

3. I waive the guarantee because I can easily find another patron after the thing is composed (my copyright).

4. It is understood, however, that what you get is not subject to any deletions or alteration of sense and is to be taken intact, or not at all.

5. I must be informed of the deadest dead-line and shown the final proof with ample time to check it.

6. My soul is mine. What you are going to get is an elegant and accurate shadowgraph on the brightest of walls.

If the complexity of the matter suits you, please let me know at once. I am leaving for Davos on the 18th but the Montreux-Palace will forward anything.

Best regards.

Vladimir Nabokov

1. Of the *New York Times Sunday Magazine*. On 6 June Collins proposed "the ultimate interview": VN interviewing VN. Although the *Times* agreed to VN's conditions, the project did not reach fruition.

TO: **GLENN COLLINS**                 TL (XEROX), I p.

Montreux-Palace Hotel
1820 Montreux, Switzerland
August 20, 1975

Dear Mr. Collins,

I had been looking forward eagerly to that delightful essay. For more than a month I hunted butterflies around Davos. Then I took a bad tumble down a steep slippery slope and was laid up for several days. Other worries cropped up in the meantime. When I returned to Montreux in the beginning of August a landslide of correspondence had to be disposed of. And my butterfly net remains hanging on the branch of a fir at 1900 metres like Ovid's lyre.

I realize now that I shall not be able to realize our project in the "near future". We must cancel it—or postpone it to a much later date.

With regret and gratitude,

yours
Vladimir Nabokov

TO: **FREDERIC W. HILLS**                 CC, I p.

Palace Hotel, 1820 Montreux
Switzerland
December 13, 1975

Dear Fred,

I thank you for your cable of December 13th and for your readiness to represent me again at the *Playboy* award ceremony.[1] I am sure you will do it much better than I could suggest. I would imagine you might include in your brief speech something on the lines of the following lines (as this wizard of words would put it):

I am delighted when Playboy's best readers appreciate the stories

translated by my son Dmitri from Russian originals written by me
half a century ago.

Véra and I wish you a merry Christmas.

It might be wise to find out when *The New Yorker* plans to publish
the two stories that will remain after "Christmas" as this would en-
able you to advise me of the exact date on which your collection will
be free to come out.

Cordially yours,
Vladimir Nabokov

1. VN had received a *Playboy* Editorial Award for his story "The Admiralty Spire."

TO: **JOHN WAIN**[1]                                TL (XEROX), 1 p.

Montreux-Palace Hotel
1820 Montreux, Switzerland
January 16, 1976

Dear Mr. Wain,

We certainly remember you and your delightful visit to Montreux.
VN regrets very much that he cannot possibly participate in your
project. As you perhaps know, the warm friendship between EW and
VN, which began in 1941, was later obliterated by minor and major
clashes, echoes of which may be found in VN's STRONG OPIN-
IONS. Psychologically it would be very difficult for VN to ignore
in a biographic paper the Pushkin controversy which revealed not
only ignorance of Russian on EW's part, but also a bizarre animosity
that he appears to have been nursing since the late nineteen-fifties.
Furthermore, VN is immersed in the writing of a new novel,[2] and
would not be able to fit any other work into his tight schedule.

With best regards from VN and me,
(Mrs. Vladimir Nabokov)

1. British novelist, poet, and critic Wain had invited VN to contribute to a volume of essays on Edmund Wilson.
2. "The Original of Laura." Uncompleted and unpublished.

TO: **SAMUEL ROSOFF**

Palace Hotel
Montreux
31 January 1976

We are heartily enjoying your sunny grapefruit, which arrived safe and sound the other day. Many thanks!

Ever since my appendicitis in the spring of 1917, I had assumed for some reason that no one would ever again put me under (loss of consciousness represents for me the worst coalescence of the worst possible nightmares). None the less, three and a half months ago, I had to undergo a much more serious operation. My recovery was rather trying but now I am better, except for hopeless insomnia. I have gradually gotten back to my writing, and am working on the first third of a new novel.[1]

Véra is deluged with correspondence from a crowd of publishers and hordes of unknown well-wishers; in this, however, she is assisted by our secretary. Mityusha is currently singing with the Lyon Opera, and recently completed a superb Italian translation of my *Transparent Things*. I am still at war with Field, who turned out to be a rat, and am forcing him to delete or alter all sorts of tripe in his book about me.

I would like to know how things are with you, and if you are well. My wife and I send you our most cordial greetings, my dear friend.

V[2]

1. "The Original of Laura."
2. Translated from Russian by DN.

TO: JOAN C. DALY                    TL (XEROX), 3 pp.

Montreux-Palace Hotel
1820 Montreux, Switzerland
February 2, 1976

Dear Miss Daly,

My husband managed to surface from the deep involvement with his new novel just long enough to consider the matter of Field's book and the alterations he accepts or does not accept. I am transcribing his notes:

*to pp. 9–20* (as defined in your letter of Jan. 5, 1976): This has to stop after the words "... the blood of Peter the Great in me." The twenty words that follow will have to be struck out (including my "remark").

*p. 29*: VN insists on an absolute and unequivocal deletion of all allusion to his sister's "pinkishness"—there just is not a shade of truth in it.

*pp. 54–5*: The passage on p. 54 in its present form may be permitted to remain + the first eleven lines on p. 55 [through "... the Russian aristocracy."] The rest of p. 55 and the first paragraph of p. 56 must go, including all that refers to the Wittgensteins' supposed return to their estates in the wake of the Nazi army. For one thing this is most probably just gossip; for another VN does not wish to be the source of such "information".

*p. 5* (Will power—o.k.)

*p. 59* All of it must be deleted, as also all dialogue between the Nabokovs—unbearably false both in tone and substance as presented by Field.

*p. 0* (derivation of the name Rukavishnikov): This must be deleted absolutely. Quite apart from all other considerations, the derivation invented by Field—from "hand" (*ruka*) and "cherry" (*vishnya*)—is, unfortunately for Field, quite impossible etymologically. Russian grammar refuses to cooperate. And while Sergey N. does not have to be an expert on VN's mother's genealogy, he is positive that he never offered the derivation of the name adopted by Field.

In the main, SN is specializing in the Nabokov genealogy. And he is in no way related to the Rukavishnikovs.

*p. 22* It is hard to convey to you the complete absurdity of the statement involved. 1) This was before the workmen's unions and syndicates came into being, and VDN would have sent all those unsubordinate—nay, rebellious—servants packing on the spot. 2) *Any* peasant would have been only too happy to carry his bags for him: he had done very much for them, and also he was very generous. The "confidential" information Field imparted to Mr. Grossman and Mrs. Sifton will not do, says VN. Unless Field names his source, and that source is other than the absurd Vonlar-Larsky book, but proves to be serious and trustworthy, Field absolutely cannot use that information. One of Field's snide purposes that runs in a more or less concealed shape throughout his book is to undermine VN's credibility and the accuracy of his recollections. As VN was present when his father returned, and Field's legendary witness was not, Field cannot be permitted to use his anonymous "witness"'s testimony.

*p. 247* All reference to the student who is the subject of this passage shall have to be deleted. It would take too long to explain all the circumstances that demand such drastic treatment.

*pp. 272–273* The entire passage (*all* reference) to Piotrovsky must be deleted. No subtle changes can make it palatable.

*p. 274* We never saw or heard of a memoir by Cannac. He was a rather pleasant young Frenchman who appeared in Berlin a short time before we left. The conflict VN had was not with the poet Piotrovsky but with the painter ... (please do not mention this name to Grossman, Mrs. Sifton, or Field), and Cannac was not present. I was there and recall every word.

*p. 29* The emendation of this passage is satisfactory.

*p. 299* Please have Field delete the entire sentence from "I know of" (or "There have been instances") to "... his artistic stature."—or specify the "instances."

*pp. 305–* O.k. after deletion of from "standing on this little islet" to "... that is all."

*p. 342* O.k. after revision.

*p. 35* VN says he does not accept Mrs. Fondaminsky's version asking "why should I sanction somebody else's error?"

*p. 373* Not acceptable. Our whole attitude toward money precluded viewing the Bobbs-Merrill advance as "tangible recognition" or a "memorable experience." This is another gaffe (or goof) of Field's.

*p. 374* The last version ("They saw to it that this made no difference where he was concerned.") is o.k.

*p. 38* VN accepts the last variant you propose "Nabokov answered shortly. It was, of course, a silly question .... on Paris."

*p. 389* I would not mind proclaiming from the top of the Empire State building that I consider serving the FBI or the CIA both honorable and patriotic but I refuse to see what this has to do in a book about my husband. Please have the passage deleted.

*p. 39* She was neither tall nor strapping, nor, actually, eccentric, and it was she who had sold CAMERA OBSCURA to Bobbs-Merrill.

*p. 39* letter to whom? from whom? what date? Without this information Field may not publish his "statistical" summation.

*p. 42* O.k. except for the 4 lines near the end ("Afterwards, the company ...... long conversation with N-").

*p. 44* Yes, must be cut after "awkward moments" through "but that visit was also not a success."

*pp. 44–447* Insert somewhere in line 5 or 6 "on Wilson's recommendation". Line 17 leave "the payments" out! Too much is quoted (though indirectly) from a genuine letter of E.W. to Katharine White?

*pp. 45–48* All allusions to the tenant, named or unnamed, have to be dropped completely and unconditionally, from "In the house they had on Seneca Street..." (p. 465) to and including "... Had a bad headache, enjoyed your course." (p. 468)

*p. 49* Delete passage from line 4 to line 21 (beginning "Even before it was finished" and ending "... more than twenty years later.")

*p. 472–473* VN says "Absolute rot. Never sent any student out for such a silly trifle. Let Field cite his 'good authority'."

I am afraid all the above-mentioned deletions are VN's minimum demands. He takes for granted that all his other deletions and alterations will also be settled to his satisfaction but it would be a pity for him to borrow more time from his novel-in-progress to attend to those matters until he has the assurance that his demands stated in this letter have been fully accepted by Field.

He also asks me to tell you how much he appreciates your patient and careful handling of all these often boring matters and to confirm that your guess was correct: the other lecturer at Dartmouth was Stefansson of the Wolves.[1]

Cordial greetings from VN and me,
(Mrs. Vladimir Nabokov)

1. Vilhjalmur Stefansson, Arctic explorer and Curator of Polar material at Dartmouth College.

TO: **PHILIP OAKES**                    TL (XEROX), 1 p.

Montreux-Palace Hotel
1820 Montreux, Switzerland
March 3, 1976

Dear Mr. Oakes,

I thank you for your kind letter. Yes, the Alpine choughs still walk at dawn on my window-sill, making kissing sounds.

The pictures by Ovenden[1] of that young sea-cow posing as my Lolita are, of course, preposterous, and the Academy Editions' plan to publish them has not received my blessing. Yet there is nothing much I can do about it. Recently I was shown an advert in an American rag offering a life-size Lolita doll with "French and Greek apertures".

We should be delighted to see you again. I always read your articles and the memory of your levitating novel still produces a nice tingle.

Cordially,
Vladimir Nabokov

1. Paintings and photographs by Graham Ovenden.


to: **DEREK C. BOK**[1]                                      TL (XEROX), 1 p.

Montreux-Palace Hotel
1820 Montreux, Switzerland
March 22, 1976

Dear Mr. Bok,

I thank you for your kind letter of February 11 (it arrived only to-day), informing me of the honorary degree of Doctor of Letters that the Governing Boards of Harvard have voted to confer on me.

It is with great regret that I must decline this honor. During the last twenty five years or more my firm principle has been to refuse all formal honors, fellowships, memberships and the like. It would be morally impossible for me to alter my conduct at this late date.

Sincerely,
Vladimir Nabokov

1. President, Harvard University.


to: **PROF. ALFRED APPEL, JR.**                             TL (XEROX), 1 p.

Montreux-Palace Hotel
1820 Montreux, Switzerland
April 26, 1976

Dear Alfred,

Your big gift and its satellites arrived safely, many, many thanks for your kind thoughts and congs. I am deep in *The New Golden Land*[1] and thrilled by those first American butterflies, some of which are quite recognizable. I answered 10 of your 15 exam questions: 2,

4, the lovely 5 (Bloom bit on the beach), 6, 8, 9, 10 (Joyce), 12 (Joyce), 13, 15 (Joyce) and give myself a plump B.

Now about the story-collection. I am not sure I like the idea. A collection is only then valuable when it is complete—and I hope to write a few more stories (after getting rid of my present novel, *The Original of Laura*, which will take most of the summer to finish) so anyway the thing is apt to be patchy no matter how brilliant the comments might be. Personally, I would never buy a *selection* of stories. The Germans and the Dutch are planning to bring out complete collections, and Proffer wants to gather all my stories in Russian—which has also its messy aspects but at least I'm quite sure I'll never write in Russian again.

Our summer plans are still rather shadowy. An ideal combination would be if you two visited us on our mountain, and I trust the mountain, at least, will be provided soon and would be somewhere in Switzerland.

Most cordial greetings from both of us to both of you.

P.S. Nice news in your PS about the RFHF,[2] nice!

1. By Hugh Honour (New York: Pantheon, 1975).
2. Rockefeller Foundation Humanities Fellowship.

TO: **PROF. CARL R. PROFFER**                                            cc, 1 p.

Palace Hotel, 1820 Montreux
Switzerland
May 17, 1976

Dear Proffer,

Ill health prevented me from replying earlier, and still prevents me from writing you in detail. I have now read Sokolov's[1] SHKOLA DLYA DURAKOV, an enchanting, tragic, and touching book (I translate this comment in case you might like to transmit it to the author: obayatel'naya, tragicheskaya i trogatel'neyshaya kniga). It is by far the best thing you have published in the way of modern Soviet prose.

Cordially yours,
Vladimir Nabokov

1. Russian writer Sasha Sokolov, author of *School for Fools.*

TO: **VICTOR LUSINCHI**[1]                    TL (XEROX), 2 pp.

Montreux-Palace Hotel
1820 Montreux, Switzerland
October 30, 1976

Dear Mr. Lusinchi,
    Here are the notes on books recently read, which I promised to contribute to the New York Times Book Review.
    I understand that (as in the case of my interviews etc.) these notes will be published verbatim, without any additions or omissions in the text. Please confirm this.

Yours sincerely,
Vladimir Nabokov

*Three Books*[2]

Here are the three books I read during the three summer months of 1976 while hospitalized in Lausanne:
    1. Dante's *Inferno* in Singleton's splendid translation (Princeton, 1970) with the Italian *en regard* and a detailed commentary. What triumphant joy it is to see the honest light of literality take over again, after ages of meretricious paraphrase!
    2. *The Butterflies of North America* by Howe, coordinating editor and illustrator (1975, 633 pages). It describes and pictures in marvelous color all the nearctic species and many subspecies. Nothing like

it has ever appeared here. The indifference of our philistine public to it is scandalous especially as all kinds of non-scientific coffee books—opalescent morphos and so on—are paraded yearly and presumably sell.

3. *The Original of Laura*, the not quite finished manuscript of a novel which I had begun writing and reworking before my illness and which was completed in my mind: I must have gone through it some fifty times and in my diurnel delirium kept reading it aloud to a small dream audience in a walled garden. My audience consisted of peacocks, pigeons, my long dead parents, two cypresses, several young nurses crouching around, and a family doctor so old as to be almost invisible. Perhaps because of my stumblings and fits of coughing the story of my poor Laura had less success with my listeners than it will have, I hope, with intelligent reviewers when properly published.

Vladimir Nabokov

1. Of the *New York Times Book Review*.
2. "Authors' Authors," *New York Times Book Review* (5 December 1976).

TO: **PROF. SIMON KARLINSKY**                    TL (XEROX), 1 p.

Montreux-Palace Hotel<br>1820 Montreux, Switzerland<br>January 3, 1977

Dear Semyon Arkadievich,

After several months of sickness, I spent a pleasant Christmas reading your book on Gogol.[1] I think you over-symbolize the sexual meaning of certain marginal objects, and I am sure you overpraise certain writers: how can one rank the great Griboedov with such a mediocrity as Hmelnitsky? Otherwise your book is a first-rate achievement.

I limit myself to these few lines as I am still groggy after my illness. Wishing you a joyful new year, I remain

yours cordially,
Vladimir Nabokov

1. *The Sexual Labyrinth of Nikolai Gogol* (Cambridge: Harvard University Press, 1976).

TO: *TIMES LITERARY SUPPLEMENT*  TYPED STATEMENT REVISED
BY VN, 1 p. *TLS* letterhead.
Montreux, Switzerland[1]

*The Passionate Friends* by H. G. Wells is my most prized example of the unjustly ignored masterpiece. I must have been fourteen or fifteen when I went through its author's fiction after some five winters of tacit access to my father's library. Today at 77 I clearly remember how affected I was by the style, the charm, the dream of the book, while not bothering about its "message" or "symbols" if any. I have never reread it and now I fear that the coloured haze leaves only some final details—growing a little closer to me in time—still coming through.

The last meeting of the lovers takes place under legal supervision on a summer's day in a stranger's drawing room where the furniture is swathed in white covers. As Stephen, after parting with his mistress, walks out of the house in company with another person, he says to the latter: (simply to say something and finding only a poor little statement concerning those draped chairs.)

"Because of the flies."

A touch of high art refused to Conrad or Lawrence.

1. Published with editorial alterations in "Reputations Revisited," *Times Literary Supplement* (21 January 1977).

TO: *INTERNATIONAL HERALD TRIBUNE*          TL (XEROX), I p.

> Montreux-Palace Hotel
> 1820 Montreux, Switzerland
> May 9, 1977

Sir,

Legal considerations oblige me to request an immediate explanation of the following passage in John Leonard's review (April 30, 1977), entitled "Hermit of Peking", of Trevor-Roper's book on Sir Edmund Backhouse, a forger:

".... These commercial dreams ... collapsed ... But nobody ever told anybody else that a liar on such an extravagant scale, a Nabokov of Peking, had been anything other than gullible or misunderstood."

What on earth is this meant to mean?

Several months ago in The New York Times Book Review, in reference to a chance character in PALE FIRE, the same reviewer maintained that I was spoofing a dear friend; I chose to ignore the silliness of the invention; but this is going a little too far.

> Vladimir Nabokov
> Montreux, Palace-Hôtel

copy to John Leonard, Esq.[1]

---

1. There is no reply from Leonard in the VN Archive.

---

TO: **DMITRI NABOKOV**          VN'S PORTION OF ALS WRITTEN
                                WITH VÉRA NABOKOV
                                Montreux, Switzerland

> 9 May 1977

My dearest, your roses,[1] your fragrant rubies, glow red against a background of spring rain. I wrote to our "Tribunka"[2] immediately to set things straight. Personally I think they confused me with Nixon.

I hug you, I'm proud of you, be well, my beloved.[3]

1. Sent for Mother's Day.
2. Diminutive for the Russian word for "Tribune." See preceding letter.
3. Translated from Russian by DN. This was the last letter DN received from his father.

# INDEX

# LOLITA

for Dmitri
from
the author
Aug. 1958
Ithaca

Вкорпил
от автора
Хтас 1962

# THE GIFT

For my best translator, Dmitri Nabokov
from his father

ATHENAEUM 1963

Babochka babochka Nab.
♂